Reflective Literacy Practices in an Age of Standards

Engaging K–8 Learners

Christopher~Gordon Publishers, Inc.
Bridging Theory and Practice

1502 Providence Highway, Suite 12
Norwood, MA 02062

800-934-8322 • 781-762-5577
www.Christopher-Gordon.com

Printed in the United State of America
10 9 8 7 6 5 4 3 2 1   09 08 07

ISBN: 1-929024-94-0
Library of Congress Catalogue Number: 2006928286

Reflective Literacy Practices in an Age of Standards

Engaging K–8 Learners

Richard C. Sinatra

Brett Elizabeth Blake

E. Francine Guastello

Joanne Marie Robertson

Christopher-Gordon Publishers, Inc.
Norwood, Massachusetts

Copyright Acknowledgments

To Camille Sinatra, antiquing companion, fishing partner, great cook, inspirational source, and terrific wife.

Richard C. Sinatra

For my son, Robbie, as he begins a new and exciting journey and for Charlie, whose journey continues to be difficult, yet full of hope—all my love and prayers.

Brett Elizabeth Blake

To my parents, Esther Mary and Frank Guastello, whose love of learning has guided my life and to my dearest and most supportive friends, Betty and Kate.

E. Francine Guastello

To my family: To my mother, Anne, who was my first teacher. To my sister, Catherine, who is and always will be my best friend. To my sons, Thomas and Matthew, who make me so proud. To my daughter-in-law Maria, who has taught Thomas to love books. To my grandson, Thomas, who brings such joy and meaning to all our lives. And lastly, to John, who believes when I don't.

Joanne Marie Robertson

Acknowledgments

Most of the topics and methodology presented in this book are grounded in the authors' own experiences in primary, elementary, and intermediate grade classrooms and in our teacher training and special project work. The many topics covered in the book are also connected to relevant issues and timely reports that affect the literacy work of teachers in the modern-day, diverse classroom. We wish to thank all those children, teachers, and administrators who have worked with us over the years and have contributed to our own growth as literacy educators.

We would like to extend a special thanks to Robert W. Blake, Professor Emeritus, for his meticulous editorial work and insightful comments that helped Brett Elizabeth Blake revise her chapter. We often take for granted those like Robert who, behind the scenes, help to make a project such as this so special!

We also wish to acknowledge our professional colleagues, secretarial staff, student assistants, and graduate students at St. John's University who contributed to the success of the book. Our teacher colleagues and students accomplished special projects with their own classroom children. You will find these projects sprinkled throughout the book, and we thank the teachers.

Contents

Introduction

The intent of this book is clearly reflected in its title. Engagement and reflection are strategic processes for us. They operate on two cumulative levels. Initially students become "hooked" or drawn into the literacy activity offered by the teacher. They then become committed to complete the activity in a successful way and, in so doing, connect to understanding achieved in the past. Our aim is to assist educators of primary- and intermediate-grade youngsters with ways of achieving compelling engagements with reflective thought. In each chapter, we include rationales and information to enhance each educator's background knowledge of reflective and authentic literacy practices and then provide ways to achieve best practices of engagement in our age of standards.

We are four voices working in a collaborative, collective way. Each brings a unique perspective in the development of the book's chapters. All have been classroom teachers; two have been building principals; and presently we share the joy and important challenge of educating teachers and administrators in literacy practices at the university level. The chapters are designed to be comprehensive in nature, and each focuses on a global aspect of literacy, such as writing and reading fusion in the early years, guided reading, creating cultural texts, poetry, literature, and informational texts. We share a "big picture" view of literacy and attempt to integrate some of the more global findings of the National Reading Panel, the National Commission on Writing, and the English language arts standards published by the joint efforts of the National Council of Teachers of English and the International Reading Association.

The concept of *engagement* and a strong belief in a balanced use of the language arts in learning processes are the threads that bind us. We share a constructivist viewpoint of learning. This viewpoint necessitates that students become actively involved in literacy practices; they make meaning as they are engaged, integrating new learnings with the old; and they benefit when viewing, listening, speaking, reading, writing, and visual representation are used in harmony. By engaging learners in these language arts components, teachers achieve a balance in how students construct meaning to support the skills and strategies teachers wish to teach. For instance, in chapter 7, we approach the critical skill of teaching inferencing or drawing conclusions in a constructivist, balanced language arts way. Students use visual representation to make outlines of their hands. Listening and speaking occur as students answer the teacher's prompts regarding ways that authors reveal a character's identity in literature. Critical and interpretive reading occur as students locate passages, lines, and dialogue to answer the queries. Students write their findings in the fingers of the outlined hand and then synthesize the finger bits into a written paragraph in the hand's palm.

Expressive ways to reveal understanding and knowledge are critical in our constructivist view of student learning. Here, writing occupies center stage as a prime way to reveal what one knows, but it is also supported by speaking and visual representation. Visual representation, in today's modern literacy arena, is technically enhanced by computer use and many engaging software programs that encourage the connection of visuals to words. In chapter 4, for instance, the reader will note how speaking through oral presentations is enhanced by software visual representation, and in chapter 9, how children use visual design and writing in researching a theme.

We are struck, however, by the underlying tension that appears to exist between the constructivist and the skills-based viewpoints of student learning. In the former, the teacher presents the larger authentic context and the guided steps to engage students in critical and reflective learning practices, while in the latter the particular skill, such as "main idea" or "paragraph writing" or "structural endings," becomes the unit of focus, often taught directly out of a larger context. The skills-based orientation is often a top-down means of curriculum control based on more narrow interpretations of National Reading Panel recommendations, state standards, and district curriculum guidelines.

In our classroom work with practicing and novice teachers and in our district and school inservice work we have become apprised of this conflict and this tension regarding how to approach students' learning processes. Teachers become enthusiastic and engage themselves when they learn of the many strategies, techniques, activities, and classroom organizational patterns presented in this book. They learn that many types and levels of skills can be mastered by students engaged in one constructivist-oriented literacy activity. For instance, in chapter 3, we see how by following the steps of guided reading, culminating in the kidstations' grouping, the teacher has immersed children in the skills of automatic word recognition; decoding; oral reading fluency; vocabulary understanding through context interpretation; and literal, inferential, and creative level comprehension.

The chapters are liberally sprinkled with figures, charts, pictures, children's work, and anecdotes to enrich the content and to provide models for the teacher to follow. The use of the Anticipation Guides before and the Anticipation Guides Revisited after each chapter also provides a way for the teacher to involve students with the important skill of critical reading. Additional resources for the teacher in the form of Web sites, appendixes with reproducible pages, and reflective activities are provided.

Each chapter presents a comprehensive overview of a topic critical to literacy development for students from the primary to the intermediate grades. In these days of rigorous academic standards and high-stakes testing, students' success in school is related to their increased abilities to comprehend, analyze, and reflect through critical reading, writing, and technological presentations. We are of a firm belief that students need to be engaged in authentic literacy practices in order to think deeply about meaning and become reflective. We have attempted to order the chapters in a somewhat developmental way, beginning with the primary years and moving upward through the grades. Yet, as teachers are aware, literature, informational readings, poetry, and computer work cut through the grades. We close with a culminating short chapter describing a practice. We practice what we "preach." In chapter 9 we describe how a constructivist-oriented approach fuses the language arts components of viewing, listening, speaking, reading, writing, and visual representation.

Chapter Summaries

Chapter 1 — The Early Years: Reading to Write and Writing to Read. This chapter explores the creative ways that young children negotiate their understanding about reading and writing, how they construct knowledge through social interactions and relationships in their environment, and how they develop a sense of self-efficacy that supports their development as confident and capable literacy learners. It analyzes the ways that children demonstrate their apprenticeship stance through literacy profiles created by teachers.

Chapter 2 — Crafting the Way to Literacy. The crafting techniques and literacy lessons presented in this chapter are designed to help teachers (preservice, novice, and veteran) conceptualize additional ways to motivate struggling, reluctant, proficient, and English Language Learners (ELLs) to write with a sense of authorship and style. The purpose of this chapter is to help teachers understand the notion of "crafting" with picture books, and how to integrate skills, strategies, and state standards into reading and writing workshops. Examples of students' writing created in crafting workshops highlight the lessons.

Chapter 3 — On and Beyond the Path to Guided Reading. A balanced literacy framework is presented through a 5-day cycle of guided reading and writing. Within the four kidstations section of the chapter, activities are presented suitable for different grade levels and for different aspects of the language arts.

Chapter 4 — Perking Oral Presentations. A refreshing look at oral presentations, now included in most state standards, with technology provides this chapter's content. Actual models for student lessons, an oral lesson presentation framework, and an evaluation scale are also presented.

Chapter 5 — Uplifting Minds on the Wings of Poetry. This chapter explores ways in which classroom teachers can introduce poetry to all students, especially to those for whom poetry may seem particularly frightening or difficult. This may be especially true for English Language Learners (ELLs). The traditional elements of poetry are initially presented with a critical discussion of "voice" as crucial to meaningful poetry. Next, beginning lessons and strategies from an urban middle school are presented, highlighting how to encourage students to be open to expression and to interact with imagery, words, and experiences to create poetry. Finally, poetry ideas and activities are presented through sample student work.

Chapter 6 — Creating Cultural Texts and Responding to Literature With Diverse Students. This chapter demonstrates how we can help students to engage with literature through a "classroom reader response" model. Citing the important work of Louise Rosenblatt, this chapter highlights the idea of "interacting" with text, as well as the importance of "cultural texts" in helping diverse students connect, understand, and respond to literature. Strategies and activities are shared (across grade levels) including actual student samples.

Chapter 7 — Lighting the Pathways of Understanding With Literature. This chapter attempts to enrich the teacher's background knowledge on the power and value of using children's literature to engage students in a meaningful way. Six major design strategies are offered by which teachers can help their elementary students to gain insight and reflective understandings through literary readings.

Chapter 8 — Bridging the Layers of Informational Text. This chapter examines the expository text style, the style of writing found in the content area readings of science, social studies, mathematics, and computer and health education. The structure of informational text is examined, as well as why bridging the layers of informational meaning is difficult for many and why success in the reading and writing of this style is critical to achieve in school and in society. Many suggestions and strategies are offered, including one major guided reading format to help students bridge the layers of difficult meaning often posed by technical vocabulary and unfamiliar text styles.

Chapter 9 — An Integrated Literacy Approach. An approach found to be successful with many students considered to be at risk for literacy success is described. The approach makes use of trade books connected to themes and has a six-step guided reading and writing format that can be implemented each time a new reading is encountered. The approach connects to the book's thesis of engagement and the multiple uses of literacy.

Have a refreshing and meaningful read.

Chapter 1

The Early Years
Reading to Write and Writing to Read

Anticipation Guide

Before reading this chapter, please read each of the statements listed below. Based upon your prior knowledge and experience with this chapter's topics, check either "agree" or "disagree" for each statement. After reading the chapter, see if your answers change in the Anticipation Guide Revisited found at the end of the chapter.

	Statement	**Agree**	**Disagree**
1.	Learning to read and write involves the understanding that what I say can be written down on paper for someone else to read.	_____	_____
2.	By the ages of 5 and 6, children know a great deal about the form and function of spoken and written language. This understanding evolves with little or no direct instruction.	_____	_____
3.	Children learn to read and write by reading and writing.	_____	_____
4.	Early literacy learning is best facilitated when children practice reading aloud easily decodable, repetitive texts ("fat cat sat on the mat") that emphasize onset and rime patterns.	_____	_____
5.	Skills instruction must take place before a read-aloud or literacy lesson.	_____	_____
6.	Using "I wonder" questions with young children promotes critical thinking and supports conversations about books.	_____	_____
7.	Picture books are excellent tools with which to teach graphophonic, syntactic, and semantic and pragmatic strategies for reading and writing.	_____	_____
8.	Time for reading and writing should not be a factor in young children's literacy learning.	_____	_____

1

Confident Literacy Learners in a Social Context

Let's begin this book's exploration of authentic and reflective literacy practices with a short vignette that reveals how literacy and learning develop within supportive social contexts. Teachers can use this narrative, and others they have experienced, to show parents how important they are in supporting and developing their children's confidence and motivation to learn.

> Twenty-month old Thomas is attempting to trace his foot on a large sheet of paper. He outlines his toes with a blue crayon and gestures to his grandmother to do the same. She traces hers alongside. He giggles with delight and then jumps up and down on top of the writing tablet. "Thomas's foot," his grandmother says, and points to his imprint. He studies the paper. "Mima's foot," she continues. Thomas scribbles on them both with his crayon. He places his palm down on the paper, and his grandmother traces around it. Next he traces hers. This is a game they have played for several months. This day, however, Thomas makes a straight line alongside his handprint and exclaims, "D!" His grandmother claps her hands and says, "Good for you!" Thomas proudly exclaims "D" again and points to his mark on the paper. He is clearly pleased with this accomplishment and continues to draw more parallel lines. Thomas leaves spaces in between; he progresses left to right and even right to left. He is not scribbling now. Rather, he is learning to communicate through writing. This scenario is typical of many interchanges between family members and young literacy learners in which they use authentic language to communicate. Conversations naturally evolve and build upon children's interests. They are rarely contrived. Learning is reciprocal as the adult takes his or her cues from the child.
>
> Thomas labels his mark as "D" on this particular day, but the contexts for this cognitive milestone were established many months before. From the earliest days, Thomas was exposed to the rich language of books. His home environment provides strong literacy models that support the progression of his thinking about reading and writing as language processes. Both parents read to him on a daily basis. His "book basket" contains many of his favorite stories. He listens with interest to both expository and narrative texts. He watches his father prepare legal briefs and review cases. He notices the ways his mother enters data on the computer and manages her home-based business. These demonstrations reinforce and extend his understanding about what it means to be a reader and writer.

Active Co-Participants in the Construction of Meaning

This chapter will extend the numerous creative ways that Thomas, as well as his childhood peers, can be enriched in literacy development through supportive environments. We will explore the creative ways in which children negotiate their understanding of reading and writing, construct knowledge through interactions and relationships in their environment, and develop a sense of self-efficacy that supports their development as confident and capable literacy learners. We will discuss the ways in which children make visible what they know through emerging reading, writing, and speaking behaviors. We will highlight the social, dialogic, and context-dependent nature of learning through an overview of the research on emergent literacy. We will study the ways in which children demonstrate their apprenticeship stance in the literacy profiles created by novice and practicing teachers in a graduate program.

Early childhood educators have come to appreciate the dynamic, spontaneous, and affective nature of young children's literacy development. Research and reflection in the mid-1980s changed the field's perspectives about readiness, or preparing children for formal reading and writing instruction, to a philosophy of *emergent literacy*. Language development is now viewed as beginning at birth and gradually emerging over time, with the language processes of reading, writing, listening, speaking, viewing, and visual representation interacting to construct meaning.

No child is at zero when he or she enters kindergarten (Ferreiro & Teberosky, 1985). Young children begin school with sophisticated notions about the form, function, and uses of spoken and written language. The emergent literacy learner readily expresses his or her wonderings and imaginings through words, drawings, collage, play, movement, music, dance, and sculpture. Educators in Reggio Emilia, Italy, describe this self expression as the "hundred languages" (Malaguzzi, 1998). Young children are active "constructors of knowledge" (Clay, 1991). They draw on personal, social, and physical experiences to construct an understanding of the world that is reflective of cultural experiences and family literacy practices.

As we saw with Thomas, learning often occurs through personal and playful interactions with others in the home and community. Like most emergent literacy learners, he is motivated to learn and confident that he can do so. Toys support his development, and most of them are interactive. Thomas's teddy bear, tractor, play cell phone, and books talk and sing to him. He especially likes to play with his alphabet magnets, which not only state each letter's name but also make the corresponding sound. He arranges them in various combinations on the refrigerator. Even though Thomas does not really know what a letter is yet, he has begun to notice these symbols in his surroundings and tries to reproduce them. He is eager to communicate and does so through simple words, gestures, and lines that he purposefully scribes on paper. His efforts are always met with praise and encouragement. Family members view him as rich in potential. By the time Thomas begins formal schooling, he will have developed many more theories about the form, function, and uses of print. Furthermore, as chapter 7 notes, he will have developed a sense of story that will contribute to his success in learning to read and write. This understanding will continue to evolve over time, through meaningful interactions with parents, siblings, and peers in real-world literacy tasks.

Having a solid theory about the ways in which children learn to read and write helps early childhood educators to plan "developmentally appropriate" literacy instruction. (Developmentally appropriate teaching practices have been outlined by the National Association for the Education of Young Children.) By carefully observing, recording, and talking with young children—"kidwatching" (Goodman & Owocki, 2002)—teachers can discover a great deal about the theories they have formed about reading, writing, and school, and envision ways of adapting and differentiating instruction to maximize student opportunities for learning.

The challenge for contemporary educators is to understand and capitalize on the remarkable ways in which emergent learners like Thomas process, transform, and produce new knowledge with a sense of optimism and personal efficacy. Self-efficacy is related to reading and writing achievement (Walker, 2003). Understanding the ways in which young children's "can do" attitudes (McCabe, 2003), perceptions of self-efficacy (Bandura, 1977), motivation to engage (Mathewson, 1994), and critical literacy development (Cambourne, 2000, 2001; Comer, 2001) are shaped, transformed, and influenced by the significant others in their lives and by the contexts of their learning (Lave & Wegner, 1991; Vygotsky, 1978) enables early childhood teachers to conceptualize environments that sustain and extend authentic moments of self-discovery. Such environments support the child's literacy learning in the classroom, honor the child's right to quality instruction and developmentally appropriate materials, motivate the child to independently engage with texts, and ensure that the child learns in joyful and meaningful ways.

Theory Builders

Frank Smith (1988) believes that young children form a "theory of the world" about print conventions as they hypothesize about their possibilities for communication. In an effortless way, children become literate as they explore, practice, and play with the various types and uses of written language in the company of mentors. Literacy includes not only reading and writing but also ways of thinking, interpreting, visually representing, and using language in diverse contexts for a variety of purposes. Mentors might be parents, guardians, caregivers, siblings, and peers. Lev Vygotsky (1978) introduced the notion of a zone of proximal development in which apprentice learners are supported to achieve what they could not do unassisted. What children are able to do with the assistance and support of others today, they will be able to independently accomplish tomorrow. Vygotsky discussed the ways in which social interaction, dialogue, and collaboration with more capable others extends concept development and scaffolds children's thinking.

The field of early childhood education has firmly established that context plays a critical role, and that rich environments and supportive adults and peers influence children's literacy learning in shared reading and writing activities. Furthermore, children's initial literacy experiences are critical to their later academic success. The language development of preschoolers is directly related to their home environments and literacy experiences (Wells, 1985). Children's interest in literacy tasks, and their involvement in family literacy events (including but not limited to shared readings), leads to higher rates of language development. Teachers perceive these children as "more ready for school" (Goswami, 1994).

Michael Halliday (1994) talks about the ways in which early learners develop a subsequent "theory of the world as we agree upon it," which reflects their internalization of concepts and the understanding that language has "meaning potential." The young child begins to select and use language in a way that communicates meaning within a particular context. This cognitive, linguistic, social, and emotional accomplishment is normally stress free, context dependent, and meaningful for the child. In the social contexts of school, literacy learning and language development are viewed as interactive, experiential, and constructivist (Kucer, 2005). The teacher plays a critical role in envisioning, supporting, and setting the tone for learning in the classroom.

Competent Communicators

Young children are "meaning makers" (Wells, 1985). They use language to establish and maintain friendships, influence others, tell stories, ask questions, give information, or analyze and speculate about their world. They progressively "learn to mean" (Halliday, 1973, 1975) and refine their understanding through social interactions and dialogue. Let's eavesdrop on the conversation of a group of second grader as they debate the existence of the tooth fairy. The dialogue, transcribed by Jessica, a student in the literacy program, illustrates the ways in which children interpret text (spoken and written) based upon life experiences.

Priscilla:	When I lost my tooth I put it under the pillow. Then in the morning my tooth was gone and money was there.
Ronald:	What kind of money?
Priscilla:	One dollar, one quarter, and other cents. The tooth fairy puts it there.
Jacky:	The tooth fairy is not real.
Valerie:	Yes, yes, she is real.
Irina:	If there is no such thing as the tooth fairy, then where does the money come from? If it was your mom, you would feel her pick your head up.
Ronald:	Maybe it is a ghost.
Kevin:	Yeah, but how do the coins get there?
Ronald:	I told you it was a magic ghost.
Priscilla:	There is no such thing as ghosts.
Tiffany:	How does the tooth fairy know if you lose your tooth?
Cally:	She watches it on TV.
Louis:	Where does she get all the money?
Matthew:	It's magic!
Teacher:	(Addressing Jacky) Well Jacky, what do you think now? Your friends believe that the tooth fairy really does exist. They even told you why they believe in her. What do you think?
Jacky:	One time, I lost my tooth and put it under the pillow. When I woke up, the tooth was still there.
Matthew:	Maybe the money was there too and fell on the floor.
Valerie:	I think she didn't go to your house because you don't believe.
Teacher:	The tooth fairy only goes to children who believe in her?
Valerie:	Yeah, she only appears when you believe.
Jacky:	If she is real, how come I've never seen her?
Polina:	She is like Santa. She only comes when you are sleeping and she lives far away.
Kevin:	Where does she come from?
Irina:	She lives in space and she built her house from all the teeth. She probably makes houses for her friends too.
Nicholas:	No, she lives in the water.
Levi:	She lives in a huge castle.
Kevin:	How does she go in the house?
Victor:	Maybe she uses a wand.
Bryan:	I think she just uses her hands to unlock the door because she has magic powers.

> Anthony: She is very small so she can use the space between the door and the floor to get in.
>
> Irina: What if you live in a building? I live in a building. That's why I know she has to fly in through the window. But I don't know how she knows what floor to go to.
>
> Matthew: She must have a map.
>
> Kevin: She is just really smart and clever.
>
> Bryan: She lives on Jupiter and there is a magic door, and when she goes through it she goes from Jupiter to New York.

What does this transcript tell us about the literacy development of these second graders? For one thing, it's highly creative. Their comments illustrate the ways in which language is reconstruction, not imitation. The comparison of the tooth fairy to Santa Claus is quite original, as are their explanations for how she enters houses. It's obvious that the children have engaged in talks like this before. With lots of modeling by their teacher and time for practice, they have begun to appreciate "the need for precision, purpose, and audience in using language" (Lapp, Flood, & Roser, 2000). The students are developing conversational competencies that enable them to use language in socially appropriate ways. Notice how they participate in the give-and-take of the conversation, are attentive to each other, take turns, make adjustments, ask questions, provide answers, and explain their thoughts effectively. The children offer pertinent feedback and extend each other's comments as they interpret viewpoints, share knowledge, and add new information. They are good listeners who build upon one another's statements, comment and affirm one another's beliefs, and make connections to everything and everyone they know. The students respect one another's point of view as they toss around theories about what is relevant and not relevant to the reality of the tooth fairy. They have also formed theories about the power of belief and the role of magic in their lives. The line between fantasy and reality is blurred, yet we can also appreciate the knowledge base they bring to the discussion. The second graders know quite a lot about many things. They are well on their way to becoming more literate.

Jessica wrote the following in her literacy profile:

> It was interesting to see how the children's experiences and fantasies enable them to think about the world and how everything in it works. . . . As the conversation continued it seemed that everyone, with the exception of Jacky, believed that the tooth fairy did exist and was a magic being. There was a time when Jacky even seemed to believe it for a moment. She wanted to be convinced but her own experiences told her otherwise. The rest of the children still wanted to believe that the tooth fairy was real and would find any proof to validate her existence. . . . The opportunity to engage in this type of conversation with my students let me see inside the mind of a child.

Teachers play a critical role in the continued development and guidance of these types of conversations in the classroom. This kind of discourse is a cornerstone upon which to build a comprehensive early literacy program. Observational studies (Dyson, 1988) have also shown the links between talk and writing development. Through rich literacy experiences, children become confident, capable, and motivated readers and writers.

Readers and Writers

Learning to read and write involves print awareness as well as an understanding that what I say can be written down on paper for someone else to read. Through the processes of visual representation and/or writing, children make their thinking visible and explicit as they construct, articulate, and refine their thoughts. Early literacy learners delight in repeating and rewriting familiar words and phrases, and manipulating letters and words in inventive ways. They are eager to read and write and have the knowledge to represent their experiences and to create story worlds. Writing becomes a tool for thinking and concept development. Young children want to join the "literacy club" (Smith, 1988) and engage in the reading and writing activities of the significant others in their lives and communities. Writing supports reading development.

The following emergent writing samples and transcripts of students' comments provide insight into the process of becoming a reader and writer. They were collected by students in a teacher education program at St. John's University and analyzed as part of their literacy profile projects. In this project, preservice, novice, and veteran teachers were asked to document, assess, and evaluate the literacy experiences of one language learner (birth through age 8), over time, to determine his or her language competencies framed within the social, dialogic, and cultural contexts of home and/or school. The students explored children's oral language development, print awareness, concepts of reading, and book knowledge in order to reflect upon, energize, and rethink models of beginning literacy instruction and to consider the notion of the young child as "ever-expanding . . . rich in potential, and strong" (Malaguzzi, 1998), and whose literacy development begins well before formal schooling.

Eagerness to Use Print

In the beginning, emergent writers create messages with their own unique symbol systems. These symbols, including pictures and shapes, are foundational to future understanding of words symbolizing thoughts and ideas. Observe the ways in which 16-month-old Kathryn (Figure 1-1) meticulously lines her message inside an oval, perhaps demonstrating an emerging awareness of both the directionality and structure of written text. Although unable to explain her writing in words, she did express her enthusiasm through smiles and a willingness to engage in the literacy task.

We recognize that literacy initiatives such as Kathryn's are purposeful. What would appear to be just scribbles, shapes, and marks are really the beginning of her understanding of writing. She might be attending to the features of print in her environment. Oval shapes are quite typical in early writing samples. Teachers often transcribe the child's words underneath to help them make the leap to a new symbol system of letters and words.

Let's look at the unique ways in which a group of 3- and 4-year-olds use writing to communicate. Even though

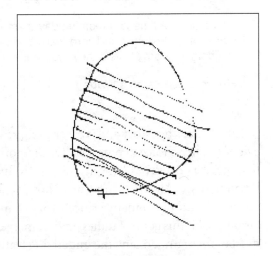

Figure 1-1. Kathryn's Writing

they are quite close in age, their perceptions of writing are quite different. In Figure 1-2, 3½-year-old Sarah scribbles an imaginative story using the book language with which she is familiar. She confidently fills two whole pages with wavy lines. It is quite readable to her, and she demonstrates not only great satisfaction in generating two pages but also a pride in retelling the story. "I gave her two pieces of paper and a pen. I just watched her," writes Emily, who is documenting Sarah's work, in her literacy profile. "She started from the bottom and wrote left to right. After she was done I asked her to read it to me and this is what she said."

"Once upon a time in a morning day there was a village princess and a pauper. Long ago Anastasia has to see the pauper. There were two bad mans. The village king worked and worked and the kingdom was saved. And they lived happily ever after. The sun will come."

Figure 1-2. Sarah's Writing

Sarah retells her story and is eager to share what she has written. The influence of the fairy-tale genre is evident in her choice of phrases ("Once upon a time . . . happily ever after"). She sets the stage by stating that the story occurred "long ago" and introduces us to two main protagonists and a couple of antagonists ("bad mans"). Always the optimist, however, Sarah concludes the tale with a sunny ending. This short piece, containing so many critical story elements (beginning, middle, and end), suggests that Sarah is familiar with this genre. Studies on the emergent writing behaviors of young children have illustrated that most of them understand the underlying features of storytelling (Applebee, 1978; Martens, 1996) before they begin formal schooling. The universal nature of a story will be further explored in chapter 7.

In Figure 1-3, 3-year-old Kayla writes a story for college student Frank. "It's a happy story," she tells him, suggesting her awareness that there are sad stories as well. She points to the symbols, especially the smiley face, to make this point. We can see the beginnings of letter formation in Kayla's writing sample, which contains various invented characters that she has embellished in own unique way. There are both curvy and straight lines that suggest she is attending to the way in which print works. We can observe how she transitions from one sign system (artwork) to another (written letters) in this sample.

Figure 1-3. Kayla's Writing

Frank writes in his profile, "I know that Kayla recognizes symbols or logos, because when we go grocery shopping she knows exactly what's in certain boxes and cans."

Children's early knowledge about words is contextual or logographic. Words represent whole units. They might understand that the cereal box says "Frosted Flakes," but they don't attend to the words. Instead, they construct meaning from the logo (context) in which the words "Frosted Flakes" appear. They use both semantic and pragmatic cues. *Semantic cues* refer to a child's ability to use the context of a sentence, illustration, paragraph, or story to construct meaning; *pragmatic cues* refer to a child's familiarity with a literacy task and its requirements. Some children might recognize graphemes, or letters, in the environmental print that surrounds them. For all practical purposes, Figures 1-1, 1-2, and 1-3 represent baby talk on paper.

In Figure 1-4, 4-year-old Denisha makes evident what she knows and what she observes in her environment when she explains what she has written. "These are words," she tells her Aunt Jennifer, "maybe like *houses* or *chairs* or *TV* and *box*. I would write you a letter about rainbows, circles, and Barbies. Don't forget about remote control TVs and people eating ice cream and listening to music." Children use life experiences to construct meaning about writing.

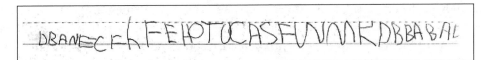

Figure 1-4. Denisha's Writing

Denisha can't seem to get the words out fast enough as she explains what she has written. She does not yet understand that words are combinations of specific letters and that there must be spaces between words (a basic form of punctuation); this is evident in her statement "These are words" when she points to the letters. Denisha does know that she must write from left to right, exhibiting her sense of directionality. Generating strings of letters is a common literacy practice of beginning writers. Denisha shows her understanding that writing involves symbols or alphabet letters. Her progression of thinking is verified in my student's observations. Jennifer writes in her literacy profile, "Denisha definitely knows the difference between drawing and writing."

In Figure 1-5, 3½-year-old Thalia, like Denisha, demonstrates her concepts about the form and function of print when she hands this note to her father as he works on her literacy profile. Thalia and Denisha demonstrate emerging knowledge of the alphabetic principle—that is, that words are composed of individual letters or graphemes.

Thalia gives her dad this extra note to include in her literacy profile. He had been analyzing the ways in which she used writing to communicate, and he had collected many samples. This simple message, adorned with flowers and hearts, shows that she understands some of the functions of writing—in particular, writing a letter to maintain a relationship. As yet, she does not fully comprehend the "systematic relationship between letters and sounds" (Adams, 1990) or even the concept of a word. In time, as she continues to communicate through writing, Thalia will begin to use letter patterns to represent sound patterns. Later, she will invent spellings for

Figure 1-5. Thalia's Writing

words, sometimes concentrating on the initial or final consonant or on the most prominent sounds. She will continue to learn to read by writing. Joseph writes the following in her profile:

Thalia always listens and follows along with our conversations. I notice that she often pauses during our talks. In the beginning I didn't know what to make of it. Eventually I came to realize that her little mind was like a computer processing everything, transforming information to meet her needs.

Awareness of Sound System

Besides knowledge of print, learning to read and write involves an understanding of the sound system of language, or its cadence, rhyme, patterns, similarities, and differences. Rich language interactions increase phonological awareness. Songs, finger plays, and nursery rhymes support children's emerging phonological awareness, build upon what children already know, and support their new understanding of relationships between letters (graphemes) and their corresponding sounds (phonics).

The child learns to perceive that spoken language is composed of individual sounds, or phonemes, which are combined to make words. The young language learner is able to discriminate between phonemes—for instance, recognizing that the one-syllable word *dog* can be broken down into three sounds, *d-o-g*, which can be blended into one spoken word.

Later, children use the shared spelling patterns of the words they see in nursery rhymes as a basis for decoding unfamiliar vocabulary. Through analogy, they compare the features and characteristics of these words to new vocabulary encountered in storybooks and school texts. Young children arrive at school with refined perceptions about rhyming words, and they are easily able to match rhyming words when asked to do so by the teacher (Goswami, 1994).

Let's look at the ways in which 5- and 6-year-olds demonstrate their knowledge of the sound system of language in their writing. As with the 3- and 4-year-olds, their pictures and writing samples reflect the diversity of their literacy development. Each of the children is developmentally progressing toward proficiency as a reader and writer.

Can you "read" 5-year-old Meredith's picture? In Figure 1-6, she contextualizes her characters between defined sky and ground lines. She draws the setting for her story.

Meredith, like many emergent writers, draws to signify meaning. In this picture she's telling you about her classmates, lined up in a row, waiting to cross the street. She indicates this with the arrows she draws in the forefront of the picture. Notice the grinning faces on the children? They are very happy. Where could they be going? Theresa, another student, explains, "I collected so many pictures from Meredith. This one was about her school trip.... She never writes much. When I asked her why she does not put words in her pictures, she said that she likes to draw to tell her story." Apprentice writers often integrate drawings and sociodramatic play into their storytelling. Artwork, dramatic play, and talk about books support their first writing attempts (Dyson, 1988).

Figure 1-6. Meredith's Drawing

Five-year-old Conor dictates a story to another college student, Josephine. His narrative demonstrates his awareness of genre ("Once upon a time"), setting ("Rainbow Island"), protagonist ("little boy"), conflict ("He swam, and he swam but he couldn't get out"), resolution ("the rainbow went in to the water and saved the little boy"), and conclusion ("The End"). "He's quite a good storyteller," Josephine writes. She has begun to focus on what Conor can do rather than what he can't.

By the ages of 5 and 6, children understand (subconsciously) a great deal about syntax, grammar, graphophones, and the semantic nature of spoken and written language with little direct instruction. Teachers' transcriptions of children's oral stories provide them with demonstrations of the conventions and form of print. They observe the graphophonic similarities and differences of words (length, shape, parts, spelling), the spacing and punctuation of sentences, and demonstrations of the types and uses of written language. Over time, we can document these changes to inform our pedagogy.

Emergent writers also use drawing and talk to support their early explorations of print (Dyson, 1988). In Figure 1-8, observe the ways in which 5-year-old Elizabeth writes her name and embellishes her picture with rainbows, flowers, and floating letters. Rainbows appear to

> Once upon a time there was a little boy who went on an Island called Rainbow Island then he was Crossing a lake and fall in to the water. He swam, and he swam but he couldn't get out. Then the rainbow went in to the water and saved the little boy.
>
> The End
> CONOR

Figure 1-7. Conor's Story

be a socially acceptable and highly valued icon in the primary grades. Elizabeth's picture seems to be in movement; the trees, flowers, and letters sway as if blown by a gentle breeze.

Elizabeth appears to understand directionality, that the letters in her name must be written from left to right. However, her concept of a word is still in process, as evidenced by the floating letters in her picture. Notice how she has carefully lined up the trees and flowers. This behavior is defined as the "recurring principle" by Clay (1975). It is the symbolic precursor of children's ability to systematically repeat letters in a word. College student Janine writes, "Ever since Elizabeth learned to write her name in nursery school she has been writing it all over the place. She's also interested in writing other people's names."

Maybe these names are represented by the letters that drift like falling leaves across the page? Elizabeth's ability to spell her name helps her to develop alphabetic awareness. Children use their names and the names of people they know as a "lin-

Figure 1-8. Elizabeth's Drawing

guistic pool of knowledge" (Owocki & Goodman, 2002) to support them as they hypothesize how letters represent specific sounds.

In Figure 1-9, 5-year-old Gabrielle writes a note to Santa Claus. The actual words are transcribed above her words by the student writing the literacy profile. Gabrielle requests in writing a camera, an alarm clock, Precious Moments, Perfection, a princess castle, a CD player, a trace projector, a Slinky Dinky Maker, and a Play Doh creativity center. Her writing makes visible her emerging recognition of letters and letter-sound relationships, or graphophonic awareness. She uses prominent initial and final letter sounds to inventively construct her list. She perceives the consonant blend of *cl* in *clock*. Her writing is beginning to look like real words. Gabrielle's literacy development is in process,

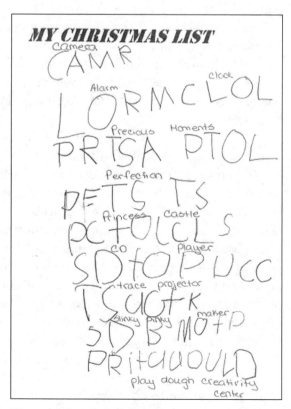

Figure 1-9. Gabrielle's Note

as evidenced by her sentence "PRITUUOULD" for the Play Doh creativity center, but she clearly understands the purposes of writing in her life.

In Figure 1-10, 5-year-old Francesca displays her emerging understandings about letter-sound relationships in her shopping list. The college student transcribes Francesca's words alongside and then notes the state standard she meets in this literacy task.

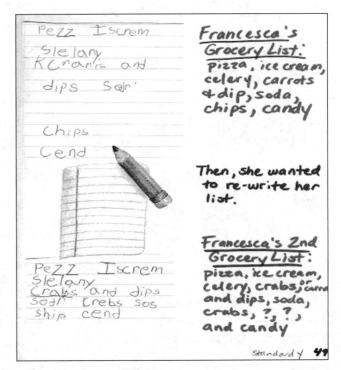

Figure 1-10. Francesca's List

Notice how Francesca demonstrates her phonemic awareness, or understanding of the ways in which spoken words have individual sound parts. "Iscrem" is not only delightful to read, it also shows Francesca's emerging awareness of sound-symbol relationships. She has created a compound word with a complex blend (*scr*) of consonants and has represented written language syllabically. "Sodr" represents the dialectical differences often seen in the ways in which children inventively create spellings. Francesca might be phonetically attempting to represent the past tense ("talkt" for *talked*). She demonstrates a solid understanding of the syllabic principle. She writes in capital and lowercase letters, which indicates her differentiation of these symbol systems. The spelling patterns reveal Francesca's transition from inventive to conventional or standard spelling. Spelling is developmental.

Teachers might "stretch" words like a rubber band (Harwayne, 2001) to help children discover their component phonemes and the sound-symbol relationships. They might blend letters to form different sounds, and blend words to form new ones. *S* and *t* are combined to form the new *st* blend. *Steam* and *boat* are combined to form *steamboat*.

Awareness of Print System

Five-year-old Cassandra demonstrates her print awareness, or recognition of letters and print in her environment, in the way that she lines her paper and writes her story in Figure 1-11. Over time she will begin to discriminate the commonalities in the print that surrounds them—for instance, the word *cat* has a *c* in it, just like the name *Cassandra*. When children begin to match letters, they demonstrate alphabetic understandings. Later, Cassandra will begin to perceive onset and rime patterns in words, evidence of her orthographic understanding. She will notice that *cat* begins with a *c* and ends with *at*. The word *bat* looks the same. Teachers call these *word families*. Children of this age will often reverse letters as they play with the symbols and gain physical knowledge of them. "Cassandra," my student writes, "is growing and becoming."

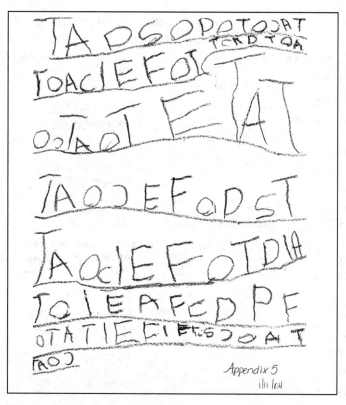

Figure 1-11. Cassandra's Writing

All of this primary understanding enables early literacy learners to be ready for formalized phonics instruction—that is, the rules of written language demonstrated by sound-symbol relationships. They will begin to ascribe phonemic values (sounds) to particular graphemes (letters), given the within-word context of those letters. For example, the letter *a* is pronounced differently in *tap* and *tape,* depending on its within-word position. Chapter 7 will discuss the value of using pattern books and books of rhyme to reinforce and extend children's understandings of phonic elements.

Children are able to write much earlier than we ever expected, and well before they are even able to read. We know that students learn to read through writing, and they learn to write through reading. We observe the ways in which they naturally integrate writing into make-believe play scenarios about real-life events. Their literacy development can be facilitated through the artful coordination of play settings and appropriate literacy props (Neuman & Roskos, 1997). The young child enjoys mimicking the real-world literacies that he or she observes in a bank, a restaurant, the neighborhood post office, the local library, or the doctor's or veterinarian's office. Setting up these types of play scenarios in early learning environments and providing children with authentic literacy materials—such as stamps and stamp pads, pencils, pens, note pads, crayons, markers, self-stick notes, memo boards, and any other props they would expect to see in these environments—makes the connections between "real-world" (Wells, 1998) and "schooled" (Meek, 1991) literacies.

Note the choices that 5-year-old Laura provides to her pretend patrons in Figure 1-12. In this sample, we see the way in which she brings everything she knows to the task at hand, or to the "Rainbow Café" script she plays with her little sister. It's obvious that Laura is familiar with menus and the wide range of purposes for which they are written. Her parents might have read menus to her, demonstrating how they are worded and organized. Laura includes appetizers, main courses, and free drinks on her play menu. Her spelling is, for the most part, conventional. Short vowels are accurately represented. Just as Laura models her own menu on those she has seen, many children will use picture books as mentor texts for their first stories.

Emergent writers learn to spell conventionally over time through a combination of implicit and explicit instruction. Young children's writing illustrates the ways in which they use letter-sound relationships in the words they want to write. In this developmental process, they will invent words and overgeneralize rules, for language learning is reconstructive rather than imitative. Research (Dyson,

1988; Graves, 1983; Teale & Sulzby, 1986) has demonstrated that when children have the opportunity to creatively express themselves, without fear of censure or emphasis upon the mechanics of the process (handwriting and spelling), they understand that writing is used for communication and has real purposes. Writing then becomes a tool for thinking and learning.

Six-year-old Jonathan writes and illustrates his story, "The Alien and the Moon." Maria transcribes her son Jonathan's words conventionally next to the story in Figure 1-13. "I am afraid of the aliens because they might destroy the electric system," Jonathan writes. Maria observes the ways in which Jonathan "tries to sound out words as he writes." This sample demonstrates Jonathan's use of this strategy, as well as his growing sight word vocabulary and understanding of common letter patterns. He spells conventionally and inventively.

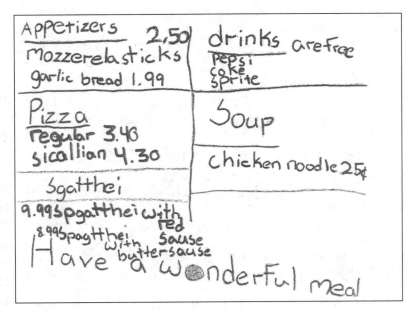

Figure 1-12. Laura's Menu

He attends to critical features of the words. Most of the initial and final consonants are correct; however, the medial sounds are still in process. He demonstrates his knowledge of grammar and punctuation. Jonathan even speculates about the existence of extraterrestrials who might do damage to the world. It is important to add that he wrote and illustrated this piece after the East Coast blackout of 2003, so this sample illustrates the ways in which children's writing reflects their culture and personal identities.

Five-year-old Daniel has a clear sense of a word, a sentence, and a story. He has chosen to write about his baseball game in Figure 1-14, and he draws a lively picture of the home run he hits to accompany the text. You can almost see the players as they run happily around the bases. Like Elizabeth's picture (Fig. 1-8), Daniel's picture has an animated quality. The players are in motion.

Figure 1-13. Jonathan's Story

Figure 1-14.   Daniel's Story

At this point, vowels and vowel markers (two vowels combined to make one sound) typically appear in children's writing. Daniel has not yet internalized that consonants must usually be doubled before adding -*ing* ("runing"), but he is an enthusiastic communicator who shares his love for baseball through drawing and writing. College student Patrick writes, "Daniel's writing has been getting increasingly better. His sentences are getting longer and more detailed. He is also starting to spell larger words." Perhaps his teacher has a collection of words posted on a word wall in the classroom that has enabled Daniel to develop a sight word vocabulary.

The use of print also involves prior knowledge, or being able to make connections between the printed symbols (words) in a text and personal experiences. The child understands a story about farm animals because he or she has visited a real farm and seen them. This background knowledge, termed *schema* by educators, facilitates reading comprehension. The symbols of written language become real for young children who can make connections with their life experiences. Chapter 8 will continue this discussion relating background knowledge to expository texts.

The "So What" Question

So what do all these pictures and writing samples mean for teachers in the primary grades? Clearly, an understanding of the complexity and diversity of children's literacy development informs instruction, assessment, and evaluation in the early years of schooling. Primary teachers who espouse a philosophy of emergent literacy consider the ways in which they contextualize learning to encourage apprentice readers and writers in their classrooms to remain confident and motivated. They build on what their students already know.

Babies and Bathwater

Having a solid theory about how children learn helps early childhood educators to plan comprehensive, developmentally appropriate literacy programs that build on what the children already know, and to teach skills within the familiar contexts of shared and guided reading and writing activities to promote understanding. We know that children bring personal and cultural experiences to bear on their school literacy tasks, and we teach in culturally responsive ways to assist them in gaining new knowledge. We appreciate the reciprocal relationship between oral and written language in this process, as well as the ways in which storytelling routines in the primary grades facilitate learning, help to bridge the literacy practices of home and school, and motivate children to be readers and writers.

We view development as social, dialogic, and context dependent. Children's skills in reading and writing develop at the same time and are interrelated rather than sequential (Teale & Sulzby, 1986). We must not toss out our theories or dismiss the seminal research on emergent literacy, including more than 100 years of observational work that illustrates the complex and highly cognitive processes of the young child's literacy development. One-dimensional models of literacy instruction will not meet the needs of our culturally and linguistically diverse student population. Sound theory leads to sound and equitable instruction, assessment, and evaluation in the primary grades. Chapter 6 will explore a "cultural text" model that engages non-English-speaking and culturally diverse student populations in reader response in meaningful ways.

"What Works"

The field has reconsidered "fat-cat-sat-mat" rigidly controlled phonics approaches to early literacy learning. Teachers know from knowledge, experience, observation, and evaluation of children's development "what works" in the foundational years. (See the What Works Clearinghouse Web site, www.w-w-c.org.) Strategy lessons in literacy-enriched environments, with ample demonstration and modeling of skills and strategies, flexible grouping arrangements, and lots of time for talk about reading and writing allow the early learner to practice new skills in a supportive atmosphere, facilitating self-confidence, love of reading and writing, and ownership of learning. Chapter 3 will present one flexible grouping arrangement called "kidstations," through which the teacher can differentiate instruction.

Strategy lessons integrated with literature-based instruction produce high levels of student engagement with books, skill in word identification, fluency, comprehension, and written composition abilities (Baumann & Ivey, 1997). During read-alouds, children learn not only about the sound system of language—its cadence, rhyme, patterns, and similarities—but also about the commonalities between letters and words. The teacher is able to extend concept development during the read-aloud by asking children questions about letters, word families, rhyming words, and words that share similar patterns. Minilessons, integrated with the children's own writing, extend these concepts.

Romancing young writers with the vibrant language and textual imagery of picture books is one of the best ways to prepare them to write independently. Using picture books wisely enables teachers to plan skills instruction within the context of authentic reading activities. Through modeling, support, and exploration of quality literature in classroom communities of writers, children begin to elaborate upon early writing genres, and new forms and purposes of expression emerge (Bissex, 1980; Kamberelis, 1999).

Making the Most of Our Time

Allington (2005) writes, "To achieve the highest quality educational outcomes requires that we make every moment of the school day count." Teaching and learning are facilitated when we consider how we integrate theory and practice into our literacy lessons and how we make effective and efficient use of academic time in our classrooms. In this reflective process, teachers make visible what they value with each instructional decision. How they model what it means to be literate impacts the unfolding sensibilities of their students. Through demonstrations, they afford children the time to construct their own understanding of reading and writing. Through collaboration, they afford them the time to refine these perceptions with their support and the support of their peers. In constructivist classrooms, teachers emphasize the personal, social, and cognitive aspects of literacy learning. They make time for reading aloud to children, journal writing, and sharing and celebrating their students' accomplishments.

Time for Reading Aloud

One of the most important activities in the formative years is reading aloud to children (Bus, Van Ijzendoorn, & Pelligrini, 1995). When teachers read aloud in the primary grades, it enhances children's oral and written language as well as their comprehension (Morrow, 1992). Expressively reading aloud to English language learners is a very effective teaching practice for improving their reading and writing proficiencies (Coyne, Simmons, & Kame'enui, 2004; Hickman, Pollard-Durodola, & Vaughn, 2004; McKeown & Beck, 2004). Chapter 3 has suggestions about read-alouds and reading to, reading with, and reading by children.

Routinely reading aloud supports children's literacy development and sets the context for the processing of the written language that's involved in reading and writing. Fox (1993) writes as follows:

> Topics and ideas are hard to find, it's true, but they're harder to find if children are living in a literary desert. . . . We need to water the desert so that writing will bloom. By watering the desert, I mean providing children with the most wonderful literature available: the classics, the new, the beautiful, the revolting, the hysterical, the puzzling, the amazing, the riveting. (p. 67)

By establishing a classroom read-aloud routine, you water the children's "desert" and seed it with wonderful writing ideas. These ideas will be explored further in the next two chapters.

Time for Journaling

Teaching children to write can never be reduced to simply copying letters. Teaching is an artful combination of personal philosophy and effective instructional strategies. Journaling can be an integral part of developing a community of writers in the classroom. Teachers might model the ways in which writers keep a notebook for their percolating ideas. Wood-Ray (1999) adds, "When students are taught to see how writing is done, this way of seeing opens up to them huge warehouses of possibilities for how to make their writing good writing" (p. 11). As they read and analyze texts, they begin to see themselves as capable writers.

Teachers encourage children to "read like writers" when they discuss the ways in which authors bring life to language. They use "I wonder" or curiosity questions to stimulate conversation as they talk about the ways in which authors restructure and craft words and phrases in picture books. These types of questions, classified as "interpretive probing" by Owocki and Goodman (2002), foster children's critical thinking about the decisions authors make as they write. Teachers can ask students to select their favorite words, phrases, or repetitive lines from texts read aloud in class, or from poetry, songs, magazines, newspapers, and even menus, and write these words in their own writer's notebooks or on the classroom word wall. Teachers might even suggest that students draw a picture to illustrate the word.

Time for Sharing and Celebrating

Teachers often make time to share and celebrate children's literacy accomplishments. As the classroom community of writers reflects upon one another's ideas, shares transactions, and records new observations in writers' notebooks, a nurturing and playful space is created in which students and teachers stretch their thinking and imagine new possibilities for writing. This leads to greater self-efficacy, persistence, motivation, and engagement in reading and writing activities. These types of interactions are familiar to children and mirror the experiences they have with family and community members who demonstrate, share, and celebrate their literacy growth and development. We'll end this discussion where we began, as we look at Thomas's language development within a supportive and celebratory context.

Thomas smiles as his grandmother hands him the cell phone. His father has just called, and Thomas wants to talk. "Ha-woa," he says. He has begun to utter simple phrases composed of nouns and verbs to create salutations, directives, and exclamations. "Da-da," he continues, "White—car—vroom—vroom." His mother adds, "Yes, Daddy's coming in the white car very soon." He simultaneously engages in a conversation with both his mother and father as he nibbles on some rolls. As he talks on the phone he varies the pitch, intonation, and pacing of his words. "Oh, no," he says at one point. This "toddler speak" (composed of conventional and invented words) reflects the ways that Thomas is observing and mimicking the language use of the significant people in his life. The conversation continues for several minutes as his father patiently listens. This builds Thomas's self-esteem as a communicator. His parents are confident that he will be speaking in longer and more complex sentences very soon. They celebrate each literacy milestone on the way.

Conclusion

Oral language and written language are learned in similar ways. Emergent literacy learners use what they know to construct their own understanding of how language works. They are motivated to listen, speak, read, write, and visually represent as they acquire these language processes within meaningful and nurturing contexts. Caretaker demonstrations provide feedback and support existing knowledge structures. Children learn about the purposes and pleasures of reading, writing, and communicating as they actively explore its uses and functions.

The National Association for the Education of Young Children (NAEYC) and the National Association of Early Childhood Specialists in State Departments of Education (NAECSSD) (2003) highlight the importance of implementing curriculum that is "thoughtfully planned, challenging, engaging, developmentally appropriate, culturally and linguistically responsive, comprehensive, and likely to promote positive outcomes for all young children."

As early childhood educators reflect upon what they value and the ways in which they teach, challenge, and motivate emergent readers and writers in their classrooms, they might ask themselves the basic questions raised in this chapter:

- Does the literacy curriculum make sense to my students?

- Is it comprehensible and authentic?

- Does it enable my students to connect existing knowledge structures about the form and function of print to their new literacy tasks?

- Does it capitalize on what my children already know?

- Will it sustain their joy and enthusiasm for learning?

- Can I create positive memories about school and learning with this curriculum?

- In what ways will I support and extend my students' perceptions of self-efficacy?

As noted in this chapter, primary teachers have the ability to motivate young readers and writers through enriched learning environments, meaningful social interactions with peers, and an artful combination of literacy materials and skills instruction. Romancing young writers with the vibrant language and textual imagery of picture books is a way to prepare them to write independently. Furthermore, a literature-based curriculum can assist primary teachers to help students remain confident and motivated readers and writers. Teachers who understand the developmental nature of reading and writing will make time for read-alouds and writing workshops. They will have high expectations for their students. They too are confident and capable literacy learners in their own classrooms, and they can easily meet and satisfy most state and federal standards in the primary grades while teaching skills and strategies in meaningful and authentic ways. Therefore, these teachers have the capability to create environments that nurture the nation's future readers, writers, and critical thinkers.

The literacy lessons presented in the next chapter are designed to help teachers conceptualize ways to engage and motivate children who are struggling, reluctant, proficient, or English language learners with quality literature and samples of craft lessons that have proved successful with writers in the primary grades.

Anticipation Guide Revisited

After reading this chapter, confirm your initial predictions about each statement. List the page number that supports each response.

Statement	Agree	Disagree	Verification
1. Learning to read and write involves the understanding that what I say can be written down on paper for someone else to read.	_____	_____	_____
2. By the ages of 5 and 6, children know a great deal about the form and function of spoken and written language. This understanding evolves with little or no direct instruction.	_____	_____	_____
3. Children learn to read and write by reading and writing.	_____	_____	_____
4. Early literacy learning is best facilitated when children practice reading aloud easily decodable, repetitive texts ("fat cat sat on the mat") that emphasize onset and rime patterns.	_____	_____	_____
5. Skills instruction must take place before a read-aloud or literacy lesson.	_____	_____	_____
6. Using "I wonder" questions with young children promotes critical thinking and supports conversations about books.	_____	_____	_____
7. Picture books are excellent tools with which to teach graphophonic, syntactic, and semantic and pragmatic strategies for reading and writing.	_____	_____	_____
8. Time for reading and writing should not be a factor in young children's literacy learning.	_____	_____	_____

Additional Resources

Web Sites

www.starfall.com
Activities for pre-K to grade 2

http://yn.la.ca.us/cec/ceclang/ceclang-elem.html
Alphabet books

www.lil-fingers.com/index.html
Storybooks for toddlers

www.starfall.com
Activities for children pre-K to grade 2

www.storyplace.org
Digital interactive library that features dual-language texts from pre-K to grade 6; a great way to bring books to children!

www.alphabet-soup.net/alphabite.html
Online and offline alphabet activities

www.learningplanet.com/parents/mom/alphabet/alphabet.htm
Hands-on alphabet activities for parents and children

www.literacycenter.net
Letters, words, and numbers

www.readwritethink.org
Comprehensive resource site with great lesson plans

http://edupuppy.com
A pre-K through grade 2 with fun activities

www.mcrel.org/resources/literacy/ela/index.asp
Early literacy assessment system to support instruction

http://kinderkorner.com
Resources for pre-K to grade 2

http://funschool.com
Interactive games—but lots of advertising!

www.pbskids.org/rogers/R_house
Features Mister Rogers' neighborhood; children can build their own neighborhood with interactive icons.

For Further Reflection

1. Family literacy practices influence young children's motivation to read and write. In what ways were you encouraged to become a reader and writer by family members, caregivers, or significant others in your life?

2. Do you remember learning to read and write in school? If so, what types of books, activities, and learning environments facilitated or impeded your literacy development? Do you remember how you felt about your capabilities as a reader and writer? Did you like to read and write? Why or why not?

3. Make a list of anything you can remember about your early schooling experiences in first, second, and third grade. Afterwards, try to reorganize the list. You might consider whether you highlighted the teacher's characteristics, the features of the instructional environment, or the types of literacy tasks you were asked to complete. Do these memories have implications for your own teaching and learning?

References

Adams, M. J. (1990). *Beginning to read: Thinking and learning about print.* Cambridge, MA: MIT Press.

Allington, R. L. (2005, August–September). President's message: Urgency and instructional time. *Reading Today,* p. 17.

Applebee, A. N. (1978). *The child's concept of story: Age two to seventeen.* Chicago: University of Chicago Press.

Bandura, A. (1977). Self efficacy: Toward a unifying theory of behavioral change. *Psychological Review, 84,* 191–215.

Bandura, A. (1997). *Self-efficacy: The exercise of control.* New York: Longman.

Baumann, J. F., & Ivey, G. (1997). Delicate balances: Striving for curricular and instructional equilibrium in a second-grade literature/strategy-based classroom. *Reading Research Quarterly, 32,* 244–275.

Beach, S. A. (1996). Facilitating young writers' development. *Reading Psychology, 17* (2), 181–190.

Bissex, G. L. (1980). *Gynys at work: A child learns to read and write.* Cambridge, MA: Harvard University Press.

Bredekamp, S., & Copple, C. (1997). *Developmentally appropriate practice in early childhood programs.* Washington, DC: National Association for the Education of Young Children.

Bus, A., Van Ijzedoorn, M., & Pelligrini, A. (1995). Joint book reading makes for success in learning to read: A meta-analysis on intergenerational transmission of literacy. *Review of Educational Research, 65,* 1–21.

Cambourne, B. (2000). Is an educationally relevant theory of literacy learning possible? 25 years of inquiry suggest it is. In N. K. Padak (Ed.), *Distinguished educators on reading: Contributions that have shaped effective literacy instruction,* (pp. 59–65). Newark, DE: International Reading Association.

Cambourne, B. (2001). Turning learning theory into classroom instruction: A mini-case study. *The Reading Teacher, 54* (4), 414–417.

Calkins, L. (1994). *The art of teaching writing.* Portsmouth, NH: Heinemann.

Clay, M. (1975). *What did I write? Beginning writing behavior.* Portsmouth, NH: Heinemann.

Clay, M. (1991). *Becoming literate: The construction of inner control.* Portsmouth, NH: Heinemann.

Comer, B. (2001). Negotiating critical literacies. *School Talk, 6* (3), 1–2.

Coyne, M. D., Simmons, D. C., & Kame'enui, E. J. (2004). Vocabulary instruction for young children at risk of experiencing reading difficulties: Teaching word meanings during storybook readings. In J. F. Baumann & E. J. Kame'enui (Eds.), *Vocabulary instruction: Research to practice* (pp. 41–58). New York: Guilford Press.

Dyson, A. H. (1988). Appreciate the drawing and dictating of young children. *Young Children, 43* (3), 25–32.

Dyson, A. H., & Freeman, S. W. (1991). Writing. In J. Flood, J. M. Jensen, D. Lapp, & J. R. Squire (Eds.), *Handbook of teaching English language arts* (pp. 754–774). New York: Macmillan.

Ferreiro, E., & Teberosky, A. (1985). *Literacy and schooling.* Portsmouth, NH: Heinemann.

Fox, M. (1993). *Radical reflections: Passionate opinions on teaching, learning, and living.* San Diego, CA: Harcourt Brace Jovanovich.

Goodman, Y., & Owocki, G. (2002). *Kidwatching: Documenting children's literacy development.* Portsmouth, NH: Heinemann.

Goswami, U. (1994). Reading by analogy. In C. Hulme & M. Snowling (Eds.), *Reading, development and dyslexia.* London: Whurr.

Graves, D. (1983). *Writing: Teachers and children at work.* Portsmouth, NH: Heinemann.

Halliday, M.A.K. (1973). *Explorations in the functions of language.* London: Arnold.

Halliday, M.A.K. (1975). *Learning how to mean: Explorations in the development of language.* London: Arnold.

Halliday, M.A.K. (1994). The place of dialogue in children's construction of meaning. In R. B. Ruddell, M. R. Ruddell, & H. Singer (Eds.), *Theoretical models and processes of reading* (4th ed., pp. 80–82). Newark, DE: International Reading Association.

Haneda, M., & Wells, G. (2000). Writing in knowledge-building communities. *Research in the Teaching of English, 34* (3), 430–457.

Harwayne, S. (2001). *Writing through childhood*. Portsmouth, NH: Heinemann.

Hickman, P., Pollard-Durodola, & Vaughn, S. (2004). Storybook reading: Improving vocabulary and comprehension of English-language learners. *Reading Teacher, 57* (8), 720–730.

Kamberelis, G. (1999). Genre development and learning: Children writing stories, science reports, and poems. *Research in the Teaching of English, 33* (4), 403–460.

Karweit, N., & Wasik, B. (1996). The effects of story reading programs on literacy and language development of disadvantaged preschoolers. *Journal of Education for Students Placed at Risk, 4*, 319–348.

Kucer, S. B. (2005). *Dimensions of literacy: A conceptual base for the teaching of reading and writing* (2nd ed.). Mahwah, NJ: Erlbaum.

Lapp, D., Flood, J., & Roser, N. (2000). Still standing: Timeless strategies for teaching the language arts. In D. S. Strickland & L. M. Morrow (Eds.), *Beginning reading and writing* (pp. 183–193). New York: Teachers College Press.

Lave, J., & Wegner, E. (1991). *Situated learning: Legitimate peripheral participation.* New York: Cambridge University Press.

Malaguzzi, L. (1998). No way: The hundred is there. In C. Edwards, L. Gandini, & G. Forman (Eds.), *The hundred languages of children* (pp. 2–3). Greenwich, CT: Ablex.

Martens, P. (1996). *I already know how to read*. Portsmouth, NH: Heinemann.

Mathewson, G. C. (1994). Model of attitude influence upon reading and learning to read. In R. B. Ruddell, M. R. Ruddell, & H. Singer (Eds.), *Theoretical models and processes of* reading (4th ed., pp. 1131–1161). Newark, DE: International Reading Association.

McCabe, P. (2003). Enhancing self-efficacy for high-stakes reading tests. *The Reading Teacher, 57* (1), 12–20.

McKeown, M. G., & Beck, I. L. (2004). Direct and rich vocabulary instruction. In J. F. Baumann & E. J. Kame'enui (Eds.), *Vocabulary instruction: Research to practice* (pp. 13–27). New York: Guilford Press.

Meek, M. (1991). *On being literate*. Portsmouth, NH: Heinemann.

Morrow, L. M. (1992). The impact of literature-based program on literacy achievement, uses of literature, and attitudes from children from minority backgrounds. *Reading Research Quarterly, 32* (1), 54–77.

National Association for the Education of Young Children & National Association of Early Childhood Specialists in State Departments of Education. (2003). *Position statement: Early childhood curriculum, assessment, and program evaluation.* Available online at: www.naeyc.org/about.positions.asp.

Neuman, S. N., & Roskos, K. (1997). Literacy knowledge in practice: Contexts of participation for young writers. *Reading Research Quarterly, 32* (1), 10–33.

Owocki, G., & Goodman, Y. (2002). *Kidwatching: Documenting children's literacy development.* Portsmouth, NH: Heinemann.

Smith, F. (1988). *Joining the literacy club: Further essays into education.* Portsmouth, NH: Heinemann.

Spandel, V. (2004). *Creating young writers.* New York: Pearson.

Teale, W. H., & Sulzby, E. (1986). *Emergent literacy: Writing and reading.* Norwood, NJ: Ablex.

Vygotsky, L. (1978). *Mind in society: The development of higher psychological processes.* Cambridge, MA: Harvard University Press.

Walker, B. (2003). The cultivation of student self-efficacy in reading and writing. *Reading and Writing Quarterly, 19,* 173–187.

Wells, G. (1985). Preschool literacy-related activities and success in school. In D. R. Olson, N. Torrance, & A. Hildyard (Eds.), *Literacy, language, and learning: The nature and consequence of reading and writing.* Cambridge, UK: Cambridge University Press.

Wells, G. (1996). *The meaning makers: Children learning language and using language to learn.* Portsmouth, NH: Heinemann.

Wells, G. (1998). Real literacy in a school setting: Five-year-olds take on the world. *The Reading Teacher, 52* (1), 8–17.

Wood-Ray, K. W. (1999). *Wondrous words: Writers and writing in the elementary classroom.* Urbana, IL: National Council of Teachers of English.

Chapter 2

Crafting the Way to Literacy

Anticipation Guide

Before reading this chapter, please read each of the statements listed below. Based upon your prior knowledge and experience with this chapter's topics, check either "agree" or "disagree" for each statement. After reading the chapter, see if your answers change in the Anticipation Guide Revisited found at the end of the chapter.

Statement	Agree	Disagree
1. Children who are struggling, proficient, reluctant, and English language literacy learners comprehend reading and writing strategies if they are presented in meaningful instructional contexts.	_____	_____
2. Children must know how to read before they are able to write their own stories.	_____	_____
3. *Crafting* refers to the decisions authors make about the wording, structure, and genre of the stories and books they write.	_____	_____
4. Repetitive language, contrastive structures, or circular picture book patterns enable children to predict, expand sight word vocabulary, and refine understanding of the form and function of print.	_____	_____
5. To be a teacher of readers and writers, you must be a reader and writer yourself.	_____	_____
6. Picture books aren't sufficient to meet state standards for the teaching and learning of the English language arts.	_____	_____
7. Teachers can write their own writing workshop curriculum in the early grades.	_____	_____
8. The National Reading Panel outlined specific criteria for teaching writing in the primary grades.	_____	_____

Introduction

The purpose of this chapter is to help teachers understand the notion of crafting with picture books, and how to integrate skills, strategies, and state standards into writing and reading workshop lessons. Crafting is an approach to language arts instruction that focuses upon the decision-making aspects of the writing process— that is, the purposeful ways authors choose to compose and pattern their stories, poems, or books using descriptive language, varied narrative structures, point of view, or type of genre. Read-alouds, group discussions, and interactive writing lessons characterize this workshop model. Reading and writing workshops in grades K–3 can be enhanced when texts are selected that match children's natural curiosity, identity, sense of humor, and level of cognitive development. Examples of the ways in which teachers in urban and suburban schools have implemented, extended, and modified crafting lessons that capitalize on children's natural desire to learn are provided throughout the chapter. These examples present ways in which teachers in the early grades can plan writing to meet the needs of all their students.

Why Crafting?

Sprinkled throughout the chapter are college students' (preservice, novice, and veteran teachers') reactions to their crafting coursework and its implications for teaching and learning in their own classrooms. These students were enrolled in a "Teaching Literacy Through Literature" course in which they were asked to create a storehouse of crafting texts to share with peers and teaching colleagues. One preservice teacher wrote, "In the field, as a student teacher, I've heard and seen the confusion felt by teachers trying to grasp the concept of a reading/writing workshop." Another made plans for the future: "I would like to have books in my classroom library with different structures of writing such as seesaw, repetition, listing, cumulative, and circular to show the use of each writing style." As you read this chapter, you might envision goals for your own classroom and discuss what could prevent you from accomplishing your objectives.

Let's examine the following vignette, called "Secret Agent Man," to see how crafting with picture books motivated Matthew to write:

> I was reading *Hairs/Pelitos* to Mrs. Walsh's second graders, pointing out the similes [Sandra] Cisneros uses to create pictures with words. We made a list of the descriptions on chart paper. The children especially liked the phrase "My papa's hair is like a broom, all up in the air." Matthew, whom the teacher called the "secret agent man," was particularly engaged with the picture book illustrations and crafting lesson. My goal was to create a class simile book with the children's own sentences. That's when I noticed that Matthew was missing from his desk. I alerted the teacher, who smiled and said, "Oh, he must be on a special mission." It seemed that Matthew, a bright child, would sometimes just disappear. Later, he would tell his teacher that he had to go undercover for the government. "He's here, don't worry," Mrs. Walsh added. Matthew, I was told, was able to find creative ways to camouflage his presence within the four walls of the classroom. I began to think of the reasons reluctant, struggling, and proficient learners might literally and figuratively camouflage themselves within the contexts of their school literacy tasks. Perhaps they do so for survival? It became my mission to hook Matthew and his classmates into the joy of reading like a writer.

In Figure 2-1, we see the way he has modeled his piece upon Cisneros's style. What a proud and creative way to describe a receding hairline!

Figure 2-1. Matthew's Piece

Teaching by the Book: Writing by Example

Modeling with picture books is one of the most powerful ways to promote strong writing in the primary grades. As children become aware of different genres, they begin to appropriate them in their own writing. Simultaneously, they learn about the mechanics of the process, by trying it out, writing often, copying what they see in the environment, and listening to good literature read well. Children learn to read and write by spending time reading and writing, and their dual language processes develop concurrently. Furthermore, the act of writing generates ideas (NCTE, 2005). There is no need to postpone writing until children know all their alphabet letters, because many develop strong writing skills simply through exposure to print-rich environments (Schickedanz, 1998). Although the literary format of picture books provides a strong model for writing instruction, young children can be supported to fine-tune their skills in reading and writing through the adoption of a comprehensive literature-based approach.

Emergent readers and writers are capable of participating in the social interaction, talk, and language-enriched contexts of literature circles and writing workshops that encourage authentic and purposeful reading and writing activities (Haneda & Wells, 2000; Neuman & Roskos, 1997). One of the best opportunities for hearing the descriptive language of strong writing comes from "sitting on the story rug and talking about children's books" (Lapp, Flood, & Roser, 2000, p. 187). It is through rich literacy experiences that children's stories become longer and more complex (Beach, 1996; Dyson & Freeman, 1991).

Teaching Children to Read Like Writers

Contemporary notions about craft writing, reading like a writer, or workshop models of literacy learning (Calkins & Pessah, 2004; Fletcher & Portalupi, 2002) have long roots in teaching, learning, and writing instruction. Ken Goodman (1996), Donald Graves (1983), and Frank Smith (1988) were some of the first to write about the relationship between reading and writing as well as authentic moments of teaching and learning in writing communities. College student Edna, however, remembers her early writing experiences as follows: "Writing to me was penmanship. It was torture."

Smith (1988) states, "To learn to write, children must read in a special kind of way" (p. 17). Children who read like writers do more than comprehend what they read. Wood-Ray (2004) clarifies, "When you read like a writer, you also notice and think about *how* a text is written. . . . everything they [children] notice about how books are made becomes something they might try when they make them" (p. 14).

Fletcher and Portalupi (2002), among others, refer to this concept as *craft writing*. Craft writing can be defined as a discussion and analysis of the purposeful ways in which authors use language and story formats to compose and pattern their books. In a crafting workshop, teachers talk about writers' techniques, including graphic structures, story patterns, writing conventions, different genres, illustrations, and whimsical ways with words that seem to dance across the page. Time is set aside to notice, describe, and talk about what writers do and how they write. This develops children's reflective abilities and meta-awareness about writing as something more than just a simple "formulaic set of steps" (NCTE, 2005). In a workshop setting, primary students learn about imagery, structure, and descriptive language as they illustrate, frame, and extend their own writing with added details and extensive description.

Emergent writers can be shown how to identify the crafting techniques an author uses and how to make theories about the reasons that he or she drafted a particular piece, in a particular way, and for a particular audience. Teachers of craft writers enjoy the ways in which their children process and respond to the books they read aloud in class, and they delight in the ways in which apprentice writers show them what they know, what they like, and what they question in their own writing samples.

English Language Arts Standards Integrated With Crafting

The four workshop formats presented later in this chapter sufficiently meet, and might even surpass, national and state standards for the English language arts (ELA). The standards presented are from New York State. They are congruent with national standards, those outlined by the National Council of Teachers of English and the International Reading Association. Through workshop "crafting" lessons, the ELA standards given below in italics are met.

Students will listen and read to acquire information and understanding; collect data, facts, and ideas; discover relationships, concepts, and generalizations; and use knowledge from oral, written, and electronic sources. They will read, write, listen, and speak for critical analysis and evaluation.

This is the essence of a crafting workshop! As students read and discuss texts and analyze authors' techniques, they begin to see the differences between and among genres and use this knowledge to create their own stories, poems, and written pieces. These "published" works become part of the classroom library, enabling children to reflect upon their accomplishments and appropriate new ideas from their peers.

Students will speak and write to acquire and transmit information, ask probing and clarifying questions, interpret information in their own words, apply information from one context to another, and present the information and interpretation clearly, concisely, and comprehensibly.

The analysis of an author's craft during reading and writing workshops addresses this standard comprehensively. As children ask probing and clarifying questions and suggest why an author might have used a certain technique in a picture book, they connect to what they already know and stretch their thinking to include alternative possibilities. As they interrogate the books they read, they make connections across the texts and contexts of their previous literacy tasks and experiences.

Students will read, write, listen, and speak for literary response and expression, comprehending, interpreting, and critiquing imaginative texts in every medium; draw on personal experiences and knowledge to understand the text; present interpretations to the content and language of the text; produce imaginative texts that use language and text structures that are inventive and often multilayered. They will read, write, listen, and speak for social interaction.

This is a given! Reading and writing workshops are lively, happy, and noisy places. Primary students respond to stories in multilayered ways. They might talk about their favorite parts, dance, sing, sculpt, draw or write their impressions, or try crafting their own version of the story. We know that literacy learning is social and dialogic in nature, and it is facilitated with demonstrations and time set aside for reading, writing, speaking, and thinking!

The Crafting Appeal

The apprentice writer, like the novice and proficient one, is delighted to discover that the writing "wheel" doesn't have to be reinvented. Instead, he or she can read with the eyes of a writer, identify and talk about an author's techniques, and then borrow the idea. It's a pressure-free approach that's guaranteed to entice the most reluctant writers. In both general and inclusive classrooms, we find students eager to craft stories after shared conversations about books. Through the incorporation of picture books and conversation in the writing classroom, emergent writers build a repertoire of genres and styles as well as a greater understanding of the process and techniques that writers use to jump-start and invigorate their writing. A college student, Dianne, wrote, "I've learned that crafting eases students into writing by taking away the scary composing element. They are not on their own because they can stand on the shoulders of their writers." Another student, Amy, writes about her own epiphany: "Crafting has taken away a fear I had. Writing for me was always a continuous struggle for perfection."

"If You Give a Teacher a Book. . ."

Picture books represent poetry between two covers. Their repetitive language, contrastive structures, and circular patterns enable children to predict, expand sight word vocabulary, and refine their understanding of the form and function of print. Many teachers are surprised to discover that they have been crafting all along but just didn't refer to it by that term. To borrow the technique of Laura Numeroff's *If You Give a Mouse a Cookie* (1985), if you give a teacher a picture book, there is a good chance that he or she will find a wonderful use for it.

For example, when teachers read big books to the class and then engage in an interactive writing activity using the wording or structure of the text, they are helping students to read like writers or to craft their writing based upon an author's model. Primary teachers can use Charles Shaw's *It Looked Like Spilt Milk* (1994) or Eric Carle's *Little Cloud* (2001) as models for first books, writing their students' words underneath the illustrations they create with white paint or cotton balls and dark blue paper. *Brown Bear, Brown Bear, What Do You See?* by Bill Martin (1983) has a strong repetitive pattern that is most appropriate for crafting in the primary grades. Students are quite able to spot Martin's writing technique and to appropriate his ways with words in their own books.

Let's now examine four ways to work with picture books in the primary grades. These make use of speech bubble, list, seesaw, and circular story patterns. Teachers' use of these formats or story patterns extends young children's literary understanding and facilitates their development as competent, motivated, and self-monitoring readers and writers. Additional story patterns, presented in chapter 7, will encourage deeper understanding and writing of the narrative style for intermediate and middle school students.

Speech bubble books include those texts that blend pictures and words in a cartoonlike format. Characters' words or thoughts are embedded within speech bubbles, and the story is dialogue driven. These types of picture books appeal to the young craft writer because their format is familiar, easy to read, and pleasing to replicate. The combination of visual and written language in speech bubble books enables primary children to bridge what they already know to what they have yet to learn. They are the perfect way to transition into craft writing in the primary grades.

List texts include those picture books that focus upon a single topic (person, place, group of things) and list it in some related fashion. This craft or format pleases the novice writer and is developmentally appropriate for early childhood instruction. Primary children appreciate the fact that people make lists for all sorts of things. The structure of this category is familiar and comprehensible. Children have seen family members write lists for groceries or errands they need to run.

The *seesaw* format refers to picture books that weave or flip back and forth through wording, concept, or story structure. Seesaw texts allow the young child to compare and contrast different yet similar concepts. Seesaw picture books also facilitate prediction, which is the heart of the reading process. As with the list story structure, the apprentice writer is developmentally and cognitively able to retrace and re-create the seesaw pattern.

A story in the *circular* format begins and ends at the same point in time or setting, thus coming full circle, as the name implies. Young writers enjoy both the directional pattern of this story structure and the sense of security it gives them. They have little difficulty emulating its craft, because it's reminiscent of their early "and then I woke up" stories.

A Storehouse of Ideas to Get You Started

The crafting techniques and literacy lessons presented in this chapter are designed to help you in the process of reconceptualizing ways to motivate students who are struggling, reluctant, proficient, or English language learners to write with a sense of authorship and style. Each lesson is framed in the same manner: a recommended picture book, its synopsis, a brief excerpt, key strategies to teach using the book, crafting and extension lessons that connect the skills instruction to an authentic reading and writing activity, suggested text sets, and an articulation of the English language arts standards addressed in the lesson. These lessons are not scripts, they are suggestions. The lessons are formatted in a concise fashion to afford you the opportunity to add your own ideas, complementary texts, and lesson extensions. Each lesson, with adaptation and modification, works well in general, inclusive, and English language learners' classrooms from kindergarten through grade 3.

The picture books presented in this chapter typify structures that will delight, motivate, and engage writers in the primary grades and assist their teachers in planning for instruction in a workshop setting. Their structures integrate nicely with an early writing curriculum, for they are similar in pattern to the types of writing children already do. The selections are arranged categorically; however, boundary lines between crafting techniques are almost always blurred. Single-craft-technique picture books are rare to find. There are list books that seesaw or are written in a circular fashion. They might even include illustrations that contain speech bubbles. Teachers can decide which aspect or craft they wish to focus on in each text, and then compile text sets of additional books. Joann, a college student, writes, "I find myself looking for interesting uses of language, punctuation, text structure, print, and illustrations." Another student, Mario, writes, "As I read the children's books, and saw their structure, I was amazed that I hadn't recognized the patterns before." Marianna plans, "In the future I will use these experienced writers (mentors) to assist me in teaching. I will be looking at writing differently, and will be reading with an author's eyes." Some suggestions for compiling text sets for these structures are presented in this chapter as well in the Additional Resources section at the end of the chapter.

Putting on Writers' Glasses

We tell primary students that good writing comes from the heart but that it always begins with a plan. As we read together, we pretend to put on our "writer's glasses" to discover and talk about how each author has planned and crafted the story. We think about where we've seen the writing techniques before and then discuss how we can borrow the ideas. Once the crafting concept has infiltrated students' thinking, they begin to notice it everywhere. Jennifer, a college student, writes, "I am beginning to read like a writer. Last night watching the Yankees game I was listening to the commercials—the rhymes, the flow, the phrases. I've never really listened or noticed commercials on purpose!" Pia adds, "Everything I read 'like a writer.' It's like reading a new language for the very first time." Another student, Kevin, writes, "To explain the shift in my thinking it was like I was in park, but now I'm in drive. Actually, I feel as though I had been in the wrong car all along!" Let's use the glasses to begin our analysis of four story patterns appropriate for crafting in the primary grades.

Speech Bubble Crafting

Matching instruction to children's emerging literacies facilitates their growth and proficiency in reading and writing. Starting with something the children already know, such as picture books with speech bubbles, or "talking clouds" (as some second graders called them), is a fitting way to begin craft study. Primary children have seen this craft in comic strips and television cartoons. In fact, they typically place these types of bubbles above characters' heads in their own pictures, embedding two- or three-word phrases within them. Over time, teachers observe the ways in which these snippets of speech embedded within bubbles are transformed into stories that are dialogue driven. Primary students enjoy reading fancifully crafted texts. Therefore, you might begin craft conversations in first and second grade with speech bubble books.

In Figure 2-2, we see how first- and second-grade children in a culturally and linguistically diverse suburban school district fell in love with the idea of storytelling through this structure. Speech bubble fever soon took over the school, as demonstrated in the photo above. The children used them in their illustrations for both narrative and expository writing

Figure 2-2. Speech Bubble Story—Bilingual

pieces. English language learners wrote their first sentences in Spanish and English. A shared language evolved among the children about craft and what it means to be a writer.

Second graders then took speech bubbles and incorporated them into a simple story narrative. The simple, cartoonlike structure of Figure 2-3 demonstrates one of the ways in which writers in the primary grades organize their stories. The incorporation of onomatopoeia (i.e., "honk honk") illustrates how the children appropriated features of different texts and crafts in their writing as they developed their own style. The children were exposed to onomatopoeia in a writing workshop held a few days before.

Figures 2-4 and 2-5 were written after conflict management was discussed in class.

Figure 2-3. Speech Bubble Story—Onomatopoelia

Figure 2-4.   Speech Bubble Story—Sisters' Conflict Management

Figure 2-5. Speech Bubble Story—Work

Finally, Figure 2-6 was created after the children saw a live performance of *Alice in Wonderland*.

Figure 2-6. Speech Bubble Story—The March Hare

The picture book that started the speech bubble epidemic is presented below.

Sample Speech Bubble Lesson

Title and Author: *Don't Let the Pigeon Drive the Bus!* by Mo Willems (2003).

Synopsis: Primary children absolutely adore this irrepressible pigeon's antics and attempts to "drive the bus." This little blue bird has captivated their hearts and minds. The story is told entirely in speech bubbles, and you will find that the children begin to answer the pigeon's questions as you read aloud. They giggle and smile as they enter his story world, making it an interactive experience. They love this book so much that they will ask you to read it again and again.

Excerpt: "Hey, can I drive the bus?"
"Please?"
"I'll be careful."
"I tell you what: I'll just steer."

Objectives: The main purpose of this lesson is to engage children in an interactive guided reading, writing, and sharing activity that will introduce them to the notion of crafting, or borrowing ideas from authors. A second goal is to begin classroom conversations that will enable students to talk about the process and learn what writers do when they compose. In developing a schema about the structure and wording of texts, students will begin to understand audience and purpose in their writing.

Crafting Lesson: You might begin this lesson with a conversation about the way Willems crafts his story through the use of speech bubbles. Ask the children to tell you what they notice about how the book is written. Write down all their observations on large chart paper, combining and extending statements when possible. In conversation, guide them to recognize the unique storytelling technique of first-person narrative drafted through speech bubble dialogue. Avoid naming the craft. Instead, ask the children what they would call Willems's technique, and add these names to the chart. *Talking clouds, dreaming clouds, talking bubbles,* and *thinking bubbles* were some of the names the second graders I worked with suggested. Finally, ask the children if they have ever seen this craft before. Have companion texts ready to share with the class to make this visible. Discuss the ways in which authors borrow ideas. The children are now ready to practice, or borrow, the craft of this picture book. You might use pages from wordless picture books, such as Mercer Mayer's *Frog Goes to Dinner* (1974), or use cartoon strips to support beginning stories. Draft the first one together to demonstrate how to tell a story through talking bubbles.

Text-Set Extension: Willems's sequel, *The Pigeon Finds a Hot Dog!* (2004), is appropriate, as are *Goodnight, Gorilla* by Peggy Rathmann (1994) and *Watch Out! A Giant!* by Eric Carle (2002b). Other texts that complement this craft study are *Tea for Me, Tea for You* by Laura Rader (2003), a cumulative text with rhyme, numeric concepts, and speech bubbles; *Two Eggs, Please* by Sarah Weeks and Betsy Lewin (2003), a short book that explores the concept of difference with thinking bubbles; *Don't Forget the Bacon* by Pat Hutchins (1976), a repetitive and cumulative story that holds the interest of primary readers and writers; *The Magic School Bus* series (Cole, 2002), which makes liberal use of this crafting technique and is quite popular with the little ones; and finally, *Mrs. Watson Wants Your Teeth* by Alison McGhee (2004), which will captivate first graders, who can relate to the anxiety of entering first grade and meeting a new teacher as well as losing two front teeth. The story, told in speech bubbles, tickles their fancy.

Standards Connection: The national and state standards addressed in this lesson are as follows:

- Promoting phonemic awareness through analysis of initial and final consonant sounds in words
- Using context picture clues to decode and comprehend
- Strengthening spelling skills and building sight word vocabulary
- Learning about quotation marks and dialogue through speech bubbles

List Book Crafting

List books focus on a single topic (person, place, or group of things) or theme. The young child naturally gravitates toward books written in a listing structure, because he or she enjoys writing lists. Clay (1975) suggests that listing is appealing to young children because they can take "stock of their own learning" through the ordering of pictures and words in a "systematic" way. She writes that children's early writing "shows how spontaneously they arrange or order the things they have learned into inventories" (p. 31). They write lots of lists, as we saw with Francesca and Gabrielle in Chapter 1.

List texts with highly repetitive, strongly patterned structures also provide early learners with ample opportunities to predict, comprehend, expand sight word vocabulary, communicate understanding, and refine their awareness of the lyrical nature of language. The following texts are most suitable for the apprentice writer, who will often copy the words or letters he or she knows over and over to construct longer messages. This writing behavior, known as the recurring principle (Clay, 1975), is most pleasing to the young child, who is often proud to read back what he or she has written. Primary teachers note how emergent literacy learners string letters together, write groups of words spelled inventively, and eventually construct simple sentences containing conventional and inventive spellings. Children's first narratives or stories are often chains of simple, egocentric sentences, such as "I went to the store. I went with my grandma. I got a teddy bear." Therefore, list books make sense for emergent writers, for these abbreviated texts mimic their own writing. As outlined by the National Research Council (1998):

> Once children learn to write letters, they should be encouraged to write them, to use them to begin writing words, and to use words to begin writing sentences. . . . Writing should take place regularly and frequently to encourage children to become more comfortable and familiar with it. (pp. 323–324)

You can accomplish all of these suggestions with list books.

As with all crafting techniques that you incorporate into the writing curriculum, it is best to start small and practice the craft yourself. Try drafting a few list pieces crafted with the books or poems you plan to use with the children in your own writer's notebook. In doing so, you're learning to craft in order to teach crafting.

Frank, a college student, writes:

> This idea of having a writer's notebook was not one that I was so comfortable with last year. However, after realizing the great importance of providing students with a model of your expectations, I will be using one in the forthcoming year.

Another college student, Roxane, shares:

> I never considered myself to be a strong writer, it was just something I had to get done in school. However with positive feedback from a teacher, my writing would have improved. This class allowed me to break down my wall and just write.

Sample List Book Lessons

Alphabet books are the list books with which primary children are most familiar. You might stockpile a set of these texts to teach the alphabetic principle, and so much more, to the young writers in your class. Children of all ages enjoy these books, and these texts model the strong crafting techniques of wording, text structure, and descriptive writing coupled with vivid illustrations. Let's examine two list books that have led to successful writing lessons.

LESSON 1

Title and Author: *Animalia* by Graeme Base (1996)

Synopsis: This is a delightful alphabet book with inviting illustrations and amusing alliteration. The children will love hearing you read the tongue-twisting menagerie of words, and they will enjoy viewing the illustrations to search for the objects listed.

Excerpts: "Great green gorillas growing grapes in a gorgeous glass greenhouse"
"Lazy lions lounging in the library"
"Eight enormous elephants expertly eating Easter eggs"

Objectives: The purpose of this lesson is to provide an enjoyable shared reading experience while promoting children's phonemic awareness. Another objective is to talk about clusters or blends of letters, supporting children's graphophonic awareness of letter-sound associations, onset and rime, and word parts.

Crafting Lesson: Begin this lesson with a read-aloud. Then, through talking, ask the children to notice what guides them to observe not only the letters but also the technique of alliteration and vivid imagery. Discuss the rich, descriptive language. Write the children's observations and comments on chart paper for later reference. Next, ask if they have seen this technique before. (Some of my students mentioned Sandra Cisneros!) They have now established a solid base of literary knowledge from which to draw, enabling them to connect new crafts to ones they have previously analyzed. A fine companion text is *The Book of Shadow Boxes: A Story of the ABCs* by Laura Seeley (1958). Seeley structures her alliterative sentences poetically. She writes:

> Bananas and butterflies
>
> Both start with B's,
>
> And little blue bubbles
>
> That bounce in the breeze.

At this point in this lesson, encourage the children to borrow the idea. Brainstorm some alliterative words and playfully combine them to model the first sentence. Children can work in pairs on their own invented sentences, which can then be displayed on a bulletin board or in a word study center.

Figures 2-7, 2-8, and 2-9 show how Ms. DeAngelo's fifth graders explored and replicated Base's crafting techniques in the alphabet books they created for primary students.

Figure 2-7. List Book Story—Sally the Snake

You might transcribe some of the adjectives from *Animalia*, or from the children's own sentences, into their writers' notebooks. They can illustrate them to facilitate comprehension, retention, and word recognition. College student Stephanie writes, "I have learned that for writing to make the most sense, it should be taught in context, not in isolation."

Crafting Extension: You might use the children's first or last name, and the accompanying alphabet letter, with an alliterative description, such as "S—Sammy sings songs." The children can illustrate these pages for an alphabet chart or book. Third graders, with the assistance of teachers and peers, can write and illustrate their own alphabet books to be read to students in kindergarten. An alphabet

Figure 2-8. List Book Story—Prickly Pineapples

Figure 2-9.   List Book Story—Whistling Whales.

book by Alice Lyne (1997) called *A, My Name Is...*, further extends this classroom craft study. The author cleverly writes the following stanza to accompany the jump-roping alligators:

> A a
>
> My name is Alex,
>
> My best friend's name is Angie,
>
> We live in Alabama.
>
> And we sell alligators.

Text-Set Extension: A college student, Danielle, writes in her reflective paper, "I try to talk across the stacks [text sets] and notice craft techniques with my students." An example of "talking across stacks" is introducing the concept of onomatopoeia with *Alphabeep: A Zipping, Zooming ABC* by Debora Pearson (2003). Children living in urban and suburban areas will relate to the illustrations and will enjoy the sound effects of the text. Or try Dr. Seuss's *ABC* book (1963/1996a). The rhythmic writing and capricious illustrations facilitate both uppercase and lowercase letter recognition. Children can make sets of "Big *A*, little *a*" playing cards for a "Go Fish" game. Teachers can personalize alphabet letters for the classroom bulletin boards, copying the craft of Dr. Seuss's book. These words can become part of the class word bank, classroom thesaurus, or personal word lists. *A Is for Angry: An Animal and Adjective Alphabet Book* by Sandra Boynton (1987) can supplement your text set for this craft study. *America Is. . .* by Louise Borden (2002) has magnificent illustrations depicting parts of the country, each accompanied by a listing poem. *The Alphazeds* by Shirley Glaser (2003) presents the letters in an interactive story with speech bubbles. Explore *Z Goes Home* by Jon Agee (2003) to discover where alphabet letters might be hiding in your classroom. A nice companion text is the photograph collection *Alphabet City* by Stephen Johnson (1995). As children develop print awareness, *I Read Signs* by Tana Hoban (1983) will integrate beautifully into this text set.

Standards Connection: The national and state standards addressed in this lesson are as follows:

- Facilitating letter recognition and understandings about letter-sound relationships in the primary grades

- Helping emergent learners to put sounds and letters together to write their first words

- Enhancing graphophonic awareness (sound-symbol relationships, root words, prefixes, and suffixes) of the ways to decode and compose unfamiliar words

- Using context and picture clues to decode

Lesson 2

Title and Author: *The Important Book* by Margaret W. Brown (1949)

Synopsis: The pictures in this simply told narrative alternate between black-and-white and color illustrations. Each page reveals a topic or subject that is richly defined according to its unique characteristics. The first and last sentences in each stanza are always the same and contain the words "The (most) important thing about . . ."

Excerpt: "The important thing about you is that you are you.
It is true that you were a baby, and you grew,
and now you are a child,
and you will grow into a man,
or into a woman.
But, the most important thing about you is that
You are you."

Objectives: The purpose here is to engage children in a shared reading and group discussion on how to write a new story that copies the style of the book. You'll also be able to place children in small writing groups to draft this new piece.

Crafting Lesson: In this lesson, proceed as before. Integrate all components of the workshop model: reading aloud, talking, making theories, connecting, brainstorming ideas, and modeling the craft. Students will then be ready to collaboratively draft and edit their own "Important" poems, which can be anthologized into a classroom "Important Book." If multiple copies of this text are available, students can pair up to take turns rereading the book to familiarize themselves with the sound and cadence of the structure and ways with words. This craft can even be used for expository writing about content area concepts. For example, "The important thing about a community is . . ." An example of this crafting lesson is presented in Figure 2-10. Observe the delightful ways this first grader expresses her appreciation for snow.

Crafting Extension: *My Grandpa Is Amazing* by Nick Butterworth (1992b) is about a very "cool" grandfather who rides motorcycles, loves to dance, climbs trees to rescue cats, makes flower arrangements, and is a positive portrayal of senior citizens in the 21st century. The simple listing craft, similar to *The*

The important thing about snow is that it's white like marshmellows.
It can be slippery and chilly like ice.
It is slushy, frosty, and freezing.
It is bright, cool and white.
But the important thing about snow is that it's white like marshmellows.

Figure 2-10. List Book Story—Snow

Important Book (Brown, 1949), is easily retraced and re-created by the primary-grade children. The use of an ellipsis predominates in the text structure and allows the children to understand that this child has endless things to say about his grandfather.

> My Grandpa is amazing.
>
> He builds fantastic sand castles . . .
>
> And he invents wonderful games . . .
>
> It's great to have a grandpa like mine.
>
> He's amazing.

This book, as well as *My Dad Is Awesome* (1992a), *My Mom Is Excellent* (1989), *and My Grandmother Is Wonderful* (1991), all by Nick Butterworth, allow the young child to make connections between family life, significant others, memories, and school-related literacy tasks. The additive crafting formula is easily retold in a class big book. Proficient literacy learners can create their own pieces about caregivers, sisters or brothers, favorite teachers, or even pets.

> My _____ is amazing.
>
> He/She can_____.
>
> And _____.
>
> And _____.
>
> It's great to have a _____ like mine.
>
> He/She is amazing.

Text-Set Extension: *Water* by Frank Asch (1995) is exquisite! Asch lists and defines the properties of water, illustrating its rainbow essence and fluid quality through natural watercolor renderings.

> Water is rain.
>
> Water is dew.
>
> Water is ice and snow.

Teachers can use this book to show children how to describe an object by defining its properties. English language learners will especially benefit from the combination of written text and visual representations. Students might think of other topics and describe and list simple sentences on a classroom experience chart. For example, "Bananas grow in Mexico. Bananas grow on trees. Bananas grow in bunches. Bananas can be green. Bananas grow to be yellow."

Cuckoo Can't Find You by Lorianne Siomades (2002) is another simple list book with three-dimensional drawings and rhyming words.

Fox can't find her socks.

Stork can't find his fork.

Snail can't find his pail.

Goat can't find her boat.

Students can pair up to write and illustrate a rhyming line for a class story using the author's structure and ways with words:

_____can't find her _____.

_____can't find his _____.

Zoo-Looking by Mem Fox (1996) is a repetitive list book in which young Flora realizes that the animals in the zoo are just as interested in her as she is in them!

She looked at the giraffe

and the giraffe looked back.

She looked at the panther

with its coat of silky black.

. . . She looked at her father

and her father looked back.

The pattern of the book can be framed for the children to explore and play with in their writing:

One day _____ went to the _____.

She/He looked at the _____

and the _____looked back.

She/He looked at the _____

with its _____.

She/He looked at the _____

and the _____looked back.

Does a Kangaroo Have a Mother Too? by Eric Carle (2002a) is a simple list book with a question-and-answer structure that will complement this text set. The structure is as follows:

Does a _____have a mother too?

A _____ has a mother

Just like me and you.

Have You Seen My Cat? (1987) and *From Head to Toe* (1997), both by Eric Carle, as well as *Can I Keep Him?* by Steven Kellogg (1971), also demonstrate this crafting technique.

Standards Connection: The national and state standards addressed in these lessons are as follows:

- Reinforcing phonemic awareness of consonant sounds
- Understanding syllabication
- Recognizing rhyming words
- Building knowledge of letter-sound correspondences
- Developing awareness of vowel rules
- Building a sight word vocabulary and spelling skills
- Writing sentences that can be read by others
- Moving from inventive to conventional spelling
- Using the syntactic structure of predictable sentences and repetitive language
- Relating personal experiences to the text
- Using a simple story structure as a model for descriptive writing

Seesaw Story Crafting

The apprentice literacy learner enjoys the contrastive and predictable style of the seesaw tale. Clay (1975) discusses the apprentice writer's ability to compare two things that are at "the same time similar and different." She writes, "Sometimes the urge to see all things in black and white is a handicap to clear thinking, but it is a special kind of structuring to establish opposites" (p. 36). Seesaw texts are an excellent way to support and extend the young child's perceptual and cognitive ability to compare and contrast and to promote critical thinking. One group of second graders classified these books as "Teeter-Totter Tales."

Sample Seesaw Lesson

Title and Author: *When I Was Little* by Jamie Lee Curtis (1993)

Synopsis: This bright and colorful memoir of a 4-year-old is written in the seesaw pattern of "When I was little I _____. Now I can _____." Children are captivated by the humorous text and accompanying illustrations. Kindergartners are quite able to follow the craft pattern, as demonstrated in the following samples. This text is an excellent introduction to autobiographical and memoir writing.

Objectives: The purpose of this lesson is to use a shared reading experience to create a "then and now" story, encouraging children to compare and contrast concepts in their own writing.

Craft Lesson: Proceed as before with this lesson, and introduce the concept of prewriting with a simple graphic organizer. Provide one for the children to work on together. This organizer, or planning sheet, can be quite simple. Draw a line down the middle of the paper, and on one side write "When I was little...," and on the other write "Now that I am big..." After students have brainstormed their ideas, including drawing them, they can be encouraged to write a simple sentence. Afterwards, they can confer with the teacher about the wording and spelling for the final copy. In this way, primary students begin to understand that writing includes rewriting. Observe the ways two first graders transformed their organizers into pages for a class book in Figures 2-11 and 2-12.

Figure 2-11. Seesaw Story—Reading

Figure 2-12. Seesaw Story—Fear

Crafting Extension: Eloise Greenstein's *As Big as You* (2002), introduces the concept of a simile. For example, "When you were born . . . you were as quiet as a mouse." Afterwards, the children can brainstorm "then and now" lists, bring in photographs of when they were "little" to further activate memories for writing, and try writing some similes. This crafting lesson can be supplemented with an additional read-aloud of Ann Jonas's *When You Were A Baby* (1991).

Text-Set Extension: *Tough Boris* by Mem Fox (1992) and *That's Good! That's Bad!* by Margery Cuyler (1991) are examples of the seesaw text structure and are most appropriate for primary writers. The descriptions and imagery of *Quick as a Cricket*, a rhyming and seesaw text by Audrey Wood (1982) is perfect to reinforce this crafting structure and also the use of similes and antonyms:

> I'm as quick as a cricket,
>
> I'm as slow as a snail,
>
> I'm as small as an ant,
>
> I'm as large as a whale.

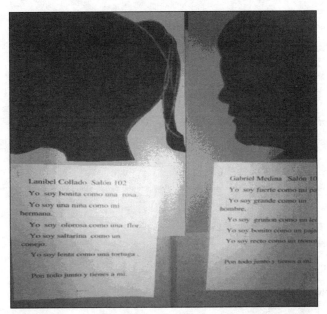

Figure 2-13. **Seesaw Story—Spanish Simile Poems.**

In Figure 2-13, the simile poems of second graders, who were predominantly English language learners, are displayed. They are formatted with each child's silhouette, and the text is written in Spanish.

Simile quilts created by first and second graders are featured in Figures 2-14 and 2-15. The teachers pieced together children's individual simile sentences and illustrations ("I'm as cute as a kitten" and "I'm as small as a pebble"), unifying them with a quilting square modeled on the last line of *Quick as a Cricket* (Wood, 2002). "Put it all together and you've got me!" write the first-grade teachers.

Figure 2-14. **Seesaw Story—First-Grade Simile Quilt**

Figure 2-15. **Seesaw Story—Second-Grade Simile Quilt**

Incredible Me! by Kathi Appelt (2003) celebrates individuality in rhyme and seesaw. A shift occurs in the middle of the story as Appelt shifts from "nobody" to "I," with further elaboration at the end:

> Nobody wears a smile like this.
>
> Nobody blows the kiss I kiss.
>
> Nobody whistles the way I do.
>
> Nobody chews the way I chew.
>
> I'm the cat's meow.

I'm the dog's top flea.

I'm the *one,* the *only*

most marvelous *me!*

This pattern can be easily copied for the children and used to supplement memoir writing.

As the children use the crafting technique to create memoir poems, or write cards for a special someone, they can alter the format a bit.

Nobody _____ the _____ you do.

Nobody _____ the _____ you do.

Nobody _____ the _____ you do.

You're the _____.

You're the _____.

You're the one, the only, most marvelous you!

Finally, *If You Were Born a Kitten* by Marion Dane Bauer (1997) provides children with the opportunity to write in a seesaw fashion and also to adopt the perspective of another creature. This, in effect, can begin discussion in the primary grades about personification. The descriptive language of the text and the illustrations are appreciated by the children, and they have often asked me to reread this book. Examples of students' writing emulating craft, and the ways they were adopted by their primary teachers, are presented in Figures 2-16 through 2-20.

Figure 2-16. Seesaw Story—Mouse

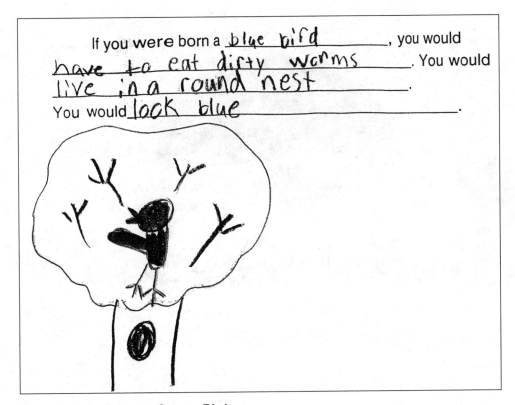

Figure 2-17. Seesaw Story—Bird

Figure 2-18. Seesaw Story—Giraffe

Name. _____ _____   Date November 5, 2004

Writing

If you were _a baby lion_, you would _lick your soft fur._

Figure 2-19.   Seesaw Story—Lion

If you were born a ___OCelot___, you would
_have litte ears_____. You would
_have litte cute paws_____.
You would_have lots of pretty spots_____.

Figure 2-20.   Seesaw Story—Ocelot

Standards Connection: National and state standards addressed in these lessons are as follows:

- Varying and enriching sentence structures to produce poetic line breaks within a cohesive narrative
- Reviewing punctuation, capitalization, and other literary conventions
- Expanding listening, oral, and written vocabulary
- Discussing style, syntax, and word choice
- Creating specificity with details
- Comparing books by different authors
- Sharing memories in writing
- Beginning to read individual stories aloud to others

Crafting With Circular Stories

Circular stories begin and end with the same setting or situation. The story structure is a particular favorite of apprentice literacy learners, who enjoy its recursive nature. Jennifer, a teacher who finds the story format fun to teach, writes, "The shift in my thinking began with the seesaw books and circular poems we read. I found out that all authors borrow ideas and words from one another." Let's look at the circular workshop lessons that follow.

Sample Circular Story Lesson

Title and Author: *If You Give a Pig a Pancake* by Laura Joffee Numeroff (1998)

Synopsis: *If You Give a Pig a Pancake* is a circular, cause-and-effect tale that delights and appeals to the sensibilities of the young child. The humorous plot revolves around the interactions of a very accommodating child and her unsatisfied pet. No matter how hard the young child tries to appease the pig, he always seems to want something else. The story crosses several crafting genres and is written in a repetitive, seesaw, circular pattern. As such, it enables children to make connections, perceive similarities and differences, and develop mental constructs for authors' crafting techniques.

Excerpt: "If you give a pig a pancake, she'll want some syrup to go with it. If you give her some of your favorite maple syrup, she'll probably get all sticky."

Objective: The purposes of this lesson are threefold: to read several books by the same author and use the same crafting technique; to schedule blocks of time for extended writing; and to allow students time to peer-edit, revise, and ultimately present their stories.

Crafting Lesson: After reading all the *If You Give a . . .* books by Laura Numeroff and discussing the crafting that the children observe, you might suggest that they try this style. The simple sentence "If you give a _____ a _____, she'll/he'll probably ask for _____" can be the starting point for an interactive writing project that can lead to an independent composition later. Numeroff's latest book, *If You Give a Pig a Party* (2005) is sure to please the little ones.

Craft Extension: *The Doorbell Rang* by Pat Hutchins (1986) is a circular tale about a mother who bakes chocolate chip cookies for her children. As they all sit down to eat, the doorbell rings. It continues to ring throughout the story, as more and more hungry children arrive. The cookie supply runs dangerously low, but grandmother saves the day. The beginning and ending sentences of this book are the same: "No one makes cookies as good as grandma." Many teachers use this book to teach mathematics concepts. Students write a circular tale about time spent with friends or family that begins and ends with the same phrase or line. Children can also write a repetitive math word problem.

Text-Set Extension: *Where the Wild Things Are* by Maurice Sendak (1991), the classic tale of exiled and imaginative Max, the "wild thing" who dresses up in his wolf suit, has captivated generations of children. It is a fine example of a circular text, beginning and ending in the same location—Max's bedroom. Students can copy and play with the deliberate use of run-on sentences and the word *and* as presented in Sendak's story.

Standards Connection: The national and state standards addressed in these lessons are as follows:

- Developing a sense of what makes good writing
- Using a range of reading strategies to decode and construct new vocabulary words
- Understanding writing strategies that make a story more interesting
- Using a variety of sentence types to retell a story
- Developing ideas in a logical and organized plan
- Creating a sequence of events in chronological order

Conclusion

Early childhood educators have the competency, qualifications, and capability to construct reading and writing workshop lessons that are both child-initiated and teacher-directed to successfully meet local, state, and federal standards. Primary lessons can be created by infusing quality literature into the literacy curriculum, immersing children in books, teaching them to "read like writers" (Smith, 1988), and supporting their craft writing through talk, interactive writing, collaboration, and group sharing. This chapter has presented the ways in which four crafting patterns enliven picture book instruction. Subsequent chapters will extend the discussion of literature-based instruction, and six more comprehensive strategies will be presented for older students.

Teachers Do It!

Research shows that teachers and their expertise make all the difference for students. Pia, a college student, highlights this point when she shares early memories as a bilingual learner in the primary grades:

> I had a teacher who made me feel so small and worthless. That same year I met another teacher who was warm and caring. I'll never forget how she looked at me, it wasn't pity, and it wasn't disappointment. She looked at me with admiration and respect. What I wrote for her she treasured and that's when I began to learn.

Allington (2002) summarizes this viewpoint succinctly: "Programs don't teach, teachers do" (p. 17). In fact, Pressley, Allington, Wharton-McDonald, Block, & Morrow (2001) document the expertise of effective teachers in first-grade classrooms, who balance skills instruction with literature and writing activities rather than just presenting a structured phonemic awareness or phonics approach. Despite comprehensive research analyses and a century of empirical studies about literacy learning in the primary years, more and more teachers have been given commercially prepared direct instruction programs and scripts to read during literacy instruction. Duffy and Hoffman (1999) point out, "Current policy mandates ignore research that tells us improved reading is linked to teachers who use methods thoughtfully, not methods alone" (p. 15). Kevin, a teacher, writes:

> I often push creative writing to the background. With the ever growing curriculum and testing, writing is the area that I overlook. Also, I have a hard time thinking of more interesting ideas. . . . I was thinking about the upcoming year and what I would like to improve upon. The answer was certainly writing. It's the one area that I need to stress.

Teachers in the primary grades must consider what they value and determine if their values are reflected in their lessons and interactions with students. For early childhood education, appropriate instructional methodology is at a crossroads. Federal and state initiatives (i.e., the No Child Left Behind Act) outline increased accountability through systematic testing, the establishment of national standards for proficiency in the language arts, and interventions for diverse populations of struggling readers and writers in the primary grades. Reading First initiatives and Early Reading First manuals (Armbruster, Lehr, & Osborn, 2001, 2002) have primary teachers and teacher educators struggling to blend the finest developmentally appropriate strategies with federal, state, and local mandates for early literacy instruction based upon reliable and replicable research. The National Reading Panel (2000) report gives few insights about the impact of writing upon children's literacy development. Scant attention is paid to the ways in which teachers might frame and structure writing instruction in the early years. The suggestions presented in this chapter offer a teacher-tested, better way, allowing educators to stand on stronger ground with federal and state policy makers.

"I Am Delicious Like a Rose"

This chapter ends where it began (a circular tale, so to speak!), celebrating the strong and vibrant nature of the child and advocating for the use of story in the primary grades. We stress the importance of a literature-based approach, particularly for English language learners, who especially benefit from the dialogue and social interaction of the four crafting approaches to workshop lessons. We marvel at the ways in which they have responded to crafting lessons, and we appreciate the ways in which they are validated and supported to acquire a new language while sustaining their mother tongue. They become competent and confident bilingual writers. Observe the proficient ways in which Kaity describes herself in a list poem, inspired by Audrey Wood's *Quick as a Cricket* (2002). Each line is translated.

Yo soy rica como una rosa.

I am delicious like a rose.

Yo so comelona como un tiburron.

I am a big eater like a shark.

Yo soy Chiquita como una hormiga.

I am little like an ant.

Yo soy feliz como una santa.

I am happy like a saint.

Pon todo junto y tienes a mi.

Put it all together and you have me.

Anticipation Guide Revisited

After reading this chapter, confirm your initial predictions about each statement. List the page number that supports each response.

Statement	Agree	Disagree	Verification
1. Children who are struggling, proficient, reluctant, and English language literacy learners comprehend reading and writing strategies if they are presented in meaningful instructional contexts.	_____	_____	_____
2. Children must know how to read before they are able to write their own stories.	_____	_____	_____
3. *Crafting* refers to the decisions authors make about the wording, structure, and genre of the stories and books they write.	_____	_____	_____
4. Repetitive language, contrastive structures, or circular picture book patterns enable children to predict, expand sight word vocabulary, and refine understanding of the form and function of print.	_____	_____	_____
5. To be a teacher of readers and writers, you must be a reader and writer yourself.	_____	_____	_____
6. Picture books aren't sufficient to meet state standards for the teaching and learning of the English language arts.	_____	_____	_____
7. Teachers can write their own writing workshop curriculum in the early grades.	_____	_____	_____
8. The National Reading Panel outlined specific criteria for teaching writing in the primary grades.	_____	_____	_____

Additional Resources

Web Sites

1. Have you read the No Child Left Behind Act or the Early Reading First initiatives? In order to become proactive and join in the conversation with educators and policy makers about developmentally appropriate teaching and learning in the primary grades, visit the following web sites to broaden your understanding of these initiatives and their implications for early literacy instruction.

    Education Commission of the States—No Child Left Behind (NCLB) Policy Brief on Literacy. Summarizes literacy components of NCLB. Any state's Reading First plan can be accessed at this site. www.ecs.org

    Early Learning Standards: Creating the Conditions for Success. Joint statement of the National Association of Early Childhood Specialists in State Departments of Education. www.naeyc.org/about/positions/pdf/position_statement.pdf

Montgomery County Maryland's Early Success Performance Plan. Learn how one district focused upon early learning to improve academic achievement. www.mcps.k12.md.us/info/CTBS2003/earlysuccess.shtm.

"What Works" Clearinghouse. A federal site for the dissemination of research. www.whatworksclearinghouse.org

2. Review Readwritethink's (National Council of Teachers of English) lessons, using Comic Creator for ideas to integrate with speech bubble crafting. Visit www.readwritethink.org, click on "Student Materials," then choose "Comic Creator."

For Further Reflection

1. Craft workshop lessons might focus on traditional genres or favorite children's tales, such as "Cinderella." Find the following deliciously repetitive and humorous book, then research the genre a bit more. Writers' notebooks can be used to record interesting words and phrases and to try out new writing techniques.

Title and Author: *Dinorella: A Prehistoric Fairy Tale* by Pamela Duncan Edwards (1997)

Synopsis: This prehistoric spin-off of the classic "Cinderella" tale is a 500-calorie alliteration treat. Children will enjoy the antics of the dinosaurs, especially Dinorella, and the ways this author has used language to bring them alive.

Excerpt: Edwards and Cole describe the two evil dinosaur stepsisters:

> "Dora and Doris did nothing all day. They dumped debris around the den. They never did the dusting or the dishes. Dinorella was dainty and dependable. Dora and Doris were dreadful to Dinorella. All day they demanded . . . "

Objectives: The purpose of this lesson is fourfold: (a) to foster reading and listening comprehension through a read-aloud; (b) to introduce versions of the "Cinderella" tale; (c) to encourage children to maintain a writer's notebook to collect their thoughts and phrases from the stories; (d) and to use notebook entries to write longer and more complex sentences.

Standards Connection: The federal and state standards addressed in this lesson are as follows:

- Reinforcing decoding skills through letter-sound associations
- Analyzing word parts and the sentences and paragraphs in which the words appear
- Reinforcing comprehension skills through contextual cues
- Attending to the story line

Crafting Extension: Find the following variations on "Cinderella," and describe how each author borrowed and modified the original idea.

> Cinder-elly
>
> Prince Cinders
>
> Yeh-Shen
>
> The Turkey Girl: Mufaro's Beautiful Daughters
>
> The Rough-Face Girl
>
> Cendrillon
>
> The Irish Cinderlad
>
> Princess Furball
>
> Kongi and Potgi
>
> The Paper Bag Princess
>
> Cinder Edna

Review the following Web sites for other versions of the "Cinderella" tale and teaching ideas:

> www.ucalgary.ca/~dkbrown/cinderella.html
>
> www.shens.com
>
> www.webenglishteacher.com/myth.html

2. Can you think of any movies or television shows that used the "Cinderella" idea?

A Storehouse of Ideas

The following tried-and-true favorites will please the young readers and writers in your classes. A few basic ideas are presented that you can adapt to best meet the needs of your student population.

LIST STORIES

Title and Author: *To Market, to Market* by Anne Miranda (1997)

Synopsis: This repetitive list text is cumulative in nature—that is, a new element is added and then repeated with the story line. This is an old crafting technique ("This is the house that Jack built"), which is quite successful at enhancing comprehension. As characters are added, a schema is established for characters and context, and children are assisted in predicting. This picture book is based on the original nursery rhyme but updated to reflect contemporary times. The pictures (color embedded within black-and-white) are incredibly amusing as the author traces the shopping trek of a frazzled but determined senior citizen and the menagerie of animals she literally carts home from the supermarket.

Excerpt: "The pig's in the kitchen.
The lamb's on the bed.
The cow's on the couch.
There's a DUCK on my head!"

Objectives: The purpose of this lesson is to create a story-sequence chart that lists the characters and events in this story.

Standards Connection: The federal and state standards addressed in this lesson are as follows:

- Using beginning and ending sounds to decode and spell
- Rereading, inferring, asking questions, confirming inferences
- Copying the language of the picture books

Crafting Extension: Just have fun with this one! You'll be laughing with the children at the hilarious illustrations. This text can be paired with *How to Make an Apple Pie and See the World* (Priceman, 1999). For more fun, try the cumulative, repetitive stories *I Know an Old Lady Who Swallowed a Fly* by Glen Rounds (1990), *The Napping House* by Audrey Wood (1984), *Today Is Monday* by Eric Carle (2001b), or *Caps for Sale* by Esphyr Slobodkina (2002), then try retracing and re-creating the craft with the children.

SeeSaw Stories

Title and Author: *You Are My I Love You* by Maryann K. Cusimano (2001)

Synopsis: This seesaw text flips between the phrasing "I am . . . You are." The picture book illustrates the mentoring relationship of a mother teddy bear and her cub. The simple wording and gentle watercolors capture the unspoken messages between mother and child.

Excerpt: "I am your calm place;
You are my giggle."
"I am your open arms;
You are my running leap."

Objectives: The purpose of this lesson is to encourage children to write using the book as a model for their own writing.

Standards Connection: The federal and state standards addressed in this lesson are as follows:

- Dictating their own stories and writing one- and two-syllable words in the primary grades
- Recognizing high-frequency words
- Comparing and contrasting characters, settings, and picture books

Crafting Extension: As students think about the special people in their lives, they will draft a stanza with teachers and peers describing the relationship. They use this simple pattern:

> I am your_____.
>
> You are my _____.

Title and Author: *It Looked Like Spilt Milk* by Charles Shaw (1994)

Synopsis: Blue and white drawings change shape as they float across the pages of this timeless treasure. The seesaw crafting of this imaginative book repeats the refrain, "Sometimes it looked like_____. But it wasn't_____. It was just a _____."

Excerpt: "Sometimes it looked like Spilt Milk.
         But it wasn't Spilt Milk.
         Sometimes it looked like a Rabbit.
         But it wasn't a Rabbit.
         . . . It was just a Cloud in the Sky."

Objectives: The purpose of this lesson is to continue adding words to the classroom word wall, promoting understanding of phonetic spelling patterns, high-frequency sight words, and rhyming word families. Expand and adapt the wall to meet the writing genres the students explore.

Standards Connection: Share ideas, facts, observations, opinions. Use words and phrases from classroom word walls, experience charts, writers' notebooks, and word banks to draft a predictable "Sometimes . . . But . . . It . . ." stanza.

Crafting Extension: Students will take a field trip outside and sketch the cloud shapes they observe in the sky. Blue construction paper and chalk, cotton balls, and/or white paint will enable them to visually represent their cloud stories. Students can print out the accompanying text using their classroom computer. Eric Carle's *Little Cloud* (2001a) works well with this lesson.

CIRCULAR STORIES

Title and Author: *The Tiny Seed* by Eric Carle (1991)

Synopsis: This vividly illustrated book traces the life cycle of a plant, from seedling to flower. It begins and ends in the fall, starting from the moment that tiny seeds are blown by fierce winds over water, grass, mountains, obstacles, and hazards to locations where they will finally take root. Winter, spring, and summer pass by quickly in this poetic narrative as steadfast and perseverant seedlings bloom and disperse new seeds to the winds.

Excerpt: "The tiny seed sails on with the others.
         But the tiny seed does not go as fast as the others.
         The tiny seed does not go as high as the others."

Objective: The purpose of this lesson is to obtain feedback from the students to improve their writing.

Standards Connection: The federal and state standards addressed in this lesson are as follows:

- Distinguishing between fact and fiction
- Writing in a third-person narrative
- Including interesting vocabulary in a circular tale

Crafting Extension: Students can illustrate, describe, and tell the story of other scientific concepts, such as evaporation, condensation, or the life cycle of a butterfly.

References

Allington, R. L. (2002). *Big brother and the national reading curriculum: How ideology trumped evidence.* Portsmouth, NH: Heinemann.

Armbruster, B. B., Lehr, F., & Osborn, J. (2001). *Putting reading first: The research blocks for teaching children to read—kindergarten through grade 3.* Washington, DC: U.S. Department of Education.

Armbruster, B. B., Lehr, F., & Osborn, J. (2002). *A child becomes a reader: Proven ideas from research for parents—kindergarten through grade 3.* Washington, DC: U.S. Department of Education.

Beach, S. A. (1996). Facilitating young writer's development. *Reading Psychology, 17* (2), 181–190.

Calkins, L., & Pessah, L. (2004). *Units of study for primary writing: A yearlong curriculum.* Portsmouth, NH: Heinemann.

Clay, M. (1975). *What did I write? Beginning writing behavior.* Portsmouth, NH: Heinemann.

Duffy, G. G., & Hoffman, J. V. (1999). In pursuit of an illusion: The search for a perfect method. *The Reading Teacher, 53* (1), 10–16.

Dyson, A. H., & Freeman, S. W. (1991). Writing. In J. Flood, J. M. Jensen, D. Lapp, & J. R. Squire (Eds.), *Handbook of teaching English language arts.* New York: Macmillan.

Fletcher, R., & Portalupi (2002). *When students write* [Videotape]. Portland, ME: Stenhouse.

Goodman, K. (1996). *Ken Goodman on reading: A commonsense look at the nature and the science of reading.* Portsmouth, NH: Heinemann.

Graves, D. (1983). *Writing: Teachers and children at work.* Portsmouth, NH: Heinemann.

Haneda, M., & Wells, G. (2000). Writing in knowledge-building communities. *Research in the Teaching of English, 34* (3), 430–457.

Lapp, D., Flood, J., & Roser, N. (2000). Still standing: Timeless strategies for teaching the language arts. In D. S. Strickland & L. M. Morrow (Eds.), *Beginning reading and writing* (pp. 183–193). New York: Teachers College Press.

McCabe, P. (2003). Enhancing self-efficacy for high-stakes reading tests. *The Reading Teacher, 57* (1), 12–20.

National Council of Teachers of English (NCTE). (2005). *Beliefs about the teaching of writing.* Available online at: www.ncte.org/print.asp?id+118876&node=633.

National Council of Teachers of English & International Reading Association. (1996). The English language arts standards. In *Standards for the English language arts.* Urbana, IL: Authors.

National Institute of Child Health and Human Development. (1999). *Report of the National Reading Panel: Teaching children to read.* Washington, DC: Author.

National Reading Panel. (2000). *Teaching children to read: An evidence-based assessment of the scientific literature on reading and its implications for reading.* Bethesda, MD: National Institute of Child Health and Human Development.

National Research Council. (1998). *Preventing reading difficulties in young children* (pp. 323–324). Washington, DC: National Academy Press.

Neuman, S. N., & Roskos, K. (1997). Literacy knowledge in practice: Contexts of participation for young writers. *Reading Research Quarterly, 32* (1), 10–33.

New York State Education Department. (1997). *English language arts learning standards.* Albany, NY: Author.

Pressley, M., Allington, R., Wharton-McDonald, R., Block, C. C., & Morrow, L. M. (2001). *Learning to read: Lessons from exemplary first-grade classrooms.* New York: Guilford Press.

Schickedanz, J. A. (1998). What is developmentally appropriate practice in early literacy? Consider the alphabet. In S. B. Neuman & K. A. Roskos (Eds.), *Children achieving: Best practices in early literacy* (pp. 20–37). Newark: DE: International Reading Association.

Smith, F. (1988). *Joining the literacy club: Further essays into education.* Portsmouth, NH: Heinemann.

Wood-Ray, K. W. (1999). *Wondrous words: Writers and writing in the elementary classroom.* Urbana, IL: National Council of Teachers of English.

Wood-Ray, K. W. (2004). *About the authors: Writing workshop with our youngest writers.* Portsmouth, NH: Heinemann.

Children's Literature

Agee, J. (2003). *Z goes home.* New York: Hyperion Books.

Appelt, K. (2003). *Incredible me!* New York: HarperCollins.

Asch, F. (1995). *Water.* San Diego, CA: Harcourt Brace.

Base, G. (1996). *Animalia.* New York: Abrams.

Bauer, M. D. (1997). *If you were born a kitten.* New York: Simon & Schuster.

Borden, L. (2002). *America is . . .* New York: McElderry Books.

Boynton, S. (1987). *A is for angry: An animal and adjective alphabet book.* New York: Workman.

Brown, M. W. (1949). *The important book.* New York: Harper & Row.

Butterworth, N. (1989). *My mom is excellent.* Cambridge, MA: Candlewick Press.

Butterworth, N. (1991). *My grandmother is wonderful.* Cambridge, MA: Candlewick Press.

Butterworth, N. (1992a). *My dad is awesome.* Cambridge, MA: Candlewick Press.

Butterworth, N. (1992b). *My grandpa is amazing.* Cambridge, MA: Candlewick Press.

Carle, E. (1987). *Have you seen my cat?* New York: Simon & Schuster.

Carle, E. (1991). *The tiny seed.* New York: Simon & Schuster.

Carle, E. (1997). *From head to toe.* New York: HarperCollins.

Carle, E. (2001a). *Little cloud.* New York: Puffin Books.

Carle, E. (2001b). *Today is Monday.* New York: Philomel.

Carle, E. (2002a). *Does a kangaroo have a mother too?* New York: Festival.

Carle, E. (2002b). *Watch out! A giant!* New York: Little Simon.

Cisneros, S. (1984). *Hairs/Pelitos.* New York: Dragonfly Books.

Cole, J. (2002). *The magic school bus, space, and the planets.* New York: Scholastic.

Curtis, J. L. (1993). *When I was little.* New York: HarperCollins.

Cusimano, M. K. (2001). *You are my I love you.* New York: Philomel Books.

Cuyler, M. (1991). *That's good! That's bad!* New York: Holt.

Edwards, P. D. (1997). *Dinorella: A prehistoric fairy tale.* New York: Hyperion Books.

Fox, M. (1992). *Tough Boris.* New York: Harcourt Brace.

Fox, M. (1996). *Zoo-looking.* Greenvale, NY: Mondo.

Glaser, S. (2003). *The alphazeds.* New York: Miramax Books.

Greenstein, E. (2002). *As big as you.* New York: Knopf.

Hoban, T. (1983). *I read signs.* New York: Greenwillow Books.

Hutchins, P. (1976). *Don't forget the bacon.* New York: Greenwillow Books.

Hutchins, P. (1986). *The doorbell rang.* New York: Greenwillow Books.

Johnson. S. T. (1995). *Alphabet city.* New York: Penguin Putnam.

Jonas, A. (1991). *When you were a baby.* New York: Greenwillow.

Kellogg, S. (1971). *Can I keep him?* New York: Dial Press.

Lyne, A. (1997). *A, my name is . . .* Boston: Whispering Coyote Press.

Martin, B. (1983). *Brown bear, brown bear, what do you see?* New York: Holt, Rinehart & Winston.

Mayer, M. (1974). *Frog goes to dinner.* New York: Dial Press.

McGhee, A. (2004). *Mrs. Watson wants your teeth.* New York: Harcourt.

Miranda, A. (1997). *To market, to market.* San Diego, CA: Harcourt Brace.

Numeroff, L. J. (1985). *If you give a mouse a cookie.* New York: Geringer Books.

Numeroff, L. J. (1991). *If you give a moose a muffin.* New York: Geringer Books.

Numeroff, L. J. (1998). *If you give a pig a pancake.* New York: Geringer Books.

Numeroff, L. J. (2000). *If you take a mouse to the movies.* New York: Geringer Books.

Numeroff, L. J. (2002). *If you take a mouse to school.* New York: Geringer Books.

Numeroff, L. J. (2005) *If you give a pig a party.* New York: Geringer Books.

Pearson, D. (2003). *Alphabeep: A zipping, zooming ABC.* New York: Holiday House.

Priceman, M. (1999). *How to make an apple pie and see the world.* New York: Knopf.

Rader, L. (2003). *Tea for me, tea for you.* New York: HarperCollins.

Rathmann, P. (1994). *Goodnight, gorilla.* New York: Putnam.

Rounds, G. (1990). *I know an old lady who swallowed a fly.* New York: Holiday House.

Rylant, C. (1982). *When I was young in the mountains.* New York: Dutton.

Seely, L. L. (1958). *The book of shadowboxes: A story of the ABCs.* Atlanta, GA: Peachtree.

Sendak, M. (1991). *Where the wild things are.* New York: HarperCollins.

Seuss, Dr. [Geisel, T. S.]. (1996a). *Dr. Seuss ABC: An amazing alphabet book.* New York: Random House. (Original work published 1963)

Seuss, Dr. [Geisel, T. S.]. (1996b). *My many colored days.* New York: Knopf.

Shannon, D. (2000). *The rain came down.* New York: Blue Sky Press.

Shaw, C. G. (1994). *It looked like spilt milk.* New York: HarperCollins.

Siomades, L. (2002). *Cuckoo can't find you.* Honesdale, PA: Boyds Mills Press.

Slobodkina, E. (2002). *Caps for sale.* New York: HarperCollins.

Van Allsburg, C. (1987). *The z was zapped.* Boston: Houghton Mifflin.

Weeks, S., & Lewin, B. (2003). *Two eggs, please.* New York: Atheneum Books.

Willems, M. (2003). *Don't let the pigeon drive the bus!* New York: Hypernion Books.

Willems, M. (2004). *The pigeon finds a hot dog!* New York: Hypernion Books.

Wood, A. (1984). *The napping house.* New York: Harcourt Brace.

Wood, A. (2002). *Quick as a cricket.* Auburn, ME: Child's Play.

Chapter 3

On and Beyond
the Path to Guided Reading

Anticipation Guide

Before reading this chapter, please read each of the statements listed below. Based upon your prior knowledge and experience with this chapter's topics, check either "agree" or "disagree" for each statement. After reading the chapter, see if your answers change in the Anticipation Guide Revisited found at the end of the chapter.

	Statement	Agree	Disagree
1.	Guided reading is one of the major components of a balanced or comprehensive literacy program.	_____	_____
2.	Teachers primarily use standardized test scores to determine how to assign students to the guided reading groups.	_____	_____
3.	Guided reading is a context in which teachers observe and scaffold each reader's development of effective reading strategies.	_____	_____
4.	Guided reading is based on the premise that a student's needs direct the teacher's decisions about grouping and text selection.	_____	_____
5.	Once students are assigned to a guided reading group, they remain with that group for the entire school year.	_____	_____
6.	Teachers focus specifically on students' lack of skill development when interacting with them during the guided reading session.	_____	_____
7.	All guided reading groups should be initiated during the first week of school.	_____	_____
8.	The text that teachers should select for the guided reading group is above the students' reading level.	_____	_____

On and Beyond the Path to Guided Reading

Chapter 3 launches into a more comprehensive view of literacy development as children emerge from natural literacy engagement into a more guided and teacher-directed format. This chapter defines the concept of *balanced literacy* and explains the stepping stones of guided reading as children continue to make their way to becoming independent and lifelong readers and writers. The term *guided* takes on new meaning as we show how students guide their teachers in the decision-making process and teachers guide their students in their literacy development. Attention is given to the determination of guided reading groups, the implementation of guided reading sessions, and the development of support to strengthen the reading and writing skills that have previously been taught. This chapter will also provide a practical framework for connecting with the English language arts standards in a manageable and effective manner.

This chapter reflects not only the best research findings from the field but also practical experiences gained from the classroom. Teachers who read this book will learn the best guided reading classroom practices; they will appreciate the goals of guided reading and what adaptations or modifications they might need to make in order for the ideal to become real. During the past 4 years we have had the opportunity to work with and learn from teachers as they implemented balanced programs under our guidance in their classrooms.

Some Thoughts About Balanced Literacy

A fundamental principle of balance is that there is no one-size-fits-all approach or program that can meet the needs of all students (Allington & Walmsley, 1995; Burns, Roe, & Smith, 2002). Teachers need to be acquainted with a variety of programs and methods in order to differentiate instruction to meet the diverse needs of their students. Over the years, various approaches to reading have developed from the field: from the bottom up (part to whole, or text based) to the top down (whole to part, or reader based). In the former, students learn letters and sounds before they are taught to read words, they learn a series of subskills, and they are conditioned to sense that meaning comes from the text. With a top-down viewpoint, the emphasis is on constructing meaning by engaging a reader's prior knowledge, experience, and language ability (Gove, 1983; Gunning, 2002; Walberg, Hare, & Pulliam, 1981).

An interactive perspective, on the other hand, attempts to combine the bottom-up and top-down models in a continual process of making predictions, generating hypotheses, and using visual and spelling-pattern cues to construct meaning (Burns et al., 2002). Rosenblatt (1994) adds that in the interaction between the reader and the text, a transaction occurs. It is during this transactive process that meaning comes into being. Years of debate among advocates of various approaches and viewpoints have resulted in attempts to mesh the best of each to provide us with an effective model of teaching reading in what is now known as *balanced* or *comprehensive* (Bauman, Hoffman, Moon, & Duffy-Hester, 1998; Fountas & Pinnell, 2001; Tompkins, 2001).

Despite the fact that balanced programs may vary, they address fundamental principles. A balanced approach, according to Spiegel (1998), is informed by research and acknowledges the teacher as an informed decision maker who develops a flexible program built upon a comprehensive view of literacy. Fitzgerald (1999) adds three constructive viewpoints. The first includes developing skill knowledge, both decoding skills and comprehension strategies, while motivating and nurturing a love of reading. The second focuses on the integration of different views, such as bottom-up and top-down approaches to address students' learning needs. The third requires the use of lots of reading materials for students. This includes trade books, literature-based readers, books with controlled vocabulary, authentic and whole pieces of literature, and even basal reading textbooks. Cunningham and Allington (1999) concur that the inclusion of a variety of instructional approaches is in itself a major way to achieve balance.

Within a balanced literacy program, skills and strategies have a place and are taught directly and individually. Strategies for word recognition, vocabulary development, and comprehension are an essential part of the instructional lessons, but balance and comprehensiveness are achieved as students use reading, listening, speaking, writing, and visual representation as modes of communication and as tools for learning content area subject matter as well. Furthermore, the techniques and conventions of writing are taught as a means to achieve cohesiveness and balance. When the use of literature is placed at the core of balanced literacy (Tompkins, 2001), the ultimate goal is to develop lifelong readers and writers (Baumann & Iney, 1997; McIntyre & Pressley, 1996; Spiegel, 1998; Weaver, 1998). It is through this balanced literacy approach that we can enable our students to become independent readers by leading them on and beyond the path to guided reading.

Stepping Stones to Guided Reading

As we learned from teachers while they implemented a balanced program in their classrooms, many had concerns about how guided reading fit in and how to manage the different groups and the "kidstations" effectively. *Kidstations* are centers, stations, or work areas at which students engage in different activities to learn, share, practice, or reinforce a skill or concept (Lenski & Nierstheimer, 2004). In addressing teachers' concerns, we began by discussing the merits of read-alouds and shared reading, because what the teacher models, demonstrates, and incorporates into direct instruction during read-alouds and shared reading is directly related to what the teacher expects to see when observing the students during the guided reading group sessions. Think of read-alouds and shared reading as stepping stones toward guided and independent reading. These practices help teachers to integrate time for reading *to* students, *with* students, and listening to and encouraging reading *by* their students (Fountas & Pinnell, 2001; Mooney, 1990). Table 3-1 illustrates the role of students and teachers as students develop the skills become independent readers.

Read-Alouds: Reading To

Reading aloud to students should not be a practice limited to primary-grade children or low-functioning readers. Read-alouds can occur for students from pre-K to high school. Teachers usually conduct read-alouds for short periods of time with the entire class. However, read-alouds can also occur with small groups of students, depending on the purpose and material selected for the experience (Huck, Hepler, & Hickman, 1993).

When implementing read-alouds, teachers often choose literature that includes a variety of genres and a multicultural flavor. Students in the primary grades often ask teachers to read aloud a favorite selection over and over. Each time the teacher reads the selection, a new skill may be taught or reinforced.

Table 3-1.   Stepping Stones on the Path to Becoming an Independent Reader

Read-Alouds

Teachers:

- Model effective reading behaviors & demonstrate how to read fluently with expression.

- Demonstrate before-, during-, & after-reading behaviors.

- Select text that is geared toward the high interest level of students.

- Choose material that is difficult for students to read independently without support.

Shared Reading

Teachers and students engage in an interactive process.

- Students have access to the text & can read along with the teacher but not entirely by themselves.

- Teachers provide direct instruction of skills that relate to reading.

- Students acquire vocabulary & make the auditory-to-visual connection between words they hear & words they can read, extending their listening vocabulary to their reading vocabulary.

- Students' comprehension is enhanced through interaction with the teacher and the text.

Guided Reading

Students read and teachers observe and guide.

Guided reading takes place in small groups.

- Students are assigned to (flexible) groups.

- After a brief introduction by the teacher, students read text on their own.

- Teacher listens to students read individually and observes the students' reading behaviors.

- If necessary, teachers will incorporate those behaviors or strategies into direct instruction.

- Students' needs direct the teachers' decisions, which focus on the students as readers.

Independent Reading

Students self-select text and can read it independently.

Students:

- Apply the skills they have learned to read independently.

- Take responsibility and ownership for their reading experiences.

- Self-select their texts as reading becomes more authentic for them.

- Choose their own topics, materials, and purpose for reading.

- Conference with their teacher to monitor their progress and elevate their reading experiences.

For example, with the story *Why Mosquitoes Buzz in People's Ears* by Verna Aaderma (1975), teachers can read it once and discuss cause-and-effect relationships; read it again and point out how the author used the technique of personification with animal characters; and read it a third time to focus on the sequencing of events.

In the upper grades, teachers may use the read-aloud as a readiness activity before distributing copies for students to read independently or with their peers. Teachers are not limited to certain selections of literature during read-alouds. Material related to content area subject matter or even current events can be incorporated into a read-aloud. Donovan and Smolkin (2000) found that for older students, reading aloud excerpts from information books led students to engage in highly meaningful discussions. Furthermore, reading aloud from information texts provides a context for scaffolding, modeling, and directly teaching comprehension (Donovan & Smolkin, 2000; Dreher, 2003). Using read-alouds with content area subject matter lends itself to clarifying concepts and constructing meaning (Barrentine, 1996: Freeman & Person, 1998).

The motivational value of reading aloud to students is fundamental to the reading act (Burns et al., 2002). It involves all students, and it usually becomes an enjoyable experience. Even the most reluctant readers (McCaffrey & Minkel, 2003) will sit up and listen to a poem, story, or relevant piece of information. This is the time when teachers model before-, during-, and after-reading behaviors so that children will develop these same behaviors.

Before reading the text, teachers demonstrate how they examine the cover, read the title or headline, and make predictions. Teachers also model how to make connections and discuss what they already know about the topic. They may even engage children in brief interchanges.

During a read-aloud, the focus is again on the teacher, who not only reads aloud but also thinks aloud as the text is read. Here again the modeling is important and may include some of the following behaviors. Students observe as the teacher stops periodically to check his or her understanding of a sentence that contains an anaphoric relationship. Students listen to how their teacher rereads a portion of the text that contains important details, to how context clues are used to determine word meaning, and to how to predictions are checked as the passage is read. The teacher may stop periodically and ask a quick question out loud to demonstrate that asking questions can help one to understand a difficult or confusing part.

Teachers also encourage students to engage in visual imagery—to visualize in the mind's eye what is taking place in the story. For instance, while reading the story *Ice Walk* by Cass Hollander (2000) to her class, one teacher encouraged her students to close their eyes and to imagine themselves walking across a frozen river. Suddenly, halfway across the river, the ice makes loud sounds and begins to crack underneath the feet of the young girl and her mother as they attempt to reach the other side. Visualizing makes the event come alive. Students are absorbed by the story and become one of the characters, feeling either the young girl's or the mother's anxiety.

After reading either some segments or the whole of a text, teachers may reflect on their initial predictions, and they often retell a portion of the text with details. They might restate facts, consider the author's purpose in writing the text, or connect what has been read to the interests and needs of the students. Teachers might ask students to consider how the reading relates to other selections they've read or to experiences in their lives.

A key aspect of read-alouds is the importance of listening. Students listen to how their teachers read with proper phrasing, intonation, and expression. Reading aloud not only involves students in listening for enjoyment but also exposes them to a variety of text structures, develops their knowledge of language syntax, increases their vocabulary, and enhances their oral language and memory skills (Adams, 1990). Many new words and concept terms can become part of the students' listening vocabulary, which will aid in the transfer of reading vocabulary in the future (Reutzel, 1997).

Reading aloud affords the struggling and low-performing reader the opportunity to be involved in the art of listening, and these students will often attempt to answer questions and participate in discussions. This practice is also beneficial for non-English-proficient students, who learn the syntax of the language through this modeling process. Gradually, all students are pulled into becoming a community of good listeners, which becomes a genuine reflective behavior often transferable to the reading process. Read-alouds stir students' imaginations, encourage creativity, and enhance students' abilities to infer meaning (Tompkins, 2001).

A read-aloud may take 5–15 minutes at a time of day deemed appropriate by the teacher. Some teachers choose to incorporate the read-aloud into their literacy block, whereas others use it when preparing to teach a content area topic.

Shared Reading: Reading With

A second major component of a balanced or comprehensive reading program is shared reading, or reading *with* children. Shared reading is usually conducted with the entire class (although it could be modified for small groups) for 30–40 minutes. Unlike read-alouds, in which only the teacher has the text and engages in reading and thinking processes, in shared reading the students also have access to the text. They share in the interactive process of engagement with the text and their teacher (Park, 1986). It was initially developed for young readers (Holdaway, 1979) and was intended to assist children in becoming more familiar with conventions of print, intonation, phrasing, and expression, as signaled by punctuation marks and different sizes of typography.

In the primary grades teachers use "big books" propped up on an easel so that all the children can see the text. Sometimes these big books are accompanied by smaller books that allow each child to follow along and read with the teacher. It is through shared reading that children engage in the central components of reading. They often develop phonemic awareness by becoming aware of the sounds in words (Ukrainetz, Cooney, Dyer, Kysar, & Harris, 2000) and by learning to read words themselves (Ganshe, 2000). Reading fluency is naturally facilitated (Fisher & Medvic, 2000). Since many stories and picture books have songs, repeated phrases, poems, and rhyming, students enjoy the opportunity to jump in and read with their teacher (Tompkins, 2001). The togetherness of sharing a reading promotes the rereading of texts that might be difficult for students to read on their own. Furthermore, the sharing and rereading of a text with children often motivates many to later read the selection on their own.

In the upper grades, students have readers, literature books, or content area textbooks. There are occasions when the teacher may use transparencies to project the pages of a text to read them with students. The process of shared reading invites students to join in as the teacher is reading. Using chapter books, poems, and dramatic stories with upper-grade students, the teacher may begin reading aloud while students follow along. Some students, who want to read aloud and are fluent enough to do so, will read along with the teacher. As some do, the teacher may wish to fade out of the process. This process is not the same as a round-robin reading situation, in which everyone must read. In this case, sharing the reading with the teacher is strictly voluntary.

As in the read-aloud, the teacher continues to model before-, during-, and after-reading strategies. During shared reading students are encouraged to do the following:

- Continue developing word recognition strategies
- Make visual connections between what they hear and what they see (Harris & Hodges, 1995)
- Acquire a more extensive reading vocabulary
- Incorporate the before-, during-, and after-reading behaviors
- Use figurative language
- Develop myriad comprehension skills
- Think about and discuss what they have heard or read (Mooney, 1995)

Park (1986) insists that shared reading is a vital instructional strategy, and when teachers incorporate it into the literacy program with confidence and enthusiasm, students respond in kind. By engaging students in the techniques of prereading, reading, responding, exploring, and applying, shared reading builds a literacy foundation, motivates students to read, and establishes social and emotional support for students, helping them to develop into a community of readers (Hicks & Wadlington, 1994). It also provides them with an ability to risk reading on their own as they journey on the path to becoming independent readers.

Guided Reading: Reading By

Guided reading is another part of a balanced program and perhaps the most critical. It provides a format designed to assist readers in processing meaning from a variety of texts with understanding and fluency (Whitehead, 2002). Guided reading allows for a context in which teachers monitor each reader's development of effective reading strategies at increasing levels of difficulty (Fountas & Pinnell, 2001). A critical aspect of guided reading is that students read materials that are used for instruction. The aim is to develop independent readers who know how to formulate questions, consider alternatives creatively and strategically, and make informed choices as they acquire meaning from text. Guided reading also empowers students to become problem solvers and provides them with the rationale for selecting specific strategies to remedy problems they encounter during reading (Kellenberger, Saunders, & Wang, 1998; LaMere & Lanning, 2000).

The basic principles of guided reading support the constructivist and transactional views of learning. In these views, teachers function as coaches who prompt and question students about the strategies they need to use and how these strategies will help them problem-solve (Hornsby, 2000). Teachers often help students to focus on cues in the text to monitor and address problems with a specific reading. During a typical lesson, students discuss the content and the strategies they used to make sense of what they read (Malik, 1996). Specific attention is devoted to levels of comprehension, types of questioning, and before-, during-, and after-reading behaviors (Burns, 2001).

Guided reading interactions often direct readers' attention to important aspects of a story. These interactions ask readers to look for significant relationships, such as making associations between story content and previous knowledge experiences (schemata), and invite readers to draw conclusions and apply the information to the real world (Durkin, 1993; Twining 1981). Ultimately, as suggested by the views of learning above, it is the students who must demonstrate how to bring meaning to and obtain meaning from the text (Anderson, O'Leary, Schuler, & Wright, 2002; Hurst, 2000).

Small-Group Interaction

Guided reading takes place within the context of small groups (5–7 students per group), where teachers listen to individual students read to determine whether each student is incorporating the strategies they learned during read-alouds and shared reading. In guided reading, a student's placement in the group is based on the teacher's understanding of the characteristics and needs of each student, the difficulty of the text, and the presentation of a text that allows fluency to occur (Roger, 1999; Simpson & Smith, 2002). This balance is achieved as teachers interact with students in small flexible groups and conduct ongoing assessment (Snow, Burns, & Griffin, 1998; Taberski, 1998). The information teachers collect through observations, conferencing inventories, running records, and other forms of assessment allows teachers to determine initial grouping patterns (Ganshe, 2000). Furthermore, when making decisions about the daily group makeup, teachers must consider each student's interests, abilities, and need for specific skill development.

Small-group configurations allow students to interact with their teacher. Within the group, students feel less threatened or embarrassed in sharing the difficulties they experience with a reading, because they know that the teacher is there to scaffold their learning. Furthermore, their peers often have similar difficulties. While working in a small group, students are more likely to take risks, attempt to use strategies, and strive to achieve the goals they have set in collaboration with their teacher (Ediger, 2000). When teachers select appropriate and interesting texts that are geared toward students' instructional levels, teachers help students to feel in control and confident in their ability to read with ease. In the picture below, the student takes the initiative to read aloud to the teacher, knowing that she is there to assist with any difficulties that may occur.

Guided Reading—A Reciprocal Process

Guided reading, in simplest terms, is a means of providing students with scaffolded instruction. It provides a framework for integrating the interaction of readers, the text, the text situation, and the teacher. By working directly with each student in the guided reading groups, teachers hone in on concepts and strategies that help to create fluent and proficient readers.

How Students Guide Teachers

There are many factors that contribute to the effective implementation of guided reading. One of these factors is the information gathered on each student to guide the teacher in making appropriate decisions about group placement. What students know, and how they show what they know, helps to guide the teacher in forming all the class groups.

During the initial encounters with a new group of students, teachers need to create and maintain literacy profiles. These profiles contain surveys or interest inventories that reveal each student's reading and writing preferences. The profiles also reveal a list of reading and writing skills that the students have acquired (Kellenberger et al., 1998). Some profiles contain a list of before-, during-, and after-reading behaviors, which the teachers check off as they observe their students read. (See Appendix A at the end of this chapter for one such listing.) The profile may also contain a list of skills that students are using independently and include evidence of students' understanding of texts as demonstrated by the completion of literacy assignments through interest inventories, conferencing with students, examining students' past reading selections, and observing the choice of books, teachers can determine the topics and different genres that students enjoy reading.

One way to group students for guided reading is by *interests*. Selecting topics based on students' interests often serves as a motivator. Students are excited to discuss what they are reading because the topic is of interest to them and they might already know something about it. Thus they feel comfortable and confident engaging in a lively discussion.

However, there are other variables that teachers might consider when arranging groups. Teachers often determine grouping patterns by *ability*. They begin guided reading groups with students who are reading orally at the same instructional level, based on the accuracy of word recognition, generally at 90%–94% accuracy (Clay, 1993). Both formal and informal assessments and the use of running records can reveal a student's independent, instructional, and frustration levels of reading. Sometimes teachers utilize the pertinent information they gather to guide their decisions in forming groups based on *skills* that need to be taught (Brabham & Villaume, 2001; Ganshe, 2000).

As students engage in the reading process, the teacher observes and listens to each student. Sitting beside each student, the teacher observes reading behaviors, looking for evidence of the student's ability to use the before- and during-reading strategies previously modeled by the teacher during read-alouds and shared reading. Teachers acknowledge the use of appropriate reading strategies and affirm the effective implementation of them. Gunning (2002) insists that students need to know what they are doing well, not just what they need to learn. Teachers monitor what the students do when they are confronted with a problem. Here is where good listening behaviors come forward. Teachers listen to ascertain whether students can use context clues in determining how to read unfamiliar words or whether they still engage in decoding strategies. Teachers listen as students reread a passage to clarify meaning or engage in self-correcting. As students read aloud, teachers listen for proper phrasing, intonation, expression, and fluency. While observing the students, teachers take notes, compose summary records on one or two students in the group, use an observation checklist of their own creation (see Appendix A), or use a checklist provided by the school district or publisher.

During the guided reading sessions, students will share some of the difficulties they may be experiencing. For instance, while reading the story *Hedwig's Journey to America* by Juanita Havill (2000), a student informs his teacher that he is having difficulty determining which events could be real. As the teacher initiates an on-the-spot discussion of fact and opinion, she notes that this student might need additional instruction to distinguish between fact and opinion as a follow-up. The teacher listens to the other students in the group and asks if they can distinguish between fact and opinion. Realizing that there are other students who have the same difficulty, the teacher notes that in addition to direct teaching, reinforcement activities should be included at one of the kidstations.

After students have completed a text, teachers can profitably engage them in a brief discussion using inferential and critical-thinking questions (see chapter 6). By evaluating their responses, teachers can determine how well students understood the selection or if they had difficulty inferring or responding to thought-provoking questions. The information gathered during these observations and conferencing encounters serves to guide the teachers in a decision-making process. Teachers might be guided in determining what skills to teach in a minilesson, what elaborating and application activities are needed at the kidstations, what reading selections are best suited to continue interest and motivation, and what students, if any, need to change groups. In a way, the students guide the teacher to address their instructional needs.

During these close and meaningful encounters, students develop ease and comfort in articulating their successes and difficulties to the teacher. This enables the teacher and the students to collaborate on realistic goals in becoming proficient readers.

How Teachers Guide Students

The successful implementation of a guided reading program involves several steps: (a) determining the reading level of each student; (b) organizing the books by level in the classroom library; (c) establishing the initial guided reading groups (which are subject to change as noted above); (d) selecting the appropriate reading materials for students to read; (e) providing time for conferencing; (f) creating appropriate literacy activities for students to implement at the literacy kidstations; and (g) scheduling time for students to demonstrate what they have accomplished at the literacy kidstations.

Determining the Groups

The teacher begins by guiding students into appropriate groups. As noted above, using a variety of assessment tools, including running records, conferencing with students, and conducting observations, teachers guide students into their initial groups based on needs, abilities, and interests. Four guided reading groups within an average class size of 25–30 students are manageable, based on classroom experiences. Ideally, there should be no more than 5–8 students in each group. Using the model presented later in the chapter, the teacher works with one guided reading group each day for approximately 25–35 minutes. We suggest that guided reading groups begin several weeks after school has started to ensure that the necessary preparations have been made.

Although interests and conferencing information will initiate grouping, teachers should understand that observations and assessment are ongoing (Fountas & Pinnell, 1996); thus grouping and regrouping students is a dynamic process. Teachers may also address the rotation of the guided reading groups by using task management boards; by establishing expectations for work, behavior, and following directions; and by designing the literacy kidstations for independent student work (Brabham & Villaume, 2001). The picture below shows students rereading a text as they prepare to use a story grammar wheel to outline a story summary.

Planning the Readings

Once the groups have been determined, the teacher selects texts that match students' reading abilities, needs and interests. Many teachers use a procedure to organize their classroom libraries known as "leveling" (Fountas & Pinnell, 1999), by which books are organized according to how easy or difficult they are to read. By knowing the readability level of texts, teachers are assisted in using those that are at students' instructional levels. There are many commercially prepared leveled-reading kits available in which the task of leveling the text is already determined. Within the kit, there are usually six to eight copies of each text, with 30 or more different text titles. The kits also provide a variety of genres and topics with multiethnic themes. However, financial restraints can prevent the purchase of such commercially prepared guided materials. Subsequently, many teachers collect and level literary and informational trade books for their guided reading groups and gradually create a classroom section with leveled books. Teachers can use leveled-reading book lists, as well as a variety of formulas such as the Fry Readability Formula (Fry, 1977), to determine the level of a book.

Many teachers incorporate the use of basal readers and anthologies in the primary grades and literature-based readers in the upper grades. Fawson and Reutzel (2000) discuss the feasibility of implementing guided reading in the primary grades with basal readers. They contend that as long as the context in the basal is at the student's instructional level, it is the manner in which the students interact with the teacher and the purpose of group instruction that make it different from the traditional basal reading groups of the 1960s and 1970s. Furthermore, many teachers make use of their basal anthologies to provide students with a variety of genres to guide reading instruction (O'Mallan & And, 1993).

Books that teachers select are expected to be read with approximately 90%–94% word recognition accuracy (a range determined to be the instructional level by developers of reading inventories). Books selected for early emergent readers focus on developing the conventions of print and story comprehension, such as understanding the elements of story structure: setting, characters, plot, episodes, resolution, and conclusion. Fluent readers tend to prefer trade books and content materials based on their own proficiency levels. Through ongoing monitoring, teachers select appropriate book levels and constantly update reading levels as students become more proficient readers. Teachers also consider some of the following:

- Are book concepts familiar or can they be made clear through a discussion or introduction?
- Is the plot interesting, and will it appeal to the students in the group?
- Do the words used in the text allow students to use context clues to determine pronunciation and meaning?
- Is the length of the text appropriate for the groups in terms of difficulty and background experience?
- Do the pictures, captions and/or graphs support the students' search for meaning, and do they support the text meaning?
- Does the text provide students with practice in problem solving and comprehension monitoring?
- Is there sufficient content to challenge students without frustrating them?

Emergent readers usually read a new book nearly every time they meet for guided reading. Older students, who generally read longer and more difficult texts, might need to spend more time reading and discussing the content of a text. As students become more proficient readers, the focus often shifts to higher level skills, with greater emphasis on constructing meaning.

The Guided Reading Lesson

The guided reading session may touch on many literacy experiences, but teachers can focus on phonics development, syntactic and semantic cues to aid meaning, and writing (Reutzel, 1997). The guided reading session with one group of 5–8 students begins as the teacher initiates some prereading strategies (Morrow, 2001).

Introducing the Text

Before students actually hold a book, the teacher may introduce the story by talking about specific aspects of the tale (Fountas & Pinnell, 2001). When students approach a new text, they are benefited by an introduction so that when they read, the gist of the whole or partially revealed story can provide some guidance for fluent reading (Clay, 1993). The teacher may guide the students to activate their prior knowledge or experience with the topic. Many teachers call attention to the title and cover of the book and then smoothly guide students through the text with a picture walk. Likewise, as part of prereading, the teacher asks students to make predictions about the story based on information gained through the picture walk. The teacher may introduce new vocabulary to facilitate the comprehension of the text or may wish to use a directed reading and thinking approach to sense new word meanings (this will be explained in chapter 7). Finally, and most important, the teacher reviews a skill or strategy that students need to use as they read the text. With older students, the teacher may guide them to observe captions, charts, pictures, and other features of the text to facilitate understanding; while skimming through the text, students can be prompted to ask questions about text features or unfamiliar words.

Reading the Text

Students are then encouraged to read the text on their own. They may read silently or quietly, depending on their need to subvocalize. The teacher sits beside one student for several minutes and asks the student to read loud enough for the teacher to hear. During earlier read-alouds and shared reading, the teacher modeled many reading behaviors, and students heard their teacher "think through" the difficulties encountered in a text. Now the teacher listens and observes students' reading behaviors for evidence of using appropriate strategies when a problem occurs. For example, the teacher observes how students react when they encounter unfamiliar words. Do they skip over them, reread the sentence to gain meaning, or attempt to use picture or context clues? Do they attempt to decode the unfamiliar words correctly? Do they check to see if what they read "sounds right"? Are students engaged in self-monitoring and self-correcting by using content clues to make sense of what they are reading? Are appropriate phrasing, intonation, and expression occurring to signal adequate understanding?

When a student hits a roadblock, the teacher provides the necessary support to enable the child to hurdle the block and continue reading independently and fluently. Vygotsky (1978) maintained that with support by a more experienced person, learners are able to do more than if attempting a new or difficult task on their own. Students who interact with their teachers and are supported by them extend their learning in the process (Antonacci, 2000). Information about each student's needs and abilities gathered during this interactive teaching and learning process will determine the kinds of activities the student will explore in the guided reading kidstations.

Post-Reading

It is not uncommon for students to read and reread a text several times during guided reading, especially in the primary grades. Afterwards, the teacher may engage students in a discussion in which connections are made between the text and the students' experiences with the text. A minilesson may be conducted to highlight a specific strategy, such as responding to new words or teaching a skill related to word identification. While engaging students in thoughtful conversation about the text, teachers often use questioning that extends across the literal, inferential, critical, and creative levels of understanding. Teachers also encourage students to reflect upon the problem-solving strategies they used while reading and how they can apply these strategies to help them read other books.

Preparing the Kidstations

By now you know that one aspect of guided reading involves a small group of students whose reading behaviors are observed by the teacher and who interact with the teacher and the text. Like most teachers, you are probably asking, "What are the students in the other three groups doing while I'm working with the guided reading group?" Teachers often report that their group sessions are delayed and interrupted by students who can't or don't know how to work on activities independently. In this section we will discuss the practical implementation of guided reading kidstations, differentiated from centers. The term *kidstations* also affords students a sense of ownership, it's their place to do their work.

Traditionally, *centers* are permanent physical areas within a classroom designed for a specific purpose (Isbell & Exelby, 2001). These centers provide students with equipment and materials with which to work independently on a given task. For instance, a designated part of the classroom could be utilized for a listening center, complete with a tape recorder and headphones. Another area of the classroom might have four or five computers that students use to develop their writing skills and to access Internet sites to conduct research. There are many types of center that can support curricula goals, such as reading centers, art centers, science centers, geography centers, and writing centers (Ford & Opitz, 2002).

However, during the past 4 years of working with teachers in various school districts, we have found that the concept of permanent classroom centers is very difficult to implement, especially in urban schools with large class sizes. Therefore, we have established the practice of guided reading kidstations, each one with a specific literacy purpose related to follow-ups of readings in the teacher-guided groups (Figure 3-1).

Prior to creating these stations, teachers need to engage in preliminary planning at the beginning of the school year. During a 5- to 7-week span, teachers should demonstrate a variety of literacy activities for each kidstation. For instance, the teacher could show the entire class how to make a vocabulary quilt as a means of learning how to use a thesaurus and apply

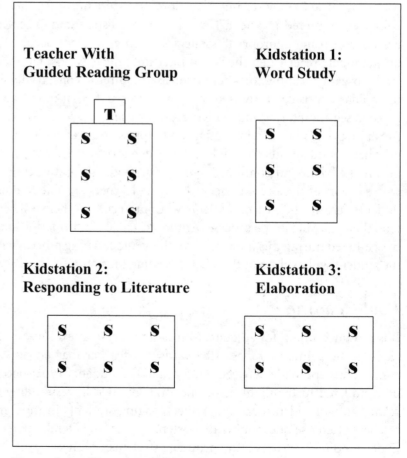

Figure 3-1. Classroom Kidstations

their understanding of new vocabulary words from the group readings (see Appendix B). The students in the picture below are taking the materials from the file holder that contains a sample word quilt and directions for making one.

The teacher shows students how to read and interpret the directions for each task and guides them through the process. By explicitly teaching students how to manage the kidstation activities, the teachers begin to create procedures and organizational strategies that encourage students to function independently (Perlmutter & Burrell, 2001). At each kidstation, the teacher should provide a sample of the activity with materials and directions. It might also be wise to show students how to interpret the directions for each task and provide ways for them to seek guidance when needed. Teachers should leave just the right amount of materials for each group. With directions and an understanding of the purpose of the activity, students become aware of how their literacy skills will be enhanced.

Effective implementation of kidstations also requires guidelines and expectations for students. Along with the students, the teacher should establish ground rules for independent engagement. Some teachers make a chart of a kidstation's courtesy tips in order to make students be considerate of the teacher and of classmates working in different groups. These tips might be as follows:

- Be considerate of your teacher and classmates in the different groups.
- Whisper, please!
- Review directions carefully.
- Look at the sample model.
- Replace all materials in the kidstation kit.
- Clean up when you have finished.

- Ask a buddy, if you really need help.
- Take pride in your work.

The purpose, of course, is to create a classroom environment that is conducive to implementing and managing the guided reading model with the kidstation activities. Students must understand the role of the teacher and the importance of individual interactions during guided reading group time. Every student will, in turn, receive individual attention and scaffolding of instruction from the teacher when his or her guided reading group meets.

Activities at the kidstations are not busywork. Students are held accountable for the work they must produce. By creating activities for students, teachers are providing opportunities to use reading and writing skills and strategies that enrich students' minds and attitudes about literacy development. The four-station model includes time for students to make presentations or demonstrations of what they have created or completed. Thus, from the onset, students realize that they must produce and perform and are held accountable for their products and performances.

Teachers should plan at the outset to have students work independently. Quite often, teachers start out by having students work collaboratively in a group. This is not always a good idea! It's better to get to know your students and see what they are capable of doing on their own. Too frequently, when students work in a group, there are two or three who sit back and let the others do the work. They might not contribute to the group, or if they do, their contributions are minimal. Then when it comes time to be graded for the work, they expect the same grade as those who did most or all of the work. Having students work independently places the responsibility on each and every student to complete the tasks at the kidstation. Teachers are better able to monitor how each student performs and encourage those who need assistance. Independent work also provides the teacher with knowledge of what each student needs to complete a particular activity successfully. Thus, each student becomes motivated to enjoy and complete an activity as an independent accomplishment.

Another reason to begin with independent work is directly related to classroom management. If you allow groups to work cooperatively at the same time, the results are often somewhat chaotic, adversely affecting the learning climate in the classroom. However, once students have demonstrated their individual responsibility and have been made accountable for their products, the teacher can provide time for an occasional group project. For instance, in a classroom with three groups engaged at the kidstations, one group may work collaboratively while individuals in the other two are working independently. The teacher may rotate the group projects so that all students have the opportunity to work as a group.

Standards, Skills, and Reading and Writing Components at Work

The kidstation activities recommended in this section support the tenets of the *Standards for the English Language Arts* (NCTE & IRA, 1996) and the essential components of reading as identified by the National Reading Council Committee on Preventing Reading Difficulties in Young Children (Snow et al., 1998). The essential components—identified as phonemic awareness, phonics instruction, fluency, vocabulary development, and comprehension instruction—are considered instrumental in the acquisition of reading behaviors that allow students to become independent and lifelong readers. The language arts processes of viewing, listening, speaking, reading, writing, and visual representation are integrated into the kidstation activities for students. Unique to this kidstation model is the aspect of speaking that occurs when students are given the opportunity to present their work to various audiences.

Kidstation 1: Word Study

Kidstation 1 focuses on word recognition, vocabulary development, and literal comprehension. It supports the first English language arts standard: *Language is for information and understanding.* To meet this standard, students recognize the words they read and hear and learn the meaning of these words. They also recall information, identify details when retelling or summarizing, collect data, discover relationships, and make generalizations based on what they have read or heard. As speakers and writers, students learn how to use words effectively, express their ideas clearly and vividly, and follow the accepted conventions of the English language to acquire, apply, and transmit information.

At kidstation 1, students work on word recognition strategies that strengthen their reading fluency. In one instance, the teacher observed in the guided reading group's daily reading that several students had difficulty reading words that contained a soft *g*, as in *huge*. During a discussion of the day's story, she gave a minilesson on hard and soft *g*. The next day, at kidstation 1, the teacher arranged for students to listen to a tape-recorded list of words with hard and soft *g*. Then students used self-correcting task cards to read so that they could generalize the rule that determines when the letter *g* is read as /g/ in *goat* or /j/ in *gym*. The teacher also created a short story with a number of words containing hard and soft *g* sounds. Subsequently, students wrote their own story or riddle using the new words they had learned that contained the sounds. During individual readings of each other's stories and riddles, fluency increased.

While listening to another guided reading group, a teacher observed that students were having difficulties with compound words, contractions, inflectional endings, prefixes, suffixes, and syllabication of multisyllable words. The teacher created an activity, Seek and Find (see Appendix C) to reinforce the learning of word parts, new vocabulary, and grammar elements. The word learning ideas for this activity were based on the story *The Wild West* by Myka-Lynn Sokoloff (2000), which had been read the day before in the guided reading session.

Likewise, there may be activities that improve vocabulary development through the use of context clues, analogies, word origins, synonyms, antonyms, heteronyms, homographs, and homophones. While discussing fears with her students, one teacher introduced the term *phobia*. Students were given a phobia puzzle to complete as a kidstation 1 activity (see Appendix D). Afterwards, one student wrote about her own "phobia"—brontophobia, an irrational fear of thunder—as shown in the picture to the right.

Another activity, focusing on the development of the literal comprehension skill of event sequencing, also came from the story *The Wild West* by Myka-Lynne Sokoloff (2000). First, students at kidstation 1 were asked to reread the story they had read the day before during guided reading, then they were provided with an activity sheet. The students were instructed to cut out the sentence strips and rearrange them in the correct order (see Appendix E). The materials for each of these activities are placed in the kidstation box for students to complete. When each student completes the activity, it is placed in the same box for the teacher to check, respond to, and compliment.

Kidstation 2: Responding to the Literature

The activities in kidstation 2 support the principles of the second English language arts standard: *Language is a means of reading, writing, and responding to literature.* This standard notes that, as readers and listeners, students learn to develop the skills of inference—reading between the lines. They engage in a deeper understanding of a text by drawing conclusions, determining the main idea, and understanding cause-and-effect relationships. As they read or listen to different genres, they learn different text structures and infer the author's purpose or interpret the author's point of view and relate texts and performances to their own lives. In kidstation 2, students work on activities that call upon their ability to use implicit and inferential levels of comprehension and to connect story ideas to their own experiences. Accordingly, with the story *The First Day* by Nat Gabriel (2000), the main comprehension skill that was discussed during the guided reading session was recognizing cause-and-effect relationships. The following day, students were given a string board activity, as shown in the picture below, where they identified the cause-and-effect relationships that were established in the story (see Appendix F).

Another kidstation 2 group used a story spin wheel to select questions to respond to in writing. Here students had to use their prior knowledge and experiences to interact with the ideas of the story (see Appendix G).

Kidstation 3: Elaboration

Kidstation 3 supports the following English language arts standard: *Language is used for critical analysis and evaluation.* It challenges students to leap beyond the text to respond to the literature in relation to their own lives, experiences, and prior knowledge. This standard asks students to analyze text, synthesize information, make evaluations, express opinions, and apply the information they have integrated with their prior knowledge. They also use language to persuade, explain, compare and contrast, make judgments, support an opinion, and engage in problem solving.

Based on the story *Head First* by Mike Dion (2000), Michele, a fifth-grade student, analyzes the feelings of the main character in the story and synthesizes these feelings, not in a descriptive essay but in a poem, thoroughly transforming the original genre (see Appendix H). Other kidstation 3 students who use this story will discuss their own fears and write an essay about how they confront them, while comparing themselves with Cindy, the main character in *Head First*. Still another group of students may be asked to compare the main character in *Head First* with the mother in Cass Hollander's *Ice Walk* (2000). They will use analysis and synthesis to compare and contrast two characters. In kidstation 3 students explore their creativity and elaborate on the ideas about which they have read. Many activities in kidstation 3 can be created by students who work in collaboration with the teacher and their peers.

Presentation Kidstation

The presentation kidstation provides an opportunity for students to exercise the fourth English language arts standard: *Language is for social interaction and presentation.* On the fifth day of each weekly cycle, students from one of the three kidstation groups make a presentation of one or more of their completed activities. This is where the element of accountability becomes evident.

After reading the story *The Sandwich Queen* by Sydnie Meltzer Kleinhenz (2000), a student from the kidstation 1 group used a story grammar wheel to recall the important elements of the story. The student depicted in the picture below wrote a story summary and, on presentation day, read his summary to the class (see Appendix I).

Prior to implementing this phase of the cycle, the teacher would be wise to spend time demonstrating and modeling the qualities of effective presentation skills. This can be done with the whole class on an interesting topic. Students should also be shown how the presentation will be evaluated. The teacher can use a simple rubric for oral presentations or a more complex one if the students have incorporated the use of technology. (Examples of these rubrics are given in the next chapter.)

Initially, the teacher may decide which type of activities would be best presented to the larger class group. A recommendation is to start with activities that are meaningful but simple for students to show and talk about so that they can concentrate on the presentation itself—that is the process of presenting. This suggestion gives students the chance to feel more relaxed and confident in their abilities to present. Later on, teachers may select more complex activities for presentations. Having the teacher decide on which activities to present will also eliminate the chance of students presenting the same kind of activity from the same kidstation. Eventually, as students become more familiar and confident with the process of presentations, they will start to select more complex activities to demonstrate to the class.

Putting It All Together: The 5-Day Cycle

Table 3-2 presents a 5-day cycle for implementing guided reading groups, kidstations, and presentation day. Note that on each day of the week the teacher is working with one guided reading group.

Table 3-2. A 5-Day Cycle for Guided Reading Groups, Kidstations, and Presentations

Group	Day 1	Day 2	Day 3	Day 4	Day 5
1	**Guided Reading**	Kidstation 1 Word Study	Kidstation 2 Understanding the Literature	Kidstation 3 Responding to the Literature	Presentations
2	Kidstation 3 Responding to the Literature	**Guided Reading**	Kidstation 1 Word Study	Kidstation 2 Understanding the Literature	Presentations
3	Kidstation 2 Understanding the Literature	Kidstation 3 Responding to the Literature	**Guided Reading**	Kidstation 1 Word Study	Presentations
4	Kidstation 1 Word Study	Kidstation 2 Understanding the Literature	Kidstation 3 Responding to the Literature	**Guided Reading**	Presentations

Many grouping models propose that the teacher work with two groups a day. Observing actual classroom grouping patterns, we have noted that the two-group structure has not proven to be productive or effective. Realistically, teachers need 30–35 minutes to conduct a meaningful guided reading session. Thirty minutes or so is a reasonable amount of time because teachers can give the introduction, discuss the meaning of potentially difficult words, and observe and interact with individual students as each reads independently.

Thirty minutes also gives students at the kidstations enough time to work on their activities.

Day 1

Once the groups are determined (remember, however, that they are flexible!), the teacher begins day 1 with group 1 initiating guided reading. After a brief introduction, the teacher encourages the students to read the selection independently. The teacher then listens to each child in the group read a different portion aloud. The teacher observes the student to determine appropriate or inappropriate reading behavior and provides guidance and support in assisting the student. The teacher may answer the student's questions about a particular part of the selection. As the teacher interacts with each student in the group, the teacher may use a checklist or log to note the types of skills and strategies the student might need to develop (see Appendix A).

Day 2

On day 2 the initial guided reading group is assigned to kidstation 1, where the students complete activities that support the building of word recognition and vocabulary or a literal form of comprehension. In their kidstation kit, students have a sample of each activity and a set of directions and materials they need to complete each task. At the same time, the teacher begins guided reading with group 2.

Day 3

Group 1 moves on to kidstation 2, engaging in an activity that allows the students to respond to the literary reading; group 2 is completing the activities from kidstation 1, and group 3 has its guided reading session with the teacher.

Day 4

Group 1 is now working at kidstation 3, actively engaged in an elaboration assignment; group 2 is at kidstation 2, with activities that enable the students to respond to the reading; group 3 is at kidstation 1, working on a word recognition activity; and group 4 is interacting with the teacher in its guided reading group.

Day 5

One group of students (group 1, initially) presents to the class the work completed in one of the kidstations. The 5-day cycle continues until all the groups have presented, so that in the course of a month (Table 3-3), each child of each group has the opportunity to be observed and evaluated giving a presentation to his or her classmates.

Table 3-3.   A 4-Week Cycle for Guided Reading Groups, Kidstations, and Presentations

Week 1	Week 2
GR KS-1 KS-2 KS-3 **PR**	GR KS-1 KS-2 KS-3
KS-3 GR KS-1 KS-2	KS-3 **GR** KS-1 KS-2 **PR**
KS-2 KS-3 GR KS-1	KS-2 KS-3 GR KS-1
KS-1 KS-2 KS-3 GR	KS-1 KS-2 KS-3 GR
Week 3	**Week 4**
GR KS-1 KS-2 KS-3	GR KS-1 KS-2 KS-3
KS-3 GR KS-1 KS-2	KS-3 GR KS-1 KS-2
KS-2 KS-3 **GR** KS-1 **PR**	KS-2 KS-3 GR KS-1
KS-1 KS-2 KS-3 GR	KS-1 KS-2 KS-3 **GR PR**

The choice of what to present is initially suggested by the teacher. Subsequently, the children may be given options. This is done primarily so that students do not present the same type of activity, or the "easiest" activity, each time.

Remember that students are not assigned to these groups for the duration of the year. A student's participation in a group depends on the student's needs. The student might need to work within two guided reading groups in 1 week if a skill needs to be reinforced. The plan of grouping must benefit the individual child in ongoing lessons and units of instruction (Ediger, 2000). The kidstation assignments are also flexible. Students do not have to participate in three separate kidstations. If the teacher sees that the students do not need any word study activities for a particular book they have read, they may be assigned an extended writing project within the context of kidstation 3 for the weekly cycle. The cycle model suggested here is a guide for the sake of management and variety. However, as teachers come to know their students and their needs, they tailor the kidstation activities to make them more flexible and meaningful for the students.

Like most teachers, you are probably ready to ask, "Before groups 2, 3, and 4 meet with the teacher for guided reading, what are they doing while the teacher begins guided reading with group 1?" As suggested earlier, before teachers start these guided reading groups and kidstations, it is important that they take the time to teach the children how to do a number of reading and writing activities. While groups 2, 3, and 4 await the day of their first guided reading session with their teacher, they may be working independently on a project based on the content of a shared reading lesson or a content area lesson. In some cases, the teacher may wish to situate the first guided reading group in the middle of the classroom while the rest of the class watches the lively teacher, text, and student interaction. In this way students also realize how important it is for them not to interrupt the teacher and their classmates during the guided reading group time.

A second question frequently asked by teachers is "Does each guided reading group read a different story?" In the beginning, the teacher may start out by using the same story or literary book; however, as the groups progress, each group may be assigned a different text. This depends on fluent reading levels and success rates with the skill work accomplished at the kidstations.

Conclusion

The planning that must precede the implementation of kidstations cannot be overemphasized. For effective use of time and classroom management, teachers must establish the ground rules and framework of the 5-day cycle. This model provides a predictable daily schedule and routine that guides both the teacher and the students with expectations, procedures, and standards. The success of the 5-day cycle gives the teacher quality time to interact with individual students in the guided reading group while planning the instruction and creating the appropriate kidstation activities that help to create fluent and independent readers, writers, and presenters.

Implementing kidstations to reinforce skills taught during guided reading sessions offers students the opportunity to apply word recognition, vocabulary development, and comprehension skills while responding to literature in a creative context. A guided reading teacher planning sheet (see Appendix J) allows the teacher to plan the kidstation activities for each group. Student accountability is an essential component of participation in each kidstation. Moreover, the kidstation approach provides time for the teacher to work intensively, without interruption, while the remainder of the class works on worthwhile reinforcement activities. The teacher is also able to assess students' progress at each kidstation and evaluate their understanding of concepts during the presentation phase. The weekly presentations make the students accountable while they develop their oral and written presentation skills.

Teachers who have used the four-group model report that the overall benefit of working with the four groups made their reading program more manageable. Because teachers took the time to model many of the independent activities at the beginning of the school year, students learned to work well independently at the kidstations. The teachers also noted that students of all abilities benefited from working at the kidstations and were able to make valuable contributions to their group. Low-achieving students took pride in the work they produced, and average and high-achieving students were challenged by the kidstation activities.

The presentation aspect of the 5-day cycle was especially appreciated by teachers and students. Students looked forward to presenting with their groups. They were proud of their presentations and experienced less and less anxiety about speaking in front of the class. The teachers indicated that over time they saw a significant improvement in students' presentation skills. They also believed that the students were more accountable for their work products because of the understanding that they would present in front of their peers. Another benefit of the model was the increased collaboration among teachers using the kidstation approach (Anderson, 2000; Hicks & Wadlington, 1994).

The response from teachers and students in an urban school district with a large percentage of children reading below grade level suggests that the model could be of value in any school, regardless of available resources, diverse student abilities, and socioeconomic levels.

Anticipation Guide Revisited

After reading this chapter, confirm your initial predictions about each statement. List the page number that supports each response.

Statement	Agree	Disagree	Verification
1. Guided reading is one of the major components of a balanced or comprehensive literacy program.	_____	_____	_____
2. Teachers primarily use standardized test scores to determine how to assign students to the guided reading groups.	_____	_____	_____
3. Guided reading is a context in which teachers observe and scaffold each reader's development of effective reading strategies.	_____	_____	_____
4. Guided reading is based on the premise that a student's needs direct the teacher's decisions about grouping and text selection.	_____	_____	_____
5. Once students are assigned to a guided reading group, they remain with that group for the entire school year.	_____	_____	_____
6. Teachers focus specifically on students' lack of skill development when interacting with them during the guided reading session.	_____	_____	_____
7. All guided reading groups should be initiated during the first week of school.	_____	_____	_____
8. The text that teachers should select for the guided reading group is above the students' reading level.	_____	_____	_____

Additional Resources

Appendix A: Guided Reading Observation Checklist

1—Always   2—Frequently   3—Sometimes   4—Rarely

Prereading Behaviors	1	2	3	4
Previews the text				
Uses prior knowledge & experience to make predictions				
Skims through the text & identifies unfamiliar words				
Examines cover, jacket, pictures, graphs, captions				
Engages in a think-aloud to clarify purpose				
Asks for assistance				
During Reading Behaviors				
Uses context clues to identify and/or understand words				
Applies phonetic analysis and/or syllabication to read words				
Reads with proper phrasing, intonation, & expression				
Rereads a portion of the text to clarify meaning				
Self-corrects while reading				
Monitors comprehension				
Checks predictions and makes adjustments if necessary				
Stops to predict outcomes or conclusion				
Reads with appropriate rate				
Reads with sustained interest and attention				
Asks for assistance				
Post-Reading Behaviors				
Checks predictions				
Determines the main idea				
Participates in discussions				
Responds to literal questions				
Responds to inferential questions				
Responds to critical thinking questions				
Elaborates upon the text				
Determines author's purpose or point of view				
Summaries the text				

Student: _____   Gr.: _____   Date: _____

General Comments and Recommendations:

_____

_____

_____

_____

Adapted from Gunning (2002) and Scott-Forseman Guided Reading Series

Appendix B: Vocabulary Quilt

Directions to make the vocabulary quilt

Materials: two different pieces of light-colored construction paper (e.g., yellow and pink), scissors, text, and thesaurus

1. Cut the two pieces of paper into 2 large squares.
2. Take one piece of paper (yellow) and fold it in half. Cut it in half from the creased side to the open side but not all the way through. Leave about ¼ inch at the end.
3. Turn the paper around, crease it, and follow the same procedure.

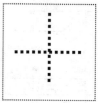

4. Now place this cut piece (yellow) over the second piece (pink) and glue the two pieces together around the edges only.
5. Next, gently take the tips of the cut piece (yellow), pull them back away from the center of the paper, and crease them down.
6. In the center of the bottom piece of paper (pink), write the new vocabulary word.
7. Now take the text. Find the sentence containing the new vocabulary word and write it on the top right flap. Then explain what it means in that sentence.
8. Next, in the top left box, write 5 synonyms for the word, using the thesaurus.
9. On the bottom left flap, find 5 antonyms.
10. On the bottom right flap, write a sentence of your own using your new vocabulary words.
11. When you are finished, sew your square to your classmates' squares to form the vocabulary quilt.

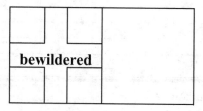

Appendix C: Seek and Find

Kidstation 1 – *The Wild West* by Myka-Lynne Sokoloff (2000)

Sit back and reread the story. Then see if you can help Chester to find the answers.

1. Find 5 compound words.

   _____, _____, _____, _____, _____

2. Find 5 contractions.

   _____, _____, _____, _____, _____

3. Find a word that ends in *-tion*. _____

4. In what season does the story take place? _____.

5. Find a word that is the opposite of:

   east_____, old _____, breakfast _____

   whispered _____, sister _____

6. Find a word that is a synonym for:

   to think about _____ pal _____ spooky _____

   tales _____ soup _____

7. Find 5 plural nouns.

   _____, _____, _____, _____, _____

8. Find three adjectives.

   _____, _____, _____

9. Find a 5-syllable word. _____

Appendix D: Phobia Puzzle

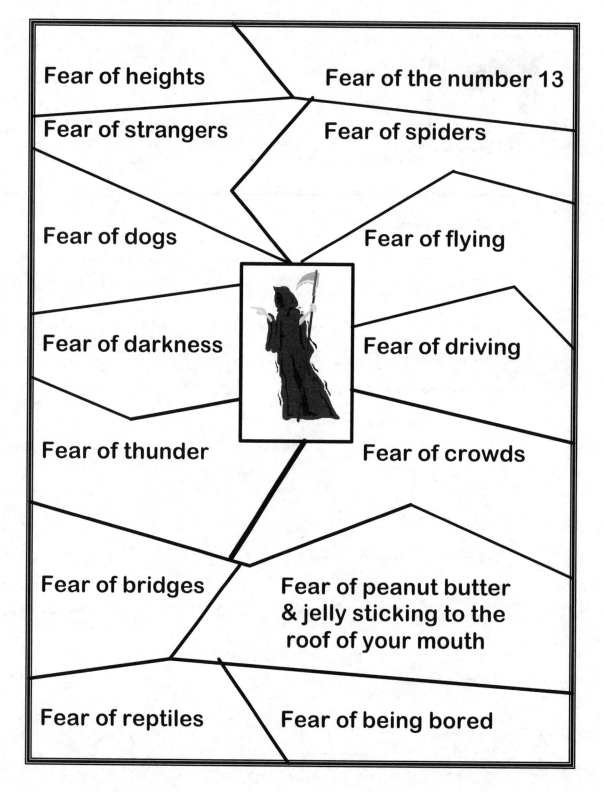

Appendix D: Phobia Puzzle (Continued)

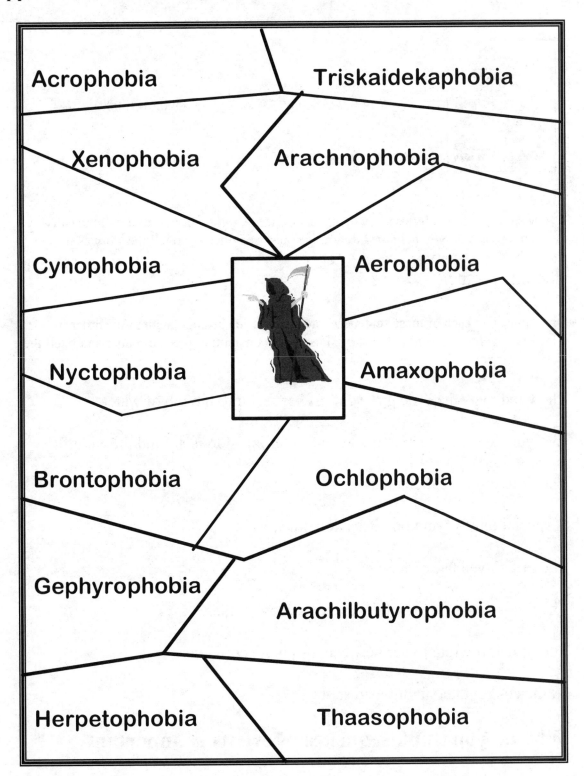

Appendix E: Sequence of Events—Kidstation 1

The Wild West by Myka-Lynne Sokoloff (2000)

Howdy partner,

I've been trying to retell this story to a friend of mine, but I can't seem to tell the story in the right order. Can you help me? Rearrange these sentences to retell the story as it should be.

Thanks, partner!

Directions: Cut each of these sentences into strips. Then arrange them in the order in which the events occurred in the story. Paste them on another piece of paper and retell the story to a friend.

The wind blew the little girl right off her feet into the tub of water.

Everyone went to sleep in the tent after telling stories around the campfire.

The little girl rode the horses.

A special family went on a vacation out west.

The girl played tag with Pete.

The family got to wear all different cowboy clothes.

The little girl wrote to her new friends on the computer.

At the cookout, the family had stew.

Why do you think sequence of events is important?

Appendix F: Cause and Effect

Directions: Use a string to connect the cause-and-effect relationships in the story *The First Day* by Nat Gabriel (2000).

CAUSE	EFFECT
Katie's mom is offered a new job.	Katie decides not to buy new jeans.
Katie recently moved from Michigan to New York.	Katie feels comfortable in her new school.
Katie's first day in school is depressing.	Katie and her mom move to New York.
Katie's mom takes her on a tour of New York City.	Katie is homesick for her family and friends.
Emma tells Katie her clothes are cool.	Katie realizes that even though New York is different, it can still be a great place to live.
Emma introduces Katie to other students at the school.	Katie is upset over small rooms, large crowds, and the fact that she didn't know anyone.

Appendix G: Responding to the Literature—Kidstation 2

Directions: Spin the wheel and choose any two activities to write about.

The First Day by Nat Gabriel (2000)

1. Have you ever moved and started at a new school? Have you ever moved to a new neighborhood? If so, describe how you felt the first time you came to a new school or neighborhood.

2. Explain what you would have done to make a new student in your class, school, building, or neighborhood feel welcome. Prepare to role-play the event with classmates.

3. What are some reasons that people move from place to place?

4. Katie's mom says, "Change is always difficult." What is your opinion? Think of a time when you had to make a change. How did you deal with it?

5. What does this story reveal about the value of a friendship?

6. What causes Katie's attitude to change at the end of the story?

7. What would you have done to help someone get to know and enjoy New York? Create a travel brochure with an itinerary of what you would do and where you would take your new classmate or neighbor.

Appendix H: Poem

Create a poem in the style of Lee Bennett Hopkins' list poem depicting the feeling and
theme of the story *Head First* by Mike Dion (2000).

Diving
By Michele Grade 5

Diving low
Diving high
Diving scared
Diving why?

Diving practice
Diving team
Diving challenge
Diving beam

Diving coach
Diving meet
Diving opponent
Diving neat

Diving bounce
Diving twirl
Diving champion
Diving girl

Appendix I: Story Grammar Wheel

After students read a story, they use the story grammar wheel to identify the elements of the story. Starting with setting, students write a description of each element in the story. This helps students to summarize the story and improve their comprehension. The outer wheel (B) is placed over the sheet (A), and students move it as they discuss each portion of the story or write their summary.

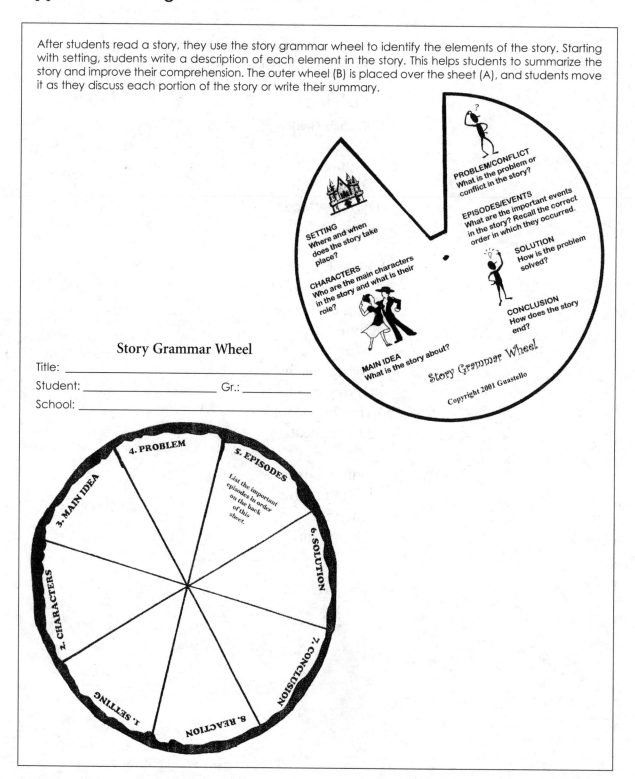

Story Grammar Wheel

Title: _____

Student: _____ Gr.: _____

School: _____

Appendix J: Guided Reading Planning Sheet

Title: _____

Author: _____

Genre: _____

Comprehension Skill: _____

Vocabulary words suggested by author and identified by student: _____

_____

_____

Kidstation 1
Word Study: What word recognition and/or vocabulary skills do the students need to develop their understanding and application of the words? What literal comprehension skill needs to be developed?

Kidstation 2
What questions might you ask the students to determine their understanding of the literature using inference and implicit comprehension? The comprehension skill of _____ was the focus of this lesson. What activities can you develop so that students can respond to the literature?

Kidstation 3
What activities will be used to allow students to elaborate on the ideas of this story? Extension activities could be multidisciplinary and include art projects as well. They can be related to but are not limited to the comprehension skill.

Web Sites

Road to Reading
> http://208.183.128.8/read/guidedr.html

Reading A–Z: The Online Guided Reading Program
A complete reading program with affordable books, lesson plans, work sheets and assessments to teach guided reading, phonics, phonemic awareness, and the alphabet
> www.readinga-z.com/

Leveled Books for Guided Reading From Reading A–Z
Inexpensive developmentally appropriate leveled books to teach guided reading.
> www.readinga-z.com/guided/

Guided Reading Through Children's Literature
Opportunities to use great kids' books for guided reading activities in the classroom.
> www.carolhurst.com/profsubjects/reading/guided.html

Guided Reading
> http://208.183.128.8/read/gr/index_files/v3_document.html

This site chronicles the activities we do in our first-grade classroom.
> http://www.msrossbec.com/greading.shtml

Information for early childhood educators and parents.
> http://www.hubbardscupboard.org/guided_reading.html

> www.mcps.k12.md.us/curriculum/english/guided_rdg.html

Four Blocks: Guided Reading
Making the guided reading block multilevel. Guided reading is the hardest block to make multilevel.
> http://www.wfu.edu/~cunningh/fourblocks/block1.html

Research Behind Guided Reading the Four Blocks Way
> www.wfu.edu/academics/fourblocks/Leadership_2004ResearchBehindGuided ReadingThe4BlocksWay-2.ppt

For Further Writing and Reflection

1. Try implementing your guided reading groups according to the model in the chapter. Write to the authors about how this model has helped you with the management aspect of implementing guided reading.

2. Have your students develop some of the guided reading extension activities from the stories they are reading. Kids have great ideas.

3. If you are not conducting guided reading sessions in your classroom, how are you monitoring the literacy strategies your students should be learning and applying?

References

Adams, M. (1990). *Beginning to read: Thinking and learning about print.* Cambridge, MA: MIT Press.

Allington, R., & Walmsley, S. (Eds.). (1995). *No quick fix: Rethinking literacy programs in America's elementary schools.* New York: Teachers College Press.

Anderson, C. (2000). *How's it going? A practical guide to conferring with student writers.* Portsmouth, NH: Heinemann.

Anderson, T., O'Leary, D., Schuler, K., & Wright, L. (2002). *Increasing reading comprehension through the use of guided reading.* U.S. Illinois Clearinghouse: Reading, English, and Communication (CS511598) (ERIC Document Reproduction Service No. ED 471413).

Antonacci, P. A. (2000). Reading in the zone of proximal development: Mediating literacy development in beginner readers through guided reading. *Reading Horizons, 41* (1), 19–33.

Barrentine, S. J. (1996). Engaging with reading through interactive read-alouds. *The Reading Teacher, 50,* 36–43.

Baumann, J. F., Hoffman, J. F., Moon, J., & Duffy-Hester, A. M. (1998). Where are teachers' voices in the phonics/whole language debate? Results from a survey of U.S. elementary teachers. *The Reading Teacher, 51,* 636–650.

Baumann, J. F., & Iney, G. (1997). Delicate balances: Striving for curricular and instructional equilibrium in a second grade, literature/strategy-based curriculum. *Reading Research Quarterly, 23,* 244–275.

Brabham, E. G., & Villaume, S. K. (2001). Guided reading: Who is in the driver's seat. *The Reading Teacher, 55* (3), 260–263.

Burns, B. (2001). *Guided reading: A how-to for all grades K–12.* Arlington Heights, IL: Skylight.

Burns, P. C., Roe, B. D., & Smith, S. H. (2002). *Teaching reading in today's elementary schools.* Boston: Houghton Mifflin.

Clay, M. (1993). *An observation survey for early literacy achievement.* Portsmouth, NH: Heinemann.

Cunningham, P. M. & Allington, R. L. (1999). *Classrooms that work: They can all read and write.* New York: Longman.

Donovan, C. A., & Smolkin, L. B. (2000). *The contexts of comprehension: Information book read alouds and comprehension acquisition* (Report #2-009). Ann Arbor, MI: Center for the Improvement of Early Reading Achievement.

Dreher, M. (2003). Motivating struggling readers by tapping the potential of information books. *Reading & Writing Quarterly, 23,* 25–39.

Durkin, D. (1993). *Teaching them to read* (6th ed.). Boston: Allyn & Bacon.

Ediger, M. (2000). *Grouping pupils for instruction.* Kirksville, MO: Truman State University. (ERIC Document Reproduction Service No. ED 441 238)

Fawson, P. C., & Reutzel, D. R. (2000). But I only have a basal: Implementing guided reading in the early grades. *The Reading Teacher, 54* (1), 84–97.

Fisher, B., & Medvic, E. F. (2000). *Perspectives on shared reading: Planning and practice.* Portsmouth, NH: Heinemann.

Fitzgerald, J. (1999). What is this thing called "balance"? *The Reading Teacher, 53,* 100–107.

Ford, M. P., & Opitz, M. F. (2002). Using centers to engage children during guided reading time: Intensifying learning experiences away from the teacher. *The Reading Teacher, 55* (8), 710–717.

Fountas, I. C., & Pinnell, G. S. (1996). *Guided reading: Good first teaching for all children.* Portsmouth, NH: Heinemann.

Fountas, I. C., & Pinnell, G. S. (1999). *Matching books to readers: Using leveled books as guided reading, K–3.* Portsmouth, NH: Heinemann.

Fountas, I. C., & Pinnell, G. S. (2001). *Guiding readers and writers.* Portsmouth, NH: Heinemann.

Freeman, E. B., & Person, D. G. (1998). *Connecting informational children's books with content area learning.* Boston: Allyn & Bacon.

Fry, E. (1977). Fry's readability graph: Clarification, validity, and extension to level 17. *Journal of Reading, 21,* 249.

Ganshe, K. (2000). *Word journeys: Assessment-guided phonics, spelling and vocabulary instruction.* New York: Guilford Press.

Gove, M. (1983). Clarifying teachers' beliefs about reading. *The Reading Teacher, 37,* 261–268.

Gunning, T. (2002). *Assessing and correcting reading and writing difficulties.* Boston: Allyn & Bacon.

Harris, T. L., & Hodges, R. E. (Eds.). (1995). *The literacy dictionary: The vocabulary of reading and writing.* Newark, DE: International Reading Association.

Hicks, K., & Wadlington, B. (1994, March). *The efficacy of shared reading with teens.* Paper presented at the Association for Childhood and Educational International Study Conference, New Orleans, LA.

Holdaway, D. (1979). *Foundations of literacy.* Portsmouth, NH: Heinemann.

Hornsby, D. (2000). *A closer look at guided reading.* Armadale, VIC: Curtain Publishing.

Huck, C. S., Hepler, S., & Hickman, J. (1993). *Children's literature in the elementary school.* Fort Worth, TX: Harcourt Brace Jovanovich.

Hurst, C. O. (2000). Guided reading can strengthen comprehension skills. *Teaching Pre-K–8, 31,* 70–71.

Isbell, R., & Exelby, B. (2001). *Easy learning environments that work.* Beltsville, MD: Gryphon House.

Kellenberger, L., Saunders, M., & Wang, J. (1998). Diagnostic training and guided reading in teacher evaluation. *Reading Improvement, 35* (4), 178–183.

LaMere, R., & Lanning, J. L. (2000). An important aspect of guided reading: Books galore! Classroom connections. *Council Connections, 5* (3), 26–28.

Lenski, S. D., & Nierstheimer, S. L. (2004). *Becoming a teacher of reading: A developmental approach.* Upper Saddle River, NJ: Pearson.

Malik, S. (1996). Reading for meaning: A guided reading approach. *Volta Review, 98* (3), 127–136.

McCaffrey, M., & Minkel, W. (2003). Reluctant students read, and "do a 180." *School Library Journal.*

McIntyre, E., & Pressley, M. (Eds.). (1996). *Balanced instruction: Strategies & skills in whole language.* Norwood, MA: Christopher-Gordon.

Mooney, M. (1990). *Reading TO, WITH and BY children.* New York: Owen.

Mooney, M. (1995). Guided reading: The reader in control. *Teaching Pre-K–8, 25* (5), 54–58.

Morrow, L. M. (2001). *Literacy development in early years: Helping children read and write.* Boston: Allyn & Bacon.

National Council of Teachers of English (NCTE) & International Reading Association (IRA). (1996). *Standards for the English language arts.* Urbana, IL: Authors.

National Institute of Child Health and Human Development. (2000). (NIH Pub. No. 00-4754). Washington, DC: U.S. Department of Health and Human Services.

O'Mallan, R. P., & And, O. (1993). Effects of the guided reading procedure on fifth graders' summary writing and comprehension of science text. *Reading Improvement, 30* (4), 194–201.

Park, B. (1986). Shared reading promotes student engagement. *Highway One, 9* (1), 29–32.

Perlmutter, J., & Burrell, L. (2001). *The first weeks of school: Laying a quality foundation.* Portsmouth, NH: Heinemann.

Reutzel, D. R. (1997). *Maintaining balance as a teacher of children: Reading instruction for all.* Paper presented at the Annual Conference on Reading and Writing, Rutgers University, New Brunswick, NJ.

Roger, K. B. (1999). Using current research to make "good" decisions about grouping. *NASSP Bulletin, 82* (595), 38–46.

Rosenblatt, L. M. (1994). The transactional theory of reading and writing. In R. B. Ruddell, M. Ruddell, & H. Singer (Eds.), *Theoretical models and processes of reading* (4th ed.). Newark, DE: International Reading Association.

Simpson, J., & Smith, J. (2002). Guided reading develops fluency. *Literacy Today, 31* (10), 2–12.

Snow, C. E., Burns, M. S., & Griffin, P. (1998). *Preventing reading difficulties in young children.* Washington, DC: National Academy Press.

Spiegel, D. L. (1998). Silver bullets, babies and bath water: Literature response groups in a balanced literacy program. *The Reading Teacher, 52,* 114–124.

Taberski, S. (1998). Make guided reading groups flexible and independent. *Instructor-Primary, 107* (6), 83–85.

Tompkins, G. E. (2001). *Literacy for the 21st Century: A balanced approach.* Upper Saddle River, NJ: Merrill Prentice Hall.

Twining, J. E. (1981). *Implications of schema theory for the guided reading of short stories.* Paper presented at the Annual Meeting of the National Council of Teachers of English, Boston. (ERIC Document Reproduction Service No. ED 211 929)

Ukrainetz, T. A., Cooney, M. H., Dyer, S. K., Kysar, A. J., & Harris, T. J. (2000). An investigation into teaching phonemic awareness through shared reading and writing. *Early Childhood Research Quarterly, 15* (3), 331–335.

Vygotsky, L. (1978). *Mind in society: The development of higher psychological processes.* Cambridge, MA: Harvard University Press.

Walberg, H., Hare, V. C., & Pulliam, C. A. (1981). Social-psychological perceptions and reading comprehension. In J. T. Guthrie (Ed.), *Comprehensions and teaching: Research reviews.* Newark, DE: International Reading Association.

Weaver, C. (Ed.). (1998). *Reconsidering a balanced approach to reading.* Urbana, IL: National Council of Teachers of English.

Whitehead, D. (2002). The story means more to me now: Teaching thinking through guided reading. *Reading: Literacy and Language, 36* (1), 33–37.

Children's Books

Aaderma, V. (1975). Why mosquitoes buzz in people's ears. New York: Dial Books.

Dion, M. (2000). *Head first* (Guided Reading Series 5A). Glenview, IL: Addison-Wesley.

Gabriel, N. (2000). *The first day* (Guided Reading Series 6A). Glenview, IL: Addison-Wesley.

Havill, J. (2000). *Hedwig's journey to America* (Guided Reading Series 4A). Glenview, IL: Addison-Wesley.

Hollander, C. (2000). *Ice walk* (Guided Reading Series 2A). Glenview, IL: Addison-Wesley.

Kleinhenz, S. (2000). *The sandwich queen* (Guided Reading Series 3A). Glenview, IL: Addison-Wesley.

Sokoloff, M. L. (2000). *The wild west* (Guided Reading Series 4A). Glenview, IL: Addison-Wesley.

Chapter 4

Perking Oral Presentation Skills

Anticipation Guide

Before reading this chapter, please read each of the statements listed below. Based upon your prior knowledge and experience with this chapter's topics, check either "agree" or "disagree" for each statement. After reading the chapter, see if your answers change in the Anticipation Guide Revisited found at the end of the chapter.

Statement	Agree	Disagree
1. The development of oral language is critical to building confidence among all language learners.	_____	_____
2. There is no relationship between oral language development and academic success with reading and writing.	_____	_____
3. As students progress through the grade levels, instruction in oral language communication skills should decrease.	_____	_____
4. The national English language arts standards are specifically designed to develop *only* reading, writing, speaking, and listening competencies.	_____	_____
5. Students should not be taught oral presentation skills until the intermediate grades.	_____	_____
6. Semantic maps and graphic organizers can help students to prepare the text for their oral presentations.	_____	_____
7. Multimedia and technology present new forms of literacy that should be integrated into the language arts curriculum.	_____	_____
8. Videotaping is an effective means of documenting and evaluating students' oral presentation skills.	_____	_____

Introduction

Think back for a moment to when your college professor required that you give an oral presentation of your work to the class. No doubt you experienced a feeling of dread and anxiousness. "Oh no, I'd rather do a term paper or take an exam, but not a presentation," you thought to yourself. Many of us have felt that way at one time or another, perhaps because we were not actually taught to give formal presentations until much later in our schooling. By that time our fears of presenting in front of large groups had become daunting!

We now live in an age of global communications and vast technology. At any given moment, the TV, radio, computer, and even cell phones can connect us to someone anywhere in the world. Newscasters report information about every aspect of human life. We listen to local and world events, financial reports, medical breakthroughs, and the weather. There are political debates, celebrity biographies, talk shows, and, of course, commercials. Toddlers and seniors alike share 30-second spotlights to convince us to purchase more things than we need. We're urged to keep listening and watching! The Internet allows businesses to conduct teleconferences in which a presentation is a phone call away, and students "attend" college in the comfort of their homes with online courses and distance learning. All around us, people are constantly engaged in communicating through electronic media, carrying people's voices and images to potentially vast audiences.

Language for Social Communication and Presentations

Every profession and occupation requires effective communicators. Oral communication skills, enhanced by the power of technology, have become paramount to the success of global communication. Chapter 1 showed us how important conversation is in young children's lives and how very often their earliest writings are a reflection of their talk. Yet how are we preparing our students to assume roles as effective communicators in today's electronic and multimedia world?

This chapter supports the activity and presentation schedule discussed in chapter 3. Recall that after students produced work at their kidstations, they had to demonstrate what they created on presentation day. What better opportunity do teachers have? They can now encourage and train students to speak about something they have learned and feel comfortable about presenting. In this chapter we will add a bit more to show how teachers can capitalize on developing students' technology and multimedia skills and strengthen their oral presentation skills as they learn to communicate their ideas effectively to various audiences.

What Happens in Schools?

In many schools, individual students volunteer to participate in poetry or speech recitals, join the drama club, or speak out on the debate team. Most likely there is a teacher who coaches these students in developing the oral presentation skills required to be effective communicators. Nevertheless, these activities are voluntary, and only a small number of students engage in them and receive their benefits. What efforts exist in your schools to develop students' oral language communication and presentation skills? Shouldn't this development be approached with the same vigor and strategy implementation in our modern world that we use with reading and writing? Haber and Lingard (2001) have noted that oral presentation skills are central to a physician's ability to communicate, but little is known how and when these skills are learned. Is there a way to coach the *how* during the *when* of particular oral activities at school?

Although oral language development is often viewed as an integral part of the elementary school curriculum, little formal instruction is initiated to help children acquire competence in oral presentation. Most teachers agree that even though the curriculum contains oral language objectives, these tend to be taught and evaluated incidentally (Stewig, 1988). Furthermore, teachers seem to stress oral language development less and less as students progress through the grades. This might be a faulty point of view, because older students must continually develop proficient oral language skills in order to prepare for adulthood, when oral language is often the predominant mode of transferring and communicating information (Smith, 2003). Ward (1984) has suggested that oral communication skills need to be formally developed by elementary school children to avoid the communication anxiety often experienced by high school students, college students, and young adults as they enter the business world.

Time restraints and other measurable requirements often consume the teaching and learning process while focused development on oral language skills falls by the wayside, however unintentionally. Children learn oral communication skills if the instructional climate is shifted from using techniques that restrict oral communication instruction to those that promote and enhance it (Ward, 1984). Both formal and informal learning experiences in the primary classroom can help youngsters to develop expressive and receptive communication skills. Rapidly, however, in most school settings, the instructional climate shifts to one that focuses on printed language development with emphasis on reading and writing. It might be only during the later school years that students are called upon to engage in individual presentations or formal recitals before an audience. So where and how does the formal instruction occur?

The impact of immigration to the United States has dramatically altered the texture and needs of our classrooms. More than 45% of school-age children come from homes where a language other than English is spoken (National Association of Bilingual Education, 1992). Every day this percentage increases, and teachers are faced with a growing demand for teaching oral language skills as well as developing second-language acquisition in English. Often these students do not bring a well-developed use of their first language to school. Whether all children engage in elaborate language experiences at home is often linked to such factors as the education and literacy abilities of their parents or caregivers and the availability of these adults to nurture learning at home because of their demanding work schedules. Regardless of the reason, a lack of oral language development for students both at home and in our schools adversely impacts their literacy growth. Although reading and writing are the language modes most critical to academic success (perhaps because they are measured the most), the lack of emphasis on academically oriented oral language development, especially with second-language learners, represents a missed opportunity for coordination with reading and writing (Hadaway, Vardell, & Young, 2001).

From Oral to Other Literacy Connections

Loban (1976, 1986) advocates the need for oral language instruction to help children organize their ideas and to demonstrate and illustrate complex generalizations. His research established a firm relationship between oral language development and academic success with reading and writing (Buckley, 1992). More recently, Norton and Norton (2003) added that oral language development can be strengthened by teaching children to organize and categorize their ideas through the use of semantic maps and graphic organizers in preparation for their oral presentations.

Oral Language Development: The Springboard of Communication

In our schools, it is evident that students converse, present, perform, and draw, using oral language skills to do so. Furthermore, today's students can express themselves by using multimedia and technology to communicate ideas and projects in a variety of forms. When teachers provide students with instruction that challenges them to use multimedia and technology in creative ways, they support the enhancement of oral language development and presentation skills (Guastello, 2003).

Fountas and Pinnell (2001) have presented a literacy framework that emphasizes the importance of oral language development and presentation skills as a crucial aspect of learning. Their stages of oral language development include conversation and discussion, performance and drama, presentation, and visual presentation. Through experiences at these four stages, teachers help students to develop, refine, reshape, and effectively use language as visual and technological tools are integrated. When students are engaged in conversation and discussion, they learn to be active and attentive listeners in order to respond to others' statements. Speakers should stay focused on a topic and share information or views clearly and concisely. They also need to learn to read their audience as a means of determining if their audience heard and understood what was being communicated.

In many cases, English language learners find the situation of conversation and discussion more comfortable rather than that of engagement as presenters. By starting out as active listeners, they learn the rhythm and patterns of the English language and how to use language to express their ideas. Furthermore, such group discussion allows all students to interact and collaborate on problem-solving skills (Page, 2002).

Dramatic performances encourage students to use their creativity and experiences of language in an enjoyable manner. Whether as an improvised or a formal performance, language comes alive in their minds and in their self-expression. Those students who have difficulty reading might often shine at singing the words of a song with ease or reciting a rhythmic poem with fluency and expression. Students with reading difficulties often gain confidence in their language abilities when teachers provide opportunities for them to speak and listen through such activities as dramatic plays, choral reading, brainstorming, role-playing, and interviewing (Norton & Norton, 2003). Chapter 7 will extend the ways that oral language activities connect with other art forms to make literary figures come alive.

Standards Connections

Published standards in various states ask students to gather and share information, persuade others, express ideas, and make the ideas understandable not only in written form but by delivering individual presentations (Board of Education of the City of New York, 1997; Florida Department of Education, 2000; New Jersey Department of Education, 1996; Utah State Office of Education, 2000). In order to meet such curriculum goals, teachers must develop a sound rationale for language development, plan curriculum objectives throughout the grade levels, and implement validated learning experiences that can be documented, recorded, and evaluated (Crawford, 1996).

English Language Arts Standards

For decades, listening, speaking, reading, and writing have been the accepted forms of the language arts. Developers of the national English language arts standards have expanded the concept to include viewing and visual representation (Burns, Roe, & Smith, 2004). Prompted by the national standards, states and large school districts have integrated oral, visual, and written language along with their own standards, which require students to accomplish tasks with print, oral presentations, multimedia, and technology. Some states, such as Florida and New Jersey, have included viewing as a means by which to understand and use nontextual, visual information or to use nonverbal cues to convey messages to their audiences. Furthermore, these standard concepts are in close agreement with the national language arts standards, which require students to develop the use of the English language properly, to speak clearly and distinctly, to establish and maintain eye contact, to present information logically, and to utilize multimedia, visual aids, and technology effectively (National Council of Teachers of English, 1999).

Technology Standards

Being literate in our contemporary society now means being active, critical, and creative users not only of print but also of visual language, film, television, video, photography, and other media to enhance oral presentations and produce effective communications (International Society for Technology in Education, 2000). Visual presentation can become a critical aspect of oral language development and communication. Through such presentations, teachers can determine if students are becoming effective communicators and if they are developing the English language arts standards that ask students to use language effectively for social interaction and presentation. By using visuals—illustrations, charts, diagrams, graphic organizers, photography, videos, transparencies, and computer programs—students learn to use technology effectively to convey their intended meaning.

With a broader view of what it means to be literate, the national standards in technology (ISTE, 2000) were developed to be used as guidelines for creating activities that utilize technology and multimedia in school and life-related learning tasks (see Appendix A). Students learn not only the basic operations and concepts of technology but also how to use it as a productive tool in conjunction with reading, viewing, speaking, and listening to create technology-enhanced publications and presentations. The activities in this chapter will assist you in helping students to use telecommunications to communicate information, to publish, and to interact with peers and other audiences.

Specifically, we will demonstrate how to stimulate students' presentation skills while developing a comfort level by integrating videotaping, multimedia, and technology into their individual presentations. Furthermore, as we videotape each student's performance, progress in many skills may be documented and evaluated, thereby setting goals for more effective communication skills.

Essentially, students learn to create visuals that enhance their presentations. Through the use of various computer programs, starting in pre-K with programs like Kid Pix Studio, children can draw pictures that relate to stories or topics they wish to discuss. Older students can access the Internet for information and graphics and learn to give slide presentations complete with animation, sound, and movable text. Instruction may also include the use of the computer to make transparencies for the overhead projector and the use of videotaping so that students can monitor and evaluate their own presentation skills.

Stages of Implementation

This section will present one schoolwide communication skills program that was integrated into an existing language arts curriculum in a school with a large Spanish-speaking population. A teacher who is reading this chapter will clearly see how adaptable the ideas can be for his or her individual classroom, even if the school does not adopt them as a schoolwide endeavor. Several teachers will often volunteer to pilot such a project and then be the catalyst for implementation throughout the school.

The schoolwide program was initiated at three levels: the first for students in pre-K and kindergarten; the second for students in grades 1–4; and the third level for students in grades 5–8. An effort was made to achieve collaboration between teachers and parents throughout the stages of the program. Any teachers who were not sufficiently adept at using multimedia or technology resources to implement these stages received training during 1 week in the summer prior to the beginning of the school year. Figure 4-1 illustrates the procedural steps followed in implementing the schoolwide initiative of integrating multimedia and technology for the purpose of developing oral presentation and communication skills necessary in our modern world.

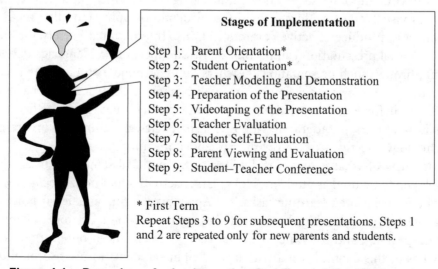

Stages of Implementation

Step 1: Parent Orientation*
Step 2: Student Orientation*
Step 3: Teacher Modeling and Demonstration
Step 4: Preparation of the Presentation
Step 5: Videotaping of the Presentation
Step 6: Teacher Evaluation
Step 7: Student Self-Evaluation
Step 8: Parent Viewing and Evaluation
Step 9: Student–Teacher Conference

* First Term
Repeat Steps 3 to 9 for subsequent presentations. Steps 1 and 2 are repeated only for new parents and students.

Figure 4-1.   Procedures for Implementing Oral Presentation Skills

Step 1: Parent Orientation

The program began with a parent orientation that explained the rationale and the objectives of the language arts program to include an understanding of the importance of developing oral language and technology skills. Parents were informed that one major purpose of the language arts curriculum was to develop language skills for social interaction, presentation, and effective communication. To prepare for oral presentations, students would learn how to use multimedia resources and technology. They would also learn how to research information, to use props and creative dramatics, and the fundamental features of oral language communication.

The parents were presented with two basic rubrics (see Appendixes B and C) that contained the criteria for evaluating their children's presentations. The parents were invited to view a videotape of a student using multimedia and the computer while giving a presentation. The student gave a PowerPoint slide presentation retelling a story he had read. After the presentation, the teacher stopped the tape and gave the parents the opportunity to evaluate the presentation with one of the rubrics. The parents asked good questions and discussed their comments with the teacher.

One of the key objectives of this stage of the program was to involve parents in the teaching and learning process by helping them to support and reinforce at home the communication skills taught in school. For the purpose of the orientation, it was important to show the parents what happens after the student presentation was evaluated. The teacher continued the video, which showed the student discussing his self-evaluation with the teacher while she shared her feedback with him. The parents watched how the two interacted and collaborated on setting goals for the next presentation. This process was important for the parents to see. It made them cognizant of the expectations for their children, gave them knowledge of the objectives of the program, and eventually made them more confident in their ability to help their children become effective communicators. It also relieved the parents of any apprehension they might have had about having their child videotaped.

Step 2: Student Orientation

Next, the process was presented to the students. At a school assembly, teachers, along with their principal, conducted a student orientation. It was equally important for the children to understand what they were about to learn and why their participation in the process was so important. The students viewed video clips of a newscaster giving a report, a candidate giving a speech, and several commercials, and were led to understand how important it is for them to be good readers, writers, listeners, and speakers.

Like their parents, the students, at different grade-level meetings, were shown a videotape of a student giving a presentation. The younger children listened to a child recite a nursery rhyme enthusiastically and with expression. Elementary students watched one of their classmates use a diagram and the illustrations he made on transparencies to explain his science project. Middle school students listened to a student deliver a speech with clarity, expression, and ownership. Each group was led to realize that effective communication skills are an integral part of their literacy development.

Students at the elementary and middle school levels were shown different rubrics, and their teachers explained the criteria for evaluating their presentations. Furthermore, the students were informed of the importance of their role in self-evaluation and in the peer evaluation process. This discussion of evaluation procedures served two purposes. First, it enabled students to comprehend the expectations for effective presentations. Second, it provided them with feedback and a framework for enhancing their performances. Student engagement in self- and peer evaluation provides learning benefits due to the give-and-take of feedback (Magin & Helmore, 2001).

The teachers explained to the students that the procedures for evaluation were presented to their parents as well. The students understood that after their performance was evaluated by their teacher, they would view their presentation and then take the recording home for their parents to view. Subsequently, their parents would share their comments with them. Upon returning to school, they would conference with their teacher to discuss their presentation with evaluative feedback suggested by their parents.

Step 3: Teacher Modeling and Demonstration

In compliance with their district's curriculum and state standards, the teachers planned the type of presentation the students would develop during each trimester. Teachers began each trimester by modeling skills in the mechanics, delivery, and interpretation of oral presentations. Through oral reading and various types of recitations, the teachers demonstrated voice quality, pronunciation, diction, eye contact, poise, variation in tone, use of gestures, and expression. Depending on the grade level and type of presentation, the teachers also demonstrated how to use multimedia—such as the overhead and slide projectors, computers, or simple props—when delivering a presentation. They showed the students how to use props, such as costumes or signs, how to create transparencies to be used with overhead projectors, and how to use specific computer programs such as Excel, PowerPoint, Inspiration I and II, The Bank Street Writer, mPower, Kid Pix, Paintbrush, Hyperstudio, and Hypercard. This stage also presented a great opportunity for teacher collaboration. The language arts teachers helped the students to develop the content of the presentation whereas the computer teacher instructed students on how to use various computer programs and other media equipment.

In the early grades—pre-K and kindergarten, specifically—the initial focus was on using props and, in some cases, costumes to motivate the children. The children also used pictures they had drawn or other items they created. However, as early as kindergarten, children can learn to use simple computer programs like Kid Pix or Paintbrush, which allows them to create pictures with a written sentence or two about their pictures. These pictures tell stories, which the children can use for their oral presentations.

In the higher grades students were taught how to use Excel, mPower, and Inspiration to create their own graphic organizers, diagrams, and charts. The teachers showed the students how to create transparencies to be used with overhead projectors as they explained the uses of images and diagrams. The instruction also included learning how to research and access information from the Internet and how to download images for their presentations. In many cases, PowerPoint, mPower, and Inspiration presentations were created, complete with animation, sound, and timing segments.

Step 4: Preparation of the Presentation

The students were given 2 months to prepare their presentations. As part of their language arts or reading classes, they concentrated on developing the content of their presentation. This preparation time helped them to integrate all their literacy skills. For instance, pre-K and kindergarten students might draw a picture of their favorite part of a story or several pictures as part of their retelling while their teachers assist them with wording. Others might participate in a recitation of nursery rhymes or poetry. They met with their teachers periodically to present their visual drafts and/or preliminary written presentations and receive constructive feedback.

At the elementary and middle school levels, some form of written preparation should be developed as the framework for the presentation. It could be a biographical sketch, an outline, or a particular graphic organizer. Outlines and organizers help students to connect ideas they are developing as part of their technological slide presentation.

The students also practiced and refined the technology skills they were learning. They had the opportunity to rehearse their presentations and conference with their teacher periodically during the 2 months of preparation. The picture here shows students preparing their text for their PowerPoint presentations.

Step 5: Videotaping of the Presentation

The students viewed their tape 3 times a year: once in December, a second time in March, and a third time in June. Toward the end of the first trimester, in December, the students gave their individual presentations to their teacher and their classmates. The parents and other adults assisted with this initial level of the videotaping process.

Sometimes, students who are anxious about giving presentations in front of their peers will request being videotaped in the presence of only their teacher. However, as students gain familiarity with the process and observe their classmates' presentations, they will eventually feel more comfortable to present to their peers. The sooner students achieve a comfort level as presenters in the lower grades, the less anxious they become as they progress through the grades (Guastello & Sinatra, 2001).

Learning about different types of audiences is an important part of developing presentation skills. Students began by presenting in front of their teacher and peers. As they became more confident in their presentation abilities, the audience became larger and more varied. Presentations may be given at school assemblies, to parent groups, and even to seniors in the community. In some schools, local officials and business professionals are invited to listen to various presentations related to their professions. The goal of real audience variety is to develop effective communication skills while reducing the anxiety many students experience when giving presentations.

Videotaping of each student usually took 3–7 minutes, depending on the type of presentation. Time allocation understandably depends on the grade level; older students are usually more accomplished in the use of language and the nature of the presentation. Presentations may also vary in terms of the use of props, costumes, multimedia resources, and technology.

The language arts teachers scheduled a few students a day for about a week. During the in-class videotaping session, the presenters were observed by the teacher and their classmates. Observing peers became a means of support and served to help the observers learn from the strengths of their fellow classmates' presentations.

Step 6: Teacher Evaluation

As the student delivered the presentation, the teacher used an appropriate rubric to evaluate the student's performance. The teacher focused on mechanics issues such as voice quality and pronunciation, delivery style, and interpretation skills as well as the effective use of props, media, or technology. The teacher's evaluation informed parents of how they could support their child's efforts to improve the quality of the presentation (see Appendix B).

Step 7: Student Self-Evaluation

Before the teachers shared their evaluations with the students, each student had the opportunity to view his or her presentation at school or at home with the family. During this viewing, the students complete their own self-evaluation, using the form in Appendix B. This gave the student the opportunity to note strengths and identify presentation inhibitors. The teacher subsequently shared her evaluation with the student.

Step 8: Parent Viewing and Evaluation

The students took the videotape home to be viewed by their parents and other family members. After viewing the tape, the parents completed the same form as the student and teacher did. The parents often included comments or asked questions about the teacher's scoring of a particular aspect of their child's presentation. This communication between home and school reinforces the collaborative rapport between the two. Consequently, the students gained from the comprehensive support and encouragement.

Step 9: Student-Teacher Conference

When the students returned to school with their tape and their parent's evaluation, the teacher summarized all three evaluations (teacher's, parent's, student's). The teacher and student then met to discuss the evaluations and develop a plan for improving the student's presentation skills in preparation for the next trimester. As the students became more comfortable with the process and knowledgeable of the components of an effective presentation, the teachers included peer evaluations as a valuable tool in the process (Patri, 2002).

Cumulative Documentation

Each trimester and subsequent year, the same videotape was used to record a student's presentation. The video then became a cumulative documentation source of each presentation, allowing the teachers and the students to monitor the progress being made over time. Each teacher wrote a summative evaluation at the end of the year and passed the evaluation and the videotape to the next teacher. In this report, the teacher also included the presentation goals for each student for the upcoming school year.

After the initial orientation for the parents and students, only steps 3–9 are repeated during each of the three phases of implementation.

A Model for Implementing Oral Presentations

Table 4-1 presents an annual schedule for conducting a comprehensive program centered on the videotaping of students' oral presentations. In most instances, the program works most effectively when implemented in the three trimester phases. During each phase, different grade-level students focus on a specific type of presentation.

Table 4-1. Annual Schedule for Oral Presentations

Time Period	Grade Level	Type of Presentation
Phase 1 **September to December**	Pre-K & Kindergarten	Show-and-tell presentation with props
	Grades 1–4	Story retelling with transparencies and overhead projector
	Grades 5–8	Story retelling with Excel and PowerPoint
Phase 2 **January to March**	Pre-K & Kindergarten	Oral recitation of nursery rhymes with props and costumes
	Grades 1–8	Poetry recitation with Kid Pix pictures and clip art, Internet images or Inspiration presentation
Phase 3 **April to June**	Pre-K & Kindergarten	How-to presentation with props and pictures
	Grades 1–4	Expository demonstrations with Internet pictures and graphic organizers
	Grades 5–8	Compare and contrast presentations using Excel and PowerPoint

Phase 1: September to December

When young children enter school, teachers begin the process of preparing them to read and write. There is more and more pressure to meet the requirements of the English language arts standards (NCTE, 1999), and even pre-K and kindergarten teachers are readily teaching with that mindset. Most teachers assume that children old enough and intelligent enough to be in school can talk and that these "talkers" are good communicators. However, most of what children know about language is what they have learned incidentally at home, during play, or in day care centers. Effective oral language communication is not inherent (Holbrook, 1983). Therefore, schools must have an integrated language arts program that develops and enhances oral language competencies. Such a curriculum should be designed to address the children's needs but must also take into account their interests, life experiences, and prior knowledge of language.

PRE-K AND KINDERGARTEN: SHOW AND TELL

You might wish to start with having children talk about something that is familiar to them. Show and tell—the sharing of a personal experience—is a familiar and effective learning activity that be used to develop oral language and thinking abilities. Teaching and learning experiences in this stage of the process should begin with teacher modeling. A focus for this first presentation might be to explain what an object is and how it is used. For instance, the teacher might talk about a simple but important object such as chalk and its uses in different places. As the teacher presents, the focus should be on clarity and poise.

One teacher brought in her Polaroid camera and showed the children how to take pictures. She explained that she often takes pictures of her family and friends and even her students. Picture taking, she shared, helps her to remember important people and events in her life. The oral presentation was short and effective enough to inform the children about the use of the camera while demonstrating the process of presentation skills.

Subsequently, the children brought home a letter explaining to their parents that the first presentation will be of the show-and-tell type. The parents were encouraged to help their children select something special to share with their classmates. With the object in hand, each child explains why the object is special and why the classmates might like to learn about it. The teacher probes with questions, which helps each child to think more deeply about the object and its uses and what should be included in the presentation. Consistent modeling and discussion is provided by the teacher.

By early December, the children are ready to give their show-and-tell presentation, which is videotaped. A paraprofessional or even a parent will often volunteer to manage the videotaping while the teacher observes the student. It is important that the climate is kept informal, supportive, and relaxed. Young children are often excited at the prospect of viewing themselves and watching the tape later with their parents. Of course, at the pre-K and kindergarten levels, the main goal is to develop a comfort level for speaking in front of an audience and to help the children progress in giving coherent presentations.

The parents view the videotape and use a simple rubric to evaluate the performance (see Appendix B). They also read the teacher's evaluation and anecdotal comments. The parents' role in this home-to-school exchange is to support and encourage their children while the teacher focuses on the mechanics and the delivery of the presentations.

GRADES 1–4: STORYTELLING WITH THE USE OF GRAPHIC ORGANIZERS AND TRANSPARENCIES

First, second, and third graders are at an opportune age to learn on oral language communication and presentation skills because they are often not reluctant to present in front of their peers. Some worthwhile activities that promote oral language development among these children are oral readings, poetry recitations, retelling stories, reading self-constructed stories, and demonstrating a how-to project.

One of our favorite activities involved retold stories with the use of a graphic organizer, transparencies, and overhead projection. During the first trimester, the students were introduced to a story grammar graphic organizer in the form of a story grammar wheel, as discussed in the last chapter. The teacher made a transparency of the organizer and demonstrated how to identify story elements as she recalled a story she read to the class. Using the information recorded on the transparency on the overhead projector, the teacher showed children how to record story grammar elements on the wheel. The teacher modeled the technique several times during the trimester. She provided the children with the opportunity to do the same. After the students selected a story they wished to retell, they filled in the information on the story grammar wheel with teacher guidance and support. By the end of the first trimester, the students were then video-taped using the overhead projector and the graphic organizer as a guide in presenting a retold story to the class.

Figure 4-2 depicts Martin's story grammar wheel, which he used to retell the story *The River Rescue* by B. G. Hennessy (2000). After printing the details on a piece of paper and revising and editing his work with his teacher, Martin was shown how to make a transparency to use as a prompt when retelling the story. One viewpoint suggests that storytelling and retelling support language learning, especially when the needs of diverse students are met (Whaley, 2002).

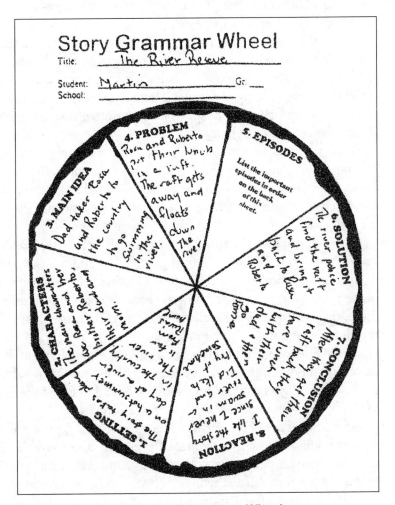

Figure 4-2. Martin's Story Grammar Wheel

Another activity of the grammar wheel allows for the integration of writing skills in more detail. Here the teacher would show children how to use the wheel as a guide for writing a story summary based on story grammar features. Children previously used the story wheel activity as a guide in presenting an oral report, but now they were to write a summary of a book or story. Students in grades 2, 3, and even higher are often required to write book reports. A written summary based on the use of the story grammar wheel allows for both a variation of the book report and a way to present orally. This also could be an energizing activity for kidstation 1 (see chapter 3).

At the end of this first phase, the students gave their presentations and viewed their tapes to self-evaluate their performances. Their parents then viewed the tape and shared their comments with the teacher. The teacher reviewed all the evaluations, conferenced with each student individually, and helped each to set goals for the next presentation.

GRADES 5–8: STORYTELLING WITH THE USE OF EXCEL AND POWERPOINT

By the time students reach the fifth grade, many have extensive computer skills. They are well versed in accessing information from the Internet and can use basic word processing programs and programs like Excel and PowerPoint quite well.

We asked students at this level to begin by selecting a book they have read. Using Excel, they created a graphic organizer that assisted them in mapping out the elements of story grammar. The organizer helps them to generate text, visualize abstract thoughts, and make the connections in the story plot through the sequencing of frames. It acts as an overall summarization guide. Furthermore, mapping out the story in written form allows for a smoother transition from written to expressive oral language (Guastello & Sinatra, 2001).

While the students engaged in completing their maps, the teachers interacted with revisions and editing. Upon completion of the graphic organizer map, the students transferred the information from the map and wrote the text in the frames provided in PowerPoint, where they could make appropriate enhancements with pictures or images. At the end of the first trimester, they were videotaped giving their story summary in a Powerpoint presentation.

One such story is "The Stone Boy" by Gina Berrault (see Appendix D). It was told and illustrated in a PowerPoint presentation by a fifth grader. The slides described the setting of the story, provided a detailed description of the characters, identified the problems and conflict in the story, showed the sequence of events, explained how the conflict reached resolution, and stated the conclusion. Furthermore, the student, Miguel, elaborated on a creative level by providing his reaction to the story. Once the slide presentation was completed, Miguel printed it, made some revisions, and edited the text. Upon conferencing with his teacher, he added graphics, animation, and sound features that increased the creativity of his project and became a highly motivational feature for those who viewed his slide story. When Miguel gave his presentation, he did not read the text from the screen, but used the slides as prompts to discuss and elaborate on the content.

After Miguel gave his presentation, he viewed his tape at school and completed his self-evaluation. At that point, his teacher encouraged peer evaluation as well. Then Miguel took the tape home and viewed it with his parents, who engaged in constructive dialogue with Miguel in evaluating his presentation. By the time Miguel returned to school, he was ready to confer with his teacher to outline his goals for the next presentation.

Phase 2: January to March

Many children today come to school with knowledge of Disney stories and cartoon characters, but few have experience with the fun and fantasy of learning the rhythm and rhyme found in the classics of the oral tradition, such as the Mother Goose stories or children's poems.

PRE-K AND KINDERGARTEN: NURSERY RHYMES

To motivate and excite young children and prepare them for performance, pre-K and kindergarten children were taught a number of nursery rhymes during the first few months of school. Through repetition at home and at school, the children memorized them. While teaching the nursery rhymes to the children, the teachers showed them how to use rhythm, gestures, and expression. For instance, one teacher used the nursery rhyme "Humpty Dumpty"; the students pretended to sit on a wall and then gently fell over. She gestured and used expressions to show that "all the king's horses" (she extended her right arm outward) and "all the king's men" (she extended her left arm outward) "couldn't put Humpty back together again" (turning her head from left to right). Books were made available to the parents from the school library so that rhymes, poems, and children's picture book classics could be read aloud at home.

At the end of the trimester each child was expected to recite one nursery rhyme. In some instances, the parents provided the children with costumes to coordinate with the poem's meaning, and the teachers showed the children how to use props and gestures during the presentation. These performances were as endearing and enchanting as those we often see young children accomplishing on TV!

GRADES 1–8: POETRY RECITATION USING PROPS, PICTURES, PHOTOGRAPHY, AND INTERNET IMAGES

In September, students in grades 1–8 and their parents were given three poems to help prepare for the presentation in March. Using one poem in a demonstration lesson, the teachers discussed an author's style, the use of imagery, symbolism, and an interpretation of the author's ideas. The teacher would model the oral recitation of a poem with gestures and expression. Having the children memorize and recite poems or use props or costumes might not be innovative as it was with the younger children, but using multimedia and technology in a presentation provided ways for the students to demonstrate their understanding of, reaction to, and interpretation of a poem.

Students in grades 1–3 learned how to use Kid Pix and Paintbrush to draw their interpretation of a poem and how to make a transparency of the picture that would be projected during the recital. The picture here shows the students as they recited a winter poem from their own creative writing.

Students in grades 4–8 used pictures from clip art or the Internet as visual props when they recited their poems. The pictures students selected reflected their interpretation of the poem and the author's intent. To prepare for this presentation, the teachers conferred with the students to ensure that the content was understood and that the pictures were appropriate.

The students were subsequently motivated to create their own poetry, which became the focus of their presentation the following year. This will be discussed in chapter 5 with more ideas for integrating poetry writing with oral recitation and technology.

Phase 3: April to June

In phase 3 the teachers had the children share in a class experience and then draw a picture to represent their favorite part of the experience. Using an illustration, the children "talked" about the experience and why it was important or fun for them.

PRE-K AND KINDERGARTEN: HOW-TO DEMONSTRATION

One teacher photographed each of her 16 kindergarten students as the class prepared its class fish tank. Each child was photographed doing something specific. After the pictures were developed, the children received their particular picture in the preparation sequence. The children recalled what their job was for preparing the fish tank, and with the teacher's assistance, they arranged the pictures in the correct sequence to create a story board. Using the procedures of the Language Experience Approach, she wrote a description of each child's action as the child dictated to her. The teacher glued each picture to an index card on which she printed the child's description of the activity. The pictures with the printed event sequence were displayed for all the children to see.

As the story board was put together, the teacher would read each child's description of the event and introduce sequence and transition words as she progressed in the teaching of event sequence. After reviewing the process a few times, the teacher was able to show the students how to use the picture clues and descriptions to create a story of how they made a home for the fish. The teacher then videotaped each child as he or she displayed his or her photograph and explained his or her contribution to the task.

GRADES 1–4: EXPOSITORY PRESENTATION

For their final presentation of the year, students in grades 1–4 had to demonstrate how to make something and explain the process clearly and specifically to their classmates. As with the other taped presentations, the teacher modeled the process first. Students in grades 1 and 2 drew their steps on a transparency and worked with the teacher to formulate the text. The teachers stressed the concept of sequence and the use of appropriate transition words as students explained their procedures. Then the students used the transparencies as an organizational guide to explain how they accomplished their assignment of sequencing the steps in making something. The same type of assignment can be done with either Paintbrush or Kid Pix Studio, and the student can present the process demonstration with the use of the computer.

Students in grades 3 and 4 often participate in science or math fairs. Having selected their topic for the fair, they used clip art or pictures from the Internet to illustrate their topic. The pictures helped them to organize their oral presentation and portray specific detailed information about their topics. The students may give such an oral presentation of their topic before they enter it in the fair. This procedure presents a perfect opportunity to integrate technology and oral presentation skills into a content area project.

GRADES 5–8: COMPARING AND CONTRASTING

For the final phase of the first school year, students in grades 5–8 were given the assignment to compare and contrast two objects and convey this information to their classmates. They started with concrete objects. The students used Excel to create two graphic organizers to accomplish the task. The first, a T-chart (Figure 4-3), is designed to help students determine the features of comparison and contrast. The names of the objects to be compared are placed in each of the two ovals. Then the students use critical thinking and analysis skills to list features that are alike and different. Under each oval they describe the unique characteristic of each feature.

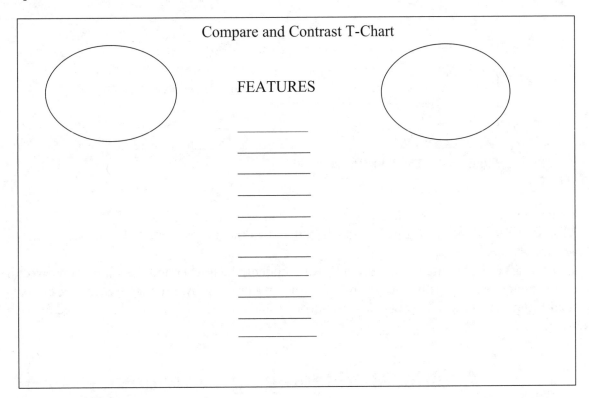

Figure 4-3. T-Chart

The second graphic organizer, The Four Ovals (Figure 4-4) helps students to organize similarities and differences in distinct paragraphs.

Using either of these two graphic organizers, the students prepared their presentation for videotaping. These graphic organizers can be made into transparencies to be used with an overhead projector or can be projected directly from the computer. The two assignments encouraged the students to organize and construct compare-and-contrast designs not just with concrete objects but also eventually

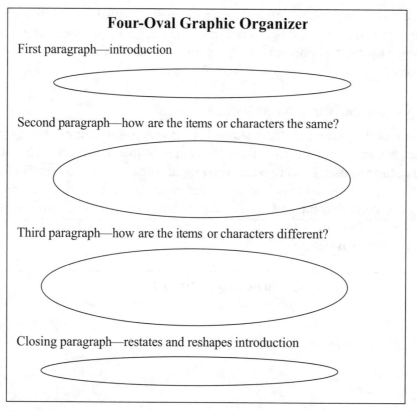

Figure 4-4. The Four Ovals

with characters in a story, with different genres, with concepts in science, and with historical events in social studies. Once students learned the process, they had the means to apply it to any content area subject matter.

After the last oral presentation was given by each student, the teacher and the student reviewed the three presentations and together determined the student's progress over the three trimester presentations and set goals for the following year. The videotape and the evaluations were then passed on to the next grade.

Additional Videotaping Activities

In the previous chapter, we suggested that students become more accountable for their work by having the opportunity to give a presentation based on an activity they have completed. Some of the many kidstation presentations on day 5 of the cycle can be videotaped as a means of documenting and evaluating students' oral presentation skills. Such presentations can include book and movie reviews, student-created original stories, improvisation talks, and biographical, geographical, or historical reports. Students can practice the fine art of debate through group and individual persuasive presentations, explore the use of dramatic storytelling skills, and demonstrate research projects. The picture to the right shows a student discussing her autobiography as she completed her elaboration activity at kidstation 3.

After discussing the format of persuasive essays, students can be engaged at kidstation 2 with the assignment of formulating a persuasive essay from a list of suggested topics. In the picture below a graphic organizer and overhead projector are used to organize the points in a persuasive essay.

Story Board Photo Essays

Children in the early grades often experience learning through hands-on activities and through participation in school-sponsored field trips. Parents often accompany children on these field trips and take pictures of their children. A pre–field trip orientation with parents will inform them of ways to take pictures so that they can be used in a story board photo essay. Children become excited when talking about events they actually experienced, especially when viewing a photo sequence in their hands. Teachers should encourage parents to use such a display of photos when preparing to go on vacation with their family. In September, these story boards can become the focus of the first oral presentation. As students learn how to use cameras to tell a story, they can create their own story boards when the pictures are developed. Other activities are shown in Table 4-2.

Table 4-2. Presentation Ideas

Primary Grades	Intermediate and Junior High Grades
Nursery rhymes	Storytelling and retelling
Alphabet rhymes	Poetry recitation
Number rhymes	Speech recitation
Phone etiquette	Debates
Emergency calls	Discussions
Poetry	Expository—How-to
Story retelling	Mathematics
Show and tell	Science fair
How-to	Historical
Story creations	Autobiographical and biographical
Personal narrative stories	Giving directions
Weather reports	Master of ceremonies
	Commercials

Teachers can assist children by providing them with instruction and opportunities to develop presentations that use visual aids (objects, pictures, video, slides), actions such as gesturing, props, audio (recorded music, sound effects from the computer), technology, and multimedia tools to develop the comfort and ease of giving oral presentations.

Bringing It Home: Involving the Parents

The success of any literacy program is strengthened by involving the parents in the teaching and learning process. Unfortunately, parents are often left out of the learning equation. Parents are sometimes perceived as uninterested or too busy to become involved in assisting their children. Parents are also not always sure how to help and what the school expectations are for their children. Therefore, the school should make every effort to include parents in a program that they would find enjoyable and profitable for their children. When implementing the schoolwide program of oral language development and effective communication skills, parents will learn that oral language is valued and that it will be evaluated. The process should begin, as noted earlier, with a parent orientation in the program.

The initial parent orientation is important to inform them about the program and to give them the opportunity to listen to and view actual oral presentations at various grade levels. For each presentation, the parents are given a grade-appropriate rubric. The teachers explain the criteria in the rubric and the parents score the presentation. Once they have scored the presentation, they discuss their scores and provide a rationale for their evaluation. The teacher simultaneously scores the same presentation. The parents and teachers then compare their scores and share insights. Both teachers and parents learn from the experience and come to a consensus for an appropriate evaluation. In time, most parents' evaluations of a child's presentation are consistent with the teacher's. Once the videotape is viewed by the parents, the teacher and student set goals for the next presentation and the teacher monitors the child's progress.

It is a good move to elicit the help of parents with videotaping in the schools. Some parents, especially those in professional fields, will volunteer to give a presentation and demonstrate how to use computers and multimedia to enhance a presentation. Some parents volunteer to be the audience as students become more confident in their ability to speak in front of others.

Parents can also reinforce oral language skills at home by engaging their children in talk situations. For instance, they can ask their children to discuss what they have read, explain how to prepare a meal, present their opinion about current events, recite poetry, or retell an experience the family just had. Whatever the quality and/or quantity of language instruction children receive in school, their chance for language success begins in the home (Holbrook, 1983).

Parents should receive notification from the school indicating what type of presentation their child will be developing during the trimester. After the first videotaping and evaluation, the parents should be informed of the next type of presentation and the skills their child will be learning to improve their oral communication. Parent participation becomes a significant aspect of the program because they are expected to view the tapes and provide related feedback.

The Benefits of Oral Presentation Instruction

The program described in this chapter views the nature of oral language and the process of language acquisition as a developmental process as children progress through their school years. The implementation of videotaping as students enhance their presentations with multimedia and technology answers the question of how and when students are taught these vital skills, which will also enable and motivate the students to become effective and confident communicators.

FOR THE STUDENTS

The development of oral presentation skills allows children to recognize that an important element for success in all areas of learning is the ability to communicate competently (Holbrook, 1983). Students will come to realize that oral communication can be integrated throughout the curriculum, with presentation experiences occurring in all the content areas.

As students view their videotaped presentations, they see themselves as others see them. They answer questions they might ask of others, such as "How did I look? How did I sound? Did I get my message across? How well did I integrate technology and multimedia into my presentations?" Videotaping allows students to gain a sense of how they appear to their audiences and provides them with immediate and practical feedback, such as identifying their style inhibitors and revealing whether they addressed a topic well enough. Being able to self-evaluate their presentations empowers them to recognize their strengths and weaknesses while motivating them to collaborate with their teacher to plan realistic goals for improvement.

In most schools where such programs have been implemented, the teachers report an increase in students' oral class participation as they become more comfortable expressing their ideas and opinions. Teachers also note that students who have difficulty with written expressive language have benefited from the organizational strategies used to prepare the oral presentations. Many students also reported that they enjoyed bringing home their videotapes and sharing them with their parents. Initially they did not feel comfortable, but as they began to see themselves improving they became proud of their accomplishments and were eager to show their parents. Students also indicated that they were encouraged by their parents and appreciated their support. Perhaps the greatest benefit to students was the comfort level they developed over the years, feeling less inhibited and less anxious about speaking in front of an audience.

FOR THE TEACHERS

In preparing students for videotaping experiences while using technology, teachers need to be proficient in the use of multimedia and technology themselves in order to model the different types of presentations. Using technology broadens the teachers' repertoire of instructional techniques. Furthermore, Glenn (1996) advocates the use of technology and multimedia as an effective means of enhancing oral presentation skills. The videotaping of students' performances provides the teacher with valuable documentation as well as a visual depiction of a student's skill level in verbal and nonverbal communication.

FOR THE PARENTS

Inviting the parents to be an integral part of this program reinforces their important role in their child's education. Parents are every child's greatest source of motivation. However, the parents' role as collaborators becomes heightened when they know what the school's expectations are for their children and when they have the knowledge necessary to help their children reach those goals.

The parent orientation informs the parents of the goals and objectives of the program and provides them with the knowledge of the different types of evaluations their children will experience at different grade levels. It also shows the parents what videotaping offers as an instructional tool, thereby relieving anxiety about the videotaping process. The opportunity to view their child's tape with the teacher's evaluation assists the parents in supporting their child's efforts to improve their presentation skills. Parents are delighted to see the progress of their children over the years, and they appreciate the school's efforts to produce effective communicators.

Conclusion

Bennett (2002) remarked that until schools can permit a major alteration in the way that teaching is carried out, teachers will continue to miss out on the improvement that the integration of multimedia and technology can bring to the learning process. Speaking and presenting in front of an audience, participating in group or individual presentations, mastering pronunciation of progressively challenging and descriptive vocabulary, and communicating ideas effectively are essential skills for children from every linguistic and cultural background, especially those being reintroduced into the mainstream (Hadaway, Vardell, & Young, 2001). We hope that the program stages and suggestions offered in this chapter will help teachers to stimulate children's natural inclination to "talk with style."

Anticipation Guide Revisited

After reading this chapter, confirm your initial predictions about each statement. List the page number that supports each response.

Statement	Agree	Disagree	Verification
1. The development of oral language is critical to building confidence among all language learners.	_____	_____	_____
2. There is no relationship between oral language development and academic success with reading and writing.	_____	_____	_____
3. As students progress through the grade levels, instruction in oral language communication skills should decrease.	_____	_____	_____
4. The national English language arts standards are specifically designed to develop *only* reading, writing, speaking, and listening competencies.	_____	_____	_____
5. Students should not be taught oral presentation skills until the intermediate grades.	_____	_____	_____
6. Semantic maps and graphic organizers can help students to prepare the text for their oral presentations.	_____	_____	_____
7. Multimedia and technology present new forms of literacy that should be integrated into the language arts curriculum.	_____	_____	_____
8. Videotaping is an effective means of documenting and evaluating students' oral presentation skills.	_____	_____	_____

Additional Resources

Appendix A: The National Educational Technology Standards for Students

Standard Category	Student Applications
Basic Operations and Concepts	• Students demonstrate a sound understanding of the nature and operation of technology systems. • Students are proficient in the use of technology.
Social, Ethical, and Human Issues	• Students understand the ethical, cultural, and societal issues related to technology. • Students practice responsible use of technology systems, information, and software. • Students develop positive attitudes toward technology uses that support lifelong learning, collaboration, personal pursuits, and productivity.
Technology Productivity Tools	• Students use technology tools to enhance learning, increase productivity, and promote creativity. • Students use productivity tools to collaborate in constructing technology-enhanced models, preparing publications, and producing other creative works.
Technology Communications Tools	• Students use telecommunications to collaborate, publish, and interact with peers, experts, and other audiences. • Students use a variety of media and formats to communicate information and ideas effectively to multiple audiences.
Technology Research Tools	• Students use technology to locate, evaluate, and collect information from a variety of sources. • Students use technology tools to process data and report results. • Students evaluate and select new information resources and technological innovations based on the appropriateness of specific tasks.
Technology Problem-Solving and Decision-Making Tools	• Students use technology resources for solving problems and making information decisions. • Students employ technology in the development of strategies for solving problems in the real world.

ISTE (2000)

Appendix B: Oral Presentation Evaluation

Student: _____

Grade: _____ Date: _____

Topic: _____

Type of Presentation: _____

Time Limit: _____

Evaluation Criteria	Point Range	Self-Evaluation Points Awarded	Teacher Evaluation	Parent Evaluation
MECHANICS • Voice quality (projection) • Pronunciation (correctness) • Diction (endings)	0–10 0–10 0–10			
DELIVERY • Audience contact (eyes) • Poise • Sincerity (ownership of speech) • Variations of tone (high-low)	0–10 0–10 0–10 0–10			
INTERPRETATION • Appropriate gestures or props • Effectiveness or emphasis • Overall realism	0–10 0–10 0–10			
TOTAL				

Teacher's Comments:_____

_____

_____

_____

Parent's Comments: _____

_____

_____

_____

Presentation Goals: _____

_____

_____

Appendix C: *Multimedia Presentation of a Four-Point Rubric*

Student:_____

Date: _____ Grade: _____

Title of Presentation: _____

Type of Presentation: _____

	4	3	2	1
Content of Presentation	The project flows well, keeps the attention of the audience, and contains relevant information to support ideas.	The project flows well and is somewhat interesting. It contains most of the details to support ideas.	The majority of the project is disjointed and the content is not sufficient to support ideas.	The project does not flow at all, is poorly constructed, and does not contain relevant information.
Language & Mechanics	The information is accurate, well written, and complete with proper grammar, punctuation, and vivid language.	The majority of the text is accurate and uses proper grammar. The language used is clear and the punctuation correct.	The project uses an acceptable amount of text. Language is only satisfactory. There are several errors in punctuation.	Information is missing. There is little use of vivid language and there are many errors in grammar and punctuation.
Delivery	Clear pronunciation, poised, fluent, uses gestures appropriately. Good posture, good voice quality, and is pleasing to listen to.	Understandable pronunciation, some hesitation, not enough eye contact, not so poised, not enough gestures, relies on notes somewhat. Is easy to listen to.	Fair pronunciation, hesitation, little eye contact, unfocused, relies on reading from slides too much. Is not easy to listen to.	Very poor pronunciation, very choppy, no eye contact, reads from slides. Not pleasant to listen to.
Graphics & Images	Images used to enhance the text are most effective and placed appropriately.	Images used to enhance the text are satisfactory. Placement of images good.	Images used to enhance the text are ineffective and not placed appropriately.	No images or graphic used.

Content of Presentation _____   14–16 Excellent, 11–13 Very Good, 9–10 Satisfactory
Language & Mechanics _____
Delivery   _____
Graphics & Images   _____
Total Score   _____

Parent's Signature: _____Date: _____

Appendix D: Stone Boy Presentation

The Stone Boy

By Gina Berriault
Presented by
Miguel S.

SETTING

The story takes place in a small country town in Corinth County. It appears to take place on a farm with lots of land and animals.

CHARACTERS

Arnold is the younger brother of Eugene and Nora. Arnold is 9 years old. He lives on a farm with his family.

Eugene is the tall, strong, older brother of Arnold. He is 15 years old and the oldest child in the family. He seems to be a very caring brother.

PROBLEM/CONFLICT OF THE STORY

Eugene is killed in an accident. Arnold cannot seem to justify his reaction to the accident. He seems to have difficulty expressing his feelings. As a result, other family members think he is made of stone and has no feelings.

PLOT/EPISODES

One morning, Arnold wakes up his older brother, Eugene. Their father had asked them to pick the peas in the field. Eugene was to help Arnold with this task.

Even though it was not duck season, Arnold wanted to take his gun. Eugene reminded him that it was against the law to shoot the ducks.

As Eugene and Arnold were approaching the rows of peas, they had to climb over a fence. Arnold's gun got caught on the fence and fired.

Eugene was lying on the ground perfectly still. Arnold called out to him several times, but Eugene didn't respond. Then Arnold put his hand under Eugene's head. It was filled with blood. Arnold stood next to his brother's body for a few minutes, then he left him to go pick the peas.

It was only after Arnold had picked the peas and went back to the house that he told his father that Eugene was dead. Quickly, his father ran to get Eugene, and then Arnold and his father had to make the trip to the county seat to see the sheriff. Everyone was shocked and amazed that Arnold was so heartless that he did not run for help right away.

Everyone in the family tried to get Arnold to explain why he hadn't come for help or why he hadn't cried at the funeral of his brother.

His sister, Nora, ignored him, and his mother found it very hard to speak to him. His father spoke to him when he had to give him directions.

CONCLUSION

One night Arnold went to his parents' room and knocked on the door. When they called him in, he did not respond.

The next day his mother asked if it had been he at the door. Arnold just looked at her. When she asked him what he wanted, he answered, "Nothing," and he walked out the door.

SOLUTION

The conflict within Arnold was not resolved. It did not seem that he could express his grief or even begin to explain to others why he did not run for help when Eugene was shot.

REACTION

I didn't like the way this story ended. I felt sorry for Arnold. I am sure he loved his brother. But maybe because he felt so guilty and shocked about his death, he couldn't express his feelings. I think that his family should have realized this and not made him feel bad about it. The story taught me the importance of expressing my feelings.

Web Sites

Elementary Schools
http://northport.k12.ny.us/aspiration/elementaryschool.html

SJUSD: Elementary School Curriculum
www.sanjuan.edu/curriculum/elementary/

ProTeacher: Space Lesson Plans for Elementary School Teachers
www.proteacher.com/110020.shtml

McNair Elementary School
www.fcps.k12.va.us/McNairES/geninfo.html

Check Sheet for Oral Presentations
www.cs.cmu.edu/~rapidproto/assessment/presentation.html

Articles for Elementary School Teachers—2000
http://k6educators.about.com/library/weekly/mprev00.htm

Evaluating Oral Presentations
http://mendota.english.wisc.edu/~WAC/page.jsp?id=110&c_type=category&c_id=49

Science Fairs in Elementary School
www.ericdigests.org/2000-1/fairs.html

Teachers—Preschool, Kindergarten, Elementary, Middle, and Secondary
www.bls.gov/oco/ocos069.htm

Technology Resources

Breyer, M. (1999). *How to give a presentation: Grades 6–8.* Westminster, CA: Teacher Created Materials.

Bryant, M. H. (1996). *Integrating technology into the curriculum.* Westminster, CA: Teacher Created Materials.

Gimotty, S. L. (1999). *Computer activities through the year: Grades 4–8.* Westminster, CA: Teacher Created Materials.

Hayes, D. S. (1997). *Multimedia projects.* Westminster, CA: Teacher Created Materials.

Hoffman, B. G. (1999). *Classroom computer center: Grades 3–4.* Torrance, CA: Schaffer.

Norris, J. (1998). *Activities using the World Wide Web.* Monterey CA: Evan-Moor.

Ryan, C. D. (1999). *Classroom computer center: K–2.* Torrance, CA: Schaffer.

Skinner, D. F. (1999). *Integrating technology into the language arts curriculum.* Westminster, CA: Teacher Created Materials.

For Further Reflection

1. Before starting the oral presentation instruction with your class, have your students write about how they feel giving oral presentations in front of their peers and an audience. Then after a year of implementing the training and videotaping, have them write again about their comfort level of giving oral presentations and compare the difference.

2. How confident are you about giving oral presentations? Do you think that teaching your students the fine points of giving oral presentations would improve your comfort level and delivery?

References

Bennett, F. (2002, December). The future of computer technology in K–12 education. *Phi Delta Kappan, 83* (8), 621–625.

Betts, R. (1994). On the birth of the communication age: A conversation with David Thornburg. *Educational Leadership, 51*, 20–23.

Board of Education of the City of New York. (1997). *Performance standards: English language arts.* New York: Author.

Buckley, M. H. (1992). Focus on research: We listen a book a day; we speak a book a day. Learning from Walter Loban. *Language Arts, 69*, 622–626.

Burns, P. C., Roe, B. D., & Smith, S. H. (2004). *Teaching reading in today's elementary school.* New York: Houghton Mifflin.

Crawford, R. (1996). Documenting and evaluating oral language development in the classroom. *Reading Horizons, 36* (4), 285–296.

Donovan, F., & Sneider, C. (1994). Setting and meeting the national standards with help from technology. *Technology & Learning, 15* (1), 40–44, 46–48.

Dugger, W. E., Jr. (1999). Putting technology education standards into practice. *National Association of Secondary School Principals Bulletin, 83* (608), 57–63.

Florida Department of Education (2000). *Sunshine standards.* Tallahassee, FL: Author.

Fountas, I. C., & Pinnell, G. S. (2001). *Guided readers and writers: Grades 3–6.* Portsmouth, NH: Heinemann.

Freeley, A. J. (1996). *Argumentation and debate* (9th ed.). Belmont, CA: Wadsworth.

Glenn, R. J. (1996). *Using video to enhance content and delivery skills in the basic oral communication course: Summarizing the uses and benefits.* Paper presented at the 1996 Kentucky Communication Association, Lake Cumberland, KY.

Guastello, E. F. (2003, March). Multi-media and oral presentation skills: A perfect match! *Today's Catholic Teacher,* pp. 16–19.

Guastello, E. F., & Sinatra, R. (2001). Improving students' oral presentation skills through the use of technology and multi-media. *The Language and Literacy Spectrum, 11*, 5–17.

Haber, R. J., & Lingard, L. A. (2001). Learning oral presentation skills: A rhetorical analysis with pedagogical and professional implications. *Journal of General Internal Medicine, 16* (5), 308–315.

Hadaway, N. L., Vardell, S. M., & Young, T. A. (2001). Scaffolding oral language development through poetry for students learning English. *Reading Teachers, 54* (8), 796–806.

Hennessy, B. G. (2000). *The river rescue.* Glenview, IL: Scott Foresman.

Holbrook, H. T. (1983). Oral language: A neglected art? *Language Arts, 60* (2), 255–258.

International Society for Technology in Education (ISTE). (2000). *National educational technology standards for students.* Engene, OR: Author.

Kanning, R. (1994, April). What multimedia can do in our classrooms. *Educational Leadership, 51*, 44–48.

Loban, W. (1976). *Language development: Kindergarten through grade twelve.* Urbana, IL: National Council of Teachers of English.

Loban, W. (1986). Research currents: The somewhat stingy story of research into children's language. *Language Arts, 63*, 608–616.

Lucas, S. (1995). *The art of public speaking* (5th ed.). New York: Random House.

Magin, D., & Helmore, P. (2001). Peer and teacher assessments of oral presentation skills: How reliable are they? *Studies in Higher Education, 26* (3), 287–299.

National Association of Bilingual Education. (1992). *Professional standards for the preparation of bilingual/multicultural teachers.* Washington, DC: Author.

National Council of Teachers of English (NCTE). (1999). *The list of standards for English language arts.* Urbana, IL: Author.

New Jersey Department of Education (1996). *New Jersey core curriculum content standards.* Trenton, NJ: Author.

Newman, D. (1992, December). Technology as support for school restructure and school restructuring. *Phi Delta Kappan, 74* (4), 308–315.

Norton, D. E. (2003). *Through the eyes of a child: An introduction to children's literature.* Upper Saddle River, NJ: Merrill Prentice Hall.

Norton, D. E., & Norton, S. E. (2003). *Language arts activities for children.* Upper Saddle River, NJ: Merrill Prentice Hall.

Page, M. S. (2002). Technology enriched classrooms: Effects on students of low socioeconomic status. *Journal of Research on Technology in Education, 34* (4), 389–410.

Patri, M. (2002). The influence of peer feedback on self- and peer-assessment of oral skills. *Language Testing, 19* (2), 109–132.

Shreiner, B. H. (1995). *Enhancing eighth-grade student presentations of scientific research with technology.* Doctoral dissertation, Nova Southeastern University, (ERIC Document Reproduction Service No. ED 389 276)

Smith, C. B. (2003). *Oral language development as a precursor to literacy.* Bloomington, IN. (ERIC Document Reproduction Service No. ED 482 005)

Stewig, J. W. (1988). Oral language: A place in the curriculum? *The Clearing House, 62,* 171–174.

Utah State Office of Education. (2000). *Pre-K Standards (Guidelines).* Salt Lake City, UT: Author.

Ward, B. S. (1984). Oral communication in the elementary classroom. In C. J. Thaiss & C. Suhor (Eds.), *Speaking and writing, K–12: Classroom strategies and the new research.* Urbana, IL: National Council of Teachers of English.

Whaley, C. (2002). Meeting the diverse needs of children through storytelling: Supportive language learning. *Young Children, 57* (2), 31–34.

Wright, R. T. (1999). Technology education: Essential for balanced education. *National Association of Secondary School Principals,*

Chapter 5

Uplifting Minds on the Wings of Poetry

Anticipation Guide

Before reading this chapter, please read each of the statements listed below. Based upon your prior knowledge and experience with this chapter's topics, check either "agree" or "disagree" for each statement. After reading the chapter, see if your answers change in the Anticipation Guide Revisited found at the end of the chapter.

Statement	Agree	Disagree
1. One reason we write poetry is that it is a basic way to learn about our culture and become a member of our culture.	_____	_____
2. Traditional poetry is focused on how selective language elements fit together and how these elements lead to an interpretation and a meaning.	_____	_____
3. Nontraditional poetry, found in popular culture today, is not highly structured nor sophisticated and is therefore not appropriate for beginning writers.	_____	_____
4. Developing voice in poetry is a major avenue through which students can achieve ownership and control over their writing, thereby writing better poetry.	_____	_____
5. Responding to poetry is a linear process that should be taught in sequence so that beginning writers (especially) can not only understand the meaning but also understand the process involved in writing good poetry.	_____	_____
6. There is always only one "correct" interpretation of a poem.	_____	_____
7. Reading a poem out loud to students is encouraged, even among older students.	_____	_____
8. Poetry is often the last component of the language arts curriculum to be taught.	_____	_____

Introduction

> I whish I were a chill slimmy monster
>
> Yo Yo Daniel
>
> He is a bad monster so Daniel
>
> Crawled to the Monster and
>
> The bug ate him and
>
> The cock-a-roach ate him too.
>
> *—Evan, May 2003*

Evan and his fourth-grade peers were writing "wish poems." They were provided with prompts from Koch's (1970, 1973) seminal books on how to teach children to write poetry. Most of these fourth graders told us that they had never written any "good" poetry before—"only for the tests," and most of them lamented the fact that they "didn't know how to," anyway. Evan's fourth-grade teacher was reluctant, too. "We've done acrostic poetry before, but not much; we just don't have the time." Teachers often use acrostic poetry because it is a simple way to connect the content vocabulary of a particular lesson to the content topic. (Examples of acrostic and many other kinds of poetry can be found later in the chapter.)

We provided inservice workshops to fourth- and fifth-grade teachers in a district—a diverse, working-class, immigrant suburb 40 miles outside New York City—specifically around writing and poetry. We found, among the 100 or so participants who attended each workshop, that most of them did very little writing at all with their students in their classrooms. In most cases, we also found *only two or three* teachers in each workshop who thought that he or she understood, had time for, and could justify (because of state standards and exams) taking time out of a busy schedule to teach poetry writing. Nevertheless, when we did some poetry writing of our own—complete with peer conferencing, editing, and working together to connect our writing to the state and city standards—most of the teachers would then say, "It's amazing" or "It's cathartic" and "My students would love it."

What Is Poetry?

Poetry, traditionally defined, is a "division of literature; a piece of literature written in meter; verse" and/or a "compressed form of literature [that] expresses great depth of meaning" (*The American Heritage Dictionary*). Poetry by its very nature defies traditional definition, however, and is therefore best described, perhaps, as a genre that uses a nontraditional writing style and language.

Consider how Ruth Gordon (1993), a children's author, expresses her understanding of poetry: "Poetry is the onion of readers. It can cause tears, be peeled layer by layer, or be replanted to grow into new ideas. And it adds taste, zest, and a sharp but sweet quality that enriches our lives".

This is Blake's (1990) ideas on why we write poetry:

> Poetry is a basic way for individuals to learn enough about their culture to become a welcome member of it. Through writing poetry we tell people some things they didn't know or hadn't put into words before. But we write poems in order to know. (p. 19)

This is Martin's (1988) advice on why we need to teach poetry:

> Teaching people to write poems requires first of all that for a limited period of time they will be forced to open their eyes and ears, to take off the blinders and let the images pour in—a necessary first step toward taking life seriously and even, I suspect, a good way to start taking responsibility for themselves and for the world they can finally see. (p. 36)

Poetry is indeed a specific genre of literature, one that includes as some of its elements the notions of rhythm and rhyme; that evokes emotions and depth of meaning; and that may help us as human beings to construct and to reconstruct our own realities. In the classroom, poetry can become an open invitation for students to respond, experience, and celebrate through language.

The Elements of Poetry

The essence of traditional poetry lies in language, with the line (rather than the sentence in prose) as one of its defining, basic elements. A line in poetry can be represented by only one word, but even that one word carries meaning. Hancock (2004) explains that in traditional poetry, both meaning and "selective language elements" are "essentially language related," in which language is creative, evocative, and meaningful, and there is no emphasis on character or plot or point of view. These selective language elements include the following:

1. *Rhythm*—a patterned movement or variation caused by the regular recurrence of contrasting elements of sound or speech; in poetry or rap music, rhythm is indicated by how certain words are stressed, by either volume or emphasis.

2. *Rhyme*—a regular correspondence of sounds, especially at the end of lines. The Dr. Seuss books are noted for their rhyme and experimentation with rhyme: "The cat in the hat"; "The cat in the hat comes back." This element also includes (a) *alliteration*—The repetition of initial consonant sounds, such as "beautiful, boisterous boy from Bankok"; and (b) *assonance*—the repetition of internal vowel sounds, such as Yates's "dolphin-torn, gong-tormented sea."

3. *Imagery*—the use of vivid or figurative language to represent objects, actions, or ideas, such as "the seasick sky," which evokes images of a putrid greenish blue, unsettled, disturbed, even "wavy" sky.

4. *Figurative language*—making use of figures of speech, such as (a) *simile*, in which two essentially unlike things are compared, introduced by "like" or "as" (e.g., Shakespeare's, "so are you to my thoughts as food to life"); (b) *metaphor*, in which a word or phrase that ordinarily designates one thing is used to designate another and make an implicit comparison (e.g., "a sea of troubles"); and (c) *personification*, in which an inanimate object is endowed with human qualities or is represented as possessing human form (e.g., "hunger sat shivering by the road").

5. *Shape and spacing*—the characteristic surface configuration; in poetry, the arrangement of words on the page, such as a diamante or "shape" poem (these will be explained below).

Why Teach Poetry Across the Grades?

Although selective language elements are often associated with good poetry writing, they are also highly structured and sophisticated. Therefore, the insistence on the use of one or many of these elements might not be appropriate for beginning writers, and might, in fact, even deter beginning poetry writers from attempting their hand at poetry writing at all.

Precisely because beginning poetry writers can be reluctant to put pen to paper, I like to follow English professors and poetry teachers Beach & Marshall's (1991) guidelines for successfully teaching poetry, especially among the most timid and/or rookie poetry writers:

Never teach a poem you do not like.

Teach poems you are not certain you understand.

Teach poems that are new to you.

Read poems daily in your life outside school.

Give students the freedom to dislike "great" poetry. (p. 384)

The expectation of writing good poetry in the classroom is difficult and frightening for even the best students (and teachers!). In fact, for many children, and especially for beginning readers and writers, writing traditional poetry is simply not an option. According to Koch (1970), this is because poetry itself is in the *way* that children write—"a poetic tradition . . . that demands rhyme, meter, and exalted subject matter is *not* child-poet-friendly." Children must therefore have alternate, or nontraditional, models of poetry that speak to them—where the "language and syntax is not so far way . . . that he or she couldn't get close to it in feeling and tone" (p. 315). Children need to feel that they can express themselves in their own words and in their own voice. (Some examples of nontraditional poetry can be found today in popular culture, including rap and hip-hop music).

As teachers, we must prepare ourselves for teaching poetry, especially to beginning and/or reluctant students. We need to understand our students' fears and give them permission to try almost anything. We need to search for lots of good models for poetry (including the silly poetry of Shel Silverstein and the clean rap poetry of Tupac just before he died). We need to let our students experiment with rhyme and rhythm, with shape and form, and most of all with voice. It is in finding their voices that the best writing, and hence the best poetry, shines through. Indeed, Duthie & Kubie (2004) acknowledged (in their work with primary grade students) that even though poetry is the most neglected genre in our classrooms and a genre not readily accessible to children, it is the one that helped them to become excited to read and write more while also discovering their voices.

Finding Voice

Voice is an elusive, complex, and controversial topic. To most writing classroom researchers (Atwell, 1987; Blake, 1995a, 1997; Calkins, 1983, 1986; Graves, 1983; Murray, 1968), voice is central to the process of writing, particularly in poetry. Expressing one's voice effectively is the primary means of achieving ownership and control of one's writing as students are given opportunities to learn the value and purpose of peer review and collaboration, shared knowledge, and community. Students who are successful in moving back and forth among the recursive stages of the writing process, for example, are more willing to revise and edit, produce pieces that exhibit higher textual readability, and develop their own individual voice.

Voice in poetry is perhaps elusive, but it is no less central. To learn to write poetry requires a great sense of voice. It forces one "to open eyes and ears, to take off the blinders and let the images pour in" *before* one can allow one's voice to speak through poetry. (V. Martin, cited in Blake, 1992, p. 19). In poetry, voice becomes transformed through a greater understanding not only of oneself but also of one's culture and one's world. Anne Sexton (according to Erica Jong, cited in Blake, 1992) said that writing poetry "relates the poet to the sacred essence of all humanity . . . the whole life of us writing is the one long poem" (p. 19).

Poetry for Diverse Students

For most children, gaining and/or expressing one's voice through poetry is absolutely essential to their wanting to write, and being successful at writing, poetry at all. This could be particularly important for diverse students. (Here the term *diverse* is used to refer to students who are different from the mainstream, including those students who are poor, second-language learning, labeled with a learning disability or a special need, and/or black, Hispanic, or other than Anglo-American.) These are students whose voices have traditionally been silenced (Blake, 1995a, 1995b, 1997, 2004), yet when they are heard, they share vibrant reflections of their distinct experiences and perceptions of the world.

Voice is therefore particularly crucial for diverse students for two major and connected reasons. First, these students have long been reported to "demonstrate sustained difficulties" with traditional school "narrative structure" (Reid & Button, 1995, p. 602)—particularly narrative structure that requires students to use and understand sophisticated linguistic strategies such as cohesion, for example. This parallels what Koch (1970) said above, that rigid adherence to traditional poetic rhyme can actually impede a child's attempt to write poetry at all.

This is certainly not to say that diverse students cannot use sophisticated linguistic strategies, only that diverse students are not exposed to these traditional, so-called sophisticated structures as often as mainstream students are. Delpit (1988) describes the "culture of power" and the tendency for minority students to be excluded from it and particularly from the language of power. Street (1995) discusses "schooled" versus "local" literacies, and Blake (2004) describes the "culture of refusal" and "out-of-school" literacies. These structures, precisely because they are deemed mainstream, are not the kind of linguistic structures that capture urban language in all its richness.

In reality, however, it is precisely because there are more flexible rules (at least, there *appear* to be so) that the structure itself can seem less inhibiting, affording students genuine opportunities to control or to own what they write. Poetry therefore gives students the opportunity to gain a measure of control over their writing through personal and creative expression, a measure of what is often called linguistic freedom.

The second reason that voice is particularly crucial for diverse students is that because we might not listen to their voices as much as we do the voices of "great importance," poetry as a way of knowing affords these students great teaching and learning opportunities. Their poetry can teach us about who they are, help us to discover "what it is like to be them . . . and what the world seems like to them" (Reid & Button, 1995, p. 603), and teach themselves about who they are as human beings in this world. Poetry can help to motivate these students to want to write more, and it can also help them to feel better about themselves and their place in the world.

Responding to poetry can have a similar effect on students. Robert Blake (father of Brett Blake, one of the authors) and Anna Lund (1986) conducted a study of student responses to poetry that reveals how poignant and thoughtful student responses can be when they are given the freedom to respond in unrestricted ways. Essentially, the researchers found that students responded to complex poems in very sophisticated ways, validating the belief that students can respond to poetry and can feel brave enough to create their own poetry. Some of the crucial findings from the study have important implications for us as classroom poetry teachers:

1. Reading a poem is not a simple or linear process. Readers need time to read over particular lines and to think about the poem; they should not be rushed through the process. A poem "needs to grow on us" (p. 72).

2. When students say they do not like a poem or poetry in general, they often mean that they are afraid they cannot understand the meaning. Furthermore, they believe that the teacher is the holder of the meaning and that there is only one meaning.

3. Younger students read and respond differently from "English majors and experienced teachers in many immensely important ways" (p. 72). This does not mean that these students do not read poetry successfully; they merely bring to the reading different backgrounds and experiences. This may be especially crucial for diverse and/or English language learners (ELLs).

4. There are as many responses to complex poems as there are students in the class. It takes time for students to learn how to read and respond to poetry, and certainly to write poetry. Students need many opportunities to develop confidence so that they can respond in meaningful ways to complex poetry. Students thus need many opportunities to both write and interpret poetry—especially reluctant, beginning, and/or diverse students.

Even professional poets struggle with writing and interpreting poetry—even their own works. Theodore Roethke, a prolific author of several poems who won the Pulitzer Prize in 1954 for "The Waking," was one such poet. Even though he was thought to have succeeded in "making magic out of inarticulateness" (Kirsch, 2005, p. 90) through his poetry, when he was asked what his poems meant, he was at a loss, saying, "Believe me, you will have no trouble if you approach these poems as a child would, naively, with your whole being awake, your faculties loose and alert" (p. 91). Roethke believed that the meaning or interpretation of a poem could best be intuited, not elucidated.

To highlight this point, below is an example of Brett Blake's son Robbie's response to reading Roethke's "My Papa's Waltz." At the time of the reading, Robbie was a freshman in high school and wanted to get it done in class, quickly, and "without much thought" (as well as to "get it right and not look stupid" he later said). He therefore chose to respond in a safe and popular way. His interpretation was indeed the one that most readers (and certainly most teachers) have been told is correct—the meaning that could be *eluci-dated* or explained, not the meaning that could be *intuited* or interpreted.

"My Papa's Waltz" describes a dance around the kitchen by a young child and his father when he comes home from work. Many people interpret this poem to be one of a drunk, abusive father who forces his child to dance, clumsily, around the kitchen with him. Stanzas that refer to the smell of whiskey on the father's breath that "could make a small boy dizzy" help to conjure up these interpretive images. Think, however, of alternate meanings as you read Roethke's actual poem and Robbie's response. How might you help students to see this poem differently? Hint: Have you had a similar experience with your father in which the "dance" was a positive and loving moment? If students can interpret this poem in multiple ways, why might that be beneficial to their writing their own poetry?

Here is Robbie's response:

> The poem "My Papa's Waltz," by Theodore Roethke (1966), describes a scene where a drunken father comes home and dances around the room with his son. This dance is thought to be very sloppy and noisy as a result of the father. The way that the poet describes the dance itself is very interesting. The father's movements and actions are referred to many times like in the part of the poem that describes the end of the dance, "you beat time on my head with a palm caked hard by dirt then waltzed me off to bed still clinging to your shirt" (lines 13–16). Also, it is intimated that the father's actions are not that which were accepted. The mother was upset with the show of her drunken husband. He was dirty and his hand was injured; he may have been in a fight prior to his coming home.

In the next section, we will shift our focus to an urban classroom. Here you will find samples of beginning poetry writing from students who are ELLs and those who have special needs. For many of these students, attempting an interpretation or a response (like Robbie's), let alone writing an original poem, was very scary. Many of these students simply had not engaged with poetry before.

Stephanie's Middle School Classroom

"Failure is ingrained in their school career," Stephanie, a teacher, told us. "The fear associated with reading and writing can paralyze these young learners. If that is not the direct result, then they turn toward acting out in order to hide their perceived academic inadequacies."

Introducing Arnella

When Stephanie first met Arnella, she had just returned from the principal's office because she had allegedly "committed willful assault on a staffperson with a weapon." (Arnella had in fact attempted to strike the staffperson with the end of a pencil). Frustrated with her constant disruptive behavior, the school counselor asked that Arnella be placed in Stephanie's classroom and that Stephanie take appropriate disciplinary measures immediately. To comply with that request, in part, Stephanie asked Arnella to write about the experience. This is what Arnella had to say (unedited):

> I wish I was in [another school] because I hate this school. because I don't know any body in this school and im going to be bad while im here and I wish I was suspended. You can do nothing for me because I don't want you to.

Stephanie's classroom was unique. In her urban classroom, each of her fifth- and-sixth grade students had been labeled with either a behavioral or an academic learning disorder. Furthermore, at least half of her class was learning English as a Second language (ESL); all were poor, and most (according to what Stephanie had heard other teachers and administrators say) were considered "uneducable," as evidenced by their state assessment scores in reading and writing. (Her students' tested reading and writing abilities were solidly on a first- or second-grade level). Indeed, Stephanie reported, most of her students did struggle with reading and writing, so much so that even choosing a topic for these students could be absolute torture, and the students would give up. Nevertheless, Stephanie persisted. First she insisted that all her students write (even as a disciplinary tool). After she introduced a unit on poetry, she discovered that her students could write. Moreover, they were motivated to write more and to write well. (It is very important to note here that most standardized state exams now test for poetry. In fact, a poem has appeared on New York State's fourth-grade and eighth-grade standardized English Language Assessment (ELA). See page 171 for a list of children's poetry from the last three years' New York State fourth-grade ELA exam. The appendix gives sample questions from the exams. By integrating poetry interpretation as a kidstation 3 activity (see chapter 3), teachers give students the opportunity to engage in creative thinking as they explore ways to sharpen topic ideas.

Haiku and Diamante Poetry

Stephanie's unit on poetry began with a walk outside. She encouraged her students to pick up objects—sticks, rocks, snow in the winter—and to hold them, feel them, close their eyes and describe them, and even talk to them. Back inside, with the students seated with their objects, fresh from the physical activity, and curious, she would introduce a particular form.

Next she would model poetry that she or some other students had written, using their objects and the poetic structure of the haiku, for example. Haiku is probably the most familiar syllable-counting poem used in classrooms today. It is a Japanese poetic form consisting of 17 syllables arranged in three lines of 5, 7, and 5 syllables, respectively. Haiku poems almost always have nature as their theme, and present a clear, single image of it. Haiku is very precise and concise.

Finally, without little further "formal" instruction (except, of course, for the form and various samples), she would let her students write. Here are some examples.

Arnella became one of Stephanie's most prolific poetry writers, beginning with a simple haiku:

> I have a snowball
>
> It is part of nature
>
> It snows all Winter

After instruction, Arnella also wrote diamante poems. These are in a structure that is well liked by teachers and students because it is simple and subtly introduces grammar and form. Diamante poetry is a seven-line contrast poem written in the shape of a diamond. One formula is as follows:

Line 1: One noun as the subject

Line 2: Two adjectives describing the subject

Line 3: Three participles (ending in *–ing*) telling about the subject

Line 4: Four nouns (the first two related to the subject and the second two related to the opposite)

Line 5: Three participles (ending in –*ing*) telling about the opposite

Line 6: Two adjectives describing the opposite

Line 7: One noun that is the opposite of the subject

Below, Arnella describes her bed at home, covered with soft pillows and a basket that held her favorite things:

Basket

Orange yellow

Carrying holding stuff making

Fruit candy clothes food

Sleeping keeping using

Purple soft

Bed

After writing this poem, Arnella exclaimed to Stephanie, "I like to go outside and walk around because finding stuff and writing is easy!"

Introducing Josh

Josh had a history of difficulty in school. He had repeated both kindergarten and first grade and had been socially promoted from fourth to fifth grade because of his age and size. Nevertheless, his overall skills were measured at a first-grade level, and he experienced extreme difficulties with any reading or writing task. An initial sample of Josh's written work looked like this:

> School is but [butt] because we do to much work in class. I will have Gym all day we will play basketball in Gym all day.

Josh, too, seemed to respond well to Stephanie's unit on poetry. Like Arnella, Josh wrote a poem (though freestyle, not a haiku or diamante) after returning from a walk outside:

Stick

It dropped from a tree

And fell to the ground

I found it outside

In some leaves

There it was

On the ground

Where I saw it

I picked it up

It is rough

It was alive

Now it is dead

The wind came by

And killed it

Later, however, after Josh felt successful with his freestyle poem, he did indeed try his hand with diamante poetry, seemingly finding and expressing his own sense of identity through this poetic form:

Me

Restless Tired

Running Playing Hanging

Ball Book Hall Shoes

Rapping Shopping Reading

Big Bad

Me

Ball

Oval Big

Throwing Running Kicking

Football Basketball Baseball Soccer Ball

Bouncing Passing Shooting

Round Hard

Rock

Aware of Josh's love of sports and of talking about himself, Stephanie pushed him to write more. As she continued to push him to write, she reports that she saw an amazing change in him:

> Josh had had a fear of written language. He was a helpless reader with few word attack strategies and he didn't have a good recall of sight words . . . it was just jumble to him. However *poetry was him*. There really was not a lot of jumble because it was about his thoughts and feelings. He became the expert . . . he was in control of his learning for once.

Guidelines for Teaching Poetic Writing

Before offering some guidelines on how to teach poetry to beginning students, we will review some of the ideas inherent in the *processes* of writing and revising poetry—that is, how a writer creates a poem from beginning to end. We know about this from talking and working with professional writers and poets—those who can articulate their metacognitive awareness about language and processes. (These activities were co-designed by Robert W. Blake, professor emeritus, State University of New York.)

First, the student (writer) makes use of formulas, patterns, or models, presented by the teacher and like those used by other poets, to begin his or her writing. (Think of Stephanie's use of haiku and diamante.)

Second, the poet-student starts with a feeling—the "something moves me" feeling—and lets an image or images come from the feeling. The poet-student may also start with an image or object and let that evoke the feelings. Think of Arnella's snowball. Or, the poet may begin with an idea or a theme—think of Josh's notion of "being bad"—and let the associated words flow from there.

Finally, during the revising process, the writers help to create and re-create their poetry by doing the following:

1. Condensing: eliminating unnecessary words or using one word for several, as the poet continually moves toward the essence of what he or she is trying to say.

2. Finding patterns in the first draft, perhaps concentrating on a single pattern and refining it.

3. Tinkering with words: adding, deleting, or substituting (for more powerful images, perhaps), and moving words around.

Once we teachers understand this process, we are ready to "teach" the writing of poetry to our students. Remember, as we noted earlier, although so-called traditional poetry can contain one or more selective language features like metaphor, instruction for beginning writers might not be at all necessary and in fact can hinder beginning students from wanting to attempt to write poetry at all.

The teacher teaches students to write poetry by doing the following:

1. Inundating them with poetry of all kinds, from all ages, through professional and student models

2. Encouraging them to respond freely (both intellectually and emotionally) to the poems, maintaining a free and flexible classroom atmosphere in which students are not inhibited from responding and are encouraged that there is not one right answer

3. Letting them take risks in writing poems, allowing them to learn by their failures, and giving them opportunities to try many kinds of poems

4. Supporting their voices so they'll create poems about matters that affect them deeply and use words that are naturally theirs

5. Encouraging them to write poems about what they honestly see, think, and feel, realizing that this process can be unnerving for teacher and student alike but at the same time knowing that the only important writing is truthful writing

6. Helping them to be open to experience, to interact with other creatures and objects as well as humans, to observe, to savor, to feel, to think, to evaluate experiences, and to put what they have perceived into words

7. Assuring them that he or she (the teacher) is going to evaluate their efforts not by correcting errors in grammar or form, but only by describing what they can do to improve their work

8. Helping them to set goals in writing as the basis for future assessments (i.e., concerning imagery or choice of words) and helping them to set goals for statewide exams that increasingly choose poetry as a measure of a student's knowledge

In the next section, we first present some guidelines for generating poetry ideas. Then we describe some activities that have worked well in generating poetry from beginning-level students in diverse classrooms. Finally, we present more actual samples of students' poetry, as well as more templates for various types of poetry.

Devising Poetry Ideas as Student Activities

The concept of the *poetry idea* was developed by Kenneth Koch (1970, 1973). It is an especially fertile way to stimulate students to create poems. As they react to the poetry ideas and produce poetic writing, they learn to read poetry better.

When you make a poetry idea the basis for a lesson, you find the essence of a poem that appeals to you and that you believe will be attractive to the students. Making the poetry idea accessible to the students helps them to discover their own thoughts, emotions, and voice.

Below are some guidelines for using poetry ideas, accompanying activities as poetry ideas, and actual sample poems from a diverse classroom as the students responded to a particular poetry idea.

Guidelines for Generating Poetry Ideas

1. Find a poem that intrigues you and that you believe might interest your students. Whether it is difficult or easy is not the crucial issue. What is important is that its main idea will engage your students.

2. Look for the essence of the poem, its main feeling or idea. Try to summarize it in a few words or a single phrase.

3. Read the poem out loud to your students and make it dramatic. Try to convey the excitement you feel for the poem.

4. Explain difficult words or ideas or, better yet, have the students explain in their own words through their own experiences what the words mean to them.

5. Help your students to feel close to the experience of the poem; have them somehow associate the poem with their own backgrounds.

6. Try to state the writing activity derived from the poem in a few words or sentences, such as "Choose six of your favorite words and write a poem using them." This transition becomes the basis of a poetry activity.

7. Have the students jot down words, images, or ideas connected with their experience. Encourage them to let the words flow.

8. Offer suggestions for opening lines yourself, call for others to come up with opening lines, and write them on the blackboard.

9. When enough ideas are generated, let the students start writing.

10. Collaborate, share, and celebrate!

Poetry Activities

WRITING A "BAD CHILD" POEM

Prewriting Activity. Did you ever do something as a small child that you knew was wrong but that you got a great kick out of? As the teacher reads a poem expressively, put yourself in the child's place. Try to feel as the author does!

For beginning students the teacher should use Shel Silverstein's (1996) wonderful, silly poem "One Sister for Sale." For more advanced students, read Roethke's (1966) poem, "Child on Top of a Greenhouse." (Hint: Read both of these poems out loud.)

Writing Activity. Think back to a time when you did something you knew was wrong but was so thrilling to do, such as eating your dessert before supper, throwing water balloons on Halloween, or even being mean to your brother or sister. Hint: You might first describe the "bad" thing you did and then end with the excitement it gave you—like selling your sister or throwing the water balloons on trick-or-treaters.

WRITING A "SIX FAVORITE WORDS" POEM

Prewriting Activity. What are some words that you especially like? In his poem, David Wagoner (1999) tells us his six favorite words, which he "sets loose like birds in the landscape." The teacher should begin by reading this wonderful poem aloud to the students.

The Words

Wind, bird, and tree,
Water, grass, and light:
In half of what I write
Roughly or smoothly
Year by impatient year,
The same six words recur.
I have as many floors
As meadows or rivers,
As much still air as wind
And as many cats in mind
As nests in the branches
To put an end to these.
Instead, I take what is:
The light beats on the stones,
And wind over sater shines
Like long grass through the trees,
As I set loose, like birds
In a landscape, the old words.

From *Traveling Light: Collected and New Poems.*
Copyright 1999 by David Wagoner. Used with permission of the poet and the University of Illinois Press.

Writing Activity. How would you describe the kinds of words the poet keeps returning to? Jot down, as quickly as you can, 10 words that you like. Then cross out 4 of the words, leaving only 6 words that are your very favorite. Now use your special words in a poem. You might write them down first in a few lines, as Wagoner did, and then use them again in separate lines, showing the significance of each word to you. You can also use the words in any natural way you wish.

SAMPLE FAVORITE WORD POEMS

Prewriting Activity. Make a list of 20 words that you like. You can use names, words from other languages, names of cities and countries, words that suggest sounds, brand names, names of colors—any 20 words. Once you have 20, cross out 5.

Writing Activity. Write down your favorite 15 words. Put them in any order that you like. If you care to, fool around with different combinations. Read them aloud in a silly way.

WRITING A "WISH" POEM

Writing Activity. Using your favorite 15 words from the last exercise, begin each line with "I wish." Be as crazy and weird as you like. You might even want to read it aloud like a rap song!

Name _____   Date _____

I read _____ 's poem entitled _____

- -

1.   This is what I liked about your poem:

2.   These are the words I liked best in your poem:

3.   These are the words that I didn't understand or that confused me in your poem:

4.   You are using your "voice" best when you use these words:

5.   Here are some things that you might want to work on:

6.   If I were going to rewrite your poem, I might do this:

Figure 5-1.   Peer Conferencing Guidelines

Rewriting Activity. In pairs use the form shown in Figure 5-1 to help change or add to your poem. Figures 5-2, 5-3, and 5-4 show student samples of favorite words used in "wish poems."

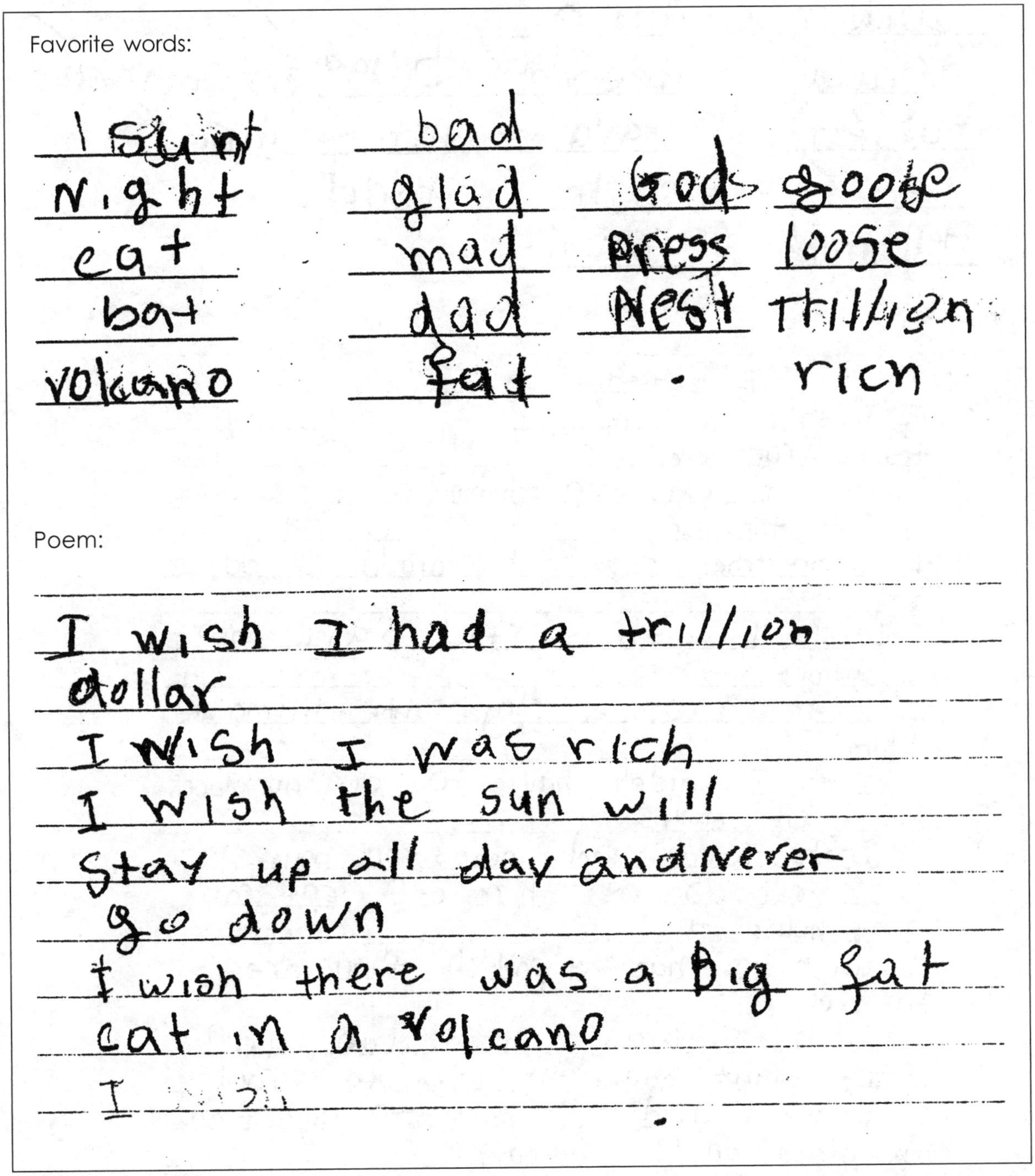

Favorite words:

Isint	bad		
night	glad	God	goose
eat	mad	press	loose
bat	dad	Nest	trillion
volcano	fat		rich

Poem:

I wish I had a trillion
dollar
I wish I was rich
I wish the sun will
stay up all day and never
go down
I wish there was a big fat
cat in a volcano
I wish

Figure 5-2. Jose's "Wish Poem"

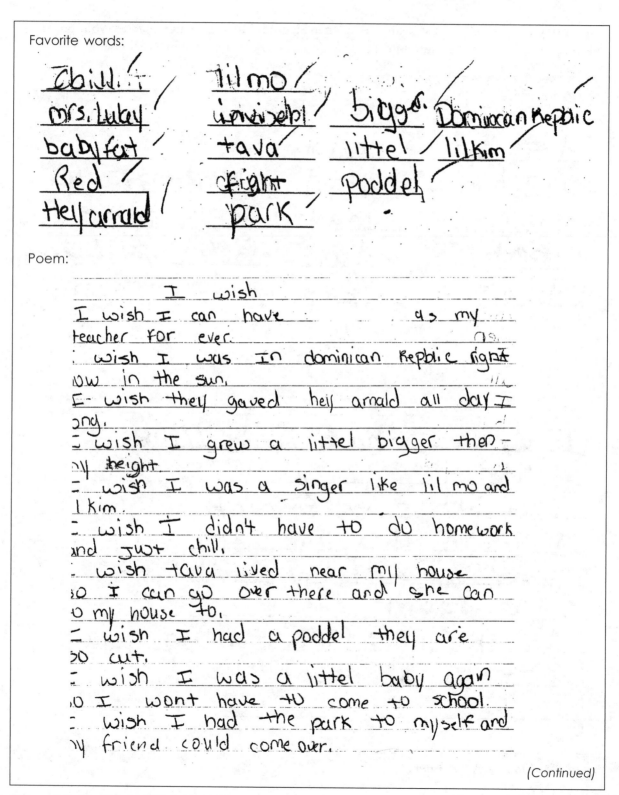

Figure 5-3. Leticia's "Wish Poem"

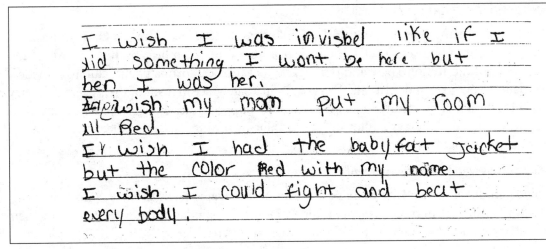

Figure 5-3. Leticia's "Wish Poem" *(Continued)*

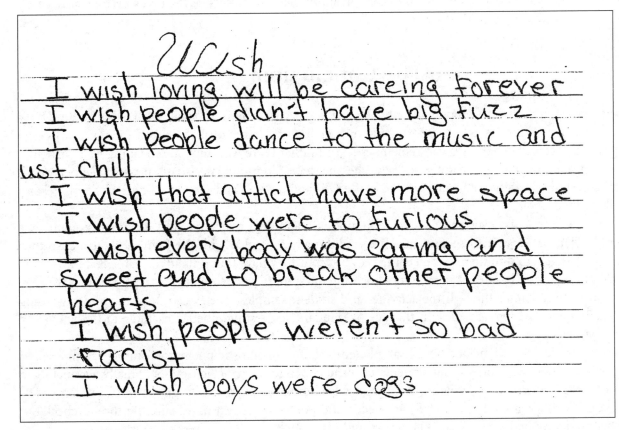

Figure 5-5. Maria's "Wish Poem"

PERFORMANCE AND CELEBRATION ACTIVITIES

Students should share their poetry in front of the whole class. Indeed, according to Opitz & Rasinski (1998), poetry is meant to be read aloud, to be shared so that others can hear both the words of the poem and the voice of the author. These authors suggest that teachers form a poetry club to provide a forum for students to perform and celebrate their poetry in a safe space in front of their peers. A poetry club, a more formal version of a read-aloud, gives students opportunities to select, practice, and read either a favorite poem from another author or one of their own to the class. Furthermore, these authors suggest, teachers might want to do the following:

1. Read aloud several poems to students as a model.

2. Provide students with plenty of time to select and rehearse poems. For example, if poem selection occurs on Monday, students could spend the remainder of the week practicing their poems; trying out their poems in different voices at different rates.

3. Invite students to sign up for a poetry club, which can then be held for a specified amount of time on a Friday, for example. When it's time for the poetry club, students might also want to be prepared to include other information about their poem, such as their reasons for sharing and/ or writing a particular poem.

Conclusion

Poetry is often the last component of the language arts curriculum to be taught. That is because both teachers and students are afraid of poetry as a genre, and many of us have bad memories of being taught poetry in school. We can remember learning that there was only one meaning to a particular poem, and that the one meaning was *never* the one we had in mind! We also often associate poetry with rhyme and a "traditional" structure that is often difficult to read and even more difficult to model and thereby reproduce.

Poetry can cause even more trepidation among beginning, reluctant, and/or diverse students like ELLs. This is because these students have traditionally struggled with the English language, so they often struggle to find their voice. Furthermore, even if they have found their voice, the rest of us often don't listen to it, because it represents something different from the mainstream. However, as we have seen in this chapter through the activities and student samples, poetry can offer fun and rewarding reading and writing activities. In this age of standardized testing, poetry teaching and learning is a must!

In conclusion, we include here a sample template for an acrostic poem, two simple examples, and some sample ideas for helping students to write concrete poetry (Figure 5-5). Finally, we include a copy of a "poetic license" (Figure 5-6), an idea we borrowed from a colleague of ours, Lindamichelle Baron, a children's author, teacher, storyteller, and poetry writer extraordinaire. Be sure to check out her book on poetry, *The Sun Is On: Poetry and Ideas* (1999).

Concrete poems are different from other poems in several ways.

Concrete poems may show a few words or a single word repeated in designs that reflect the meanings of the words. Unlike traditional poems, they may be read in any direction—up, down, diagonally, or even backwards.

Can you figure out this concrete poem about a jet plane breaking the sound barrier? Remember, you can read concrete poems in almost any way.

Supersonic Jet

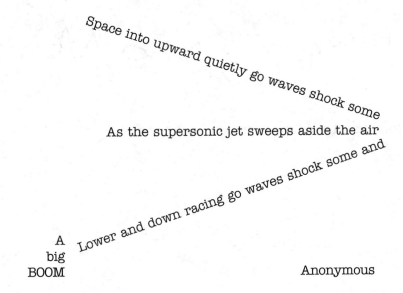

As the supersonic jet sweeps aside the air

A
big
BOOM   Anonymous

Directions: Some concrete poems are made up of single words arranged in ways that suggest their meaning:

Make up a concrete poem from one of these words, or choose your own word.

I	black	he
rose	we	sidewalk
light	snake	lightbulb

Other concrete poems include the name of some thing and action associated with it, arranged so that the design suggests the meaning of the words.

Figure 5-5.   Concrete Poems

Write the name of a simple thing and an action associated with it. You may add a word that expresses how you feel when you think of the word. Then arrange the words so that the pattern suggests the meaning of the words.

Example:

        A motorcycle vrooms!

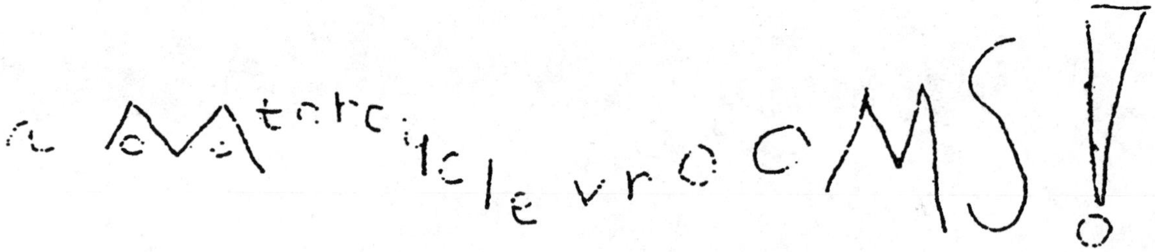

Use the blank space provided below to design your own poem.

Figure 5-5. Concrete Poems *(Continued)*

And still other concrete poems make use of one or two simple words, arranged in a novel way. Use the blank space provided below to design your own novel poem.

Choose two words that sound alike and can be connected in some way. Arrange the words so that the pattern reflects the meaning:

Suggested words:

        life, loaf   house, haven

        spaghetti, slippery   meat, muscle

Figure 5-5. Concrete Poems *(Continued)*

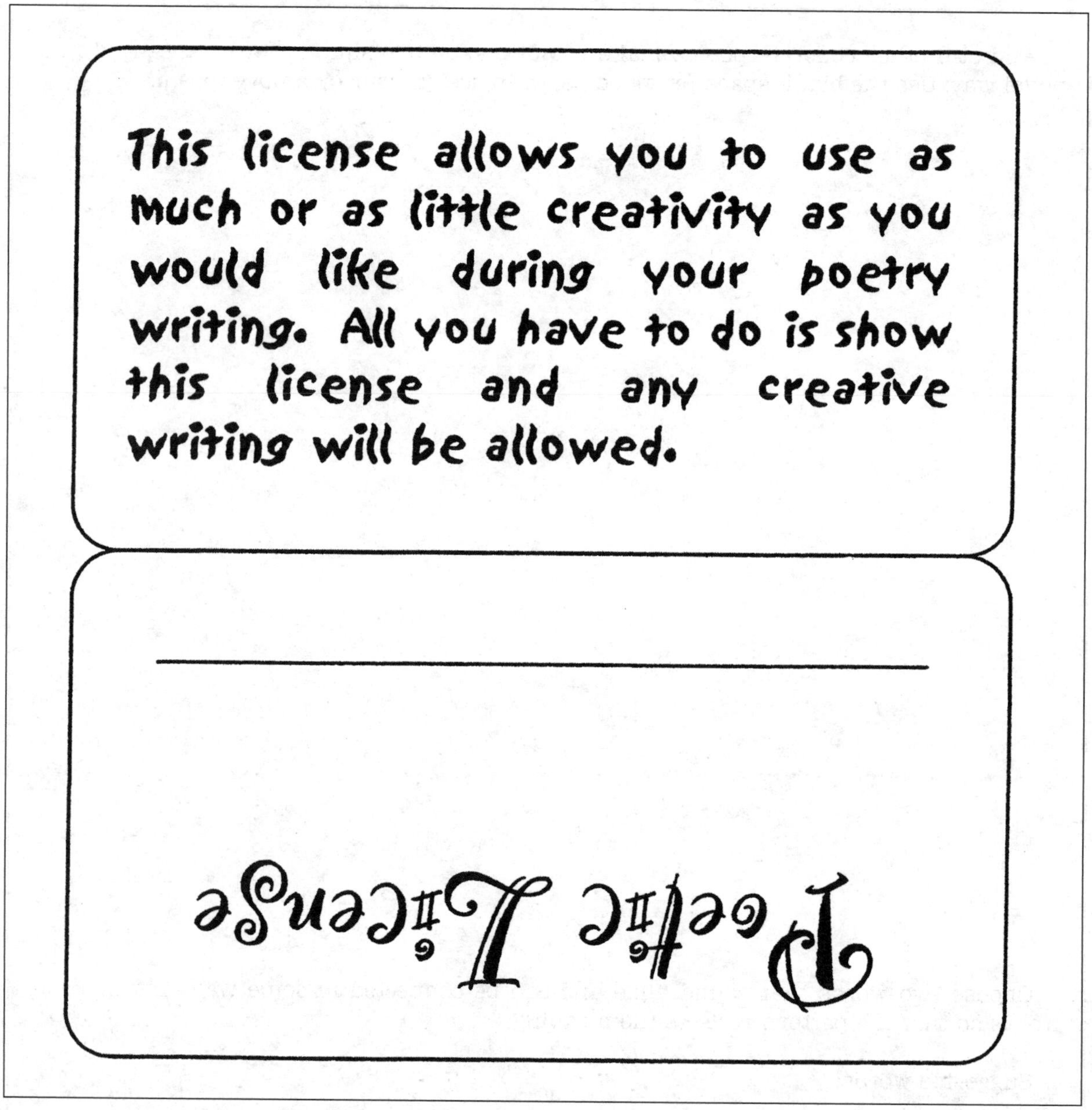

This license allows you to use as much or as little creativity as you would like during your poetry writing. All you have to do is show this license and any creative writing will be allowed.

Poetic License

Figure 5-6. "Poetic License"

Acrostic poetry is often used most successfully in teaching students content vocabulary in a content area lesson. We have also used acrostic poetry with much success as an "ice-breaker" the first week of school by having students list all the letters in their name and describing themselves! Following are two examples:

Amphibian

A	Amazing
M	Marvelous
P	Pet
H	Hovering
I	In (my)
B	Bathtub
I	Interesting
A	Amphibian
N	Nesting!

Brett

B	Beautiful
R	Ravenous
E	Energetic
T	Terrific
T	Teetotaler

Anticipation Guide Revisited

After reading this chapter, confirm your initial predictions about each statement. List the page number that supports each response.

Statement	Agree	Disagree	Verification
1. One reason we write poetry is that it is a basic way to learn about our culture and become a member of our culture.	_____	_____	_____
2. Traditional poetry is focused on how selective language elements fit together and how these elements lead to an interpretation and a meaning.	_____	_____	_____
3. Nontraditional poetry, found in popular culture today, is not highly structured nor sophisticated and is therefore not appropriate for beginning writers.	_____	_____	_____
4. Developing voice in poetry is a major avenue through which students can achieve ownership and control over their writing, thereby writing better poetry.	_____	_____	_____
5. Responding to poetry is a linear process that should be taught in sequence so that beginning writers (especially) can not only understand the meaning but also understand the process involved in writing good poetry.	_____	_____	_____
6. There is always only one "correct" interpretation of a poem.	_____	_____	_____
7. Reading a poem out loud to students is encouraged, even among older students.	_____	_____	_____
8. Poetry is often the last component of the language arts curriculum to be taught.	_____	_____	_____

Additional Resources

Appendix: Poems on the New York State English Language Arts Assessment

2002:   "Trees" by Harry Behn
In this poem, Behn describes trees as the "kindest things" he knows and tells us how we and others, like resting cows, enjoy trees.

Sample Questions

1. The main idea of the poem is to
   a. show how trees change as the season changes
   b. show how we should be as kind as trees are
   c. remind us to appreciate the special things about trees
   d. remind us of how we felt about trees when we were small

2. This poem is probably trying to
    a. teach the reader to identify different trees
    b. share with the reader a feeling about trees
    c. remind the reader of a lullaby about trees
    d. entertain the reader with funny stories about trees

2003: "To a Rabbit Hurrying" by Grace Cornell Tall
This poem, told in the first "person" by another forest animal, pleads with the little rabbit to stay and play to celebrate spring.

Sample Questions

1. Why is the rabbit running fast?
    a. It is happy.
    b. It is afraid.
    c. It is looking for food.
    d. It is looking for a friend.

2. Which word best describes the tone of the poem?
    a. playful
    b. surprised
    c. careless
    d. fearful

2004: "Do You Know Green?" by Anna Grossnickle Hines
In this poem, *green* symbolizes the coming of spring and the sprouting of new green leaves of grass of life.

Sample Questions

1. This poem is mostly about the
    a. coming of spring
    b. beginning of a new day
    c. colors of different plants
    d. different kinds of trees

2. In the poem, the word *green* stands for
    a. time that passes
    b. things that grow
    c. an imaginary creature
    d. a forest animal

Author Discussion

Although each poem differs in length, use of figurative language, and rhyming scheme (the poem from 2004 does not even rhyme), none of the sample questions asks for a student's response or interpretation. It is assumed there is one right answer. This may be clear with a few of the questions, but it is not at all clear with all of the questions, especially question 2 for the 2002 poem! Think back to the chapter and what the poet Roethke had to say about what his poems meant.

Adapted from: New York State Education Department. (2002, 2003, 2004). *New York State Testing Program*, English Language Arts. Albany, NY: Author.

Web Sites

www.poets.org

www.favoritepoem.org

www.onlinepoetryclassroom.org

www.poetryteachers.com

www.gigglepotz.com/kidspoetry.htm

www.nesbitt.com/poetry/howto.html

For Further Reflection

1. Write about an experience you had in being taught poetry in school. Were you free to experiment? Did the teacher hold the only "true" meaning? Were you afraid? Describe your feelings.

2. Using all the letters of your first name, write an acrostic poem. Describe yourself in the most vivid language you can think of!

References

Atwell, N. M. (1987). *In the middle*. Upper Montclair, NJ: Boynton/Cook.

Beach, R., & Marshall, J. (1991). *Teaching literature in the secondary school*. San Diego, CA: Harcourt Brace Jovanovich.

Blake, B. E. (1995a). Broken silences: Writing and the construction of "cultural texts" by urban, pre-adolescent girls. *Journal of Educational Thought, 29*, 165–180.

Blake, B. E. (1995b). Doing number 5: From process to cultural texts in an urban writing classroom. *Language Arts, 72*, 396–404.

Blake, B. E. (1997). *She says, he says: Urban girls write their lives*. Albany, NY: SUNY Press.

Blake, B. E. (2004). *A culture of refusal: The lives and literacies of out-of-school adolescents*. New York: Lang.

Blake, R. W. (1990). Poets on poetry: Writing and the reconstruction of reality. *English Journal*, pp. 16–21.

Blake, R. W. (1992). Poets on poetry: The morality of poetry. *English Journal*, pp. 16–20.

Blake, R. W., & Lund, A. (1986). Responding to poetry: High school students read poetry. *English Journal*, pp. 68–73.

Calkins, L. (1983). *Lessons from a child*. Portsmouth, NH: Heinemann.

Calkins, L. (1986). *The art of teaching writing*. Portsmouth, NH: Heinemann.

Delpit, L. (1988). The silenced dialogue: Power and pedagogy in educating other people's children. *Harvard Educational Review, 56*, 379–385.

Duthie, C., & Kubie, E. K. (2004). Poetry in live directions for your imagination! *The Reading Teacher, 46*, 14–23.

Gordon, R. (1993). *Peeling the onion: An anthology of poems*. New York: HarperCollins.

Graves, D. H. (1983). *Writing: Teachers & children at work*. Portsmouth, NH: Heinemann.

Hancock, H. (2004). *A celebration of literature and response*. Upper Saddle River, NJ: Pearson.

Kirsch, A. (2005, August 8). Primal ear: Roethke, Wright, and the cult of authenticity. *The New Yorker*, pp. 90–99.

Koch, K. (1970). *Wishes, lies, and dreams: Teaching children to write poetry*. New York: HarperPerennial.

Koch, K. (1973). *Rose, where did you get that red? Teaching great poetry to children*. New York: Vintage Books.

Martin, V. (1988, February 7). Waiting for the story to start. *The New York Times Book Review*, pp. 1, 36.

Murray, D. (1968). *A writer teaches writing: A practical method of teaching composition*. Boston: Houghton Mifflin.

Opitz, M. F., & Rasinski, T. V. (1998*). Good-bye round robin: Twenty-five effective oral reading strategies*. Portsmouth, NH: Heinemann.

Reid, D. K., & Button, L. J. (1995). Anna's story: Narratives of personal experience about being learning disabled. *Journal of Learning Disabilities, 28*, 602–614.

Street, B. V. (1995*). Social literacies: Critical approaches to literacy in development, ethnography, and education*. London: Longman.

Children's and Adolescent Poetry

Adoff, A. (1995). *Street music: City poems*. New York: HarperCollins.

Baron, L. (1999). *The sun is on: Poetry and ideas*. Garden City, NY: Harlin Jacque.

Creech, S. (2001). *Love that dog*. New York: HarperTrophy.

Lansky, B. (2000). *If pigs could fly and other deep thoughts: A collection of funny poems*. New York: Meadowbrook Press.

Roethke, T. (1966*). Roethke: Collected poems*. Garden City, NY: Doubleday.

Seuss, T. G. (1958). *The cat in the hat comes back*. New York: Random House.

Silverstein, S. (1996). *Falling up*. New York: HarperCollins.

Wagoner, D. (1999). *Traveling light: Collected and new poems*. Urbana, IL: University of Illinois Press.

Chapter 6

Creating Cultural Texts and Responding to Literature With Diverse Students

Introduction

Why is everything that I read about white people and boys? Why is it that everything I read is soooo boring?

—Chantal, 1993

Chantal, a fifth-grade African-American girl, spoke to one of us often about the literature she was reading in her urban classroom. Her responses more often than not reflected a typical student's response among the urban elementary, middle, and junior high students we have taught and worked with over the last several years. Mostly non–native speaking (i.e., their first language was not English), often African American, sometimes labeled as having "special needs," and always poor, these students held a common perspective about the value of literature: There was little sense in bothering to respond—to "talk"—to this literature because it did not, and could not, "talk" to them.

Recent research points out that educators have failed to attend to the literary needs of all students and, in failing to do so, have not made their language arts and "English classrooms . . . spaces of community for non-mainstream and oppositional students" (Hines, 1997, p. 117). As our urban *and* suburban public school classrooms become increasingly diverse, the value of focusing on programs with limited literary offerings and response strategies needs to be carefully scrutinized, questioned, and challenged.

In this chapter, we will first discuss, from a theoretical perspective, the elements of reader response and classroom reader response as we present actual student samples and examples of tasks that might work in your own classroom. Next we will discuss the notion of critical responses as we frame them within a "cultural text" (Blake, 1997) perspective. This perspective will show how the creation of cultural texts is crucial in our urban and/or diverse classrooms if we are to find ways to engage these students in reader response and, eventually, the reading of good literature (see the next chapter for a fuller discussion of ways to assist students in reading good literature). Before we begin examining how this dynamic interaction can happen, however, let's briefly define and describe a traditional response to text in today's classrooms, as well as a reader response approach. We'll end this chapter with an exploration of what constitutes a classroom-based reader response approach and examine what a classroom reader response program might look like in both a lower elementary and an upper elementary classroom. In this way it will become clear how we can move from critical reader response to cultural texts in our classrooms with diverse students.

The different response models are summarized in Table 6-1.

Table 6-1. Types of Responses

TRADITIONAL LITERARY RESPONSE	CLASSROOM READER RESPONSE	MORAL	CRITICAL READER RESPONSE
1. The teacher emphasizes the text primarily.	1. Although a worthwhile text is a necessary element, the primary emphasis is on the student's oral or written response to that text.	1. An ethic of justice is based upon the idea of equality—that everyone should be treated the same.	1. Critical response is an ideological orientation associated with gender, class, and race.
2. The teacher guides the student to find the "correct" meaning within the text.	2. The student creates his or her own personal meaning for the text, with the sophisticated help of an especially trained and sympathetic teacher.	2. An ethic of caring rests on the concept of nonviolence—that no one should be hurt.	2. A critical response is a culturally relevant, ideological discourse.
3. The teacher directs the student to answer specific comprehension questions about the elements of a literary text, such as setting, plot, characters, and theme.	3. The student gives an initial response to a literary piece and then uses personal knowledge of literary elements to support the interpretation.	3. While the ethic of justice has traditionally been associated wih males and the ethic of caring with females, a more complex and satisfying idea of morality would include both viewpoints.	3. It assumes that students' texts are artifacts of an oppressive society.
4. The traditional method is essentially objective, detached, inductive, and scientific. Emotions and personal opinions are not emphasized.	4. Feelings, memories, associations, and intuition (perceptions arrived at without rational thought) are not only allowed but form the core of reader response.	4. Readers, recognizing this dual nature of morality, might come to realize that a judgment by a character in a literary work can be interpreted according to the context in which the dilemma is framed.	4. Critical response is one powerful way to shape nondominant discourses and ideologies as it challenges dominant discourses and ideologies.
5. The student usually shares his or her responses with the teacher only.	5. The student shares his or her responses with other children in small groups and with the whole class, including the teacher, within a learning community. Each student thus sees his or her individual response grow, becoming enriched and validated by the responses of peers and the teacher.		

Traditional Literary Response

Traditional literary response is based on the notion that the teacher must guide the student to find the "correct" meaning as he or she directs the student to answer specific comprehension questions about the elements of a literary text, including those around setting, plot, characters, and theme. In this traditional practice, emotions and personal opinions are not emphasized; instead, the teacher places primary emphasis on meaning from the text.

Traditional response is reflected most clearly in students' stances or subject positions toward texts. Beach (1994b) describes *stances* as "ideological orientations or perspectives associated with gender, class, or race, i.e., the stance of white male privilege" and as "reflections of cultural models/discourses . . . acquired from social practices in specific social contexts" (p. 1). Stances reflect society. All students, then, adopt multiple, often competing stances, some of which resist the teacher's articulated stances or the stances of those who are perceived as good students. Still other stances simply reflect what students are taught to believe are good responses. However, most students do not resist; they simply respond the way they are taught, according to what the teacher perceives to be correct.

Reader Response Theory

Reader response theory, on the other hand, posits that literary meaning comes from the reader, the text he or she is reading, and the experiences that the reader brings to bear on the text. That is, there is always more than one interpretation of what a literary text means, and this meaning can constantly shift. There is no one inherent meaning in any reading of a literary text. (Throughout this chapter, by *text* we mean a literary text as opposed to an informational text—a difference that will be treated in more depth in the next two chapters.)

It is widely believed that today's notion of reader response theory comes directly from the early work of Louise Rosenblatt (1938/1968), later reinterpreted and used widely after this work was republished. Her essential thesis about response is the following:

> Sound literary insight and esthetic judgment will never be taught by imposing from above notions of what works should ideally mean . . . the reader, too, is creative . . . the literary experience must be phrased as a transaction between the reader and the text. (pp. 33–35)

Nevertheless, Rosenblatt's work contained much more. It was a result of her interactions with philosophers, psychologists, and anthropologists of the day and was based on her experiences teaching literary criticism to university students, dealing with how students actually respond to literary texts. Besides stating her claim that reading literary texts should be seen as a transaction, she also asks nearly all the big questions that we educators have been wrestling with since then:

1. As teachers, how do we foster literary transactions?

2. How do we teach students to develop sensitivity to the way in which the elements of a literary text relate to an organic whole?

3. What student needs and interests should we be aware of?

4. How does reading literature help us to understand ourselves?

5. How does reading literature help us to understand our society within a broad context of feelings and ideas?

In 1978, Rosenblatt expanded her original premise that reading literature is a transaction between the reader and the text by positing that there are two kinds of readings: aesthetic and efferent. An *aesthetic* reading relies on the reader (or student) living through an emotional experience in order to make an interpretation. In an *efferent* reading, the reader takes away factual information. However, Rosenblatt recognized that many texts contain examples of both aesthetic and factual writing, so that in reading any one text (e.g., *Moby Dick* by Herman Melville [1988], which contains not only aesthetic storytelling but also much factual information about whaling), the reader might have to transact with it in more than one way. The aesthetic reading is essentially ambiguous, imprecise, suggestive, and emotional, and its words generally have a connotative value. The efferent reading is unambiguous, precise, and declarative; its words are denotative. (In today's classrooms, we usually associate aesthetic reading with literature and efferent reading with informational text—see chapters 7 and 8 for a more in-depth discussion). Following is Rosenblatt's (1978, p. 54) description of how we read a poem, story, novel, or play:

1. When we first meet a text, we determine by linguistic cues the kind of stance we should adopt. (Stances are based on many factors, including race, gender, and class, and are discussed more fully below).

2. We develop a tentative framework for understanding the text.

3. As we read, we develop expectations about what will happen, and these expectations affect our further reading.

4. Either we find our expectations are met, or, as we read further, we change our expectations.

5. If this process goes well, and we are satisfied with our reading of the text, we create a final interpretation.

In the nearly 30 years since Rosenblatt's 1978 work, reader response to literature has been examined extensively among middle-class suburban students, particularly at the secondary level (Beach & Hynds, 1991; Beach & Wendler, 1987; Blake, 1989; Langer, 1994). However, these explorations of students' responses have focused primarily on response to mainstream literature, although recently there have also been accounts of how students respond to multicultural literature, with an emphasis on exploring the particular cultural stance or subject position a student takes with regard to the text (Altieri, 1994; Barton, 1994; Beach, 1994a; Enciso, 1994). Oral response to literature (explained in depth in chapter 4) has also been explored more carefully as talk in the classroom has taken a more central position in the language arts (Blake, 1992; Weiss, Strickland, Walmsley, & Bronk, 1995). More recently, even state assessment boards have taken notice: The New York State Education Department (1997), for example, requires the following in standard 2 of its English language arts framework:

Students will read, write, listen, and speak for literary response and expression. Students will read and listen to oral, written, and electronically produced texts and performances, relate texts and performances to their own lives, and develop an understanding of the diverse social, historical, and cultural dimensions the texts and performances represent. As speakers and writers, students will use oral and written language for self-expression and artistic creation.

Classroom Reader Response

A *classroom reader response* model seeks to put into practice the theoretical notions that Rosenblatt (1978) originally posited. That is, it attempts to form a guide to help teachers understand, so that they may then guide students to a real and meaningful response.

There are five major assumptions underlying classroom reader response (Blake & Blake, 2002). These assumptions essentially broaden Rosenblatt's original notions, and we have outlined activities for both lower elementary and upper elementary or middle school students consistent with this framework. The five major assumptions are as follows:

1. *The primary emphasis is on the reader's response to a text.* In this approach, the emphasis is not solely on one's examination of a text as a text but is principally on the reader's response to a text. The work itself is not insignificant, for we all know that *Huckleberry Finn* is in a different category from the yellow pages of a phone book, for example. The practical result of this implication is that each reader is recognized as existing uniquely—a result of many factors, such as age, gender, race, experiences, culture, and linguistic background—and that the reader's response is a mysterious combination of these factors.

2. *The reader creates personal meaning.* Rather than finding someone else's meaning—whether it is the teacher's or that of the teacher's previous professors—the reader creates his or her own meaning. The implication here is that the reader is literally creative, trusting him- or herself to create more rich and varied responses.

3. *Feelings are allowed.* Readers are allowed, even encouraged, to respond emotionally. Within a classroom reader response approach, feelings are okay. Readers can admit their feelings because it is through emotions that readers enter a work.

4. *Memories and associations are encouraged.* When readers permit memories evoked by a text to arise from their unconscious—when they accept associations related to these experiences, to other works of literature, and even to movies, television shows, and popular songs—they are able to relate literature to their own lives in a powerfully significant way.

5. *Intuition is invoked.* After readers have allowed themselves to become emotionally involved in a piece and have let themselves experience the piece through memories and associations, they learn to trust themselves to give an immediate, intuitive reaction to the piece.

An engaging activity in chapter 8 asks readers to interact emotionally with an informational text. Generally known as the double-entry response, it has the reader tell what the author says on the left side of a page and what he or she feels or thinks about what the author says on the right side of the page. This activity would also work quite well with an expressive literary work and would be highly suited as an elaboration activity for kidstation 3 (see chapter 3).

An Elementary Classroom Reader Response Program

In this section, we show how a group of first-grade students read, discussed, and responded to a children's picture book, *Jesse Bear, What Will You Wear* (Carlstrom & Degen, 1989).

For the first reading of the book, the teacher has the children sit together in a circle and asks them to read their books silently. Then they all read the book together out loud, and when they are finished, they talk in the group about their initial impressions of the book and why they liked it:

Krysten: The whole book rhymes and I think it's neat.

Jolene: I like Jesse because he was a bear and because my sister's name is Jesse.

Lindsay: I read the book before and after and I think it is funny.

Brian: I think the book is good!

The teacher then asks for volunteers to retell the story.

Jolene: I will! Jesse Bear had dirt on his shirt and ants in his pants.

Teacher: Would you like Jesse as a friend?

Jolene: I would love that!

Teacher: Why?

Jolene: Because he looks so cuddly and cute.

Brian: I would like him for a friend because Jesse has neat toys.

Krysten: I'm almost like Jesse Bear. I get up, get dressed, play outside, have lunch, play some more, have dinner, take a bath, put on my pj's and then go to bed.

The children go back to their seats and write a response to the book. They are encouraged to illustrate their responses. Here is how they responded (unedited):

Krysten: (drawing a picture of Jesse Bear in his red shirt and jockey shorts with blue stars) I't all rime's. And I't says in the morning at nighte in the after noon. And Jesse Bear rime's with is clothes like with noon at nigte in the morning. And I like this story very much I injoy this book.

Lindsay: (drawing and coloring a picture of Jesse's dirty shirt and a picture of Jesse with his red shirt and his blue pants) The book was good. Because Jesse Bear was funny. He said I'll wear my blue pens and my red shirt. The at noon he said I'll wear my blue pj's. At night I wear white pj's with peanda [panda] bears on it.

Brian: (with a picture of a brown Jesse, looking somewhat like a happy seal, reclining in an immense expanse of blue water in an old-fashioned claw-footed bathtub) I like Jesse Bear because I like the part when he's in the tub and it talls all of the times in a day and it is a very good book and there is very good carters [characters].

Jolene: (with illustrations in purple, green, and red that include Jesse at the breakfast table, Jesse reading, and Jesse in bed) The book has bears in it. It had singing in it.

> There was a mama bear a papa bear in it and a little bear. Jesse was taking a bath. He had a pipe. He had sors [stars] on in the morning. He had a tesrt [T-shirt] on in the morning.

As we can see from the above example, these elementary-age children were able to respond to literature both orally and in writing, allowing feelings to arise, making use of personal memories, and making connections to people, places, and events in their lives. At this initial stage, therefore, even very young children can learn the elements of classroom reader response.

A Middle School Classroom Reader Response Program

It is important in the upper elementary or middle school classroom to choose pieces to which young people feel connected and/or that challenge them, so they are willing to respond. (As we will see in the next section, certain groups of students have been turned off to literature altogether, so we must help them create their own pieces, or cultural texts, to which they can respond.) In many middle schools, however, a provocative (or scary!) piece is often all that it takes to compel students to want to respond. Robert Beloof's poem "A Spring Night" (1965) is one such piece. Watch what happens as students are asked to give initial, feeling, and memory responses to this poem, which describes a father-son relationship beautifully but hauntingly. Beloff's stanzas "could of [sic] hated him" and "could of [sic] loved him too," illustrate how complex such a relationship can be, and it will speak to many of our students.

We give the *initial response* task to our students so that they can become used to responding intuitively and without inhibitions to a literary work. The initial response is a crucial feature of classroom reader response. With it, we want to wean students away from the idea that they need to approach a text or a poem in a scientific or necessarily rational way. Rather, we want students to learn to trust their immediate, intuitive responses to literary texts and then to choose significant evidence in the works to substantiate their personal interpretations. We continually stress that they should trust their own interpretations, so that in any response, from the simplest to the most sophisticated, the students will start with an intuitive sense of what the work means to them. Here is an example of a task we ask of students:

> In a short paragraph, write out what_____ [name of poem, story, novel, play] means to you. Don't worry about what anybody else thinks it means, including your teacher. Also, at this time, don't worry about spelling, punctuation, or other writing errors, and don't worry about getting the "right" meaning. We really want to now what you believe the piece means. Write as quickly as you can about your feelings and thoughts without stopping to think about them too much.

Here is what two students, untrained in classroom reader response, wrote after their first reading of "A Spring Night."

> *Melissa:* I thought this was a sad poem about a father who either couldn't or didn't want to see his son. If there's a will, there's a way.

> *Charlie:* I liked this poem because it showed how a father feels when not able to see his son. Or didn't want to.

The *feeling response* is what Bleich (1978) calls the "affective" response. We want students to understand that feelings are okay and that not only can they trust their feelings, they will be lauded for relating their feelings to their overall interpretations. Here is the task we ask of these students:

> As you read this poem (or story, etc.), how did you feel? Jot down in a few sentences what your feelings were. Here are some samples of the kinds of sentences you might use to show you're writing a feeling response: I felt (sad, happy, disgusted, bored) as I read this poem. I (laughed out loud, cried, felt sad) as I read this poem.

Here is what some students wrote:

> *Kim:*   The poem started out sad, and I expected it to wind up happy, when the way I see it, it remained sad. I really don't care for this poem. Sorry.
>
> *Kathy:* I found the poem being sad.
>
> *Mike:*   My response to the poem is that it was dull. Cuff is a very withdrawn man he doesn't care. I think he was trying to communicate with his son and be a friend to him. He wanted someone to talk to.
>
> *Chris:* It's rather depressing but easy to read. The father hardly ever thought about his son. He didn't really have any feelings for him. Eventually he realized he liked him.

In the *memory response* task, we ask students to let their reading bring up memories and associations triggered by the piece that in turn illuminate for them the meaning of the poem. Quite often, we find this task to be the most powerful one for allowing students to relate literature to their lives. Here is the task we use to help students see how their own experiences are related to feelings, images, or events evoked by a poem:

> What memories come to mind as you read this poem? Don't worry about what the recollections are, or how far-fetched they may seem to you at this time. Your memories are a valuable part of reading literature because they help you understand the poem. Here are some sample sentences you might use in your memory response: This poem reminds me of a time when_____. This word, this line, or this particular part brought back memories of _____.

Here is an especially poignant memory response by one student:

> *Diane:* I really didn't understand it all. What I did understand I liked because I could relate to it with our relationship with my father. Sometimes it feels like my own father resents me but we still get along.

What happens at the upper elementary or middle school level, however, when students, like Chantal (in the quote above), become disenfranchised by, uninterested in, and resistant to any the literature they are reading? What role can the creation and use of "cultural texts" play in reader response? How do students like Chantal move toward a critical reader response as they develop an understanding, and perhaps even an appreciation, of literature?

Critical Reader Response

Rosenblatt's (1978) transactional theory of reader response, which describes a poem that exists in the mind of the reader and a text the reader is transacting with, has for years successfully provided a useful theoretical direction for the literature classroom. As students learned that there was no one true meaning, they were encouraged to bring their own interpretations to the discussion of a text. Students were afforded opportunities to resist imposed interpretations while understanding that, theoretically, all interpretations were valid, creating what Blake & Blake (2002) call a "community meaning."

Rosenblatt's (1978) challenge to a traditional, text-centered approach that renders the reader invisible continues to be important. However, it is crucial to extend Rosenblatt's transactional approach to make the diverse reader visible. This is what we call a *critical reader response* model—it helps the teacher to encourage diverse, often disengaged, readers to generate their own texts, called *cultural texts*, so that they can and will engage and respond to text.

The critical reader response model (Blake, 1997, 2004) is based primarily on the notion that through a certain ideology or stance one can look critically at a text's or an author's assumptions and perspectives about, for example, gender, race, or class. These ideologies and stances are grounded in critical, feminist, postcolonial, and other theoretical frameworks.

The critical reader response model assumes, therefore, that reading and responding to a text is dependent not only on the author's stance and the reader's stance but also on *society's* stances—specifically those that are embedded in mainstream literature and in the institutions of mainstream teacher training (i.e., many university programs). Here, expectations and perceptions of diverse students are used to make judgments (usually negative) about what these students have to say and how they express themselves. Attitudes around the correctness of Standard English and heterosexuality, for example, are elevated to the forefront of this thinking and form the repertoire of society's understanding of what constitutes a good response. Any response that falls outside these parameters is not deemed worthwhile.

Many of the diverse students with whom we have worked, like Chantal, know this and consciously resist and reject not only mainstream literature but also the so-called right or best answers demanded of them on standardized tests. In practice, then, it makes sense to begin with texts and authors whose ideological stances are familiar and appealing to diverse readers. In urban classrooms, where many students have had little exposure to literary texts that connect to their lives, it makes sense to begin with the students' own texts. Blake (2004) calls these student texts "cultural texts"—texts that truly reflect the students' own ideologies and stances.

The critical reader response model requires, at least in its initial stages, texts that students are willing to engage with—recall again Chantal's comment. The critical reader response model not only provides an alternative framework from which students can respond to literature (outside what Beach [1994a; 1994b] calls the "traditional, White male privilege" stance) but also affords opportunities for students to create the literature of the classroom. These student-generated cultural texts, then, become the vehicle for response in the classroom.

Critical Reader Response in Middle School

In the diverse urban classroom, students' stances are often formed from society's assumptions and judgments of who they are and who the students are capable of becoming. Diverse students often do not have a repertoire of positive stances and/or ideological discourses from which to read, write, and respond, because urban students "have internalized self-contempt from years of official neglect" (Bigelow, 1990, p. 439). They simply have not been given models on which to base positive responses, and in our experience, their responses often reflect this self-contempt and neglect.

According to Enciso (1994), because the cultural models on which students base their stances (and, she argues, their identities) are not necessarily well defined and are constantly shifting, helping students to create cultural texts and to learn to respond critically can be crucial in helping students to reshape and redefine not only their cultural stances but also their identities. As a result, students can challenge, through response, the judgments and assumptions made about them by the mainstream culture.

Cultural Texts

According to Bakhtin (1981, 1986), the act of composing and responding to a text is always an act of "dialogism." That is, when a writer uses words, he or she "necessarily engages or responds to past and present discourses," as each word "smells of the context . . . in which it has lived its intense social life" (Ewald, 1993, p. 332). A cultural text, therefore, is a text that "smells" of a particular context. Among urban, diverse writers, it is a text, perhaps, that releases scents of gender, race, and class; a text that reflects their particular aspirations, struggles, and realities (Figure 6-1). Cultural texts are the "stuff" of students' lives, created and responded to in ways that incorporate the semiotics of a culture (Blake, 1995). Cultural texts are inherently "dialogic" and "answerable" (Bakhtin, 1981, 1986) as multiple voices in a classroom conflict and collide in response to one another. Creating one's own cultural text can be "personally transforming" (Rogers, 1997, p. 102) as students' writings help them to connect their lives to other texts and literature.

The major emphasis on creating cultural texts with students is a shift from the process of writing and responding to the actual product that the student creates—highlighting not only *how* the text is socially and culturally constructed from notions such as gender, race, and class but also *what* the text actually says, revealing issues of gender, race, and class that are particularly central to urban, poor, ethnically diverse students. The issues the texts raise, therefore, form the literature of the classroom, and both the students and the teacher can use such texts as points of critique for further discussion and examination. As students learn to read each other's texts and respond to them in critical ways, they can then move, or be hooked, to similar issues in "real" (often described as traditional or classical) literature. Moving from cultural texts to critical response to reading "good" literature can provide models on which these diverse students can begin to engage with literature and response, perhaps changing their learning altogether.

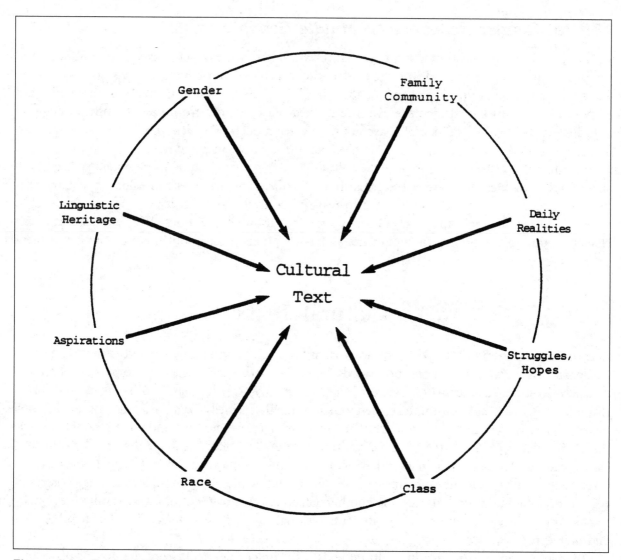

Figure 6-1. Cultural Text Elements

Michael's Middle School Classroom

Michael's fifth-grade classroom of 28 students was situated in a poor neighborhood on the west side of Chicago. Most of his students were English language learners (ELLs); all qualified for a free lunch as determined by family income. Many of his students had recently transitioned out of bilingual education and, for a number of reasons, were reading, writing, and testing in both English and Spanish at first- and second-grade levels. The principal at the school was desperate. "Try anything," she proclaimed to her faculty as the dropout figures for that particular middle school rose above 70%.

We therefore implemented a classroom reader response program that included the notion of student-generated cultural texts as literature in the classroom. Here is how some of the students' initial responses—to books they were reading, written as journal entries to the teacher—read:

Dear Teacher:

Today I am reading another book called *The President in American History*. This is a very good book to me. It's better than the book I read before and it's called *The War of 1812*. And it's boring. But I think the book that I'm reading right now is better than I read before. Well I'll see you for now, Mr. [*name of teacher*].

Dear Teacher:

What can I tell you, Mr. [*name of teacher*], I am just in the third page. I just don't get it that it says she has brothers, but she doesn't. (*Response to* Her Seven Brothers).

(The next day, from the same fifth grader)

Dear Teacher:

I think I don't like this book anymore. I think I am getting bored of it so I am just going to read my favorite page.

To successfully implement a classroom reader response model, we need to first model to students the elements that are described above; namely, that students are free to respond in emotional and intuitive ways. One concrete way to get students to change their responses from one of "being bored" is to use the fourth assumption of classroom reader response: Memories and associations are encouraged. Students are urged to relate what they're reading to their own lives—movies, music, computer games, community, school, even family. Below (and in Figure 6-2) is how one young girl responded to what she first described as a "boring" book—*The World War II at Monte Cassino*, by Sanford (1991)—relating it to stories her father told her:

> When Larry was in the army he had to eat army food and he said it tasted alful [awful] and he didn't like it. When my dad was in the army he had to eat army [food] too. And he didn't like it either. What I like about this book is that it reminds me of my dad. That's the only thing I like about this book!

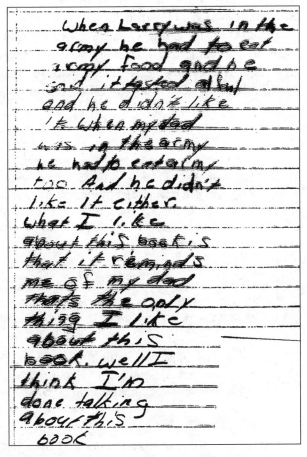

Figure 6-2. Response to World War II Book

In Michael's classroom, we began by allowing the students to free-write, or to write on any topic they wished, but we quickly found out that it was best to set themes for the week according to specific curricular requirements. One of those themes, for example, was a focus on nonfiction writing and included the topic "endangered species." Here is an example of a typical student-generated piece (unedited):

Alligators

Alligators are ancient, and lived when the dinosaurs lived about two hundred million years ago. The name alligator is from a Spanish word, "el lagarto" which means the lizard. Lizards do look like miniature alligators. Alligators are found in only two parts of the world: a few in eastern China, most in the warm southeastern United States especially Louisiana and Florida. Alligators live in water, beside water, half in and half out of water. They stay in ponds beside an algae-covered pond in swamps, marshes, lakes, rivers, streams, and sometimes in people's swimming pools, fish ponds, and in water or golf courses.

Because of texts like the one above, the students became activists, of sorts, responding to animal rights issues and talking about the human rights issues faced by homeless people. Their student-generated cultural texts prompted them to respond to how they helped people in their lives or to write about the injustices they saw in the world around them. These cultural texts, often very powerful, generated some of the richest critical response we had ever seen any group of students do. It truly was not until these students began to create and engage willingly with their own texts that we began to understand that student-generated texts could serve as initial sites for response that were much more authentic and connected to these students' lives. Here are three more examples (unedited):

Cheetahs

Cheetahs are a very large cat with spots that is something like a leopard and is found in Southern Asia and Africa. Cheetahs run very fast and are the fastest animal in the world. Also they are called hunting leopards. Either of the two cats are native from India to Africa, south of the Sahara. The common cheetahs stand about 3 feet tall at the shoulder and measure 6 feet long from its nose. But the cheetahs are in danger from man and this is terrible. Something should be done.

I like to write about animals and freedom and stuff like that. Like those poor butterflies [kept in a box in the classroom]. You know, animal rights and stuff. Yea, because those poor dolphins, I mean they make tuna out of them!

One day I found 200 hundred dollars in the street and I saw a little poor woman and she could not talk and my mom told me to give the money to the poor woman. So I did. She gave me a cross of Jesus and she was nice. I was the only one who gave her a lot of money and I started to bring food to her.

Writing about endangered species and then responding freely to the issues and causes that these students considered important in their lives (rather than historical pieces on World War II, which, though certainly important, is arguably not monumental in these students' daily lives) not only provided a number of empathetic responses but also gave students the opportunity to offer solutions that were perhaps more connected to their ways of seeing society. Mainstream conceptions of the world are woven through the texts our students are required to read. The diverse learners in Michael's classroom could not connect with many of the initial trade books they were required to read and therefore did not find them meaningful. Nevertheless, when given the opportunity to create and respond to their own texts, the students became engaged.

This is not to say that everything that students read and respond to must be meaningful in personal ways. However, assuming that all of our students agree on certain perceptions of the world, and thereby read and respond in like ways, is not fair. An extended critical reader response model provides a viable alternative approach for the diverse, urban, and/or reluctant classroom.

Rosenblatt's transactional theory of reader response, we believe, is necessary but not sufficient when one is attempting to engage students in urban classrooms like Michael's. Rather than continuing to transmit mainstream culture—and the expectations and assumptions of the dominant culture—through the literature we share with our students, we educators need to help them critique and transform culture through their own texts, and eventually, we hope, through a serious study of other meaningful literatures.

Connecting to Literature

Creating cultural texts and allowing for meaningful and critical responses helps even the most reluctant student to begin to see the benefits of connecting to good literature.

Engagement with good literature offers many positive opportunities for entertainment, good feelings, and learning. Engagement can occur in many ways: through reading, listening, viewing through picture walks, reflecting, emotive thinking that accompanies writing, and artistic creation of aspects of a literary work. We can account for six positive benefits that involvement with literature brings to children and adolescents. Two of these benefits bring perspective in understanding cultures and diverse peoples. These perspectives may be particularly important in engaging diverse and multicultural students in reading literary texts. The final four benefits are woven into the next chapter and reveal how the reading of good literature can truly light students' pathways to understanding, reflective thinking, and creativity.

Perspectives of the Human Condition

First, good literature reveals humans and creatures that have human qualities at their best (and sometimes at their worst!). These characters strive for something in spite of adversity. These strivings are often designated "conflicts," and resolving these conflicts generally becomes the classical basis of the plot. There are conflicts of characters against characters, characters against nature, characters against the supernatural, or a character against her- or himself. Bruner (1996) labels the drama of the conflict as "Trouble" (with a capital *T*), and says that it makes the storytelling worthwhile in the first place. The Trouble arises out of the complications caused by the one who acts, the acts themselves, the goals pursued, and the means one takes to achieve a resolution.

As younger students listen to and/or view and read, they learn to sense struggle and perhaps to overcome and forbear. They learn to understand, appreciate, and emulate the best characteristics of the human condition. This also occurs through literature when animals and other creatures personify human qualities, something nicely exemplified in the picture book *The Dandelion Seed* (Anthony, 1997). A dandelion seed that is carried away by the wind on one part of the earth has wonderful human qualities of anxiety, fear, curiosity, and wonder as it is blown through unknown territory. Finally, after it is allowed to root, grow, and ripen to become a "parent," it releases new seeds to become part of the wind. All but one is carried away. The mother plant then tells her one clinging seed not to be fearful. Like a good parent, the plant advises her offspring that the wind, the sun, and the rain will look out for it. She tells the young seed to let go and watch what happens, and the final page shows a young boy blowing the lone seed off to a distant place. Seeing the seed float away by following its parent's advice helps to alleviate young children's fears and can make the young reader feel good. (Also, wouldn't this delightful picture book make a wonderful source for writing emotional and meaningful student-generated cultural texts?)

The reader feels good because something positive was achieved, and he or she is left with a sense of optimism about the future. Through stories, children can be shown how to understand human qualities, how to widen their perspectives about others, and how to become more tolerant of and empathetic with the characters they face (Emery, 1996). Stories also help readers to make sense of their lives, to think with mental pictures, and to desire that characters do and be good, maintains Kilpatrick (1993). He adds that through stories, caring parents and thoughtful teachers can assist children in identifying with models of courage and virtue in ways that problem-solving exercises and much of classroom discussion doesn't fulfill. Moreover, Wiggins and McTighe (1998) believe that a curriculum based on the structure of stories offers students and teachers the potential of greater engagement and deeper understanding than content instruction based on the logic of explanation. This deeper understanding occurs when storytellers teach readers about people, situations, and ideas as the mystery or dilemma is unraveling.

The literature we use to help students accomplish these tasks, however, must be good literature. By "good" literature we mean literature that, based on several criteria, has won awards or been well received by experts such as teachers, librarians, and, most important, children. It is important to note once again, however, that just because good literature might speak to a classroom of white middle-class children doesn't necessarily mean that it will speak to a classroom of diverse learners. Hence it behooves us as teachers to make sure that the literature we choose to share with our diverse readers does accomplish this, rather than disengaging them from reading and responding to literature at all.

Friedman and Cataldo (2002) reinforced this notion as they examined the main characters in contemporary award-winning children's books. Because the main characters were about the same age as middle school students, generally from 10–15 years old, Friedman and Cataldo found that many of the young adolescents were able to connect to the emotional and moral-cognitive complications faced by the literary characters, whose struggles were similar to those found in these young adolescents' daily lives. Remember, students will be much more willing to read, write, and respond to texts to which they can connect.

A Link to the Past and Other Cultures

The second wonderful quality of good literature is that it provides a link, a connection to the past and to different cultures; a crucial attribute when working with diverse learners. Students' understanding of the human experience takes on greater depth as they partake of the folk and cultural stories that have been passed on through generations of peoples, including ones that they might have even heard at home!

In one context, Norton (2001) points out that literature has contributed to a heightened sensitivity to the needs of all peoples and provides a major way to develop understanding across cultures. She adds, in another context (2003), that students' world understanding increases as they learn of early cultural traditions, learn how cultures shared traditions as variations of stories are read, learn to appreciate the culture and art of different countries, and learn about the languages and dialects that are used by peoples across cultures. This genre may be called *multicultural literature.*

Multicultural literature has many benefits for all students. Moore, Moore, Cunningham, & Cunningham (2003) indicate that the greatest asset of multicultural literature is that it reflects the diversity of heritage in the larger culture. The content rather than the form of the writing differs, and it deals with issues of race, religion, ethnicity, socioeconomic status, age, gender, and exceptional ability. In the selection and use of multicultural literature, Rasinski and Padak (1998) suggest, teachers should have two primary goals. First, their students should learn about and appreciate peoples of other cultures by celebrating what is good and special about these people, and second, they should provide motivating, satisfying reading experiences. Indeed, Blake (1997) asserts that as mainstream children engage with multicultural literature, diverse students in the classroom become better understood by others, thus empowering them while giving them additional opportunities to want to engage with the texts they read.

The use of literary selections about peoples from other cultures does not necessarily mean that students will become culturally conscious or sensitive. Teachers need to help students make connections to their own views about peoples of different cultures, color, and languages. One way to raise students' consciousness about diversity, suggests Boyd (2002), is through reading about, writing about, and discussing issues presented in multicultural literature.

An issue such as separateness is admirably presented for elementary students in the book *The Other Side* (Woodson, 2001). Annie, a lonely young white girl, wishes to befriend Clover, a young black girl, and her friends, who seem to engage in playful, youthful activities. However, a wooden fence separates the white from the black properties. The story, told in the third person through the voice of Clover, addresses the issue of separateness (and, of course, on a larger scale, racism), in a questioning, childlike way. Clover thought that Annie never had anybody to sit on the fence with. Then Clover asks her mother about the necessity of fences, and her mother tells her that it's always been like that with fences. Eventually, Clover feels brave enough to chat with Annie by the fence. Annie also acknowledges that her mother said she couldn't cross to the other side of the fence, but her mother didn't say anything about not *sitting on* the fence, so she reaches down to pull Clover up. As both girls sit side by side on the fence throughout the summer, the other black girls eventually join them. Clover suggests that someday the fence—old as it is—will be knocked down, and Annie agrees. A book such as this can and does engage all students to read and respond richly.

The use of multicultural literature in the classroom, therefore, not only supports diversity in the classroom but also teaches children about cultural issues that are rarely covered in schools. It encourages students to question traditional prevailing views about people of color and of different cultures, as well as their perceptions of themselves as mainstream or diverse students. Many contemporary authors and illustrators of multicultural literature for K–12 students are including relevant illustrations, author's notes, forewords, or afterwords to help teachers and students understand and reflect upon the cultural, social, and political themes presented in their books (Perini, 2002). Such notes provide useful facts and information about the authors' backgrounds, their reasons for telling the story, and background information about the historical climate and prevailing views of the time.

Conclusion

Good literature provides readers with three wondrous experiences (Barone, Eeds, & Mason, 1995). First, literature can engage readers in vicarious experiences they might otherwise miss; second, it allows and challenges readers to view peoples and events from perspectives they might not be able to attain on their own; and third, it provides a mental stimulus for readers to act differently because of the broader outlook they have achieved from the reading experience.

Nevertheless, a student must *want* to engage with such good literature. An extended critical reader response model and the use of cultural texts as a precursor to the introduction of good literature might be necessary in any classroom. This practice encourages all students to read and respond to literature as it accounts for the experiences and identities of diverse students and acknowledges and connects their experiences with social justice issues such as violence and racism, issues that unfortunately can be much too commonplace among these students.

Rather than continuing to transmit mainstream culture—and the expectations and assumptions of the dominant culture—through the literature we share with our students, we educators need to help students critique and transform culture through their own texts and eventually, we hope, through a serious study of other meaningful literature, such as exemplary multicultural literature. In this way, we not only acknowledge the crucial interpretations that all readers bring to text, we also help them learn to make meaningful, critical connections between the text and their own cultural identities as diverse readers.

Anticipation Guide Revisited

After reading this chapter, confirm your initial predictions about each statement. List the page number that supports each response.

Statement	Agree	Disagree	Verification
1. Traditional reader response is based on the notion that the teacher guides the student to find the correct meaning.	_____	_____	_____
2. According to Louise Rosenblatt, the literary experience can be described as a search for the one true meaning.	_____	_____	_____
3. One major assumption in a classroom reader response model is that feelings and emotions are important.	_____	_____	_____
4. A cultural text reproduces society's expectations and perceptions of students' lives.	_____	_____	_____
5. In good literature, human values are often depicted and revealed to readers as characters who work through problems and challenges.	_____	_____	_____
6. The greatest asset of multicultural literature is that it forces other students to appreciate diverse students.	_____	_____	_____
7. A classroom reader response model seeks to put into practice the theoretical notions Rosenblatt suggested.	_____	_____	_____
8. An extended, critical theory of reader response is necessary as a precursor to the introduction of good literature in the classroom.	_____	_____	_____

Additional Resources

Web Sites

Center for Applied Linguistics
www.cal.org

Dave's ESL Café
www.eslcafe.com

ESL Lounge
www.esl-lounge.com

ESL Magazine Online
www.eslmag.com

Kathy Schrock's Guide for ESL and Foreign Language Educators
http://discoveryschool.com/schrockguide/world/worldrw.html

Multicultural Resources for Children
http://falcon.jmu.edu/-ramseyil/multipub.htm

Enhancing Student Literacy in Secondary Schools
www.bced.gov.bc.ca/irp/ela1112/tpc/toc.htm

Teaching Ideas: Reading
www.ncte.org/teach/read.html

For Further Reflection

1. Think about a time in school when you were asked to respond to a poem or a story. Were you able to respond honestly, with emotions, and not be afraid of having the wrong answer? Write about your experience.

2. Go back to "My Papa's Waltz" and "A Spring Night" in this chapter. Respond to each poem using the following questions as a guide: How does this poem make you feel? Do you have any memories from your childhood that make you think of this poem? Is the poem essentially a happy or sad one? Cite words or phrases from the poem substantiating your position. Would you teach this poem to your students? Why or why not? If yes, how might you teach this poem to your students?

References

Altieri, J. (1994, December). *An examination of multiethnic readers' preference for literature portraying diverse cultures.* Paper presented at the Annual National Reading Conference, San Diego, CA.

Bakhtin, M. (1981). *The dialogic imagination.* Austin, TX: University of Texas Press.

Bakhtin, M. (1986*). Speech genres and other late essays.* Austin, TX: University of Texas Press.

Barone, T., Eeds, M., & Mason, K. (1995). Literature, the disciplines, and the lives of elementary school children. *Language Arts, 72,* 30–38.

Barton, J. (1994, December). *The influence of culturally based literature instruction on reader stance: Grade 4.* Paper presented at the Annual National Reading Conference, San Diego, CA.

Beach, R. (1994a, December). *High school students' responses to portrayal of racial discrimination in short stories.* Paper presented at the Annual National Reading Conference, San Diego, CA.

Beach, R. (1994b, December). *Research on stance and response to literature.* Paper presented at the Annual National Reading Conference, San Diego, CA.

Beach, R., & Hynds, S. (1991). Research on response to literature. In R. Barr, M. Kamil, P. Mosenthal, & P. Pearson, (Eds), *Handbook of reading research II* (pp. 453–489). New York: Longman.

Beach, R., & Wendler, L. (1987). Developmental differences in response to a story. *Research in the Teaching of English, 21,* 286–297.

Beloof, R. (1965). A spring night. In D. Aloian (Ed.), *Poems and poets.* New York: McGraw-Hill.

Bigelow, W. (1990). Inside the classroom: Social vision and critical pedagogy. *Teachers College Record, 91*, 427–448.

Blake, B. E. (1992). Talk in non-native and native peer writing conferences: What's the difference? *Language Arts, 69*, 604–610.

Blake, B. E. (1995, August). Broken silences: Writing and the construction of "cultural texts" by urban, pre-adolescent girls. *Journal of Educational Thought, 29*, 165–180.

Blake, B. E. (1997). *She says, he says: Urban girls write their lives.* Albany, NY: SUNY Press.

Blake, B. E. (2004). *A culture of refusal: The lives and literacies of out-of-school adolescents.* New York: Lang.

Blake, B. E., & Blake, R.W. (2002). *Literacy and learning.* Santa Barbara, CA: ABC-CLIO.

Blake, R. W. (1989). Explorations and new directions for teaching literature: An introduction. In *Reading, writing, and interpreting literature* (pp. vi–xxiii). Schenectady, NY: New York State English Council.

Blake, R. W., & Lunn, A. (1986). Responding to poetry: High school students read poetry. *English Journal, 75*, 68–73.

Bleich, D. (1978). *Subjective criticism.* Baltimore: Johns Hopkins University Press.

Boyd, F. B. (2002). Conditions, concessions, and the many tender mercies of learning through multicultural literature. *Reading Research and Instruction, 42*, 58–92.

Bruner, J. (1996). *The culture of education.* Cambridge, MA: Harvard University Press.

Emery, D. (1996). Helping readers comprehend stories from the characters' perspectives. *The Reading Teacher, 49*, 534–541.

Enciso, P. (1994). Cultural identity and response to literature: Running lessons from "Maniac McGee." *Language Arts, 71*, 524–535.

Ewald, H. R. (1993). Waiting for answerability: Bakhtin and composition studies. *College Composition and Communication, 44*, 331–348.

Friedman, A., & Cataldo, C. (2002). Characters at crossroads: Reflective decision makers in contemporary Newbery books. *The Reading Teacher, 56*, 102–112.

Hines, M. B. (1997). Multiplicity and difference in literary inquiry: Toward a conceptual framework for reader-centered cultural criticism. In T. Rogers & A. Soter (Eds.), *Reading across cultures: Teaching literature in a diverse society* (pp. 116–134). New York: Teachers College Press.

Kilpatrick, W. (1993). The moral power of good stories. *American Educator, 17*, 24–35.

Langer, J. (1994). A response-based approach to reading literature. *Language Arts, 71*, 203–211.

Moore, D. W., Moore, S. A., Cunningham, P. M., & Cunningham, J. (2003). *Developing readers and writers in the content areas, K–12.* Boston: Allyn & Bacon.

New York State Education Department. (1997). *English language arts learning standards.* Albany, NY: Author.

Norton, D. (2001). *Multicultural children's literature: Through the eyes of many children.* Upper Saddle River, NJ: Merrill Prentice Hall.

Norton, D. (2003). *Through the eyes of a child: An introduction to children's literature* (6th ed.). Upper Saddle River, NJ: Merrill Prentice Hall.

Perini, R..L. (2002). The pearl in the shell: Author's notes in multicultural children's literature. *The Reading Teacher, 55*, 428–431.

Rasinski, T., & Padak, N. (1998). Selecting and using multicultural literature: In M. F. Opitz (Ed.), *Literacy instruction for culturally and linguistically diverse students* (pp. 180–183). Newark, DE: International Reading Association.

Rogers, T. (1997). No imagined peaceful place: A story of community, texts, and cultural conversations in one urban high school English classroom. In T. Rogers & A. Soter (Eds.), *Reading across cultures: Teaching literature in a diverse society* (pp. 95–115). New York: Teachers College Press.

Rosenblatt, L. M. (1968). *Literature as exploration.* NY: Noble & Noble. (Original work published 1938)

Rosenblatt, L. M. (1978). *The reader, the text, the poem: The transactional theory of the literary work.* Carbondale, IL: Southern Illinois University Press.

Weiss, K., Strickland, D., Walmsley, S., & Bronk, G. (1995). Reader response: It's okay to talk in the classroom! *The Language and Literacy Spectrum, 5,* 65–70.

Wiggins, G., & McTighe, J. (1998). *Understanding by design.* Alexandria, VA: Association for Supervision and Curriculum Development.

Children's and Adolescent Books

Aloian, D. (1968). *Stories and storytellers.* CA: Addison-Wesley.

Anthony, J. (1997). *The dandelion seed* (Chris Arbo, Illus.). Nevada City, CA: Dawn.

Carlstrom, N. W., & Degen, B. (1986). *Jesse Bear, what will you wear?* New York: Little Simon.

Melville, H. (1988). *Moby Dick.* New York: Penguin Books.

Sanford, J. (1991). *The World War II at Monte Cassino.* New York: Penguin Books.

Woodson, J. (2001). *The other side.* New York: Putnam.

Chapter 7

Lighting the Pathways
of Understanding With Literature

Anticipation Guide

Before reading this chapter, please read each of the statements listed below. Based upon your prior knowledge and experience with this chapter's topics, check either "agree" or "disagree" for each statement. After reading the chapter, see if your answers change in the Anticipation Guide Revisited found at the end of the chapter.

Statement	Agree	Disagree
1. Only when children enter school do they begin to learn how to tell stories through the oral language tradition.	_____	_____
2. The oral storytelling tradition among peoples within cultures and countries formed the basis of the folklore of fables, myths, epics, and fairytales.	_____	_____
3. Teachers can use pattern books and books of rhyme to help children learn a phonic element.	_____	_____
4. In traditional plot structure, a precipitating event occurs to initiate conflict or tension, which serves as a catalyst for the development of the story.	_____	_____
5. In good literature human values are often depicted and revealed to readers as characters work through their problems and challenges.	_____	_____
6. Words used in the oral language are more vivid and rich than those used in written language.	_____	_____
7. The basic premise of the Great Books method of shared inquiry is to engage the reader in literal comprehension.	_____	_____
8. Story mapping, the graphic representation of content being read, has been recommended by a national panel as a means of improving reading comprehension.	_____	_____

Introduction

This chapter focuses on the richness of literature to convey meaning, sensitivity, and enjoyment for readers at all age levels. It complements the discussions in earlier chapters about the use of picture books with their internal motivating structures; the balance achieved through the classroom practice of read-alouds, shared readings, and guided reading; and the value of using poetry and multicultural literature to engage students from diverse cultures. This chapter extends that discussion and offers teachers six major classroom design strategies by which they can help their primary and intermediate students gain insight and reflective understandings through literary readings. We begin by looking at the major components of literature and why they exert a powerful influence on how one reads and writes a literary piece. We hope that this initial discussion will enrich the teacher's knowledge base and provide additional information on why the use of children's literature is a powerful vehicle of instruction.

Most of us would undoubtedly agree that *literature* means a story, sometimes cast in a fanciful way, sometimes in a realistic way, and other times in a futuristic way. We often use the words *story, tale, narrative,* and *fiction* interchangeably to capture the essence of literature as a creative and inspiring use of the imagination. We recall from our English literature classes the study of Samuel Taylor Coleridge's *Rime of the Ancient Mariner* (published in 1798), in which we were asked to engage in a "willing suspension of disbelief" as it unfolded. Coleridge asked his readers to knowingly suspend their understanding of the natural order of things by interjecting imagination and fantasy into possible real-world happenings, just while reading the story.

The Natural Oral Tradition

Smith (1994) has observed that creating stories is a natural condition of human thinking. He calls this the "narrative basis of thought." We think in sequence and causality as the mind engages in the planning and recollection of everyday events. We plan this and arrange that, and because of how we planned, we anticipate. When outcomes occur the way we wish, we may feel joy and satisfaction. If outcomes occur contrary to our expectations, we experience sorrow, tension, acquiescence, or even fortitude (determined to try again).

This notion that the narrative is essential in human thought prevails in the research and study of children's development with literacy, as we noted in Chapters 1 and 2. Hayward and Schneider (2000) add that narratives reveal the actual use of language by young children in social and school circumstances, and the analysis of children's oral narratives is more important to study than the isolated use of language. Children who were not able to relate a satisfactory narrative before the first grade had problems when they had to follow the narrative structure in written texts (Peterson, 1993). As children and adults relate their natural order of thinking about events to others, a story is born. When the story is written down, sprinkled with much imagination and vivid language and bound in book format, literature is brought forth to be read by others.

It is generally acknowledged that the traditional folklore of fables, myths, epics, folktales, and fairy tales grew out of the oral storytelling traditions that existed among peoples within cultures and countries (Norton, 2003; Saltman, 1985). In fact, in *The Riverside Anthology of Children's Literature,* Saltman designates the rich tradition of folklore from all countries of the world as "The Oral Tradition: The Cauldron of Story." Multicultural literature, since it generally focuses on peoples from different cultures, religious groups, racial groups, and world regions, also has its roots in the bubbling cauldron of oral tellings and retellings of unique peoples.

The Components of Literature

Let's look at the major components of how literature is planned by writers and encountered by readers. The major components are the following:

- *Genre*, the traditional or classical form of the literacy style
- *Format*, the way the work of literature is packaged to be read
- *Storytelling stance*, the way in which the story is told by the author
- *Structural elements*, the features within stories that are universal to the literary style

These are illustrated in Figure 7-1. Using these components and the artistry of the written language, writers deliver meaning and sensitivity to their reading audiences. Readers, on the other hand, gain more and more meaning and pleasure as they transact with the many guises and styles of written literature. We also noted in chapter 6 that many modern-day students transact well when their individual voices are heard about a text's potential meaning.

Genre

Genre, in its broadest meaning, is a way of sorting all kinds of written and art forms. When genre refers to the content of what is said and how it is said in written form, its major classifications are poetry and prose (Glazer, 2000). Prose can appear as biography or informational writing—nonfiction— or as literature, or fiction.

Literature, in today's world of print prolifera-

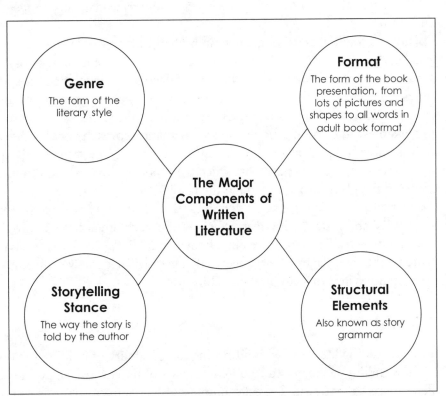

Figure 7-1. The Major Components of Literature

tion, can appear in many guises and styles. Most often teachers use the word *genre* to distinguish the specific type of literature they will ask their students to read. Many teachers tend to distinguish the reading of literature as "make-believe happenings" from the reading of informational text, which describes real-world happenings.

Authors can provide reasons why stories and history support and mirror one another, because the story of life itself offers a progression of history (Langer, 1995), and historical fictional works can be excellent vehicles for teaching history (Rudman, 1995). Barzun (2002) explains that history provides us with a story of colorful events and persons of other times in order to help us gain the wisdom to live in our times, whereas literature provides us with a story of how life could be lived or should be lived in any time. The reading of both history and literature rids the world of provincialism, or narrowness of thinking, that can occur with the sameness of our everyday existence. Kilpatrick (1993) adds that by exposing our children to stories and histories, we provide them with strong examples of moral character and the virtue of doing good to aid our children's own character development. Freeman and Person (1998) provide another dimension of why informational books may be considered a genre of children's literature. Though conceding that the expository writing style of informational books is different from the style of a narrative, they also note that modern-day informational books often contain the same lyrical quality and imaginative language that appear in children's storybooks.

The genres of literature fall into three broad categories: folklore, fantasy, and realism (Tompkins, 2003). These three traditional forms of story presentation are further categorized. Folklore includes myths, fables, epics, folktales, and fairy tales; fantasy includes stories of animals and objects with human qualities, ghost stories, and science fiction; and realism includes adventures, mysteries, and historical fiction.

Thus the traditional use of genre to indicate the literary style of a written work remains a major way to categorize the world of classic and modern stories. Just enter any bookstore or library, and you'll see designated areas for mysteries, adventures, fairy tales, science fiction, and so forth. Some anthology authors have imposed an even larger concept over that of genre and individual author. Keating and Levy (2001) present an anthology of seven universal themes such as "parents and children," "friends and enemies," and "people alone." Such a thematic approach is believed by the authors to be relevant and meaningful to the reader's experiences and growth development. Rudman (1995) takes an issues approach to children's literature in which the problem situations found in stories mirror what actually occurs to people in society. Through the reading of issues regarding personal and social concerns, the reader is faced with problems and conflicts that arise out of real-life happenings such as divorce, sibling rivalry, abuse, death, or old age. Such an approach offers a way to provide guidance and protection through story reading, a practice often known as *bibliotherapy*. Whatever larger form the perspective of genre might take, Slavin (1994) believes that genre provides a way through which meaning is made by readers and writers to focus on the teaching of texts.

Format

Imagine reading literature without having the capability of holding the book itself. From the time of infancy, children are exposed to different kinds of book formats, progressing from those with lots of illustrations to those with a greater number of words in continuous text. Books, both hardcover and softcover, remain the "golden rule" of literature reading. Many modern-day children certainly have computer access at home and at school, but the reading done on the computer is usually informational and expository. It is still a storybook that a child holds while he or she is sitting in a waiting room or during quiet and recreational reading time at home and in school.

The publishing industry divides books into two categories: trade books and books "outside the trade." Scharer (1994) indicates that the latter are published for a particular commercial or educational audience and include textbooks, basal readers, dictionaries, encyclopedias, research publications, and government documents. Such books are generally not found in our local retail bookstores. Children's trade books, which are available through retail stores and book dealers, are generally grouped into three broad categories: (a) picture books, (b) storybooks and children's literature, and (c) information books. Picture books and children's literature are the focus of this chapter, and information books will be discussed in the next chapter.

Picture books are those that contain illustrations, artwork, and photographs with relatively little or no text; many useful crafting lessons for these were presented in Chapter 2. This category contains a number of book formats, all centered around the nature and extent of picture use (Glazer, 2000). Wordless picture books, such as *The Snowman* (Brigg, 1978) and *Tabby* (Aliki, 1995), tell the story through pictures only. Another picture book type, such as *Hello Toes! Hello Feet!* (Paul, 1998), has both narrative and illustrations, with each supporting the other to tell the tale. Then there are concept books, which use pictures in a very educational way for young children; the two most popular types are alphabet and counting books. Concept books also attempt to explain ideas and relationships, such as *Chidi Only Likes Blue: An African Book of Colors* (Onyefulu, 1997), in which the young child learns how colors represent ideas in Nigerian culture.

Books in the formats described above can also appear as toy, board, pop-up, and "big" books. These books have appeal for young children and involve them visually and kinesthetically with unique features. Toy books might contain a touch-and-feel component; board books often have a cardboard quality, are laminated, and might be shaped to represent their topic. Pop-up books have characters that seem to come alive; they jump out as pages are turned. "Big" books are used by primary-grade teachers to engage small groups of children in read-alongs and book discussions. An important quality of big books is that the entire enlarged text is associated with the accompanying pictures, and children are encouraged to read with meaning (Glazer, 2000).

Books that are designed to help young children with their own initial reading experiences, rather than being read to or engaging in read-alongs, are often called easy-to-read books or beginning-to-read books. This format still contains a lot of pictures to indicate the story, but it is characterized by a limited vocabulary and short sentence length. This is believed to assist the young reader with ease of reading, a process known as *fluency,* because of the redundancy of print features. Norton (2003) suggests that these beginner books act as transitions between basal readers and the library trade books that children will encounter in school and community settings. She also notes that the control of word choice to fit the needs of the emergent reader can result in tales that have a contrived language. This occurs because authors have difficulty writing stories naturally, in a way that captures their creative thought processes, if they have to use words in certain spelling patterns selected from regulated and controlled lists.

Other picture book arrangements that are fun, inventive, and interesting for young children to read include predictable books, patterned books, and cumulative tales. These books help children predict what will come next while cumulatively building on what was presented earlier. They present a fun way to engage children in early reading because there's often a great deal of rhyming accompanied with chanting or singing. Since many of the books are presented as retold tales, they might have been part of an oral tradition as well. We see the representation of such a singing, lyrical quality in *Down by the Bay* (Udave, 1999), *I Went Walking* (Williams, 1996), *Bringing the Rain to Kapiti Plain* (Aardema & Vidal, 1981), and *The Grouchy Ladybug* (Carle, 1977).

Teachers may also use pattern books and books of rhyme to focus on the learning of a phonic element after the tale has been read and enjoyed. The phonic element would have an alphabet letter (or letters) presented in a regular, predictable way to match its sound or phoneme equivalent. A pattern is established in which several words (like a refrain) or even a whole line or sentence is repeated over and over again, so that the engaged reader can predict the words that are coming. Some patterns may also have rhyme, as done by Bill Martin (1983) in *Brown Bear, Brown Bear, What Do You See?* and by Dr. Seuss [Theodore Geisel] in *I Can Read With My Eyes Shut!* (Geisel, 1978). With one or both of these books, teachers can focus on the /ee/ phoneme (or the long *e* vowel sound) that is prompted by the *e* or *ee* spelling at the end of words such as *me, be, see, tree, bee, knee, three*. (Teachers can add *he, we*, and *she*, but not *the*).

As we move further away from the various types of picture book and easy-to-read book formats, we enter the larger arena of children's literature. Here the printed narrative tells the story, and illustrations and artwork are used to enliven and enrich the tale. In picture books, the illustrations are central to the meaning of the story, whereas with most children's literature in the elementary grades and beyond, text comprehension itself is central to understanding the story. All genres are represented in the rich world of children's literature as books with some, little, and eventually no illustration. They range from thin bound volumes of illustrated books to chapter books to junior novels and short stories and, finally, to full-length novels. Chapter books are popular today because they present a longer story in chapter-by-chapter format, allowing teachers to engage their students in character and plot development over a period of readings. Tompkins (2003) recommends that teachers reflect upon the scheduling of the chapter-book reading. For instance, they should consider how many chapters will be read per day, how students will respond to the reading, and how and when key points will be explored.

Chapter-book readings model the way that most older students and adults read novels. Great literature, as found in the novel, helps readers reflect upon the conflicts that are formed when characters interact with the institutions of society and how these conflicts become resolved, suggests Jacques Barzun (2002). The novel, he adds, teaches the young what life is about.

Storytelling Stance

The storytelling stance is the perspective from which the author tells the story. This is often referred to as the *point of view* of the story, and authors generally use three type of narrative approaches (Keating & Levy, 2001): first-person narration, third-person narration, and objective narration.

In first-person narration, the author tells the story through one character. This character reveals what he or she is thinking or planning to do by stating his or her own thoughts. The reader knows that this tale is being told through a character's voice because the familiar pronouns *I, me, my*, and *mine* are used. For instance, in the delightful picture book *Playing Right Field* (Welch, 2000), the story of a young boy who is always relegated to baseball's right field is told through his voice. He rues that the good players always play the best positions, whereas the worst players, besides being selected last to make up a team, are sent out to stand in right field. Through the course of the story, as he is absent-mindedly playing his position, a ball is hit in a critical game and his teammates yell and point at him. As he puts on his glove to block out the sun, the ball plops into his glove. Now the unlikely player is suddenly the game's hero. He now believes that's why he was sent out to right field.

Sometimes the narrator is the author, and at other times the narrator is a central or minor character who reveals through his or her words the nature of the tale. Quite often young writers use the first-person narrator's voice when they tell personal narratives. Because they have lived through an experience, they can relate firsthand to what they want to write about as they look back with mental imaging. So they tell the story, "I remember when . . ." If they can enliven the experience with colorful words, their retelling of a personal, even prosaic, adventure will be well told.

In third-person narration, the author tells the story through one or more characters. These characters reveal what they are thinking, planning, or doing as the author tells the story through their eyes. Here the pronouns refer not to self but to others: *he, she, they*. The characters tell what is going on in their minds and express their opinions about others and events that have occurred or that will take place.

When the author steps out of the characters' thoughts and tells a story while looking at characters and events, an objective narration occurs. Keating and Levy (2001) liken the author to a filmmaker or video recorder. The characters are revealed as to how they appear, what they say, what they do, and how other characters interact with them. Like a filmmaker, the author is allowing us to look in on the characters and see how they shape the development of the story. Here the action and the interactions shape the story, and readers make inferences and conclusions based on the events the author has unfolded.

When taking the objective narrative stance, an author might let us in on how a character is thinking in first person by using dialogue. For instance, when Corduroy (Freeman, 1976), a toy bear, looks for his lost button in a department store, he finds himself in front of what looks like stairs, not knowing that the stairs are escalator steps. The author then shows Corduroy moving up the escalator, with the bear thinking out loud that he is moving up a mountain. Authors of contemporary realistic fiction often tell the tale through the first-person point of view or through the third-person voice of one character when writing for children age 8 or older (Norton 2003). In this way the focus on one character's experiences creates a greater bond with youthful readers who might have had similar experiences.

How does point of view develop with the emergent writer? Let's look at 7-year old Cosima as she works through the writing of two stories: one finished with some satisfaction and the other not, because of something she couldn't produce at the moment of her writing. Look at the beginning of both stories (Figures 7-2 and 7-3). Do you think that earlier life experiences of being read to with the traditional stories of folklore, fables, and fantasy brought about the universal opening of "one day"? Other children might use "once upon a time." After the "one day" announcement, the mental camera rolled to peer in on the escapades of a rabbit and a pig. In her mind, Cosima had the concept of story sense: a character does something (an action), and there appear to be outcomes. She is leading us with transitions in story development with the use of "after that," "because," and "so."

Why was the rabbit story completed and the pig story not? There was another important process going in in Cosima's mind that influenced her actual creation of the stories: orthography, or correct spelling. For whatever reason, she was concerned with the standard spelling of words and didn't wish to write the words as they sound (inventive spelling). She did have many words registered correctly in

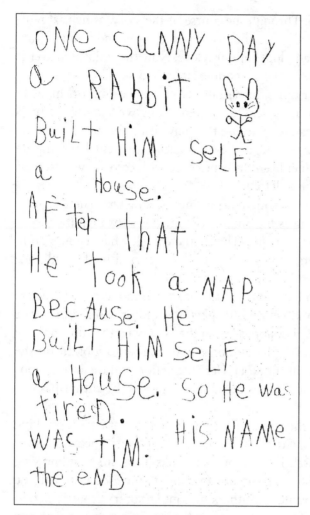

Figure 7-2. Cosima's Rabbit Story

ONe DAY a Pig
Went to the
BeAch BecAuse
it WAs hot.
he woRe HIS

Figure 7-3. Cosima's Pig Story

her mind's eye, and she laboriously sounded out each word as it was written to be sure of the spelling. She would practice a word first on nearby scrap paper, writing *built* as "bilt," *because* as "becas," and *tired* as "tird." Then she asked if these were correct. With adult feedback from her grandpa, she moved on with story development.

In the pig story, after she wrote the words, "he wore his" she turned to her grandpa and whispered, "How do you spell 'polka-dotted bathing suit'?" Grandpa was involved in a meeting with his peers, and it would have been rude for him to stop to work through the sounding-out and spelling process with a 7-year old. So without help forthcoming, Cosima said, "Oh, bother!" and concluded the story with three star-shaped polka dots. It would have been most interesting to learn the resolution of the story after the pig donned his bathing suit, but Cosima's creative mind was short-circuited by a need to have the words spelled correctly.

Structural Elements

The structural elements found across the genres of literature are also known as *literary elements,* or aspects of fiction. At the primary and intermediate school levels, these literary elements are generally recognized as theme, plot, characters, setting, outcomes, and resolution. Sometimes point of view is included as a literary element as well. Teachers generally refer to these features as *story grammar.*

Written literature has an underlying universal structure that is held together by the nature of the narrative. The narrative moves on in time and provides the "glue" for all developing stories. Hayward and Schneider (2000) suggest that because narratives are understood and produced according to a set of organized principles, they can be described and analyzed through such models as story grammar. Pradl (1994) adds that even with the endless diversity of story forms and content, researchers have noted that particular narrative structures remain constant. For instance, he tells of one researcher who analyzed 100 Russian folktales and found that even while the characters and details varied, the same types of actions were occurring in each tale.

By their very nature, cumulative folktales are structured on chronology. These folktales move along with the repetitive, sequential ordering of the action, and each character is connected to some previous occurrence (Norton, 2003). In John Langstaff's *Oh, a-Hunting We Will Go* (1989), each animal that is captured by the children is temporarily placed in a different holding place, followed by the children's chant to let the animal go. The cumulative action also moves forward as each character interacts with the next, and then abruptly halts and reverses itself when the problem causing the action is solved. This occurs quite humorously in Verna Aardema's *Why Mosquitoes Buzz in People's Ears* (1975). King Lion calls a council of the animals and has to work backwards through events to figure out why Mother Owl will not awaken the sun and cause day to come. King Lion figures out that because the iguana had put sticks in his ears to ward off a pesky mosquito, a series of cumulative misunderstandings occurred among the animals, resulting in the death of one of Mother Owl's owlets, an action that made her resolve not to call forth the sun. When Mother Owl learns that the mosquito was the initial cause of her owlet's death, she becomes satisfied and hoots for the sun to rise.

THEME

Besides the chronology structure of the narrative, structure in folktales, fairy tales, and fables is also contained in the theme. When these stories originated, religion was a dominant aspect of daily life. Thus the themes found in these traditional tales are similar to those found in the Bible and in the mythologies of peoples of various cultures. The purpose of these tales was to provide a lesson and to reveal truths about human nature and development. These stories were created and told by adults who used their imaginations to create inventive plots and superhuman and supernatural characters. However, in spite of the fanciful and supernatural elements, the heroes of these traditional folk stories are generally ordinary men and women (Keating & Levy, 2001). Just recall "Snow White and the Seven Dwarfs" and "Little Red Riding Hood" and you'll remember how the goodness found in human beings triumphs over the badness found in the unreal characters. Furthermore, the lesson imparted by the theme provides a structure to the development of the narrative events, which we commonly call the plot.

PLOT

Plot refers to the unfolding and sequencing of events in a story. Because events are usually connected to one another in some meaningful or dramatic way, causality is also connected to sequence. For instance, because something happened, it caused a following event to occur, which had a positive or negative impact on the first event, and so on. To envision how plot works, you might visualize a character ready to strike the balls on a pool table. As the cue ball is struck and it hits the other balls on the table, the struck balls in turn strike each other and reverberate off one another and the sides of the pool table, which provides the setting for this event. Then there's the tension created by the eight ball. If the character hits the eight ball into a pocket before its intended turn, the character loses. If the character pockets, or sinks, each ball in succession and dramatically reaches the eight ball with success, the character is the winner, or "hero," of this event.

Glazer (2000) suggests that the plot structure in picture books is revealed in different levels of complexity. One or many problems might need to be solved by a few or many characters. Sometimes two parallel plots can be developing in the story, and both plots are resolved in the conclusion. Other books use the flashback structure to interrupt the chronological ordering of events to bring us back to the past (Norton, 2003).

CHARACTERS

Characters are the movers and doers in the story. The more that characters seem lifelike and believable, the more likely readers will be to remember them through their lifetimes (Norton, 2003). Authors reveal information about characters by giving the following details:

- What the character looks like
- What the character says through dialogue
- What other characters think about this particular character
- How other characters interact with this character
- What the character thinks
- How the character acts and interacts with others and with particular events

In many good stories, characters undergo a change of perspective and develop in a stronger way because of the events that affect them. It is this sense of character development that lends both a form of plot structure and credibility to a good story. Because characters' motives are influenced by the story line itself and by the belief and values system of the reader, different readers will respond to the same character in different ways. This notion prompted Keating and Levy (2001) to maintain that one great pleasure of reading literature is that it provides a view of multiple interpretations of character.

SETTING

Setting refers to those features that allow one to sense when and where the story is occurring. These features are known simply as *time* and *place*. The use of these two words alone can be unfortunate, because readers might know when and where a story took place but still miss the richness that the setting brings to plot and character development. Also, setting shifts to accommodate the purpose or meaning of the story. For instance, in *Lovable Lyle* (Waber, 1977), most of the story occurs in the house where Lyle, the crocodile, lived with his human family, but there would be little depth to the story if the setting didn't shift to the beach where Lyle rescues the drowning girl, who had set herself up to be Lyle's enemy. Glazer (2000) suggests that setting should be regarded as an integral part of story development and not just a backdrop that can change without causing a change in plot structure.

Time is an essential ingredient of a story. We noted that plot structure itself is based on the passage of time. Time can unfold in a matter of hours, days, weeks, or months, or be suggested by seasons of the year or periods of history. How much time unfolds in *Franklin Plays the Game* (Bourgeois, 1995)? Time in this story is inferred by one's experience with how one prepares for a key, final sports event—in this case, a soccer game. After being introduced to Franklin, the turtle, and his team players, who were quite the band of misfits when it came to soccer, we see them learning to use teamwork and their bodily features to come close to defeating a bear's team in the big game. Time can also move backwards, as in the case of a flashback, or jump ahead to the future to allow the reader to peer ahead into story aspects that influence the happenings of the present. With flashbacks the author often reveals character traits, events, and experiences that occurred in an earlier time so that the reader will better understand a character or the events that are occurring in the present time.

Place can be described, as occurs with sections of a big department store in *Corduroy* (Freeman, 1976), or imagined, as with many folktales that refer to "a land of long ago" or "a forest deep and dark." Eeds and Peterson (1995) note that place adds to the mood or feeling of a story, influences both characters and their actions, and often reveals the period in which the story takes place. Norton (2003) adds that accuracy in place and time is critically important in historical fiction and in biography.

How Narrative Structure Helps Readers and Writers

Many teachers, activity books, and duplicated pages created for students present narrative structure as three main segments: beginning, middle, and end. This portrayal is unfortunate because it reduces the complexity of the narrative to a formula. On the one hand, Norton (2003) suggests that readers do expect a good story to have a beginning that introduces the action and characters, a middle section that develops the drama caused by the interacting and reverberating events, and a credible ending. On the other hand, suggest Eeds and Peterson (1995), when plot is revealed simply by the listing of story events, the reader loses a sense of how the events affect one another and how the incidents are related. Furthermore, the structure of plot may be developed in different ways, through different patterns (these will be presented later in our sections on story grammar and story mapping). Through story maps, which are visual representations of story structures, we can show readers and writers *how* different story patterns are constructed, and that the beginning, middle, and end sections have various conceptual weights in story construction.

Traditional Plot Structure

Keating and Levy (2001) point out that the traditional plot of most classical fiction has four essential structural parts: the introduction, the conflict, the climax, and the resolution. Swanson and DeLaPaz (1998) add that narratives constructed in Western cultures also reveal internal or external reactions by characters to problems or goals that are faced during the conflict, leading to a story's resolution. In the introduction, an author presents the main character or characters, the setting in which the story occurs, and the issues or problems that will cause the plot to unfold. Even with a story that begins with "Once upon a time in a forest deep and dark, there lived a . . . ," we have a setting in which the reader will know to expect an unusual or unreal character who might have a problem or face a difficult situation. Soon after the introduction, a precipitating event occurs to initiate the conflict or tension that will propel the development of the story. In the traditional tale of "Cinderella," retold by Nola Langer (1974), the initiating event occurs when the invitation is received to the prince's ball. Because the self-centered stepsisters are included in the invitation and Cinderella is not, a scenario is established in which a fanciful plot can develop to help Cinderella with her problem of attending the ball. In classical story structure, a character initiates attempts or a series of actions to resolve a problem or to reach a goal.

A traditional tale such as "Cinderella" leads to a climax in which the major problem or issue is resolved. The climax is often known as the story's *turning point*, because the propelling action of the character's resolve to overcome the problem is now reached. In traditional tales, the climax occurs very near the end of the story and is followed by a rather rapid resolution or story outcome. For instance, in Hans Christian Andersen's classic tale "The Emperor's New Clothes," when the young child yells out that the emperor isn't really wearing clothes in the imperial procession, the turning point is reached regarding the supposedly invisible clothes. After this outburst of youthful wisdom, a swift resolution occurs, with the emperor concluding that he is the biggest fool of all and possibly not the most fit in common sense.

Even in modern fantasies, such as *Lovable Lyle* (Waber, 1977), we see the classical plot structure. Lyle, the crocodile, is quickly introduced as being loved by his family, the Primms, as well as by all other humans and animals. Then one day he receives a disturbing note stating that he is hated, and it is signed by his "enemy." He therefore goes out of his way to please even more, but the hate message keeps reappearing. Finally we are introduced to a little girl, who is holding a note, and her mother, Mrs. Hipple, who won't allow her daughter to play with such creatures. The action intensifies until we find the Primms and the Hipples at the same beach. Now, what can crocodiles probably do better than humans? They can swim better, and Mr. Primm announces that Lyle is the most competent swimmer in his family, When little Clover Hipple is near death by drowning, the maligned crocodile rushes past the lifeguards to save her. Lyle holds Clover on the beach while Mrs. Hipple proclaims her sincere thanks, and everyone regards him as a hero. Is this the story's turning point and climax? Or is the climax part of the happy resolution on the next page, when Lyle receives a loving note with a request to be his playmate?

Besides the classical plot structure, Keating and Levy (2001) aptly point out that there is variation in the pattern of this structure. For instance, some stories have very little action, some have no outcome or resolution at all, and some do not depend on the propelling force of conflict. Yet Martinez and Roser (1995) suggest that stories with dramatic plot structure and an unfolding problem probably have the greatest impact in propelling children into the world of story reading.

Character Study

Character study is another way to look at the development of a good story. In other words, in some stories the plot just seems to happen, in its continuity and causality. In others, a central character or group of characters reveal thoughts, plans, beliefs, and attitudes about the events. In still others, a central character might work through a problem or dilemma and gain insight and understanding that enriches his or her life. Often a character is faced with a complication, which is something that interferes with or upsets his or her pattern of life (Franklin, 2002).

Complication does not necessarily entail conflict, which is the underlying force of the plot in most traditional stories. In a character development story, the plot develops as the character faces and struggles with the complication(s). The character shows resolve with the struggle and digs in deeper and deeper to overcome it. The most essential element in this story line is that the character undergoes change because of the struggle and reaches a point of insight. In good stories, the character determines what happens, and meaning is derived from how close the insight resembles what would occur in real-world happenings (Franklin, 2002). When characters cope with problems and situations that are universal in nature, they teach readers to understand the richness of such values as goodness, love, honor, hope, and faith and the offensiveness of such traits as instigating fear and evil (Eeds & Peterson, 1995).

Story Grammar Analysis

When teachers bring the structure of stories and literature to children, they often use the strategies of story grammar analysis, story maps, and even story boarding. These variations all refer to the same generic construct of the features of stories such as character, setting, problem or conflict, precipitating or initiating event, and plot, with attempts, outcomes, consequences, and resolution.

Two popular story grammar representations in the literature have been provided by Stein and Glenn (1977) and Gordon and Braun (1983). A story grammar was defined by these authors as a set of rules that determines how stories are generally organized. The rules include the use of the component parts of typical stories (the literary elements), the types of events that occur at various points in a story, and the relationship among the component parts of the story. According to Stein and Glenn's (1977) story grammar structure, a well-formed narrative has the following six components:

- *Setting*, in which the main character is introduced and which reveals the place and time in which the story occurs

- *Initiating event*, which is an action, a natural event, or an internal process that causes the main character to begin an action or to respond to something

- *Internal response*, which can appear as an understanding, an emotion, or a goal of the main character

- *Attempt*, which is the action the main character takes to reach his or her goal

- *Consequence*, which is an event or an ending to indicate that the main character has or has not attained his or her goal

- *Reaction*, which is an understanding, a feeling, or a final action that reveals the main character's attitude about the consequence

These authors used the term *episode* to note that an event occurs in a specified context of setting and has a chronological sequence.

Gordon and Braun's (1983) schematic representation of story structure also includes the concept of episode, but they connect the movement of episodes to the shifting of settings. Their overall story grammar model includes the four essential elements of setting, theme, plot, and resolution. Theme is revealed either by the author's message or by the main character attaining his or her goal. Setting is characterized as an initial major one supported by a number of minor ones to accommodate the number of story episodes. Each minor setting includes the features of location, time, character, and the ongoing state of the story. Important in their story grammar model is the notion that plot is composed of a series of episodes, with each episode occurring in a particular minor setting. Episodes move on through the thinking relationship that accompanies the connectives—*and, then,* and *because.* Each separate episode of the plot includes five elements: (a) a starter, or initiating event; (b) internal responses of the main character through emotions, thoughts, plans, or goals; (c) actions or attempts to execute a plan to achieve a goal or subgoal; (d) outcomes or events that resulted from (c); and (e) reactions expressed through thoughts, feelings, or responses to the outcomes (d) of an earlier action (c). Although Gordon and Braun point out that their schematic representation might be thought of as ideal, or an average story grammar structure, their visual representation might have helped give rise to the popular story mapping representation of beginning, middle, and end. Their visual diagramming of episodes as they occur in evolving settings does provide one way to construct story maps for classroom instructional use.

VanDongen and Westby (1986) postulated that if young children have frequent exposure to story representations and have opportunities to compare and contrast different plot structures, they will begin to internalize four structural patterns, which they likened to narrative macrostructures inherent in literature. They named these structures the episodic pattern, the cumulative pattern, the circle pattern, and the progressive narrative pattern. Some of these patterns were introduced for use with young children in chapter 2. Assisting older students in visualizing these patterns and presenting those offered by other story grammar models will follow shortly.

How the Reading of Good Literature Lights Our Pathways

In the last chapter we noted two ways that good literature engages readers and lights the pathways of their minds. We saw that reading good literature can simply make one feel good, and it can also help us see what life was like in the past and in other cultures. Reading about how others attempt to overcome adversity and conflict allows us to become closer to, respectful of, and appreciative of peoples from other cultures. Below are four additional ways that the reading of good literature enriches our students' lives.

It Enriches a Knowledge Base

A strong benefit of literary readings is their power to enrich a knowledge base and the understandings of informational content covered in such disciplines as science, social studies, arithmetic, and health. We noted earlier that some authors believe the distinctions between the two writing styles of fiction and non-fiction were beginning to diminish especially in the writing of historical accounts. How often have you or one of your students concluded that the reading of a particular historical novel revealed more about the conditions of a particular war, a period of history, or the plight of a people than the readings in a history textbook? Fictional trade books have the capability of acting like a magnifying glass to enlarge and augment one's personal interaction with the book's topic (Vacca & Vacca, 2002).

In the broad genre category of "realism," fiction authors use factual and historical information to make their tales ring with accuracy, but authors can teach important concepts about life through folklore and fantasy as well. Look at the picture book *The Dandelion Seed* (Anthony, 1997). The intent of the author might not have been to teach about the concept of seed dispersal. However, in the picture walk and reading of the tale, the concept of how seeds find their way into new soil is explained. The young child can learn that those little bushy things on top of the dandelion are actually its seeds and that they travel and root themselves by currents of wind.

It Enhances Imagination and Language Power

Another great benefit of literary engagement is the stirring of the imagination though the language and visualizations offered by writers and illustrators. Literature is an art form in which authors strive to use the power of words to make us see, feel, and experience their topic at a most deep and profound level. When the author teams with an illustrator, as occurs with picture books, both work in harmony to use words and illustrations to make the experience rich and vivid in the perceiver's mind. As readers (or listeners) are pulled mentally into stories, they may engage their minds to follow the story line initially, but then the mind re-creates the characters, settings, events, and outcomes as imaginary. The stronger the pull, the more vivid the images and the more they may last through a lifetime. What adults cannot mentally play back episodes of such traditional tales as "The Three Little Pigs," "Snow White and the Seven Dwarfs," and "Goldilocks and the Three Bears"?

Glazer (2000) suggests that a major goal of implementing a literature curriculum for young children is to stimulate children's imagination. By listening to a broad array of stories, children engage in the imaginative projections of many authors and learn that the structural elements of literature are interrelated. As people tell and read stories, they also elaborate and re-create them to coordinate with their own views and perspectives.

We noted in earlier chapters that the structure of the narrative initially develops through talk used in the home, the local community, and with young children's social and learning groups. Children, parents, and playmates talk about the experiences they have had, and the ability to sequentially order the narrative becomes more and more developed as an ever increasing store of words is added to children's tellings and retellings. In some cultures, the structure of a narrative is shaped as traditional stories and tales are told orally and passed on to each new generation. Au (1995) tells about young Hawaiian children who engage in the oral tradition of "talk story," in which the children's personal experiences are narrated with folk usage in the telling or retelling of a tale. Here children tell stories together, each providing segments of personalized information, and the story builds with their taking of turns.

When a parent, a grandparent, an older sibling, a guardian, or a teacher reads aloud to a child, two important outcomes occur. One is that the narrative structure begins to take a more formal hold within the child's mind. The second is related to the author's use of language to build word power and to add additional fuel to the child's imagination. In the one great act of storybook reading, the conditions of viewing, listening, speaking, affective engagement, and social bonding come together as the child watches the pages of the book turn. When children hear their favorite stories read aloud, their thoughts and expectations become those of the story. They hear and see words in different sentence structures, they begin to take note of word shapes, and their attention becomes focused by the direction of the story.

Educators and researchers have long acknowledged that the home activity book reading, reading aloud, or on-the-lap reading to children is a major contributor to their vocabulary and language development, their sense of written language structures, and their powers of imagination. On-the-lap reading provides opportunities for children and adults to engage in lively talk regarding past, present, and forthcoming events in a book. Although the illustrations transmit relevant and stimulating visual information, the talk proceeds through listening and speaking interchanges about what the book's words say and how the words' meanings are supported by the use of the illustrations. The different stories that children encounter provide them with new vocabulary, new syntactic constructions, and new visualization sources that might not be forthcoming in conversation alone. Furthermore, as children become familiar with particular stories and wish to have them repeated, they question more in order to gain fuller or richer understandings.

It Provides Pleasurable Experiences

Connected to the stirring of the imagination is the power of literature to enrich our mental and affective well-being. The reading of literature simply provides access to pleasant, engaging, and fun experiences. The readings become enjoyable because they can make one feel happy or fulfilled, and they are engaging because they center one's focus and mental energy while reading and thinking. The reader who is engaged in reading for pleasure is not seeking to acquire information but wants to explore the world of authors' imaginations and story permutations. Rosenblatt (1989) calls such involved reading "aesthetic reading." During aesthetic reading, the reader experiences and enjoys the ideas, situations, scenes, personalities, and emotions that are revealed and participates in the tensions, conflicts, and resolutions that unfold. This is why engaged readers are often reluctant to have a pleasurable reading experience end, and they can become annoyed when interruptions occur during the reading experience. Good stories pull readers into the energy of the characters and allow readers to experience vicariously the tension of the unfolding stories as their own (Barone, Eeds, & Mason, 1995).

Even for very young children, teachers and day care professionals reinforce the notion of responding to literature in a pleasurable way by encouraging children to discuss their interpretations and reactions in an open-ended way (Glazer, 2000). If children are interrupted in the cycle of a story with specific detailed questions about content, they begin listening to stories to gain the information they contain and not to the language of the author or the excitement of the plot. One of us noted this reaction when reading to his own grandchildren. Each of the three had their favorite storybooks, and during our many lap readings, he was often reminded of "lap-reading protocol." For instance, when he wished to ensure, as the ever mindful teacher, that the concept of being boring was understood, he asked 5-year old Ricardo, "What did the boar do to show that he was boring to the other animals?" Immediately the look of enchantment and wonder disappeared from Ricardo's face, and admonishment occurred with the exclamation, "Grandpa, just read the words!" He knew the plot sequence from previous oral readings. Grandpa had short-circuited Ricardo's enjoyment and anticipated imagery of the author's rhythm of words by requesting, at that moment of engagement, a more mundane task.

It Connects With Other Art Forms

A final benefit of engaging children in literature is the stimulus it provides to connect with and transfer to other forms of art. Authors of literature paint pictures with words, and illustrators of literature use the words to evoke meaning and feeling through pictures. Children can express these visualizations of meaning and feeling into art forms such as the visual arts, drama, music, and poetry. We saw this occurring with young children in Chapters 1 and 2.

The use of drama to respond to literary readings enriches children's understanding of literature and narrative structure in many ways (Galda & West, 1995). As children re-create scenes, become the characters, and plan ways to respond to the plot and meaning of the story, they become more reflective about literature and knowledgeable about language. Benefits occur, for instance, when children create puppet figures pasted on the ends of popsicle sticks to represent the thematic meaning of *The Great Kapok Tree* (Cherry, 1990). As wonderful rainforest animals such as the jaguar, the unstriped anteater, the three-toed sloth, and the boa constrictor are mounted on the ends of the sticks, the children whisper a script or paraphrased rendition of that animal's words in the story to a playacting classmate. Besides puppetry, students can role-play parts, engage in pantomime, reenact a story with costumes or props, and create a play to be performed based on a literary reading. A live reenactment supported with simple costumes and/or small props allows students the opportunity to create verbal exchanges that make characters come alive as they develop the story action (Herrell, 2000).

Art, particularly visual art, can be a propelling force for the interpretation of an author's story or for the creation of episodes in a child's own original story. Through examination of the visual art in picture books, teachers can show children how illustrators communicate through art and how their illustrations contribute to the meaning of a story. Children's drawings can reflect their understanding of a piece of literature and can reveal their sensitivity to themes or messages within the story as well.

Children may be asked to read first and then visualize and interpret the story elements through pictures. Children might also be asked to create a story through pictures first and then create the language and narrative discourse for their stories. In the retelling strategy, children draw their visualizations of the story episodes and attach their own language, retold to match the intent of the original author, to the story frames. Mrs. O'Keefe of the Notre Dame School in New Hyde Park, New York, asks her fourth graders to do their monthly book reports in a number of user-friendly ways, such as through a film-frame technique, which allows them to storyboard the story. Look at Jennifer's production of *Knights of the Kitchen Table* (Scieszka, 1994) in Figure 7-4. One can follow the numbering of her visual storyboard frames and match the meaning with the text provided in each of the scenes. Besides retelling the episodes of the story in her scenes, Jennifer also tells us some of her reactions to and opinions of the story characters.

Retelling is just one of the many ways in which to engage children and youth with storytelling and great literature. In the next section we will examine some major approaches, grouping arrangements, and particular teacher-guided ways to assist children with the healthy and lengthy pursuit of literature. In no way will we be able to exhaust the topic of literature use and strategies for classroom instruction in this chapter. Earlier we noted that some authors of children's literature have exercised an issues or thematic approach to make literature relevant and meaningful to readers at particular times in their lives. Besides these approaches, teachers can design instructional units that focus on the study of a genre, an author, or an illustrator. In earlier chapters we noted that guided reading with kidstations,

Figure 7-4. Jennifer's Story Frames

the classroom reader response model, and the use of cultural texts can aid in the understanding, appreciation, and writing capability of students. We also showed how the structure of the narrative helps students in the development of oral reporting and technology productions. For more information about book recommendations, authors, reader's theater, literature resources, and more, check out the Children's Literature Web Guide (see Additional Resources at the end of this chapter).

The Use of Literature as a Design for Classroom Instruction

In this section we will look at additional ways in which literature can assist in children's engagement of wide and varied readings while teachers skillfully integrate other domains of the language arts to develop richer and deeper understandings. We will examine approaches and strategies that help children learn the structural elements of literature and how to apply these structures in analyzing and writing their own stories. Furthermore, we will show how these particular ways provide for many positive opportunities of learning, aesthetic engagement, cultural awareness, entertainment, and good feelings.

A Literature Curriculum Through Junior Great Books

The Junior Great Books program is an established and reputable literature program for children through the grades. The junior series is one program of the Great Books Foundation, a nonprofit educational organization, which publishes collections of classic and modern literature to promote reading and discussion programs for children, youth, and adults. One concept of using "great books" is to engage readers in "grand conversations" (Peterson & Eeds, 1990), in which discussion and inquiry are cultivated to achieve reflective and in-depth thinking. Equal weight is given to how one reads and what one reads; the essential focus is on reading quality books in a rich and elaborative way (Anderson, 1994). A second concept of the foundation is that reading with critical interpretation is a complex mental activity that needs to be cultivated over time. To accomplish such interpretive reading, students read challenging literature, and through an established method of inquiry and discussion, students construct meaning, draw inferences and conclusions, and weigh evidence (Great Books Foundation, 1999).

The Junior Great Books at the kindergarten and first-grade level are packaged in attractive anthologies. Each student anthology at the K–1 level is in a softcover format and contains not only nine literary selections to be implemented in a read-aloud fashion but also activity pages and space for young children to construct their artwork. From grades 2 through middle school, 12 literature selections appear in each anthology, including folktales, classics, and modern fiction. Since two anthologies are available, one for each semester of the year, students read, discuss, and respond in writing to 24 literary selections per year. Fourth graders, for example, are exposed to Scottish, Russian, Central African, Japanese, Polish, and Northern African folktales as well as classics by Rudyard Kipling, Lewis Carroll, and Kenneth Grahame. Each anthology ranges from 9 to 12 literary selections and costs about the same as one hardcover children's trade book. It is supported by a teacher's selection, an optional student activity book, and optional audiotapes. Table 7-1 shows a sampling of anthology selections ranging from the kindergarten and grade 1 read-aloud program to the literature program for grades 2 through 9.

The foundation suggests that, prior to using its approach and resource materials, teachers participate in its professional development training program, "The Basic Leader Training Course." Here teachers learn how to implement the shared inquiry discussion method with its adaptations at the various grade levels. In the shared inquiry approach to the interpretive reading of quality literature, students are led by questioning and discussion to search for more than one answer, as suggested by the reading, and are encouraged to engage in artwork and/or writing activities to reflect their interpretations of issues in stories. Students are guided with a series of *how* and *why* questions to help them reach their own interpretations and to open them up for active listening and speaking involvement.

Probably the most important feature of the Junior Great Books sequence approach is to encourage students to be active, inquisitive readers who can reveal high-level thinking in their writings, questions, artistic work, and discussion. In this process, questioning is a most important, if not the most important, technique to implement. Teachers are trained to help get students beyond a basic understanding of the written work. This basic understanding, known as the factual or literal level, is often necessary to comprehend the foundation of the work's meaning, but questions don't necessarily have to start at this level. As soon as one asks, "Why do you think that the character behaved this way?", "How do you think this setting influences the story?" and "What does this particular word mean in this part of the story and why do you think the author used it?", the teacher is engaging students at the interpretive level of comprehension. As students think deeply about various interpretations, they also evaluate and judge the meaning of the work in relation to their own lives. These evaluations become evident when students write, discuss, and reveal their thinking through their art and dramatizations. Table 7-2 lists these activities.

Table 7-1. Sample Junior Great Books Anthology Selections by Grade Level

Grades K–1		
GUINEA FOWL AND RABBIT GET JUSTICE African folktale as told by Harold Courlander and George Herzog	**THE FROG WENT A-TRAVELING** Russian folktale as told by Vsevolod Garshin	**THE BLACK HEN'S EGG** French folktale as told by Natalie Savage Carlson
FERAJ AND THE MAGIC LUTE Arab folktale as told by Jean Russell Larson	**BOUKI CUTS WOOD** Haitian folktale as told by Harold Courlander	**THE MERMAID WHO LOST HER COMB** Scottish folktale as told by Winifred Finlay

Grade 2	Grade 3	Grade 4
THE TALE OF SQUIRRELL NUTKIN Beatrix Potter	**THE FISHERMAN AND HIS WIFE** Brothers Grimm, translated by Lucy Crane	**THANK YOU, M'AM** Langston Hughes
THE EMPEROR'S NEW CLOTHES Hans Christian Andersen	**THE BLACK HEART OF INDRI** Dorothy Hoge	**WISDOM'S WAGES AND FOLLY'S PAY** Howard Pyle
THREE BOYS WITH JUGS OF MOLASSES AND SECRET AMBITIONS Carl Sandburg	**THE OPEN ROAD** (from *The Wind in the Willows*) Kenneth Grahame	**THE DANCING PRINCESSES** Walter de la Mare

Grade 5	Grade 6	Grade 7
GHOST CAT Donna Hill	**THROUGH THE TUNNEL** Doris Lessing	**AT HER FATHER'S AND HER MOTHER'S PLACE** Natalya Baranskaya
THE TALE OF THE THREE STORYTELLERS James Kruss	**THE MYSTERIES OF THE CABALA** Isaac Bashevis Singer	**THE CAT AND THE COFFEE DRINKERS** Max Steele
MOWGLI'S BROTHERS (from *The Jungle Book*) Rudyard Kipling	**THE ALLIGATOR** John Updike	**ANNE FRANK: THE DIARY OF A YOUNG GIRL** (selection)

Grade 8	Grade 9
THE SUMMER OF THE BEAUTIFUL WHITE HORSE William Saroyan	**THE STRANGE CASE OF DR. JEKYLL AND MR. HYDE** Robert Louis Stevenson
RULES OF THE GAME (from *The Joy Luck Club*) Amy Tan	**THE IDEALIST** Frank O'Connor
HIGH SCHOOL GRADUATION (from *I Know Why the Caged Bird Sings*) Maya Angelou	**THE TIME MACHINE** H. G. Wells

Table 7-2. Reading Activities

Session Number	General Activity	Grade-Level Modification
1	Selection introduction; first reading and sharing initial responses, reactions, and questions.	Read-aloud and interpretive art activity for kindergartners and first-grade students; writing down initial questions about the story and reading them.
2	Additional reading of literary selection; note taking in response to specific directives or by indicating ideas in text margins; writing interpretive questions.	For kindergartners to second graders, a second reading of the selection and sharing answers to questions raised at home.
3	Interpreting new vocabulary words in context; sharing responses, questions, and notes.	For upper grades, preparing a textual analysis of a passage for homework. For earlier grades, a dramatization of a selection may occur.
4	Shared inquiry discussion with analysis of text occurring as well.	Questioning, dialogue among students, and raising assumptions to questions are key components across grade levels.
5	Writing, creative activities, artwork, dramatizations, and/or evaluative discussion of a selection.	Creative writing, personal or evaluative essays, and engaging in steps of the writing process for grades 2–9.

The foundation describes three levels of questioning:

- *Factual questions* are aimed at eliciting one correct answer that can be verified by what the author has noted in the work; the basic *who, what, where,* and *when* are the menu here.
- *Interpretive questions* can elicit more than one answer that can also be supported by evidence from the reading; the *why* and *how* questions come into play here.
- *Evaluative questions* ask readers to decide whether they agree or disagree with the author's ideas and story meanings. These evaluative judgments are weighed against the readers' own background experiences, cognitive and affective beliefs, and values. A prompt such as "Why do you think that . . ." would undoubtedly elicit this level of thinking.

Another way that questions may be planned are before reading, during reading, and after reading. This will be discussed later. Additional information regarding the Junior Great Books can be found on the foundation's Web site (see Additional Resources at the end of this chapter).

Literature Circles

A highly popular grouping arrangement that surfaced in the 1990s and continues to be highly favored today for literary readings is the literature circle. Authentic children's literature packaged as trade books continues to be the major vehicle for circle activities, but informational books, poems, newspaper articles, and even recipes have been used to initiate and engage a circle discussion, reading, and writing

(Brabham & Villaume, 2000; Gilbert 2000). An article downloaded from the Internet presenting a controversial topic would also serve as a nice text vehicle for this group activity. Generally, teachers select and use sets of trade books are related to themes, genres, or authors that students are learning about at a particular time in the curriculum sequence (Brabham & Villaume, 2000). It is important, however, that students be allowed to choose from the offerings provided, and if only some text-sets of books are available, teachers may have students rank the books they wish to read.

Immersing children in the world of good literature is one major goal of literature circles; a second goal is to create a community of learners. Because a circle is a cooperative group arrangement, students learn from one another as they discuss, reflect upon, and react to a reading. A classroom community is created in which teams work and equality of voice is established (Gilbert, 2000; King, 2001). Roles are assigned, and rules—as in any other cooperative group situation—guide the social and democratic etiquette of the circle activity.

How does the circle work? Literature circles, also known as literature discussion groups, are based on the concept of the "grand conversation" (Peterson & Eeds, 1990). In grand conversations about the same book, participants discuss and reflect on what they have read and gain insights and interpretations from others. Generally, four or five students make up one literature circle or discussion group, but the number may be as small as two students and as large as eight (Brabham & Villaume, 2000; Burns, 1998; Hill, Noe, & Johnson, 2002). The number of students per circle group may also be governed by the number of books in each text-set.

Thus one can see that there are some issues to face in forming circle groups and deciding what to read. First there is the issue of the topic, theme, genre, or author to be studied, along with what books are available at the time of study. Ideally, six to nine books constituting many text-sets, would be available, but this might not be the case. There might be four books related to one title, three to another, and six to another.

Second, there's the issue of student choice. Self-choice and student initiative are two of the major factors in literature circle groups, according to Daniels (1994, 2002), a recognized spokesman for the literature circle concept. Students have to choose from what the teacher has available. Many books means many choices; few books means less choice for students. One way to choose is to prepare a voting procedure based on the books available to be read (Steineke, 2002). The teacher could prepare a voting form with three or four columns. One column would name the *title* of the book; one the *author*; one would be labeled *comments*; and the final one, *book's ranking*. The teacher distributes the ballot sheets to be signed by each student, gives a quick overview or description of each book, and distributes copies of the books so that students can take a peek at the contents. While the book talk is going on, students can jot down notes in the comments column. Finally, in the ranking column, students indicate the order in which they would like to read the books.

Gilbert (2000) indicates that after she has completed such an "advertising and marketing campaign" and students indicate their choices, she still has a bit of difficulty forming the groups. She can't always give a student his or her first choice, but she tries to ensure that each gets a book from the top three choices and a book that she thinks the student would like. When intermediate-grade students have their personal preferences met in what they read, they are more apt to make a stronger commitment to get the reading done well (Worthy, Broaddus, & Ivey, 2001).

The balloting procedure is one way to ensure that students form groups based on interests and choice. In this way, diversity will be encouraged and students of different reading abilities and levels will be in each group. Lenski and Nierstheimer (2004) indicate that many students prefer to form groups around friendship ties rather than by interest in a particular book. Although such groupings can yield productive results, the teacher should consider if these students will really work well together or not.

Book selection and forming the circle grouping are two aspects of the activity, but the discussion and mental engagement that follows might be the most important part. Most teacher practitioners (as we noted with the kidstation structure) recommend that a good amount of time—probably several weeks—be spent modeling and preparing students to sustain discussion on their own. Activities such as how to engage in respectful group work, how to ask predictive and probing questions, how to brainstorm and reflect upon ideas suggested by the author, how to tackle the meaning of unknown words, how to respond in writing or artwork to story ideas, and how to share written work help students to prepare for the various circle roles and jobs (Gilbert, 2000; Lenski & Nierstheimer, 2004; Peralta-Nash & Dutch, 2000). It is also important that the literature selections themselves deal with actual issues and experiences that encourage reflection, discussion, questioning, and thoughtfulness (Brabham & Villaume, 2000). The talk generated from the literacy reading is student stimulated and student driven and may be made sustainable by the implementation of particular procedures.

One way to involve students who may be reluctant to participate, who are shy, and who are not predisposed to a lot of verbal discussion is to use a "fishbowl" technique. Kong and Fitch (2002–2003) use this practice to involve culturally and linguistically diverse learners in book discussions and readings. One group of students who are knowledgeable in circle procedures may discuss a book while those who would profit from the modeling provided by their peers watch and listen, or one group could discuss a book in front of the class while a few empty "guest" chairs are used to invite class members to join in and participate. Bell (2002–2003) suggests that to help at-risk students participate in questioning and discussing, students' names could be noted on cards or popsicle sticks and placed into a container such as a real fishbowl. As names are drawn randomly, students become active voices in the activity, and their interest and attention should continue to remain focused as their names are put back into the fishbowl.

Students' roles and routines during the circle conversations may be informal or structured. Students may formulate their own questions as they read, jot down ideas on sticky notes and attach them to relevant book pages, write responses in a journal, or create a graphic organizer, picture, or other type of visualization about their thoughts. Gilbert (2000) suggests that one way to obtain user-friendly, informal written responses is to use a teacher-prepared bookmark. On the bookmark students could write words they like, words they would like to know the meaning of, questions raised during the reading, and connections they made to ideas generated by the reading and connected to their own life experiences. Whitin (2002) likes to use a sketching strategy in which her students reveal what a story aspect means to them by sketching lines, colors, shapes, symbols, or pictures. She is quick to add that the sketching idea is not the same activity as drawing a favorite part of a story. The drawing is more likely to be a literal interpretation, whereas the sketch is abstract and metaphorical in nature. Children need to be able to tell or write about how their sketch relates to the meaning of the story. These engaging activities may certainly be suitable for a kidstation as well.

More formal structural procedures may be followed to guide students to take responsibility for their own conversation and reflective talk. Seven such roles have been identified, but they may be collapsed and combined to match a fewer number of participants in a literature circle group. Table 7-3 provides the names and a short description of the seven possible roles described by users of the literature circle procedure (Burns, 1998; Daniels, 1994, 2002; Peralta-Nash & Dutch, 2000; Schneider, 2000).

Table 7-3. Roles and Activities in Literature Circle Groups

Role	Responsibility	Questioning Prompt(s)
Discussion Director	The role of the discussion director is to provide a small set of provocative questions to generate interesting conversation. The questions should be directed to elicit high levels of thinking such as at the interpretive and evaluative levels.	Questions could begin with such prompts as *why, how, what do you think,* and *if.*
Illustrator	The illustrator creates some kind of picture or visual representation relating to the reading. The picture could be of a scene, a character, or even a feeling obtained from the reading. The group members take turns discussing the meaning of the picture.	"What feelings or meaning do you get from this picture as it relates to the story?"
Vocabulary Enricher	This group member looks for important meaning-bearing words in the day's reading and also makes note of unfamiliar or puzzling words. The words are presented and discussed when the groups meets.	"What do we think this word means as used by the author on page ____?"
Literacy Luminary or Passage Picker	This student finds short sections of the reading to read aloud because he or she thinks these are the most interesting, most important, most revealing, or will provide a good laugh. These passages could be read aloud by group members and discussed as to their effectiveness in the overall reading.	"Why do you think this passage was selected to be read?"
Summarizer	The student summarizes the reading and presents the summary to the circle group.	"Is there anything else we should add to the summary?"
Connector	The connector's role is to determine what connections can be made between aspects of the reading and other events, people, places, or a book that was read in the past or is being currently read.	"What occurred in today's reading that helped you make a connection to your own experience?"
Quotation Chooser	If the reading contains speaking characters, the quotation chooser selects dialogue from various characters. The group members then identify the appropriate character when the quotation is read.	"Which character spoke these lines?"

The role of the quotation chooser could be assumed by the literacy luminary, since specific sections of the reading have to be located. The discussion director could summarize the selection before beginning the thought-provoking questions. Even though students are assigned specific roles, any member of the group may raise issues, questions, or comments that belong to someone else's temporary role domain.

For instance, one member who isn't the vocabulary enricher may ask to have a word meaning clarified, and another, who is not the group's connector, may make a personal link to his or her life to share with the group.

Assignment pages or role sheets could be created for each role and serve as supports or scaffolds to help students fulfill the mental activity associated with each job. For instance, the discussion director might be provided with a page containing a short job description, model questions, and blank lines where actual questions would be written. The vocabulary enricher might have a columned page on which new and unique words could be listed, their contextual usage recorded, and their definitions written. However, Daniels (2002), one of the original creators of such assignment pages, indicates that using the role sheets for too long a period may actually limit the conversation and ideas generated about a literary reading. In his work with students, he has observed that the pages rather than the reading become the center of their attention. They view the pages as busywork to be completed rapidly as part of an ongoing assignment and don't take the time to reflect on the reading. He suggests that the role sheets be placed face down and turned over by students only when they need a prompt or suggestion to sustain the literary discussion.

The teacher guides, models, and redirects group efforts by moving from group to group. The teacher might need to remind students of circle group etiquette and their job assignments for that day's reading. A literature circle observation form and a literature circle individual evaluation form could also be used by teachers to record group happenings, to assess each child's progress, and to assist in assigning grades (Gilbert, 2000). The evaluation forms might have a rating scale to indicate how a child performed during each circle role.

In the procedure of assigned roles, students can meet in secondary groups after their own book has been discussed and examined. That is, all the discussion directors, connectors, illustrators, vocabulary enrichers, and so forth, meet to talk about the book their group read from the perspective of their assigned roles. Through this regrouping procedure, students learn of the books read by the other groups (Gunning, 2003). This second grouping allows a student who had a limited role in the initial group to "shine" more in the second group because of the learning and interaction gained from his or colleagues.

The Retelling Strategy

Retelling is a highly motivational and versatile way to authentically engage children in a literary reading. It is motivational because children use their own language and thought processes based on what they visualized and interpreted in an author's story. It is versatile for several reasons. First, it can be used repeatedly as a learning strategy. With each new story and each new author, the story line, language, and vocabulary changes. The language of instruction is prompted by the authors themselves as children weave new insights and word meanings into their own language patterns and understanding. Second, its versatility lies in the number of ways a retelling can be done. A story can be retold orally, artistically, through writing, through multimedia computer presentations, and through the creation of children's own books.

To retell something implies that one is telling something in the order it happened. If something is read, like a piece of literature, and it was being told to someone, the storyteller would want to keep the listener in the same suspenseful and plot-unfolding state as the original author did. When children retell an author's story, they reconstruct the story in their minds using their own language as well as the newly learned words of the author. Retelling, therefore, can be cast as a verbal, artistic, and written reconstruction of an author's story in the children's own words and imagery. Because of this, teachers derive insight into how children construct text in their minds, which allows teachers to witness and analyze comprehension as it occurs (Richek, Caldwell, Jennings, & Lerner, 2002).

Through retelling, teachers can determine successful levels of literal and interpretive comprehension. Sinatra (2003) has shown that the retelling strategy can be highly successful in increasing children's word-reading mastery and vocabulary development. We also advocate its use with literature because it encourages writing, artwork, and multiple drafts. We saw earlier how a retelling was accomplished through a film-frame technique and how one student numbered her visual scenes to match what she was retelling through writing.

A variation of the film-frame layout that we have used over the years to elicit a first-draft retelling effort is a simple story map. The teacher (or students) prepares the map by using sheets of standard copy paper, either 8 ½ x 11 or 8 ½ x 14, with a division down the middle. Two or three inches are left on top of the page so that students can write their names as "retold authors"; the title, author, and illustrator of the book they are retelling; and any other information desired by the teacher. Students have the rest of the blank page to make pictures and writing panels. With a ruler, three or four equal sections are marked off down the page. Students then have a page layout with picture panels on the left and writing panels on the right.

When retelling a story through artwork and writing, children shouldn't be limited to the number of panels shown on the one page. Many children need two pages or even six, seven, or eight panels to retell the story in writing and with their imaginative artwork. We believe this elaboration is a good thing. With a little guidance and encouragement from the teacher, students are writing more, writing in a cohesive way by following the story line shown in their pictures, and embedding some of the author's new words in their own sentences. A major strength of the mapping or film-frame strategy is that it enhances the development of writing, especially for students who are reluctant to write. We can see this colorful involvement in young Brian's six-panel retelling of *Corduroy* (Freeman, 1976), shown in Figure 7-5.

We generally suggest that students do the picture panels first. The teacher might have to lead students through this thinking by initially asking, "How do you see the events of this story happening? What important event happened first?" After they talk about the first major event, the teacher might say, "Now, how would you draw that idea in the first picture box?" Next the teacher would say, "What happens next? How might that be drawn?" The teacher would proceed this way until the number of visualizations are completed.

Students may look at the artist's illustrations or visualize the events in their minds. The number of picture panels produced by any one student depends on the richness of the student's imagination, his or her ability to draw, and the teacher's purpose in having the student create this draft. The major point is that for each picture panel produced, there will be accompanying written text to match the ideas generated in the picture. Some teachers, especially those of primary-grade children, create a graphic figure or an icon to represent the selection the children will retell. So *Lovable Lyle* (Waber, 1977) or *Playing Right Field* (Welch, 2000), for example, could be represented by an outline of a crocodile or a baseball glove, respectively, appearing down one or both columns of a prepared page.

The teacher should consider the whole process of story writing achieved with the picture panel maps as a "first draft." In other words, the best of authentic literacy engagement is yet to come. With a

Figure 7-5. Brian's Story Map

first draft accomplished in a fun way, the students will be motivated to do the next, "publishable" draft as either a retold book or a computer project. The teacher might then downplay the energy and creativity the children put into their initial artwork by telling children to make simple drawings using stick figures and a little coloring.

After the teacher has conferenced with each student about the first-draft story map plan, the student is ready to make a "retold book." With computers and appropriate software such as Hyper Studio, Inspiration or Kidspiration, Kid Works Deluxe, or Microsoft PowerPoint, students can use clip art and draw, color, and enter their own customized text on each card, page, or slide of their combined visual and written presentation. Without these resources, the retold book can be made the "old-fashioned" fun way, with construction paper, glue, tape, markers, and scissors. Books can be made in the shape of a story character (a shape book); in a pullout, accordion format (an accordion book); or with pop-up characters (a pop-up book). The procedures and materials needed to construct 12 different retold books can be found in Sinatra (2003).

Don't think that making retold books is just for young students and emergent readers. Elementary-level and intermediate-grade students enjoy them just as well. A wise teacher knows that students' anticipation of creating their own books, which are often displayed in the classroom, hallway, cafeteria, and auditorium, becomes a high motivator for eliciting each student's best work. That's why it's best to collect a first draft with the story maps to determine how many written panels with accompanying artwork will be forthcoming. Students are also more apt to heed the teacher's revision and editing suggestions made with the first draft because they realize that other students, and sometimes parents and other teachers, will see their works.

Teachers can also be creative by encouraging a retelling format that matches the motif of the literature selection. In a picture below (right), 7-year-old Lerato shines with glee as she pulls up her accordion panels that retell the story of *Playing Right Field* (Welch, 2000). Her teacher, Theresa Connell, had made a template of a baseball glove, held down with Lerato's right hand on the desk; a picture of a baseball, on which was written the book's name, author, and who was the reteller; and a pleated strip of construction paper, on which was written the retold story. In the other picture, 10-year-old Rodney places another leaf on the group's tree. On each leaf is written a student's retelling of *The Great Kapok Tree* (Cherry, 1990).

For the delightful story of *The Other Side* (Woodson, 2001), about a black and a white girl who try to befriend each other during the days of segregation, students wrote their retold version on the panels of a picket fence. In the story, a fence separated the two families. For *Princess Pooh* (Muldoon, 1989), about two sisters, one confined to a wheelchair and the other jealous because of the attention her sister receives, the teacher constructed a paper hat with a crown and stars. On the hat students wrote their own names, such as "Prince Rubin" or "Princess Yvonne," and attached a scrolled letter written to the jealous sister, Patty Jean, as they assumed the role of a friendly character. Reading what fifth grader Rubin Quick wrote (Figure 7-6), one can sense that he understood and was able to convey his understanding through writing.

Retellings are a strong way to involve groups of students in a total literacy event. The verbal is fused with the nonverbal, and background knowledge of the narrative is connected to the new story. Visual art helps to stimulate the verbal account that students write as they sequence the events of the plot. They utilize new and unusual words offered by the author in their retellings. They write, revise, and edit to complete the drafts of their works as apprentice authors. Others read what the apprentice author wrote, making the entire process of one retold book a highly pleasurable and authentic literary experience.

Figure 7-6. Rubin's Letter

The Use of Story Mapping to Portray Narrative Structure

Story maps are used to graphically represent the structure of stories and to display the connection of story grammar elements. This section returns us in a practical and strategic way to the discussion earlier in this chapter on the structural elements of literature and story grammar analysis. The use of story maps also supports two of the seven National Reading Panel's recommendations (2000) to improve reading comprehension by (a) making graphic representations of the material being read, and (b) learning the structure of stories as a means of remembering story content. Reading comprehension may be strengthened, because when meaning is represented by the use of mapping or a diagramming technique, a decision has been made about how to model memory or cognitive structure (Anderson & Huang, 1989).

Unfortunately, many teachers seem to use and reuse two graphic figures to represent information in both narrative and informational readings. These are the Venn diagram, showing two overlapping circles, and a topic development, or spider map, which expands from an inner figure to outer connected idea figures. The overuse of these two figures to represent the narrative style is unfortunate and even misleading, because they don't capture the thinking of chronological, chaining, and causal relationships. Authors and researchers have reported that students with and without learning problems have improved in reading understanding when they have used graphic story maps, have been shown how to chain events, and have used story grammar elements to map the structure of the narrative (Baumann & Bergerson, 1993; Johnson, Grahm, & Harris, 1997; Swanson & DeLaPez, 1998; Vacca & Vacca, 2002; Vallecorsa & deBettencourt, 1997).

When using story maps to represent the structure of the narrative, the teacher should consider adhering to the basic structural "glue" of chronology (sequencing) and causality implied in the terms *episodes* and *patterns*. We noted earlier that a character's action causes a series of events or episodes to unfold. To be sure, the setting elements of time and place have a great bearing on the development of many stories, and according to Gordon and Braun's (1983) schematic representation, episodes are governed by the shifting of setting. Nevertheless, it is the unfolding of time that sets the plot in motion and carries the characters along with it as they themselves cause twists and turns in the episodes along the way. If students understand that stories have predictable patterns such as an introduction, a stage of events in the middle, and a resolution, their understanding of how to write stories following predictable patterns is greatly enhanced (Tompkins, 2003).

We pointed out earlier that there are variations in the patterns of plot sequence. Some stories move on in a sequence of events or in minor episodes without connections of causality or without a resolution, some have a circular or problem-solution format, and some have a dramatic turning point. Without causal interactions, however, the sense of conflict or tension becomes reduced. For instance, although there is some action in *Corduroy* (Freeman, 1976) as the little toy bear looks for his button in the department store, there is no sense of drama established after his introductory wish of hoping for someone to pick him out from the other toys and provide him with his own home. Figure 7-7 shows a type of story map that captures the movement of a story by episodes. Episodes occur as the setting shifts to make the connections in the story. Notice how 8-year-old Genisis has rewritten the episodes of the storybook *Arthur Makes the Team* (Brown, 1998).

A literary plot favorite is the introduction of a problem in the story's beginning followed by the unraveling of the problem as the main character solves it. This format often occurs in the circular, problem-solution pattern, a recurring structure of traditional folktales. Here a main character often leaves his or her original setting to seek or undertake something better, more profitable, or even spiritual; to overcome challenges; to perform some good; or to solve a problem for the community. The character, in a circular way, returns to the original locale having accomplished the goal or solved the problem and is often revealed as a changed, enlightened individual.

In Armstrong Sperry's *Call It Courage* (1990), the main character, Mafatu, has to overcome a problem of fear of the sea. Through a series of dramatic actions, some occurring in the sea, he returns home to be recognized as a brave member of his island peoples. In *Rosie's Story* (Gogoll, 1994), Rosie's problem was that she didn't want red hair and freckles because she wanted to look like the other children in her class. Her problem is resolved after she writes a story about a boy with red hair and freckles and reads it to her classmates. The other children realize that they have hurt Rosie's feelings, and they indicate that they won't tease her anymore. Third-grade Bria captures the essence of the story quite nicely in the schematic we use for a story with a problem-solving format. Notice that her story map (Figure 7-8) be-

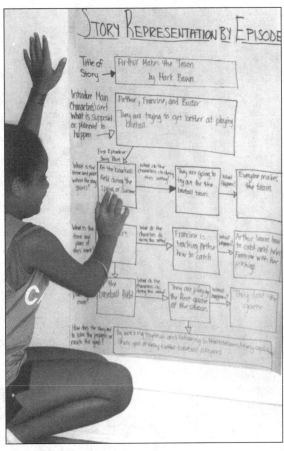

Figure 7-7. Genisis's Story Map

gins with the statement of the problem, accounts for the setting as an influence in the story line, allows her to enumerate the story action, and asks how the problem is resolved.

The traditional plot structure found in much of classical literature, and still a strong format in modern literary tales, is that of rising and falling action differentiated by the turning point. The rising action begins with the introduction, follows through with the drama and conflict of ever-building events, reaches a turning point and/or climax, and experiences a falling action during the resolution. We noted how this structure prevailed in *Cinderella* (Langer, 1974), *The Emperor's New Clothes* (Anderson, 1889/2001), and *Lovable Lyle* (Waber, 1977). This narrative structure usually engenders disharmony, tension, and action that heightens and holds the reader's interest.

The conflict arises as a central character, called the *protagonist,* struggles to overcome opposing forces, obstacles, or other characters, known as the *antagonists.* The protagonist initiates some action, often called a *starter action* or *precipitating event,* that pulls the protagonist into episodes of tension and conflict. Once propelled, the plot action begins to heighten or rise and continues rising until a peak or turning point is reached. The turning point, also referred to as the *climax* of the action, is followed by a fairly rapid falling action, known as the *denouement.* During the falling plot action, most of the subplots, involving character intrigue and conflict, are often resolved with successful outcomes, and an overall resolution of the protagonist's problem occurs. Once the central conflict and minor

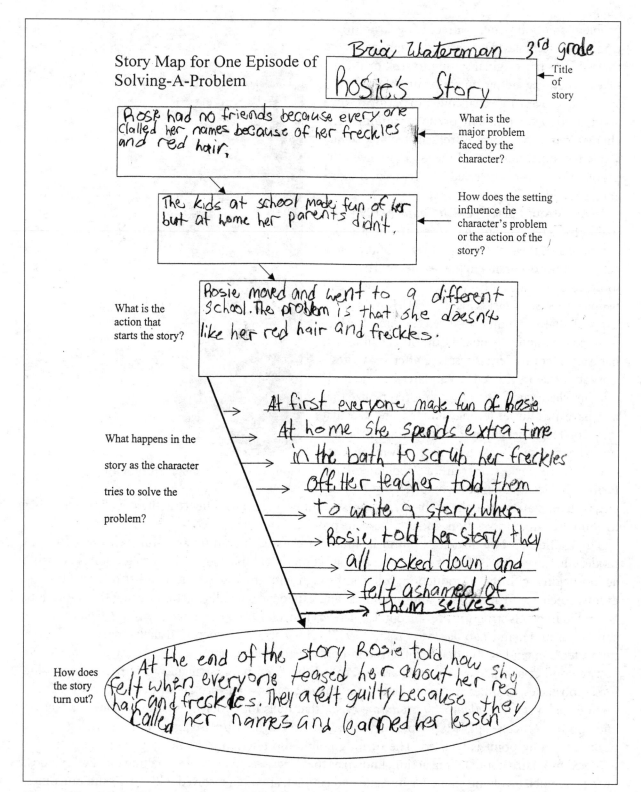

Story Map for One Episode of Solving-A-Problem

Bria Waterman   3rd grade

Rosie's Story   Title of story

Rose had no friends because every one clalled her names because of her freckles and red hair.

What is the major problem faced by the character?

The kids at school made fun of her but at home her parents didn't.

How does the setting influence the character's problem or the action of the story?

What is the action that starts the story?

Rosie moved and went to a different school. The problem is that she doesn't like her red hair and freckles.

What happens in the story as the character tries to solve the problem?

At first everyone made fun of Rosie. At home she spends extra time in the bath to scrub her freckles off. Her teacher told them to write a story. When Rosie told her story they all looked down and felt ashamed of them selves.

How does the story turn out?

At the end of the story Rosie told how she felt when everyone teased her about her red hair and freckles. They a felt guilty because they called her names and learned her lesson

Figure 7-8. Bria's Map of *Rosie's Story*

arguments are resolved, the story ends, and a theme or message often emerges.

We are reminded of our early years in the middle school classroom and can still recall drawing this classical structure on the chalkboard. The rising action was drawn with an arrow that inclined gradually upwards almost the whole length of a chalkboard; the falling action was shown with a somewhat shortened downward arrow; and the turning point, labeled at the top of the chalkboard, was located at the apex of the two arrows. We would discuss as a class where to place particular major events, and students would come to the board to write these on the graphic map. Many years later, Robb (1989) indicated that she used the same visual model to teach her sixth graders the concepts of protagonist and antagonist in an effort to enrich their understanding and provide a framework for writing.

In recent years we have taken to using the map figure displayed in Figure 7-9 to portray the classical narrative structure of the rising and falling action. Notice the map being completed by Jennifer Barile on the literary selection *Princess Pooh* (Muldoon, 1989). Once again many of the features of story grammar are listed and serve as prompts for writing. So as not to force students' writing into the narrow turning-point apex, the turning-point arrow there provides a much more ample opportunity for students to express themselves in writing. The overall structure of the step motif in the story map with a turning-point event provides a nice, clear way for students to express and write their ideas.

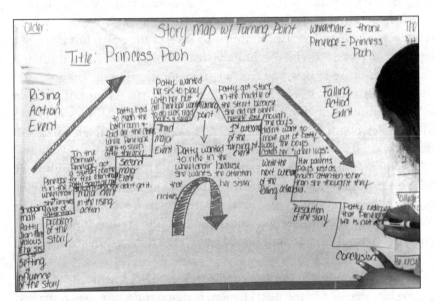

Figure 7-9. Story Map With Turning Point

We urge teachers to experiment with the narrative map structures described in this section to help students understand and compose their own works using differing macrostructure patterns. We also urge teachers to not use these structures statically! The maps are not an end in themselves, but the means to an end: helping students to comprehend the structure of a story. The maps have the common feature of focusing on plot and characters' involvement with action; their drawback is that they themselves don't help students attain interpretive, evaluative, and reflective levels of thinking. These levels of thinking occur through the discussion and questioning activity found in the Junior Great Books inquiry approach, participation in the literature circle roles, and the classroom reader response model presented in Chapter 6.

The maps can also be used interchangeably. Remember, they are representations of stories; they are idea structures. What one teacher might see as a character's problem, thus preferring to use a problem-solution map, another will visualize as a starter action, thus preferring that students examine the concept of a turning-point event. The teacher will witness much genuine student involvement with various map use. Students' pens, pencils, and erasers are constantly moving. They look back at their reading selections to check ideas and translate these ideas to add to their maps. They use writing to reveal their reading comprehension. By circulating among the children, the teacher can see how their thoughts and understanding are unfolding. Immediate teacher feedback can occur, asking individual students to clarify, redirect, or to examine a written statement more fully.

The teacher will be quite pleased when students begin to show the direction and depth of their thinking by placing their own arrows, connections, and figures on a teacher-presented map. Their graphic contributions with accompanying text reveal idea components. When students reveal ideas through mapping or other graphic representations, they have made conscious decisions to show how information connects to what they know.

The Directed Reading and Thinking Activity

The directed reading and thinking activity (DRTA) is one format for a guided reading procedure in which the teacher establishes an instructional plan for directing students through a reading with preselected segments. The teacher sets the plan for the reading and directs the plan, but does not directly teach the literary elements of the piece. As with the Junior Great Books inquiry approach and the active engagement model of the literature circles, the teacher uses questioning, discussion, and curiosity to involve students reflectively in a reading. The teacher's goal is to engage groups of children in deep, meaningful reading by stimulating their thinking through the liberal use of questions and subsequent discussion. Credited to Russell Stauffer (1969), the DRTA is a way to direct the reading and thinking process by capitalizing on children's curiosity and desire to inquire.

Many authors suggest that the DRTA could be used for stories in published basal or anthology reading series, trade books, and with expository, informational readings (Burns, Roe, & Ross, 1999; Vacca & Vacca, 2002). We suggest, however, that this guided reading strategy is a key one to use with literature-based selections. It flows in waves of curiosity and understanding, just as a reading at home might occur with parent and child. Its naturalism and authentic flow makes it refreshing to use with narrative-based selections.

A second consideration is offered by Gunning (2003), who compares the DRTA with the directed reading activity (DRA). The DRA, to be discussed in the next chapter, is much more teacher controlled and requires direct teaching, while the DRTA is more student oriented and works well when students have background knowledge of a topic. With information already in their heads, students can make more credible predictions. Because students have internalized narrative structure from repeated exposure to stories, they can more readily make predictions and hypothesize about characters' actions and plot sequences.

The DRTA works in the following way. The teacher must plan how to accomplish the reading with a group of children. The teacher notes best places to divide the reading into appropriate segments. The key concept here is *appropriate*; it is not necessarily equated to the same number of pages in each segment.

Generally, a good way to segment a reading is by the structure of the narrative and the traditional way in which a story unfolds through episodes. The teacher could determine when the introduction ends and when the initiating event happens. From this point, the teacher would determine what happens next and if there is a consequence or resolution of this event. A natural halt could also occur at a character's reactions to an event, as he or she thinks about what happened or what to do next. When the story's resolution and conclusion is reached, a theme will possibly emerge. The teacher might have selected three (beginning, middle, end) segments or any number of logical stopping points at which to segment the reading. The teacher is more or less inserting "chapters" in a story or picture book. There is no right or wrong decision here to cause the teacher anxiety.

Once the segments are selected, the teacher plans for questioning. Questions can be modeled after various types of questioning formats. Recall from the discussion of the schema in the Junior Great Books inquiry approach that questions were categorized as being on three levels—factual, interpretive, and evaluative—to elicit higher levels of thinking. The foundation emphasized the need to provoke students' thinking with *why* and *how* questions to make them consider viewpoints at the interpretive and evaluative levels of understanding.

Two other formats might be used quite well in the context of the DRTA lesson. One has to do with the presentation of questions to coordinate with the timing of the reading, such as before, during, and after each segment, and the other has to do with the connection to story grammar. Many sources suggest that questions for reading comprehension may be categorized into four types: before reading, during reading, after reading, and metacognitive. The questions from each category may also elicit various levels of thinking, from low level to high level. Before-reading questions ask students to predict, anticipate, or become curious about the events that are soon to unfold or about characters that might have been introduced through discussion or a "picture walk." During-reading questions are designed to allow students to harmonize with the reading and to determine if they are following the literal, inferential, and creative clues laid down by the author. After-reading questions help students to summarize, reflect, empathize, transfer, and react to interactions, sensations, and ideas prompted by the reading. Metacognitive questions ask students how and why a particular reading could influence them or others. Table 7-4 provides a list of questions for each category that might assist the teacher in planning for the reading segments.

One way to moderate the pace of the reading is to place student predictions on the chalkboard or chart paper. Predictions can be checked by confirming with the text. Encouraging looking back to confirm answers with retrospective questions is a valued thinking strategy of skillful reading.

Another type of thinking that is unique to the DRTA procedure is figuring out unknown words in context. With the DRA guided reading format the vocabulary is generally presented and discussed before the reading, whereas with the DRTA format the vocabulary is discussed as the author presents it, in context. In literature, authors use words in rich and creative ways, so students have the opportunity to sense how a word was used in a particular way in a particular context. A general question posed by the teacher might be, "What do you think this word means in this sentence [or paragraph or page]?" followed by "Why do you think so?" As students discuss the possible meaning of the new word, the teacher could also ask if the author provided other words in the context that might act as clues to help figure out the unknown word. The bookmark suggested earlier by Gilbert (2000) might be used by children as they write down their new words and their page location.

The DRTA provides a lively, engaging way to do a literary reading with a group of children. With sustained guidance and direction provided by the teacher, children construct meaning as they actively process the reading through the give-and-take talk of discussion and questioning. The teacher should not construct a set of pat questions for each segment, running through them in order to get to the next set of questions for the next segment. The teacher should plan questions that generally apply to any

Table 7-4. Questions to Promote Reading Comprehension During Three Stages of a Literary Reading

This guide may be used by teachers to motivate students' reading comprehension during three stages of the reading process. Some questions may be relocated and used during other stages.

Before-Reading Questions	During-Reading Questions	After-Reading Questions
• What does the title tell us about the selection?	• Has what you read made sense so far? Tell me how.	• What did you learn from this story? Was it interesting?
• Is the title interesting? Why?	• What do you think might happen in the next part? Why?	• What did you like or not like about this story?
• What do the pictures tell us?	• Are there any clues so far that might help us predict events in the whole story?	• Can you complete your story map and fill in the appropriate places with the information?
• What do the pictures remind you of?	• Can you tell me what you liked so far?	• What are your reactions to the story, the characters, or the structure of the story?
• Why do you think the author might have written this story?	• What would you wish might happen? Why?	• What can you write about now that the story is complete?
• When do you think this story took place? Why? How do you know?	• What have you found most interesting?	• What do you think the theme or moral of the story is? Why did the author write this? Was he or she trying to teach us something?
• What do you think might happen first in the beginning of the story? Why?	• Did you find some words that were difficult to read? Let's find them.	• Could you change the ending to allow the story to end in a different way? Tell me about it.
• What is the story's setting? How might this setting influence the story?	• Can you see in your mind the events of the plot?	• What do you think the author's purpose was in writing this story?
	• Who are the characters in the story? What do you think of them?	
	• Do they remind you of anyone you already know?	
	• Who do you think is the most important character? Why?	
	• What do you think is the character's problem?	
	• What are the problems faced by the other characters?	

literary reading and have these nearby as guideposts. The questions mainly serve to activate and sustain student thinking. The entire DRTA procedure is one way to encourage authentic, in-depth, and reflective engagement of a literary reading.

Writing Extensions and Interactions

Another reason we like the use of maps is that they are one way to set the stage for writing. Writing, as most teachers know, is a complex mental activity that requires a fair amount of time and effort by each individual student to produce a written piece equal to that student's competency level at that particular time in the student's life. The National Commission on Writing (2003) points out that even though the amount of time devoted to writing in school is quite low, the skills required to effectively get thoughts on paper are many. Students need to master the distinctions among the narrative, expository, and persuasive writing styles and develop a sense of voice in presenting these styles to audiences. They also need to master usage, mechanics, and presentation when they write sentences in the different styles. Also, the Commission adds, writing is a necessary means by which to show knowledge. In order to show that they understand, students must group details, rework the author's information and ideas into their own language, and communicate through writing the ideas and information they have internalized.

With the use of story maps, along with other map structures that represent expository writing styles (covered in the next chapter), students put their thoughts on paper. Besides that, the maps help students to organize their thoughts so that when the transition occurs from the map to the written paper or retold book, an organizational plan is established. In short, maps are one way to help students think and organize on paper before they write additional drafts showing a more polished effort. Indeed, as Emery (1996) indicated, story maps can effectively improve the comprehension of narratives because they provide concrete outlines, assist recall, show structural connections, and promote a means for active engagement.

We see these positive dimensions occurring repeatedly in children's written works. Earlier we showed third-grade Bria's map of *Rosie's Story*. For the question prompt "What is the action that starts the story?", Bria wrote, "Rosie moved and went to a different school. The problem is that she doesn't like her red hair and freckles." This is what five other children wrote in response to the same question prompt:

"She move to a new school. There were 17 kids in her class."

"The people made fun of her because she was different from them."

"She didn't like the way she looked. And she moved to a new school and people didn't like her."

"She was combing her hair and she saw that she had red hair and she didn't like her hair and freckles."

"The action is that Rosie was ugly with red hair and freckles that people made fun of her."

Although all six responses are somewhat different, there is a strong similarity among them in that they account for a structural element to initiate a story. Some of the students' responses might be more explicit in showing the understanding that Rosie notices she's different, as pointed out by the people in her new school setting. Another student would profit by showing a stronger connection between the 17 kids in her class and the move to a new school. Such is the nature of first-draft ideas from students. Because each student has revealed, through writing, his or her depth of understanding in response to the prompt, the teacher has the opportunity to assist the student in making stronger connections and extending thinking through writing.

Since maps serve to reveal a story plan, they become one way to show students' comprehension of a story. Once the plan is completed, we urge teachers to ask students to go on to the next draft—from the map plan to a written paper. The idea is to keep the pencil or pen flowing so that students' thinking becomes elaborated in the next writing attempt. When they transfer map ideas to their own written versions, students should fill in their own language with that of the original authors. Teachers can help students with voice change and audience perspective. This was done by Rubin's teacher, who asked students to write an account as a third-party prince or princess to Patty, the unhappy, jealous sister.

We noted that many research studies, literacy authors, and the National Reading Panel (2000) regard story mapping as a highly useful means to enhance reading understanding. Others suggest that mapping alone might not capture the full meaning of many stories. The strategy might not allow students to engage in thoughtful, inferential and reflective comprehension and might offer just one route to a story's meaning. To encourage a more robust story perspective, engage students in some of the following writing activities. They may help students reach these higher levels of understanding and reflection:

1. Students might consider the motives and perspectives of particular characters for those stories that reveal strong interactions and involvements among their characters (Emery, 1996). After students plot out the traditional story grammar features of the problem, subsequent events, and the resolution in a traditional sequential, story map format, they go back to consider different perspectives of characters to the written story events. This requires the formation of an extended story map with the events plotted out down the middle of the page and the characters' reactions and perspectives to the events written in the left and right columns of the page.

2. An alternate map model, called a *character perspective chart,* has been developed by two authors (Shanahan & Shanahan, 1997). In their chart, story grammar features are listed in columns down a page. For a literacy selection in which two or more characters have separate conflicting goals, students write answers to story grammar prompts. For instance, for the questions "What is the main character's problem?" or "What is the main character's goal?", students write answers that reflect the motives, viewpoints, and perspectives of the different main characters. The authors suggest that because readers are encouraged to enter the minds of the characters and consider the events of a story from alternative viewpoints, they gain a richer understanding of the story and its theme. By writing down the viewpoints of main characters to particular story events, students reveal how they perceive and feel about characters' motives and reactions to events in the story. Students also think and write about the story as a whole and not just from the perspective of a retelling or sequencing of events. A strategy such as viewing story events from the characters' perspectives sets the stage for many opportune and creative writing activities. Individuals or small groups of students could be asked to rewrite the story from each of the character's perspectives and present these stories back to the larger class group (a great Kidstation 3 activity!).

3 Another variation in charting the perspectives of a major character is offered by Friedman and Cataldo (2002). Their dilemma work sheet encourages reflective written comments from students. This is best done with a literacy selection in which the main character faces a dilemma or problem. Students first write the dilemma, then they write the choices that the character has in responding to the dilemma, along with the information and evidence that supports each choice. Responding to problems and choices in this way helps intermediate-grade students to vicariously experience and reflect on problems they themselves or others might face in the future.

4. An ongoing strategy to encourage writing as students read a literary selection is to use a cycle called the *transactional literature discussion* (Dugan, 1997). During or immediately after a reading, students' write their reactions and wonderings on self-stick notes. They can attach these notes at the appropriate parts in the selection and revisit these written comments after the entire reading. The comments can set the stage for a thoughtful whole-class discussion or can act as a springboard for a written paper or an extended response in a journal.

5. Teachers often ask us, "How can I help students to make inferences and draw conclusions?" One good way is to use the outline of a hand, with a character prompt on each finger. Recall from our earlier discussion in this chapter that authors often reveal information about characters in five or six ways (see page 204). One sixth-grade teacher, Jennifer Pecorella, had her group make implicit connections about the three main characters in Katie Couric's book *The Blue Ribbon Day* (2004). First she distributed three pieces of blank, unlined paper to each child. She asked each one to trace a somewhat widened outline of a hand on each paper. This step immediately gets children involved. She placed the character prompts on the chalkboard and had the children copy the prompts above the finger outline. Then each child had to work with each character in turn to answer the character prompts. This required careful rereading and analysis, most often at the inferential and implicit levels. In the palm of the hand, students then wrote a paragraph about the character, using the information displayed in the fingers. That paragraph is a good synthesizing thinking activity.

Conclusion and Connection to National Reports

This chapter has focused on the value and meaning in using quality children's literature in the literacy curriculum. We showed how written literature extends naturally from the oral tradition of storytelling, which is a prominent way that people of all cultures reveal how they think, live, believe, and imagine. When children retell stories as authors' apprentices, through artwork, storytelling, or through story mapping and writing, they engage in the tradition of telling and re-creating the story to pass on and share with others. Through these activities of mental engagement, children not only comprehend the literary work under current study but also add to their understanding that literature stimulates an inquisitive and imaginative mind.

Do the concepts and strategies presented in this chapter support the tenets of many national and state educational agencies seeking to improve literacy instruction and learning? We believe that they most certainly do. We noted that the National Reading Panel (2000) reported the use of story maps and the learning of story structure as strong ways to improve reading comprehension. This report was followed by the publication *Put Reading First: The Research Building Blocks for Teaching Children to Read* (Armbruster, Lehr, & Osborn, 2001), which noted that when students recognize the story structure categories of setting, initiating events, goals, attempts, internal reactions, and outcomes and how these become organized into plot, they experience greater appreciation, understanding, and memory for stories.

The National Commission on Writing (2003) later acknowledged that the writing of narratives was one of the styles students need to master, and they further suggested that this style should be considered a priority during the earliest years of schooling. In the early years, classroom practice should focus developmentally on drawing, talking, word engagement, pictures, and story writing.

Earlier in the 1990s, during the rise of the standards movement, the National Council of Teachers of English and the International Reading Association published their joint English language arts standards (NCTE & IRA, 1996), which, in turn, became elaborated by each of the many states. All 12 of the joint standards touch upon the domain of literature, but 5 noticeably connect to the following ideas in this chapter:

- Students should read a wide range of texts to build an understanding of themselves and other cultures, and for their personal enjoyment.

- Students should read a wide variety of literature of different genres and eras to better understand human experiences.

- Students should use their prior knowledge and experiences with literature to apply strategies to comprehend, interpret, evaluate, and appreciate texts.

- Students should apply their knowledge of language media techniques, figurative language, and genre to create and discuss texts.

- Students should develop an understanding of and respect for diversity in language use in different cultures, regions, ethnic groups, and social roles.

In the following chapter, we will continue the discussion of comprehending text and examine what agencies, government organizations, and national publications have reported about the value of informational text in our students' lives.

Anticipation Guide Revisited

After reading this chapter, confirm your initial predictions about each statement. List the page number that supports each response.

Statement	Agree	Disagree	Verification
1. Only when children enter school do they begin to learn how to tell stories through the oral language tradition.	_____	_____	_____
2. The oral storytelling tradition among peoples within cultures and countries formed the basis of the folklore of fables, myths, epics, and fairytales.	_____	_____	_____
3. Teachers can use pattern books and books of rhyme to help children learn a phonic element.	_____	_____	_____
4. In traditional plot structure, a precipitating event occurs to initiate conflict or tension, which serves as a catalyst for the development of the story.	_____	_____	_____
5. In good literature human values are often depicted and revealed to readers as characters work through their problems and challenges.	_____	_____	_____
6. Words used in the oral language are more vivid and rich than those used in written language.	_____	_____	_____
7. The basic premise of the Great Books method of shared inquiry is to engage the reader in literal comprehension.	_____	_____	_____
8. Story mapping, the graphic representation of content being read, has been recommended by a national panel as a means of improving reading comprehension.	_____	_____	_____

Additional Resources

Web Sites

Junior Great Books Foundation
www.greatbooks.org

Literature Circles
www.literaturecircles.com/article3.htm

Computer Software Programs

Inspiration and Kidspiration
www.inspiration.com

Kid Works DeLuxe
www.englishsoftware,com.au/writing/kidworks.htm

Hyper Studio
www.hyperstudio,com/hs4/index,htm/

Microsoft Power Point
www.microsoft.com/

National Reading Panel
www.nationalreadingpanel.org

National Commission on Writing
www.writingcommission.org/

Children's Literature Web Guide
www.ucalgary.ca/ndkbrown/

For Further Reflection

1. Have your children read a vivid and compelling children's literary work. After they've read it, ask them to translate their understanding and feelings into some visual representation, such as mobiles, visual art, puppetry, sculpture, or even drama. Your students can then present their revisualized work to the larger class group, sharing their expressive and aesthetic feelings.

2. Try the steps of the DRTA with a children's literature selection. Plan before-reading, during-reading, after-reading, and metacognitive questions for reading segments. See how your questions work as children provide their answers. Do your questions evoke the level of thinking accomplished through your questions? Next, coach children to create their own types of questions for ensuing reading segments.

References

Anderson, P. M. (1994). Great Books programs. In A. C. Purves (Ed.), *Encyclopedia of English studies and language arts* (pp. 545–547). New York: Scholastic.

Anderson, T. H., & Huang, S.C.C. (1989). *On using concept maps to access the comprehension effects of reading expository text* (Tech. Rep. No. 483). Urbana, IL: University of Illinois, Center for the Study of Reading.

Armbruster, B. B., Lehr, F., & Osborn, J. (2001). *Put reading first: The research building blocks for teaching children to read. Kindergarten through grade 3.* Jessup, MD: National Institute for Literacy.

Au, K. (1995). Following children's leads through talk story: Teachers and children work to construct themes. In N. L. Roser & M. G. Martinez (Eds.), *Book talk and beyond: Children and teachers respond to literature* (pp. 150–156). Newark, DE: International Reading Association.

Barone, T., Eeds, M., & Mason, K. (1995). Literature, the disciplines, and the lives of elementary school children. *Language Arts, 72,* 30–38.

Barzun, J. (with Ruth Wattenberg). (2002). Curing provincialism: A conversation with Jacques Barzun. *American Educator, 26* (6), 10–11.

Baumann, J., & Bergerson, B. (1993). Story map construction using children's literature: Effects on first graders' comprehension of central narrative elements. *Journal of Reading Behavior, 25,* 407–437.

Bell, L. (2002–2003). Strategies that close the gap. *Educational Leadership, 60,* 32–34.

Brabham, E. G., & Villaume, S. K. (2000). Questions and answers: Continuing conversations about literature circles. *The Reading Teacher, 54,* 278–280.

Burns, B. (1998). Changing the classroom climate with literature circles. *Journal of Adolescent & Adult Literacy, 42,* 124–129.

Burns, P., Roe, B., & Ross, E. (1999). *Teaching reading in today's elementary schools* (7th ed.). New York: Houghton Mifflin.

Daniels, H. (1994). *Literature circles: Voice and choice in the student-centered classroom.* Portland, ME: Stenhouse.

Daniels, H. (2002). *Literature circles: Voice and choice in book clubs & reading groups* (2nd ed.). Portland, ME: Stenhouse.

Dugan, J. (1997). Transactional literature discussion: Engaging students in the appreciation and understanding of literature. *The Reading Teacher, 51,* 86–96.

Eeds, M., & Peterson, R. (1995). What teachers need to know about the literary craft. In N. L. Roser & M. G. Martinez (Eds.), *Book talk and beyond: Children and teachers respond to literature* (pp. 10–23). Newark: DE: International Reading Association.

Emery, D. (1996). Helping readers comprehend stories from the characters' perspectives. *The Reading Teacher, 49,* 534–541.

Franklin, J. (2002). Structuring stories for meaning. *Nieman Reports, 56,* 43–45.

Freeman, E., & Person, D. G. (1998). *Connecting informational children's books with content area learning.* Boston: Allyn & Bacon.

Friedman, A., & Cataldo, C. (2002). Characters at crossroads: Reflective decision makers in contemporary Newbery books. *The Reading Teacher, 56,* 102–112.

Galda, L., & West, J. (1995). Exploring literature through drama. In N. L. Roser & M. G. Martinez (Eds.), *Book talk and beyond: Children and teachers respond to literature* (pp. 183–190). Newark, DE: International Reading Association.

Gilbert, L. (2000). Getting started: Using literature circles in the classroom. *Primary Voices K–6, 9,* 9–16.

Glazer, J. (2000). *Literature for young children* (4th ed.). Upper Saddle River, NJ: Merrill Prentice Hall.

Gordon, C., & Braun, C. (1983). Using story schema as an aid to reading and writing. *The Reading Teacher, 37,* 116–121.

Great Books Foundation. (1999). *An introduction to shared inquiry* (4th ed.). Chicago: Author.

Gunning, T. (2003). *Building literacy in the content areas.* Boston: Allyn & Bacon.

Hayward, D., & Schneider, P. (2000). Effectiveness of teaching story grammar knowledge to pre-school children with language impairment: An exploratory study. *Child Language Teaching and Therapy, 16,* 255–284.

Herrell, A. (2000). *Fifty strategies for teaching English language learners.* Upper Saddle River, NJ: Merrill Prentice Hall.

Hill, B. C., Noe, K. L., & Johnson, N. J. (2002). *Literature circle resource guide.* Norwood, MA: Christopher-Gordon.

Johnson, L., Grahm, S. & Harris, K. R. (1997). The effects of goal setting and self-instruction on learning a reading comprehension strategy: A study of students with learning disabilities. *Journal of Learning Disabilities, 30,* 80–91.

Keating, H. L., & Levy, W. (2001). *Lives through literature: A thematic anthology* (3rd ed.). Upper Saddle River, NJ: Merrill Prentice Hall.

Kilpatrick, W. (1993). The moral power of good stories. *American Educator, 17,* 24–35.

King, C. (2001). I like group reading because we can share ideas: The role of talk within the literature circle. *Reading, 35,* 32–36.

Kong, A., & Fitch, E. (2002–2003). Using book clubs to engage culturally and linguistically diverse learners in reading, writing, and talking about books. *The Reading Teacher, 56,* 352–362.

Langer, J. (1995). *Envisioning literature: Literary understanding and literature instruction.* New York: Teachers College Press.

Lenski, S. D., & Nierstheimer, S. L. (2004). *Becoming a teacher of reading: A developmental approach.* Upper Saddle River, NJ: Pearson.

Martinez, M., & Roser, N. (1995). The books make a difference in story talk. In N. L. Roser & M. G. Martinez (Eds.), *Book talk and beyond: Children and teachers respond to literature* (pp. 32–41). Newark, DE: International Reading Association.

National Commission on Writing. (2003). *The neglected "R": The need for a writing revolution.* Princeton, NJ: College Board.

National Council of Teachers of English (NCTE) & International Reading Association (IRA). (1996). *Standards for the English language arts.* Urbana, IL: Authors.

National Reading Panel. (2000). *Teaching children to read: An evidence-based assessment of the scientific literature on reading and its implications for reading.* Bethesda, MD: National Institute of Child Health and Human Development.

Norton, D. E. (2003). *Through the eyes of a child: An introduction to children's literature* (6th ed.). Upper Saddle River, NJ: Merrill Prentice Hall.

Peralta-Nash, C., & Dutch, J. (2000). Literature circles: Creating an environment for choice. *Primary Voices K–6, 8,* 29–37.

Peterson, C. (1993). Identifying referents and linking sentences cohesively in narration. *Discourse Processes, 16,* 507–524.

Peterson, R., & Eeds, M. (1990). *Grand conversation: Literature groups in action.* New York: Scholastic.

Pradl, G. M. (1994). Narratology. In A. C. Purves (Ed.), *Encyclopedia of English studies and language arts* (pp. 834–836). New York: Scholastic.

Richek, M. A., Caldwell, J. S., Jennings, J. H., & Lerner, J. W. (2002). *Reading problems: Assessment and teaching strategies* (4th ed.). Boston: Allyn & Bacon.

Robb, L. S. (1989). Mapping the "agonists." *The Reading Teacher, 42,* 549.

Rosenblatt, L. (1989). Writing and reading: The transactional theory. In J. Mason (Ed.), *Reading and writing connections* (pp. 153–176). Boston: Allyn & Bacon.

Rudman, M. K. (1995). *Children's literature: An issues approach* (3rd ed.). White Plains, NY: Longman.

Saltman, J. (1985). *The Riverside anthology of children's literature* (6th ed.). Boston: Houghton Mifflin.

Scharer, P. (1994). Trade books. In A. C. Purves (Ed.), *Encyclopedia of English studies and language arts* (pp. 1221–1222). New York: Scholastic.

Schneider, E. (2000). Shifting into high gear. *Educational Leadership, 58,* 57–60.

Shanahan, T., & Shanahan, S. (1997). Character perspective charting: Helping children to develop a more complete conception of story. *The Reading Teacher, 50,* 668–677.

Sinatra, R. (2003). *Word recognition and vocabulary understanding strategies for literacy success.* Norwood, MA: Christopher-Gordon.

Slavin, J. (1994). Genre. In A. C. Purves (Ed.), *Encyclopedia of English studies and language arts* (pp. 524–528). New York: Scholastic.

Smith, F. (1994). *Understanding reading: A psycholinguistic analysis of reading and learning to read* (5th ed.). Mahwah, NJ: Erlbaum.

Stauffer, R. (1969). *Teaching reading as a thinking process.* New York: Harper & Row.

Stein, N., & Glenn, C. (1977). An analysis of story comprehension in elementary school children. In R. Freedle (Ed.), *New directions in discourse processing: Multidisciplinary perspectives in discourse comprehension* (pp. 53–120). Hillsdale, NJ: Ablex.

Steineke, N. (2002). *Reading and writing together: Collaborative literacy in action*. Portsmouth, NH: Heinemann.

Swanson, P., & DeLaPaz, S. (1998). Teaching effective comprehension strategies to students with learning and reading disabilities. *Intervention in School and Clinic, 33,* 209–218.

Tompkins, G. E. (2003). *Literacy for the 21st century* (3rd ed.). Upper Saddle, NJ: Merrill Prentice Hall.

Vacca, R., & Vacca, J. (2002). *Content area reading: Literacy and learning across the curriculum* (7th ed.). Boston: Allyn & Bacon.

Vallecorsa, A. L., & deBettencourt, L. U. (1997). Using a mapping procedure to teach reading and writing skills to middle grade students with learning disabilities. *Education and Treatment of Children, 20,* 173–188.

VanDongen, R., & Westby, C. (1986). Building the narrative mode of thought through children's literature. *Topics in Language Disorders, 7,* 70–83.

Whitin, P. (2002). Leading into literature circles through the sketch-to-stretch strategy. *The Reading Teacher, 55,* 444–450.

Worthy, J., Broaddus, K., & Ivey, G. (2001). *Pathways to independence: Reading, writing, and learning in grades 3–8.* New York: Guilford Press.

Children's Literature

Aardema, V. (Retold by). (1975). *Why mosquitoes buzz in people's ears: A West African tale* (Leo and Diane Dillon, Illus.). New York: Dial Books.

Aardema, V., & Vidal, B. (Retold by). (1981). *Bringing the rain to Kapiti Plain: A Nandi tale.* New York: Penguin Books.

Aliki, C. E. (1995). *Tabby: A story in pictures.* New York: HarperCollins.

Andersen, H. C. (2001). *The emperor's new clothes.* Boston: Houghton Mifflin. (Original work published 1889)

Anthony, J. (1997). *The dandelion seed* (Chris Arbo, Illus.). Nevada City: CA: Dawn.

Bourgeois, P. (1995). *Franklin plays the game* (Brenda Clark, Illus.). New York: Scholastic.

Brigg, R. (1978). *The snowman.* New York: Random House.

Brown, M. (1998). *Arthur makes the team.* New York: Little, Brown.

Carle, E. (1977). *The grouchy ladybug.* New York: HarperCollins.

Cherry, L. (1990). *The great kapok tree: A tale of the Amazon Rain Forest.* Gulliver Books.

Couric, K. (2004). *The blue ribbon day.* New York: Doubleday.

Freeman, D. (1976). *Corduroy.* New York: Puffin Books.

Geisel, T. S. (Dr. Seuss). (1978). *I can read with my eyes shut!* New York: Beginner Books.

Gogoll, M. (1994). *Rosie's story.* New York: Mondo.

Langer, N. (Retold by). (1974). *Cinderella.* New York: Scholastic.

Langstaff, J. (1989). *Oh, a-hunting we will go.* Boston: Houghton Mifflin.

Martin, B. (1983). *Brown bear, brown bear, what do you see?* New York: Holt, Rinehart & Winston.

Muldoon, K. (1989). *Princess Pooh.* (Linda Shute, Illus.) Niles, IL: Whitman.

Onyefulu, I. (1997). *Chidi only likes blue: An African book of colors.* (Ifeoma Onyefulu, Photog.). New York: Cobblehill.

Paul, A. W. (1998). *Hello toes! Hello feet!* (Nadine Bernard Westcott, Illus.). New York: DK.

Scieszka, J. (1994). *Knights of the kitchen table (Time warp trio, 1)* (Lane Smith, Illus.). New York: Puffin.

Sperry, A. (1990). *Call it courage.* New York: Aladin.

Udave, C. (Retold by). (1999). Down by the bay (Consuelo Udave, Illus.). New York: Macmillan/McGraw-Hill.

Waber, B. (1977). *Lovable Lyle.* Boston: Houghton Mifflin Lorraine Books.

Welch, W. (2000). *Playing right field* (Marc Simont, Illus.). New York: Scholastic.

Williams, S. (1996). *I went walking* (Julie Vivas; Illus.). New York: Harcourt Books.

Woodson, J. (2001). *The other side.* New York: Putnam.

Chapter 8

Bridging the Layers of Informational Text

Anticipation Guide

Before reading this chapter, please read each of the statements listed below. Based upon your prior knowledge and experience with this chapter's topics, check either "agree" or "disagree" for each statement. After reading the chapter, see if your answers change in the Anticipation Guide Revisited found at the end of the chapter.

Statement	Agree	Disagree
1. The expository or informational style of writing is quite similar to the writing style of fiction or stories.	_____	_____
2. Such strategies as "questioning the author" and double-entry responses help students engage with informational text and reflect more deeply on the content.	_____	_____
3. A teacher's instructional style has little influence on how students learn informational content.	_____	_____
4. Background familiarity with particular content topics can influence how well they are understood during reading and how well students write about them.	_____	_____
5. Students' knowledge of word meanings has little bearing on how well they comprehend text.	_____	_____
6. Engaging students in authentic writing activities can assist the comprehension of content readings.	_____	_____
7. Students' perception of themselves and their intentions about learning have little influence on teachers' effectiveness during content instruction.	_____	_____
8. The directed reading activity (DRA) instructional format offers an efficient structure for engaging students reflectively in learning a content topic.	_____	_____

Introduction

In the last chapter we noted that prose writing consists of two text styles: fiction and nonfiction. Fiction asks readers to suspend their beliefs to engage in stories being woven by imaginative authors. Such stories also emerge out the natural tendency of peoples across cultures to tell about world events in ways that they could understand without the information supplied in later times that would account for such happenings. We saw in earlier chapters that the narrative, the fabric of fiction, is a major thinking process of even very young children.

Nonfiction, on the other hand, is grounded in reality. Its aim is to inform and explain. As people's knowledge of world happenings expanded through exploration, research, and experimentation, they were able to explain events to others based on evidence and factual accounts. So instead of reading stories that fantasized what air was made of or how the heavenly bodies came to be, readers could gain information written by others who actually studied these phenomena and who believed they were explaining the actual workings of them. This chapter examines the structure and style of informational text, why success in the reading and writing of informational text is important to achieve in school and in society, and some ways that teachers can help students succeed with this style.

What Informational Text Offers

Informational text is also known as expository text, and in the classroom arena, it is the reading and writing style most often associated with the content area disciplines of social studies, science, mathematics, the arts, health, and religion. Students need to master this informational text style, which is also the style of most computer programs and the Internet, to achieve success in the learning of the content disciplines while in school and beyond.

This literacy style is closest to what is needed to achieve success in the workplace as well (McKenna & Robinson, 2002). Work-type reading is what the schools should offer to help students become adults who can survive in modern-day society. Schools should not rely too much on the teaching of the narrative style and of literature, but instead should emphasize how to read math story problems and science and social studies texts to fulfill adult literacy needs (Venezky, 2000). One's thinking is strongly influenced by informational reading because facts and ideas become approachable through print (Moore, Moore, Cunningham, & Cunningham, 2003). Thus, people's beliefs and ideals are shaped by what is gained through expository reading and by how this connects to what was known in the past.

The informational text style is so important to master in highly literate and technological societies, but many students through the elementary school years and well beyond have difficulty with this discourse style. Problems arise with understanding content and how to write about it, and researchers have provided us with a number of reasons why informational text is a problematic text style for many. In general, expository reading materials often bring unfamiliar information, concepts, and terms to readers; present a writing style unlike that of the familiar narrative; and ask students to use the readings in particular ways, such as to remember great quantities of information or to accomplish written projects or experiments (Readence & Moore, 1994). Let's examine why difficulties with the expository style persist and explore some ways that teachers can assist students in achieving greater success with reading and writing in this style.

A Shift in Text Style

As children leave the third grade, they begin to do more reading in content textbooks, and it is at the fourth-grade level that many students begin to experience reading difficulties (Freeman & Person, 1998). These difficulties begin to emerge because of the shift in text style, which requires a great deal of knowledge intake from the various content disciplines coupled with a concomitant movement away from the recognizable narrative focus. We pointed out in previous chapters that the narrative story structure complements how children think and carry out their everyday lives.

Furthermore, a compelling aspect of stories told through the familiar narrative structure is the ability to imagine or visualize events as characters play them out in scenes. Writers of works of literature wish to engage their readers in an unfolding story and therefore choose their words and sentence patterns to make the characters and actions come alive on the printed page. Readers become engaged in such stories as they surrender their minds, visualizations, and emotions to the literary style of the author. Although the imagery generated during the reading of literature is prompted by the text itself, readers also extend and elaborate on the meaning and generate images consistent with their prior experiences and intense involvement with the story (Enciso, 1994).

What happens with informational readings, particularly if the topic is far removed from the experience of the reader, is that the mind can't see what's coming. The mind can't generate mental pictures to connect ideas on such topics as matter, weather fronts, or photosynthesis unless the mind has participated in previous learning or experiential encounters. Three additional qualities distinguish the narrative from expository text (Feathers, 1998). The first is point of view. A story is usually told from a character's first-person or the author's third-person perspective. Informational text lacks this familiar point of view. Instead, readers have to make their own inferences, predictions, and judgments without the help of a narrator. The second quality is the orientation of the content itself. In a narrative, a character does something that is based on what could happen in real life. Readers can identify with the characters and the actions because they have the background experience for the narrative orientation. With informational text, the reader has to orient him- or herself to the subject matter at hand, for which background knowledge is often lacking. The third quality concerns how the text ideas are connected. In a narrative, the unfolding of time occurs and the text moves on in a sequential and causal process. Although the writing of history is often based on relating sequential events, other text styles not familiar to readers might be used by authors. We'll examine these text styles later in this chapter.

We know that expository text is more demanding to most readers because of its text format, unique content, specific vocabulary, and topic unfamiliarity. Commenting on the 1998 *Nation's Report Card in Reading*, published by the National Assessment of Educational Progress (NAEP), in which 26% of eighth graders in American schools were performing below the basic level of reading, one author noted that poor reading comprehension has been identified as the major handicap of most struggling readers in the nation's middle schools (Allen, 2000). In this regard, Andrea Guillaume (1998) maintains that because reading content provides knowledge power, primary-grade children should be shown how to "read to learn" through informational text readings and not be deprived of such text because the prevailing mentality is that they must "learn how to read" first.

The Textbook as the Information Source

The content area textbook remains the main ingredient in students' information repertoire beyond the primary grades, and reading assignments are based almost exclusively on textbook readings (Vacca & Vacca, 2002). By 1997 the consensus was that textbooks were the sole instructional resource in 75% to 90% of classrooms in the United States (Palmer, 1997).

This reliance on conventionally bound print material might be due to the way that teachers remember being educated. By and large, teachers are capable and fluent readers. Textbook reading is what they remember worked for them, so they're passing on what worked. Yet Ruddell (2005) describes our textbook experiences in a not-too-memorable way. Sometime after fourth grade, the books become larger and longer, colorful pictures begin to disappear, print becomes smaller, densely packed readings begin to appear, and textbook readings are assigned for homework. Venezky (2000) adds that by sixth grade more than 75% of the reading material the child faces in school is not fiction in the basal reading series but rather nonnarrative and informational readings. By the middle grades, children need to gain meaning from science, social studies, and math texts as well as from other informational materials, often through computer interfaces, to be able to cope with the same text styles that the average adult must face.

Textbooks are generally used by teachers in two major ways: as the sole text of a content course or as a sourcebook. As a sourcebook, a text is used more flexibly by the teacher, who often selects readings in a particular way or order to meet the needs of students. The teacher might select segments out of page order and supplement the content reading with other informational sources. This might occur, for instance, when the teacher thinks it is necessary to cover content related to state standards in which students will soon be tested. Furthermore, when other informational text sources are used to augment and provide variety to a social studies textbook, for example, alternative accounts and interpretations of past historical events are provided (Zemelman, Daniels, & Hyde, 1998). Teachers often enhance textbook readings in social studies or science with trade book and Internet sources.

Pros and Cons of Sole Text Use

When used as the individual resource in a course, the textbook becomes the scope and sequence of the curriculum (Fitzgerald, 1994). A learning pitfall occurs for students when a textbook is the sole instructional resource because it becomes the only point of view in a course. In essence, the course is based on the theories and biases of the text author(s). Even though the author(s) might be objective in content presentation, what content is selected, what is omitted, and how the discussion is slanted reflect the views of the author(s).

There are other major criticisms of textbook use as well. In order to have wide application and increase potential sales, textbooks tend to be general, noncontroversial, and bland. The text is usually written for a national audience, so the authors do not take into account local issues or community attitudes toward the content. Because textbooks are geared to be understood by the greatest number of average-ability students, they may not meet the needs of those students at the high and low ends of the learning continuum. Furthermore, issues, topics, and data that might upset potential audiences or interest groups are omitted (Bernstein, 1988; Del Fattore, 1992).

Because textbooks summarize a great deal of information, they often discuss topics in a general and superficial way. In many cases, they do not treat topics with the breadth and depth of reading material necessary to develop a full and rich understanding of the concept. One of this book's authors remembers the topic of photosynthesis being covered in an entire chapter of a science text when he was a 10th-grade student. Some 30 years later, he was asked to help an eighth-grade student understand the same topic in his science text, and he was amazed to find only three or four pages devoted to an explanation of the complicated process. The author had to obtain secondary sources that contained enough text to be able to properly explain the process of photosynthesis.

Textbook publishers appear to be disregarding a basic maxim for successful understanding of a new topic: the greater the concept density of the topic, the more text is needed to understand it. Because of concept density, also known as compactness or concept load, the facts presented in one sentence are related to the information presented in the next sentence, and these have to be remembered because they have a bearing on the ability to understand the subsequent sentences in the unfolding information overload (McCormick, 2003). On the other hand, with more text comes more redundancy in the explanation of terms and concepts to help readers visualize the connections among ideas.

In many of today's content textbooks, the minimum requirements for understanding just the knowledge base of a topic seems to be the presentation norm. Much information is crammed into one text to enhance its marketability. Critics have noted that textbooks for nearly every subject and grade level present too many topics; the writing is often superficial and choppy, the content discussion is lacking in depth and breadth, and the content wanders between the important and the trivial. Content texts also often fail to capture the interest and imagination of students and help them think deeply about subjects. This is one reason that Beck and McKeown (2002) advocate the use of a "questioning the author" strategy. They suggest that students question the text author as they read, to better understand why the author presented certain information and to be better able to make explicit connections among facts and ideas in their social studies textbooks.

Despite all the criticisms, two authors suggest that textbooks can provide a number of advantages, especially for those teachers just entering the arena of content instruction (Cherryholmes, 1993; Ornstein, 1992). They suggest that textbooks can do the following:

- Provide an outline that the teacher can use in planning courses, units, and lessons
- Summarize a great deal of pertinent information
- Enable students to take home in convenient form most of the material they need to learn for a course
- Provide a common resource for all students to follow
- Provide the teacher with ideas about the organization of information and activities
- Include pictures, graphs, maps, and other illustrations that facilitate understanding
- Include other teaching aids, such as summaries and review questions
- Relieve the teacher of preparing material for a course, thus allowing more time to prepare lessons and integrate other sources

Enriching Supplements of Textbook Content

Today, however, one cannot assume that informational readings are found solely in textbooks. Most of the reading that is done on computers and through Internet sources by users of all age levels is probably expository. The more study and research students accomplish for projects, themes, topics, and reports using computers, the more likely they are to read and process the various styles of expository writing.

Although Internet materials are generally written by adults for adults, school-age children have access to another great source of informational readings: trade books. Trade books, as we noted in the previous chapter, can present literature and information to children in a highly appealing, user-friendly way. Probably sparked by the interest in using authentic children's literature in the language arts curriculum rather than stylized basal selections, authors today write about all sorts of topics so that children and adolescents have access to informational books that support the content presented in traditional textbooks. Research has indicated that the addition of trade books in the classroom helps in the development of oral language and reading ability, assists in vocabulary acquisition, and increases motivation to read at home and in school (Galda & Cullinan, 1991).

Besides providing variety in reading, informational trade books foster more comprehension of a topic or theme because they develop concepts and ideas in greater depth than a textbook segment does (Vacca & Vacca, 2002). One author notes that informational books can be a valuable resource even for kindergartners as a way to increase their vocabulary development and concept knowledge (Richgels, 2002). Another indicates that there is a rising popularity in the use of informational books in teaching elementary science. Rice (2002) notes that trade books provide a more focused and in-depth perspective of a science concept, they can be used to accommodate students with different reading abilities, they are crafted to be more interesting and less confusing than science textbooks, and they present a positive view of women and minorities at work in the sciences. Informational books about history allow readers to become more aware, deepen their feelings about historical events and peoples, extend their realm of experiences, and possibly even engage the readers to take some kind of action (Metzer, 1994).

Two authors note that informational trade books can aid children's learning of content in five ways (Freeman & Person, 1998):

1. Informational books can satisfy the natural curiosity of children as they explore topics of interest.

2. Such books assist children in understanding connections and interrelationships among concepts and topics.

3. As children compare and contrast readings from books on the same topic, their critical thinking and problem-solving skills are enhanced.

4. Children learn of distant places, ancient times, different animals and peoples, and intriguing ideas.

5. Such books help children inquire, think critically, and problem-solve as they investigate a topic.

The Classroom Instructional Mode

Added to students' problems with the textbook delivery style is the secondary problem posed by the teachers' delivery style. The dominant instructional style in the typical content area classroom is lecture (information coming at students for them to hear), text assignment or activity, and reciting (Readence & Moore, 1994). However, these authors add, research has indicated that teacher strategies are most beneficial when students are mentally and actively engaged in manipulating the information they are asked to learn. Students also seem to do best when content instruction is direct but continued and enhanced over time. Thus, the authors' ask, if particular content learning strategies are effective, why are they not implemented to supplant the instructional style of lecture-assign-recite that dominates most content area classrooms? One reason might be that teachers don't use the strategies that help students learn from their textbooks (National Reading Panel, 2000), and another might be that many content teachers simply don't know which strategies to use to help their students understand informational texts (Spor & Schneider, 1999). Another interesting point of view is offered by Schoenbach, Braunger, Greenleaf, and Litman (2003). They suggest that because teachers have not spent a great deal of time thinking about the mental processes of how to deeply understand the texts in their fields, the knowledge of how to make sense through reading is invisible and unknown to them.

Teachers also concentrate on the detailed delivery of the information of their disciplines and might perceive that their students lack adequate literacy capabilities to understand the content. They might be aware of the reading report card findings (NAEP, 1998) that indicated that although the majority of students could read at a basic level of comprehension, few were able to understand and interpret readings from informational texts (Donahue, Voekl, Campbell, & Mazzeo, 1999). According to one literacy author, if the teacher notices that students are unable to gain information from their readings, the teacher teaches around the text; the teacher becomes an "enabler" (Gunning, 2002). Thus the teacher might summarize or explain the content, have students copy notes, distribute a page of teacher-prepared notes, show a film that touches on aspects of the reading, or use other audiovisual means to address the topic. Such a procedure encourages students to minimize or even stop reading and let the teacher do the necessary deep-processing mental work.

Other authors note that teachers believe that reading has been adequately taught and mastered by students in the elementary grades (Guthrie & Davis, 2003). Therefore, when teachers teach a subject through textual readings without a focus on explicit instruction of *how* to understand the material, students experience problems with comprehension. Learning the content becomes intimidating due to a combination of lack of experience with the many concept-laden topics, inability to read with adequate comprehension, and absence of any teacher-provided ways to help students understand the content through reading.

One way to assist struggling middle school students is to connect their feelings and emotions to expository text as it is being read. The students record facts from the informational reading in one column of a response diary, and in the second column they write about their feelings related to the listed facts. Richards (2003) suggests that the response diary activity helps middle school students achieve more effective reading in four ways:

1. Students locate important information in the textual reading.

2. They integrate the processes of the language arts—reading, writing, listening, speaking.

3. Personal feelings, attitudes, and reactions to factual information are aroused, written about, and told to others during sharing time.

4. New insights and perceptions are gained when ideas are discussed with a partner and with others in the class.

Text Structure and Writing Style

A major contributor to poor or inadequate comprehension of informational text often is the written and organizational style used by an author in explaining a particular topic. Writing style is also known as text coherence, and it indicates how clearly the textual material is presented at two levels (Lenski & Nierstheimer, 2004; Meyer, 2003). One level of expository text structure has to do with how the ideas and concepts are logically arranged in the written piece. The ideas and concepts that foster global coherence and are central to understanding the overall meaning of the text are called the central thesis, the main ideas, or the macroselection level of ideas (Irwin, 1991). The sentences, their order, the transition between the ideas found in them, the use of antecedent relationships, and word choice constitute local coherence or the microselection level of text processing (Irwin, 1991; Lenski & Niersteimer, 2004).

In the last chapter we noted that children learn the macroselection level of stories early in life. With the underlying story grammar features embedded in the mind, children can unearth the meaning of new literary selections as they read them—unless, of course, they experience vocabulary overload or strange or unusual wording arrangements at the microstructure level. One might also conclude that with frequent exposure to a familiar text organizational pattern while reading literature at home and in school, students will develop mental road maps and cognitive frameworks that consistently aid them in constructing meaning from narrative texts.

Organizational Patterns

Informational text structure doesn't have a generic set of features as the narrative; rather, the expository style is characterized by a number of text organization patterns at the macrostructural level. Rowan (1994) indicates that although some define expository text by its purpose of informing or explaining, others define it by the organizational structure of its writing style, such as exemplification, causal analysis, comparison, and contrast. Authors are not in full agreement about the categories or names of expository text organizational patterns, but there is some overlap. Irwin (1991) names five patterns: spatial description, temporal sequence, explanation, comparison-contrast, and definition-example. Gillat and Temple (2000) discuss another five patterns: chronology, cause-effect, comparison-contrast, direction sequence, and exposition-explanation. Dickson's review (1999) includes reporting, explanation, persuasion, and comparison-contrast. McCormick (2003) identifies cause and effect, sequence, comparison and contrast, and classification. Vacca and Vacca (2002) discuss description, sequence, comparison and contrast, cause and effect, and problem-solution.

A study of ideas in informational writing occurred some 30 years ago in Meyer's (1975) taxonomy of expository structure types. She presented all the information from an informational reading in a detailed outline, or tree structure (Meyer, 1984). The tree structure illustrates that some content ideas are superordinate and some are subordinate. Specific details that provide additional information on the ideas above them are found at the bottom of the tree structure. From the writer's perspective, the importance the author places on aspects of the text's content is related to how the content is organized for the reader to follow. Meyer (2003) contends that students will remember more and process information faster when the reading plan is organized and will not do as well with the same information when it is presented in a disorganized way. In the picture below, we see a teacher, Theresa Connell, helping her

student Javier through the layering of ideas related to the making of good and bad choices about harmful substances so that he has a clear plan of understanding before he writes.

Teaching students about how their textbook ideas are organized or providing them with models of text organization has had a positive influence on reading comprehension and on report writing (Englert, Raphael, Anderson, Anthony, & Stevens, 1991). Text organization instruction provides writers with a framework for producing, organizing, and editing compositions (Wong, 1997). When eighth graders took a state's written essay examination before they had the opportunity to engage in text organization with accompanying concept mapping instruction, 1% scored in the inadequate category, 21% scored below average, and 79% in the average to excellent levels of writing. The following year, after text organization instruction in content area subjects, eighth graders achieved 88% in the average to excellent range and 12% in the below average category (Cronin, Sinatra, & Barkley, 1992). Low-achieving, inner-city seventh graders also significantly improved in their understanding of a study of the circulatory system when a tree map was used to organize major and minor concepts (Guastello, Beasley, & Sinatra, 2000).

Arranging Sentences Into Cohesive Paragraphs

At the microprocessing level of understanding, the sentence is a critical meaning unit. It acts as a pivotal structure in the comprehension and writing of text. The production of complex and elaborate sentences is made possible through the processes inherent in our grammar.

The processes of syntax and grammar allow for the production of an infinite number of possible sentences with a variety of word selections and arrangements. One central idea can be expressed in a variety of ways through different sentence arrangements. The central or underlying meaning of a sentence is known as its *deep structure meaning,* and the words in the sentence used to express that meaning are known as the *surface structure representations* (Pearson & Camperell, 1994). Research indicates that when children reach kindergarten and first grade, they can understand and produce complex and elaborate sentences by moving words, phrases, and clauses, and they can transform subordinate elements within sentences (Ruddell & Ruddell, 1994).

Pearson and Camperell (1994) point out additional considerations regarding sentence sense and comprehension based on their research. First, for some surface-structure representations, more thinking energy might have to be applied by the reader to achieve deep structure meaning. This could occur, for instance, when many subordinate ideas are added to a basic sentence, thereby increasing its syntactic complexity. Furthermore, if a number of ideas are embedded in a syntactic construction that separates the subject from the predicate, some sense of meaning can be lost, especially if such syntactic variations are not in one's oral language capacity. Second, those very important connector or signal words of English, such as *first, then, so, because,* or *however,* are understood and used even by young students to make implicit connections more explicit. Although a belief prevails that the longer the sentence, the more difficult it is to process, readers think of connectives between ideas and writers use connectives to express causal relationships. They add that the thinking use of connectives can serve to strengthen ideas in memory. Finally, when students combine ideas that could be expressed in simple, basic sentences into one longer, complex sentence, both maturity in writing and enhancement of reading comprehension occur. The picture below shows a teacher, Bria Rodrigues, leading her elementary-grade students into the writing of a good paragraph by using traditional signal words to connect sentence ideas.

Grouping words together to achieve smooth reading fluency is aided by the reader's sense of how grammar and syntax work. Syntactic cue features are extracted from sentences during reading to conform to the concepts of sentence construction known to the reader. If particular sentence elements and their usage, such as participles, gerunds, and appositives, are not functionally known or existent in the oral language capacities of readers, then such readers will experience a lack of understanding due to the nature of the particular sentence construction. It is wise to help students enlarge their powers of syntactic usage by writing many varied sentences rather than doing mere grammar drills.

Showing Students How Sentences Work

One way teachers can help students to overcome a lack of understanding of diverse sentence constructions is to visually and verbally show them how transformations work. Using the chalkboard or chart pages, the teacher writes an original sentence taken from the students' reading and recasts it so that the students can see how grammar works. With phrase and clause transformations, the sentence retains its same deep structure meaning, but it appears in different surface structure representations. In this way students can connect the underlying meaning of the sentence to the structures they use in the oral language while learning another way to transmit the idea in writing.

Some years ago, as a third-grade teacher, one of the authors could sense that his students were experiencing difficulty with a particular sentence in a story selection. One of the characters was asking the following question: "Why don't you make them a present of Serafina, that hard-working donkey the puppet show people sold to you last summer?" Why would third graders have difficulty comprehending this sentence? First, the antecedents of the pronouns *you* and *them* have to be identified. Next, the sentence has three connective parts: the first is the notion of the present, the second is the appositive phrase *hard-working donkey,* and the third is the clause beginning with the implied but deleted word *that* and followed by *the puppet show people sold to you last summer.* This was a sentence with combined elements that a mature, practiced reader would have little difficulty processing. To help the third graders, the teacher had to disentangle the complex parts and use simpler constructions and other surface structure representations. He wrote on the chalkboard, "Why don't you [and together with the class he substituted whom *you* meant above that word] make them [and the group substituted whom *them* meant above that word] a present of Serafina? Serafina was that hard-working donkey. Serafina was that donkey that the puppet show people sold to you last summer." Once they understood the meaning in the separate sentences, he went back to the original sentence and showed them how the ideas of the three separate sentences were combined and embedded in one structure.

The display of such an elaborate, complex sentence, the disentangling of the sentence parts to ensure understanding, and the reconstruction of the sentence elements in various meaningful ways is a very strategic way to help students with both comprehension and writing. Rearranging parts by making phrase and clause transformations helps students to understand the meaning of a difficult sentence. Such transformations retain the sentence's deep structure meaning but are rewritten in different surface structure representations so that students can connect the underlying meanings to structures they use in oral language. Transforming sentence elements directly assists reading comprehension while providing new ways for students to compose and combine sentence structures in forming their own novel sentences.

In summary, we can see that sentences carry meaning, and in portraying that meaning various syntactic constructions and arrangements can be used. We can also see that the understanding of syntax and grammar become part of one's background knowledge. How grammar works to organize complex thoughts in various sentence constructions then becomes part of one's conceptual understanding. The ability to interpret complex sentences, the order of words within them, and the use of connectors and signals such as pronoun referents is essential for gaining meaning at both the microstructure and macrostructure levels.

Prior Knowledge

Information resides in the head of a reader or writer and simply becomes the depth of knowledge that one has about anything. A reader and writer's prior knowledge reservoir is made up of three broad components of information: those contributed by one's life experiences, those conceptual understandings that have been shaped by the experiences, and those arising from one's knowledge of the words used to describe experiences and understandings. These interact with a text as it is being processed. If what is contained in the text conforms to the expectations of the reader, then the text will be read without uncertainty about the meaning. If the information in the reading is too far removed from the prior knowledge base of the reader, then loss of comprehension can occur unless the reader is able to fill in the gaps. Comments such as "What does this mean?", "I don't get it!", or "I don't know this word" might arise.

How does the prior knowledge of experiences, conceptual understandings, and words develop throughout the years? Young children, as they begin to venture out into the world, bring with them their senses of seeing, touching, listening, and speaking. As they interact with the immediate environment, they formulate their own rules about how objects and structures are put together and work. According to Piaget (1963), it is that very action of operating in the immediate environment by constructing things, pushing things, toppling things, and throwing things that children learn that events can be produced and that outcomes result from their actions. Their actions activate thinking and give rise to their intelligence. So if one child topples over a toy box and makes a display with wooden blocks and plastic animals, and an adult says, "Wow! What a great arrangement [or display or design] you made with your toys," the child hears the word *arrangement* used in the context of his or her own product. The concept of arrangement begins to form with items placed in a particular way. If another child throws a ball inside a house, a parent might say, "Please don't throw the ball in the house. You'll hit and damage something." Now the concepts of ball throwing, hitting, and damaging might begin to take shape in the child's mind as the known words *throwing, ball,* and *hitting* are added to the new idea of "damaging something."

Initially the immediate environment and later the backyards, playing fields, and trips to various locales provide the settings for active involvement and experimentation. Children manipulate materials such as toys, utensils, tools, mechanical devices, and sports equipment and receive visual and motor feedback regarding the outcomes of their behaviors. They learn how to adapt and accommodate themselves to actions caused by themselves, others, or the environment. For instance, they learn that pulling out the bottom cereal box on a shelf at the supermarket will cause the entire stack to tumble down. Active involvement and learning experiences serve to build knowledge constructs. Piaget calls each of these constructs a mental schema, which is a mental image or a pattern of action.

How Concepts and Words Connect and Build

Through action and verbal communication, children construct such conceptual skills as sequencing, sorting, classifying, and conserving. They learn that some objects go together because of some feature or property, and that some animals and plants belong to one category whereas others belong to another. Through interaction with a parent, they learn that when soda is poured from one bottle into a glass, the same quantity or volume of soda exists until it is consumed. They also learn that when clay is taken out of its box to make a creature, the same amount of clay exits. This is proved when the creature is dismantled and merged back with the unused clay in the box. Other educators have suggested that such conceptual insights can occur independently of language and take the form of images (Norton, 1997). The collection of such images then becomes each child's mental filing cabinet of organized knowledge, also considered to be the child's cognitive structures (Tompkins, 1998). Life's experiences are thus embedded in the mind as schemata (the plural of *schema*), and these schemata provide the foundation for ever-changing and emerging concepts.

Of course, words are used to explain and direct aspects of the child's activity, and these words become attached to objects and actions as the immediate environment is explored, such as we noted with the words *arrangement* and *damage*. At first, words are used for objects that appear in the immediate viewing area, but soon words are used for those actions and objects that appear as mental pictures in the child's mind. Even later, words and additional concepts are learned from reading. Many have noted that wide and varied readings are a major way to increase children's vocabularies (Gunning, 2002; Ryder & Graves, 2003).

The following example reveals how reading itself supports concept and vocabulary understanding. Initially a child visualizes a tree's leaf as green. In his or her early drawings the top of the tree is green and the trunk is brown. A bit later in life the child learns that leaves change color, disappear, and grow again as the seasons change. The colors used in the picture of the tree might therefore change to accommodate this new awareness. In the intermediate grades, the child studies the topic of plant life and sees an illustration of a leaf in a book. A whole new concept world emerges along with the vocabulary used to describe that world. Now the child learns about cells, and that cells require a certain amount of light to produce chlorophyll, the green matter of the leaf. The concept of changing colors from green to brown begins to take a sharper focus. The child learns about veins in the leaf, and this becomes a new concept. The child looks at the veins on his or her hand and understands the function of human veins. The connection is then made to the leaf veins, and the child can't wait to get out of school to examine a leaf and trace the pattern of the veins.

When writing expository accounts of information, writers often have to use a requisite vocabulary to explain the concepts of a specific topic. For instance, if the topic is photosynthesis, the writer has to use such supportive vocabulary as *chlorophyll, chloroplasts, carbon dioxide, carbohydrates, pigments,* and *reactions* to explain the process. Although each of these words can be separately analyzed and defined, the writer has a difficult time substituting easier words as synonyms to make the reading more user-friendly for a naive audience. We can sense how critically important vocabulary knowledge is for reading comprehension and how aligned words increase an understanding of certain concepts.

Furthermore, when students at all grade levels write about new topics using a freshly introduced vocabulary, we often notice how strained and forced their writing appears. They seem to use the new words of the topic in disjointed and unconnected ways. This is probably because they have not internalized the deep structure meaning of the topic in the same way that they can talk about other topics freely in the oral language. Since they can't put the words together orally without being visually riveted to the text, they have a difficult time connecting the ideas in a smooth and comfortable way. When new topics are introduced with a specialized and technical vocabulary, it is wise to have students engage in a lot of give-and-take discussion of the topic to help them achieve fluency with it in the oral language. Once they can talk about it and embed the new vocabulary in their own conversation, they will be able to write about the topic with a greater degree of deep structure meaning.

A good way to help your students build new vocabulary, connect to concepts, engage in lively discussion, and write meaningfully is to use a semantic feature analysis grid. Semantic feature analysis is a strong way to support the thinking of classifying. Beginning with a major topic, students classify and sort information into subclasses, characteristics or attributes, and examples. For instance, for the topic "Kinds of Rock," the three major types—sedimentary, igneous, and metamorphic—would follow. Each of these categories has specific types (examples), and each of these specific types has its own attributes, characteristics, and/or features. The semantic feature analysis grid links the class or category words, listed in the left column, with specific concept terms, usually attributes or examples, arranged across the top. Students place a plus sign or a checkmark in the grid when a match occurs. For instance, we would expect to see a plus sign for igneous rock matched with the words *volcanic rock, lava,* and *pumice.*

Table 8-1 shows how Yvette Morgan arranged her semantic figure analysis grid for the fourth-grade science topic "Animal Behavior." The names of the animals on the left will be easy to read for the fourth graders, but most of the terms across the top will be new concepts to the students.

Table 8-1.   A Semantic Feature Analysis Grid of Animal Behavior

Directions: Put a + if the animal has the characteristics listed across the top. (Some + marks appear as examples of matches.)

	Live in a colony	Travel in a school	Travel in a pride	Travel in a troop	Are preda-tors	Are para-sites	Nuture their offspring	Use a homing instinct	Can be a host	Migrate
Fish		+								
Lions			+				+			
Baboons				+			+		+	
Ants	+									
Polar Bears					+		+	+		
Butterflies										+
Honeybees	+							+		+
Fleas						+				
Turtles										+
Whales									+	+

The grid should be prepared so that each student has a copy and an opportunity to work with the new vocabulary. A larger copy may be prepared on chart paper. As a plus sign is added by one student, other students should confirm the match as appropriate. Then the students should be asked to use the matched words in a sentence. Later they can write sentences to show their understanding. Thus, for *polar bear,* we would see sentences such as "The polar bear uses its homing instinct to return from far distances to its home. The polar bear nurtures its young so that they can survive. The polar bear is a predator, and its favorite foods are seals, sea lions, and walruses."

Vocabulary Understanding

As noted in the last section, vocabulary, concepts, and prior understandings become linked to form a base of knowledge for each person. When new words are encountered and learned, they become connected to one's previous knowledge base and enhance one's associative knowledge of a topic or concept. Furthermore, words may reflect how one thinks and can influence how one comprehends text. Researchers have widely reported that the more robust one's oral and reading vocabularies, the more likely that a given account or text will be easier to understand (Beck, McKeown, & Kucan, 2002; National Reading Panel, 2000). Michael Graves (1994) has suggested that rich and deep vocabulary instruction connected to conceptual understanding positively affects comprehension. He adds that those who use more extensive and precise vocabularies are perceived to be more knowledgeable, competent, intelligent, and convincing.

The Idiosyncratic Nature of Vocabulary Understanding

With word understanding, nothing can be taken for granted by the classroom teacher. One child will know the meaning of a particular word, and a neighboring child will not. With the next challenging word, each child's previous knowledge base could be reversed. Witness the following account with seventh-grade Christopher to see how teacher predictions of understanding based on oral reading fluency are not always accurate.

One of the authors asked Christopher to help him model the reciprocal teaching strategy for a group of teachers. In this strategy, the teacher and student (or students) take turns reading segments of a text and then tackle the deep meaning of the text by posing queries to one another. Generally there are four consistent queries: one that requires predicting; one that requires clarifying or discussing a confusing point, such as might occur with new vocabulary or sentence structures; one that requires the asking of high-level questions, usually *why, how,* or *what if;* and one that requires summarizing (Gunning, 2003). This author likes to add a fifth query borrowed from the think-aloud strategy. This query asks students to tell about a mental picture (a visualization) they see based on their interpretation of the text segment (Kucan & Beck, 1997).

The author had selected an informational trade book, *Sheep Dog* (Ancona, 1985), for the day's reading. Christopher had good background knowledge of dogs, particularly those that are trained to work for humans, because his family had owned a guard dog and a guide dog. The author prepared five task cards that he and Christopher would hold up for the others to see as they worked through the components of the teaching strategy. They discussed the meaning of each component as noted on the task card, took a "picture walk" of the book's beginning, and then settled down to take turns silently reading, querying, and discussing the text.

The author noticed that during one of Christopher's turns as teacher, he didn't hold up the task card to note that he was going to talk about a difficult or confusing part of the text. The author thought that

Christopher should have held up the card, because of the density of concepts in one particular sentence. However, he said, "It was easy." The author asked him to read the sentence aloud, "All dogs share the predatory legacy of their wild ancestors." Not only did Christopher read the sentence fluently without halts, but he also discussed the meaning of the sentence aloud in front of the group in a very convincing way. He said, "Like the legacy of being a predator is passed down by ancestors—ancestors are the animals of the past." Christopher fully comprehended the meaning of that sentence.

During another segment of the reading, the author held up a cue card to announce that he was going to ask a good question. He asked Christopher why he thought the shepherd moved the "flock to lower pastures to graze in the mornings." With this question, Christopher looked back into the text and remained silent for a time. Then the following dialogue occurred between the teacher (T) and Christopher (C):

T: What do they do in the morning?

C: To the pasture to graze. (*looking at text*)

T: What does *graze* mean?

C: I have no idea.

T: OK. Let's figure it out. (*Reads the sentence aloud once again*) What do sheep have to do? Why do they go to the pasture in the first place?

C: I guess to graze?

T: Yes, to graze, but what does it mean in that sentence? Let's see…Can you tell us what a pasture is?

C: I know what *pasteurized* means, but not *pasture*.

T: Look at the picture. Are the sheep grazing there? What do you think the pasture might be?

C: Oh, the fields.

T: Is that a new word for you?

C: Yes.

T: (*Copies down the word* pasture *on a vocabulary card*) Yes, a pasture is a field, where the grass is. Now what do you think *graze* means?

C: Oh, the sheeps are grazing!!

T: Yes, the shepherd isn't grazing. The flock is grazing. OK, Let's go back. What's a flock?

C: Like a bunch of something—like a bunch of animals together.

T: Yes, in this case, it's the sheep.

C: Yes, the sheep.

T: OK, now why does the shepherd take the flock to a pasture to graze? I'll say one more thing and I think you'll get it. What do sheep eat?

C: Oh, do sheep eat grass?

T: Yes, sheep eat grass.

C: Oh!!! That's what *graze* means—eat.

T: Yes—eat what?

C: Eat grass.

T: Yes, usually the word is used with animals like sheep, cows, and horses. They eat the grasses found in the pastures, meadows, and fields. They put their heads down and eat or graze on the grass.

What was it in Christopher's background and vocabulary knowledge that allowed him to know words like *predatory, legacy,* and *ancestors* but struggle with words like *pasture* and *graze*? His background knowledge and interest in helping to raise various breeds of dogs contributed to his understanding of the first group of words, whereas his lack of background knowledge and experience with farms, fields, and country life led to his not understanding the latter words. Christopher was born and raised as a city dweller. However, after the thorough discussion of the meaning of those words, his application of them in a word concept map, the insertion of them in a paragraph containing blanks where the words should go, and a written essay in which he used his new vocabulary words, Christopher could undoubtedly add those new words to his storehouse.

One can see that vocabulary knowledge and concept understanding are unique and idiosyncratic for each individual. Can any one teacher know the depth of concept and vocabulary understanding for the range of students in any given classroom? A teacher can, at best, predict based on prior knowledge experiences with students what concepts and vocabulary will need to be explored in depth so that new learning can add to and reinforce the old. As Rosenblatt (2004) explains it, readers and writers, like speakers and listeners, have their own linguistic and experiential reservoir with which they interpret new words and create links to past learning.

Topics and Themes to Help Create Associative Bonds Among Words

When teachers focus on conceptually laden topics and themes, they help to create bonds of association among the many unfamiliar and technical words necessary to explain a topic or theme. We saw this occurring in the example of the topic of photosynthesis. Units of instruction, often reinforcing state content standards and accomplished through topics and themes, bring many facets of knowledge to students while the specific vocabularies both define and make the units understandable.

A topic focus generally occurs within a separate discipline such as science, social studies, English language arts, or mathematics. For instance, in science, a traditional topic unit might be the study of our solar system. Just consider some of the specific vocabulary that students would be confronting for the first time, in either the oral or written language, besides the specific names of the planets. Students would undoubtedly learn words such as *revolution, rotation, axis, orbit, light-years, universe, rings,* and *satellites,* as well as the names of the gases in the atmosphere.

One way that students can reveal a great deal of information about a given topic is through a chart structure. Notice in Table 8-2 how much information intermediate students have to "unearth" from their readings about land biomes.

A thematic unit usually occurs when teachers design an instructional unit to integrate two or more content disciplines over a period of usually 2–6 weeks. Although the theme acts as a central organizer, each separate discipline contributes its own content and thus specific vocabulary to the overall conceptualization of the theme. This could easily have occurred with the study of the solar system mentioned above. Mathematics and English language arts could have been brought into play to make an enriching theme experience for students. Naturally woven into the theme would be problem solving, required to calculate the distances between the planets and their satellites, and literary readings of space voyages.

Table 8-2.   Land Biomes Chart

Directions: Look into your study materials and complete the following chart.

Loof for	Information Findings					
The 6 land biomes studied	Rain Forest	Grassland and Savannah	Desert	Tundra	Coniferous Forest	Deciduous Forest
1. Brief description of each land biome						
2. Brief description of the weather						
3. Brief description of the vegetation						
4. Brief description of the geography						
5. Types of plants found						
6. Types of animals found						

One way to show the concepts and major vocabulary of a theme or topic is with a concept or cognitive map. A map is a visual, graphic array using such figures as boxes, rectangles, and circles to house words and phrases. The figures of the map, with words written in them, are arranged and linked in ways that express a concept and show the relationship of the whole to its parts and the parts to the whole. A logic of organization and meaning is therefore expressed. Scott and Nagy (1994) add that because semantic mapping highlights relationships among concepts, it is a stronger strategy for teaching conceptually difficult words than the practice of looking up the words in the dictionary. In the picture to the left we see

fifth-grade Miguel entering his ideas in a logical way on a concept map, and by doing so he expresses to others the direction of his thoughts.

Using Concept Maps Skillfully

Teachers need to be reminded to be skillful with concept map construction. A concept map is not the same as a brainstorming map. The latter is often accomplished prior to a reading to elicit students' background knowledge and understanding of a topic. In developing a concept map, it's not the best practice to arrange words randomly around or under a targeted concept term. The teacher should plan ahead to arrange the concept relations in the most logical way. For instance, if the concept idea is arctic life and some of the children's background ideas and new associative and related terms are *tundra, caribou, very cold, lots of snow, Eskimos, lichen, polar bear, permafrost,* and *narwhal,* it might not assist students conceptually if the terms are just arranged around the concept idea. If, however, the teacher elicits from the children how *caribou, ptarmigan, narwhal,* and *polar bear* are related, in order to add the concept of unique animals, then the ideas become organized in a conceptual, logical way. By engaging students in how the concept map should be constructed, the teacher involves them in the higher thinking processes of categorizing, organizing, and making judgments. Figure 8-3 shows how an initial brainstorming map (left) might look as students' background and new vocabulary is discussed prior to reading, and how a concept map (right) organizes information in a logical way after reading and researching.

It would be a strategic move for the teacher to call on students to provide an oral recitation of topics or subtopics to see if the students can use the words appropriately in their own language. For instance, while pointing to "unique animals" and "arctic life," the teacher could say, "Who can connect these ideas to build a paragraph?" Once a sentence is offered, a new sentence using related concept words would be added, and so on. An entire written piece may be accomplished later by children who used the new words in appropriate contexts as shaped by the teacher. The resulting selection can be read and reread, both as an aid to increasing fluency and as a way to assist low-vocabulary students in particular.

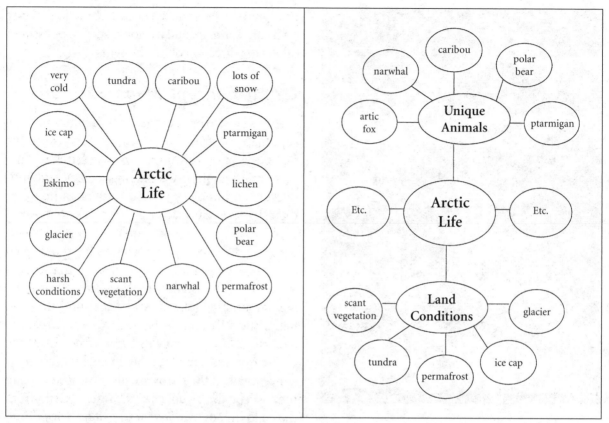

Figure 8-3. The Distinction Between a Brainstorming Map and a Concept Map in Showing Relationships

Using Writing to Strengthen Comprehension

The reader has undoubtedly noted that throughout this book, we have urged teachers to promote the use of writing to reinforce the learning of new concepts, understanding, and vocabulary words. We're also strong advocates of a reading, mapping, and writing process, as indicated in our discussion of topics and themes. Such activity, along with others in which children are experimenting with new words, requires that students make meaning connections at the syntactic, semantic, and affective levels. What occurs through writing exploration and experimentation—enhanced with evolving writing and reading experiences at home, in the computer lab, and in the classroom—is the elaboration and refinement of old writing forms and the emergence of new forms (Kamberelis, 1999).

When children begin to use their new vocabulary words in their own self-constructed sentences, they take ownership of the words. They might need several opportunities to use the new vocabulary in different contexts so that the mind can call up words more automatically when appropriate writing contexts occur. When teachers use vocabulary flash cards or vocabulary notebooks, not only should the new word and its meaning be listed, but the student should also be asked to write each word in a new sentence. In the new sentence, the writer should be asked to provide clues to readers so that they can figure out the word. In this way the writer reveals understanding while assisting readers with the comprehension process.

Another way to help your students have immediate visual access to words so that they can use them in their writings is the use of a word wall, discussed earlier. The words amassed on a word wall may come from multiple sources: from topics and themes, literature books read in class, told experiences of trips or excursions, or visitors telling or sharing unusual life stories. A word wall also serves as a focal point for the discussion of words. Words are discussed, defined, and used in oral sentences before they are written and placed on the wall. Students may borrow words from the word wall to take to their desks or kidstation centers if an opportunity arises for them to use that word in

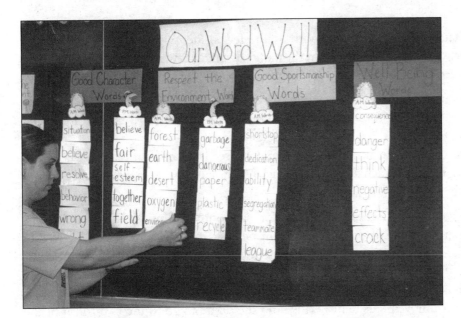

one of their own written stories or reports. A manila pocket envelope should also be hanging on the word wall for children to return the words they borrowed. The picture to the left shows teacher Theresa Connell adding a new vocabulary word to her word wall of four concept categories.

A very student-friendly way to encourage the use of new vocabulary is to use a *shape poem* activity. The teacher or students may

create an outline shape of a person, an animal, a plant, or an object that represents a topic, theme, or character in a reading. Around the shape of the outline, students use their new vocabulary in phrases and sentences and may attempt to rhyme or create a poetic affect. Note third-grade Christina's shape poem on the topic of frogs and tadpoles (Figure 8-4) and how words like *breathe, gills, stages, tadpole,* and *cycle* are appropriately used in sentences around the shape.

Students' Mindset

Apart from the content itself and its capability to connect with students' knowledge of the past is the factor of the mindset of students themselves. This factor involves their perceptions of

Figure 8-4. Christina's Shape Poem

themselves as learners, their attitudes, their interests, their motivation to learn from many diverse topics in many disciplines, and their ability to stick to tasks. Paris, Lipson, and Wixson (1994) note that skill and strategies to succeed in reading are one thing, but will is another. Will, they explain, is the motivated intent to succeed or complete a task and to behave or act in a particular way at a particular time. Will involves a learner's personal intention to act in either harmony or disharmony with a concurrent reading task.

We see the factors of personal intention and will interacting in our classrooms in many ways, as noted in the following examples:

- Why is it that the same hands are raised by the same few students each time questions are posed by the teacher? Conversely, why is it that the hands of students whom we believe know the answers are seldom ever raised?

- Why is it that some students say they like a particular school subject, like reading, arithmetic, or spelling, but hate social studies and science? Why do others in the same class say just the opposite? Do these love and hate relationships start early, due to initial successes and failures with how content is delivered, thus establishing a personal preference? Is success and failure related to reading competency or to how much thinking energy has to be employed to understand new and conceptually difficult topics?

- Why is it that when a content selection is assigned for classroom reading, the lowest achieving student of that class group is the first one to yell, "Finished!"? This exclamation is followed by a chorus of voices from students who wish to emulate the first. Although most of the students are pursuing the reading task and are interested and motivated to learn from the topic, the teacher is now challenged with a handful of students who are imminently poised to pull their classmates off-task with movements, whispering, and the desire to go to the bathroom or the water cooler.

We know that informational reading takes work. Students have to be willing—even if they are not able to relate and connect to all the pieces of information in the first reading attempt—to deliver their minds to want to learn. We teachers know that both capability and willingness aren't always on our side. We have, in our classrooms, learners who are categorized in so many ways. We have unmotivated readers, uninterested readers, disengaged readers, disenfranchised readers, reluctant readers, struggling readers, at-risk readers, readers categorized as special needs learners, and readers who have low or poor self-efficacy (which means they have negative perceptions of themselves succeeding in reading even though their mental energy is expended). Villaume and Brabham (2002) reveal ways in which student dispositions interfere with comprehension. Some resist reading and academic tasks with a lack of attention, negative remarks, sullen expressions, listless indifference, or outlandish expressions. Disenfranchised readers are those who do the school assignments in often mechanical and resigned ways, but they fall short of making personal investments and engaging in deep and reflective energy with reading and writing tasks. Thus, in any given classroom there may exist a range of fully capable readers, those who wish to succeed but are incapable of doing so, and those who might be capable but who will themselves not to be so.

One phenomenon that begins in fourth grade and continues well after is often called the *quiet crisis*. This occurs when students have achieved some literacy capabilities, but not enough to bring them up to the challenges necessary to gain full understanding of many expository readings (Hirsch, 2003; Schoenbach, Greenleaf, Cziko, & Hurwitz, 1999). Another problem surfaces in early adolescence: a downturn in students' engagement and motivation to succeed with academic tasks in general (Ryan & Patrick, 2001). The trend toward success with texts becomes especially troublesome for reluctant readers, students from economically disadvantaged backgrounds, and minority students who are not engaged in readings that are interesting and relevant to them (Newman & Celano, 2002; Worthy, 2002).

Motivating and Assisting Struggling Readers

The problems of adequate reading comprehension are even more pronounced for intermediate-level struggling readers, who are trapped in a deleterious dilemma. Since they avoid reading, they minimize the practice they would gain to become fluent and more efficient readers (Dreher, 2003). Being poor readers, they sense that they lack the competence to succeed in challenging content area reading assignments. Such students need to become motivated to make an effort in school reading tasks, and they need teacher support and positive perceptions so that they can gain competence (Ryan & Deci, 2000).

Margolis and McCabe (2003) point out the following ways that struggling readers and those lacking positive self-efficacy can be assisted to succeed:

- *Linking forthcoming work to recent successes.* This means that teachers "stack the deck" of assignments and tasks so that success follows success. Teachers also show students what strategies or mental work they need to engage in to succeed.

- *Teaching necessary learning strategies.* Here teachers engage in explicit, systematic instruction and modeling so that students can succeed in a step-by-step way.

- *Reinforcing effort and persistence.* Teachers provide help, encouragement, and praise and show students positive ways to overcome resistance while correcting errors and monitoring understanding.

- *Teaching students to be positive about their learning behavior.* Instead of saying, "I can't do it . . . I'm not too good at reading . . . I didn't really try," students need to be reminded of the words of the little blue engine that pulled the packed circus train over the mountain: "I think I can! I think I can!" With the help of such techniques as prepared cue cards or a published short list of sequenced directions, reluctant students can see that they can stick to a task to succeed.

- *Helping students formulate personally relevant goals.* With personally articulated goals set by students themselves, greater motivation to succeed in literacy and academic tasks is often achievable.

- *Incorporating the use of peers as models.* When students help students, teachers extend their effectiveness while capitalizing on the social and affective bonds that become established among peers. Often peers use language in explaining a concept or a process that is easier for other students to understand. Most of all, when peers "teach," they become more accomplished learners themselves.

Many sources agree that social interaction contributes to a greater comprehension of content and to a stronger understanding of the usefulness of what is being studied (Blackwell, 2003). Having your students engage in conversation with you, the teacher, and with one another during their readings will assist the reading comprehension process. Positive student interaction with peers to sustain and motivate the reading process, reading aloud to students, and ample time for students to just read by themselves are three ways to improve the performance of struggling readers (Dreher, 2003). When teachers provide time to "just read," the choice of materials is important as well. Although a research link between choice and reading comprehension improvement does not appear to exist, student choice of reading materials heightens interest and motivation, which in turn are catalysts to learning (Fielding & Pearson, 1994).

Worthy (2002) has summarized from reading motivation studies the following interesting results with intermediate students:

- Students desired more read-alouds by teachers and more time in school to read independently.

- Students wished to learn about good books from their teachers and liked it when teachers read segments to get them hooked and motivated to read on their own.

- Most noteworthy were the comments about teacher enthusiasm for particular books. The more enthusiastic a teacher was about a particular reading, the more likely it was that the students would want to read it.

Considerations for Content Instruction

To summarize, we can see that student disposition and interest are strong factors in learning information from expository texts. Choice becomes limited when the textbook is the only reading source. However, the teacher can obtain students' investment of their personal energy when they can choose readings from trade books and Internet sources and can form resource groups (see chapter 3). In planning an informational topic for students, the teacher might consider using the following chronology of activities:

1. Consider the concept density of the topic. Ask yourself if the students have the concept understanding and experiential background to bring to this topic. You might need to plan extensively to help students make connections with what they know and engage their curiosity to make links to the new topic.

2. Examine the predicable new vocabulary load and its connection to understanding the topic. Look to see if the meanings of new words can be inferred from the context or if a network of new concept terms should be established first so that students can see the associative and propositional links among the concepts.

3. Consider the macro and micro styles of the writing. Ask yourself if the text structure style might interfere with comprehension. Would a concept map jointly created by students after reading the topic help them to visualize the macro text style?

4. Consider your students' affective state, predisposition to learn, and willingness to commit mental energy. Are your students motivated to learn the content of this topic?

5. What will be your mode of instructional delivery to help students maximize the learning of this content? What plans and strategies layered throughout the chapters of this book should you initiate to help your students maximize the learning of this content?

One Guided Reading Format: The Directed Reading Activity (DRA)

The directed reading activity (DRA) is one format for conducting a guided reading and writing lesson. It's an instructional procedure that belongs in a class of guided reading and writing formats, in which each has a particular way that reading, writing, and social interaction proceeds. This grouping includes such formats as the guided reading and kidstation model (discussed in chapter 3); literature circles and the directed reading and thinking activity (DRTA) (discussed in chapter 7); reading and writing workshops with crafting lessons (discussed in chapter 2); survey, question, read, recite, and review (SQ3R); and the Reading Recovery program.

The DRA is presented here as one strong instructional way to proceed with the reading and study of a topic. It allows the teacher to focus on the viewing, listening, speaking, reading, and writing features of the language arts for a whole class or group, to consider the layers of depth discussed previously, and to bring in many strategies and activities that are covered in this book and that are popular today in language arts and content area instruction.

The DRA has enjoyed a long tenure in the field of reading instruction; it was one of the initial structured reading strategies that focused on students' comprehension of text (Gunning, 2002). Originally credited to Emmett Betts in 1946, the DRA supports the reading comprehension process by attending to students' background knowledge of a topic, engaging students' interest before reading, setting a purpose to motivate students to want to read, and monitoring students' understanding of the topic (Hammond, 1994). As initiated by Betts and modified by many current authors (Burns, Roe, & Ross, 1999; Gunning, 2002; Hammond, 1994; Reutzel & Cooter, 1996), the DRA consists of the following five major steps:

1. Readiness and preparation to read; "purpose" question(s) before reading

2. Reading silently, orally, or both

3. Discussion and interaction with some oral rereading with a purpose

4. Skills building that is related to specific content within the reading, or strategy-level development that has transfer value

5. Individual or group follow-up enrichment and extension activities that are related in some literal, interpretive, or applied (creative) way to the reading

We recommend the DRA for use with many content area topics because of its commonsense structure and guided instructional format. Before students are given the text assignment, a fair amount of time is given to step 1, readiness and preparation to read. The teacher sets the stage, engaging a mental hook so that students want to gain the topic information. This may take part of a class period, a whole period, or even more. A basic rule that has served the authors well over their teaching years is this: The greater the concept density of a topic, the more time needs to be spent in readiness.

The format is compatible with a whole-part-whole classroom grouping pattern. A whole-part-whole instructional framework or pattern is a way to achieve a balance in content and literacy instruction, particularly in regard to the weight given to specific skill or concept development and that given to a holistic orientation (Fowler, 1998; Strickland, 1998). Literacy has a number of processing and representation modes, and the whole-part-whole framework allows the teacher to capitalize on students' active involvement in these modes while providing for various classroom grouping patterns. In the initial "whole," the entire class is together in one group, and the students generally participate in a whole reading, listening, discussing, and/or viewing event. During the "part," either individually or in groups, the students participate in some directed skill work that has emerged or that is grounded in the context of the "whole." In the second "whole," the students practice the skill they learned by using another literacy mode such as writing, artwork, or computer representation, and they share their work with the whole group.

Reutzel and Cooter (1996) contend that the use of the whole-group or whole-class organizational pattern is an effective way to provide a "safety net" for emerging or at-risk readers, because reading is a social event and children interact positively when they share their reading experiences. Through such activities as storytelling, story dramatization, sharing of self-written stories, reading aloud and singing of songs, reading of "big" books, and group reading and writing, at-risk students are socially and linguistically involved with their more competent classmates. Moreover, such whole-class literacy activities negate some of the potentially harsh effects often associated with ability grouping or labeling at-risk children as "slow learners," "learning disabled," or "resource room students." The whole-group organizational structure is usually done during the readiness stage of the DRA.

Readiness to Read

In the readiness and preparation-to-read segment, there are four broad teacher tasks that require various amounts of instructional time, depending on the anticipated difficulty of the topic. The teacher has to (a) engage the students by relating the topic to their background experiences; (b) develop and clarify the predominant concepts underlying the piece; (c) introduce and visually portray the new vocabulary; and (d) set the purpose and motivate students to read. This looks like a tall order for the teaching of a topic, but the trick is to minimize the direct talking and engage the students in the readiness activities. Not only must they hear, they must also see and feel the importance of the information contained in the topic.

KWL

This is where the K and W parts of the KWL strategy can be used to great advantage. When the teacher asks, "What do you *know*?" and "What do you *want* to learn?" about a topic, and then directs students to write in the appropriate columns, they become engaged. During and after the reading, when they enter information under the L (*learn*) column, they will tell what factual information they gained from the reading. In an additional column, marked S for *still curious*, they will note what they are still curious to learn and if they confirmed their earlier curiosities in the W column.

The need to instill conversational involvement while generating intellectual curiosity is why many teachers use the KWL strategy when introducing a new topic or theme. Before they read or engage in the new learning topic, children can discuss or write what they know under the K column on a large chart or prepared paper. The question posed by the teacher for the K column is generally worded "What do I know about this topic (or theme)?" Once again, prior to reading, children respond to the next question, posed in the W column, "What do I want to learn about this topic?" After reading or learning about the topic through explanation or other instructional activities, children discuss or write "What I have learned" in the L column (Ogle, 1986, 1989). It is vital that each child has the opportunity to discuss what was learned and whether his or her special "want to learn" question was answered (May, 2001).

Instead of the S that we added above, some people add a fourth A column for affective responses. Here children can note their feelings, attitudes, appreciation, and values encouraged by the topic (Mandeville, 1994). The A column may also be used as a means of informal *assessment* (McAllister, 1994). The teacher might make note of the quality of each child's response, then interact to achieve elaboration and clarification of the response. We recommended the S column to encourage additional discussion, thinking, and curiosity. Children will record continuing but curious gaps in their knowledge and add questions they would still like answered. This allows you, the teacher, to whet students' intellectual curiosity even further by providing additional explanation and discussion about the topic or by eliciting their help to find the answers to the new questions through library and Internet research (Reutzel & Cooter, 1999).

To deal with informational topics, Sampson (2002) has suggested the addition of three additional columns to the KWL grid to help students deal reflectively with the information explosion on the Internet and other print and media sources. In two columns, students tell the sources of their inquiry and their learnings, and in another they tell if their original prior knowledge statements were confirmed. During the discussion, students should show that they evaluated the information they researched and didn't just take one source as confirmation for an often-believed "fact."

One helpful tip we have learned in our work with children while using the KWL activity is to keep them motivated and engaged in the reading of the informational topic. Many times the work with the KWL chart is rather static; that is, the K entries are written, the W entries are written, and after reading, the L entries are added to the chart. To make the process more active with information-seeking readers, we ask them to write down what they learned after short reading segments. These segments could be a paragraph or a section. Prepared ahead of time for children to write on are little icons, pictures, or outlined shapes of the topic they are reading about. Thus, if the topic is whales, a little whale-shaped picture could be prepared, copied, and cut out for the children to use. Note third-grade Christina's written notations on the frog icons placed in her L column (Figure 8-5). The process of writing what was learned during the reading of information-packed segments reinforces the comprehension process and makes the reading active and fun.

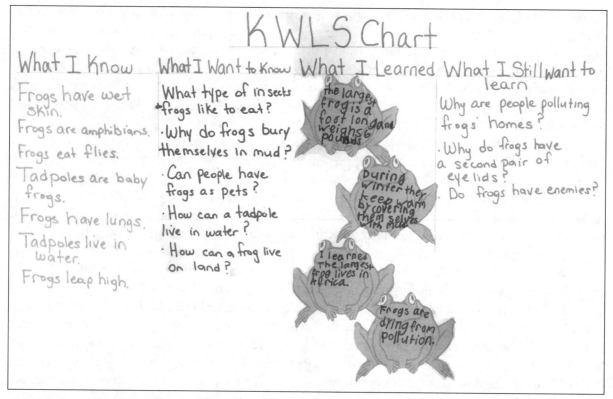

Figure 8-5. Christina's KWLS Chart

CONCEPT MAPS

At another time, when developing a concept, the teacher might want to introduce a simple but useful graphic map on the chalkboard as a brainstorming activity and have students contribute parts. For instance, one fourth-grade topic was the unusual communities in which people live. The teacher posed the question "What places on earth are difficult to live in?" and drew a circle around it on the chalkboard. The fourth graders contributed their background knowledge by making a web of such concept ideas as the sea, the deserts, the polar regions, and the very tops of mountains. When the teacher asked "Why?", other children came to the board to add their ideas relating to those four places. With that visual display on the chalkboard, the teacher motivated the children to read with the purpose question "What are two other places that humans find difficult to live in, and why is life difficult there?"

Also on the chalkboard were some of the new vocabulary words that children would encounter in the reading. The teacher was able to skillfully introduce the new words to reinforce the children's language. When one child said of a desert, "There's nothing there," the teacher reinforced the concept with the words *barren* and *arid,* and these were webbed to the word *desert.* When the concept of the difficulties arising from living on different kinds of land arose, the teacher introduced, wrote, and discussed the word *inhospitable.* Attending to the major vocabulary of the topic provides a high degree of certainty that most children will recognize and understand the words when they are seen in context.

REALIA AND VISUAL REPRESENTATION

The teacher should not forget to employ the power of artifacts, objects, and even still-life pictures to provide an experiential foundation before a reading. Think of how beneficial it might be before the study of the challenging topic photosynthesis if the teacher brought in tree leaves. What kind of thinking and discussion might emerge with questions such as "Why is this leaf green and this one brown [or yellow, orange, etc.]?" Some students might know or be able to deduce through a general class discussion that sunlight and the seasons of the year are related in some way to the green color that is the trademark of the active, growing tree. When a reading of the second most important animal (after humans) responsible for changing the face of a landscape is about to occur, the teacher might display a large picture of a beaver or hold up a stuffed animal. Many children might have heard the word *beaver* and seen it in a cartoon, but have they looked closely at its natural features to see why it's the foremost builder (and destroyer) of human property in the animal world?

One teacher about to begin the topic of immigration brought in artifacts from his grandparents and great-grandparents, with photographs showing life in America in the early 1900s. The students were sixth graders of many different nationalities and cultures themselves; they resided in a borough of New York City that is home to many different ethnic groups and languages. The teacher was immediately impressed, even taken aback, by the respect the students showed for the old and frayed photographs, birth certificates, immigration papers, and citizenship papers. They passed the artifacts to one another in hushed tones and constantly raised questions (the W kind!) about life in those times. With such a readiness activity that worked beyond the teacher's expectation, the immigration topic took hold in the sixth graders' minds, and the teacher had their curiosity and motivation to read secured.

Reading

After students have understood the major purpose question that provides a holistic mindset for them, they read the selection. It might be wise for the teacher to write the purpose question on the chalkboard, since it will act as a focus reminder for students and be there to start the discussion after silent reading. Sources call this stage guided silent reading, directed reading (either silent or oral), or just guided reading. (Recall that chapter 3 presented guided reading along with read-alouds and the kidstation procedure). The reading is guided or directed because the teacher observes students to ensure that they are accomplishing the reading task, offers assistance with word or vocabulary problems, and provides help with understanding difficulties. Gunning (2002) suggests that with a fact-packed informational reading, it might be wise to read it in segments with a discussion. Interaction with text segments could also be accomplished with the use of the prepared icons discussed earlier.

Fielding and Pearson (1994) suggest that the traditional silent-reading step doesn't necessarily have to be silent. Because comprehension is strengthened by social interaction, they suggest paired reading, especially when a pair is made up of students with different reading abilities. Additional social interaction is encouraged when students discuss the meaning with one another and with the teacher, making conversation a cognitive part of the comprehension process.

Lenski and Nierstheimer's format of guided reading (2004) includes a first and second reading after the introductory, readiness stage. The first reading, especially for young children and novice readers, is done silently or through a quiet reading. The second reading encourages oral reading guided by teacher discussion and questioning. Here children may read aloud chorally or individually.

WRITING TO PROMOTE ACTIVE COMPREHENSION

There are a number of ways to encourage active, reflective thinking during the silent reading step by making writing an essential part of the understanding process. One technique to maintain student focus would be a study guide. This could even be just a standard-size sheet of paper, divided lengthwise, with two headings: *question* and *answer*. Students can be shown how to formulate questions based on a boldface heading. If a boldface heading says "Types of Behavior" in a reading on animal responses, the student might write the question in the left column, "What types of behavior do animals have?" As the student reads the text under the boldface header, he or she answers the question on the right side of the page. With some prior training in the question-and-answer procedure, students—especially those with poor concentration habits, weak recall, and poor understanding in general—become more strategic in understanding as they read.

Less traditional but highly strategic formats for engaging students in study-guide behavior have been mentioned previously in this chapter. Richards (2003) offers a "facts and feelings response diary" to help middle school students become more affectively involved with a content reading as it is being processed. In the left column of the response journal, students list facts, and in the second column, they discuss the feelings that these facts engender. A similar format requires a double-entry response. On the left side of a page is the heading "What the Book or Author Says," and on the right side is the heading "What I Think About It." Look at the reflective comments made by sixth-grade LaShai as she did her double-entry writing on the book *Teammates* (Golenbock, 1990) about Jackie Robinson and Pee Wee Reese (Figure 8-6).

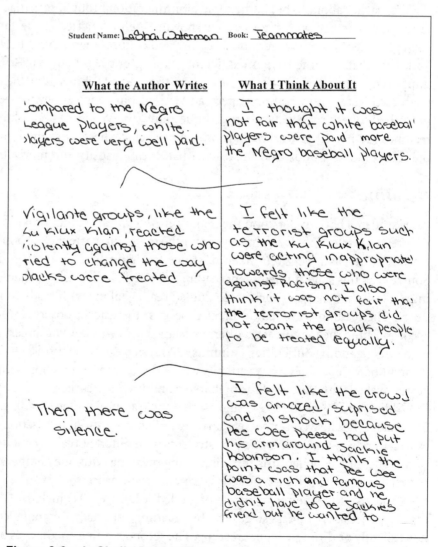

Student Name: LaShai Waterman   Book: Teammates

What the Author Writes	**What I Think About It**
Compared to the Negro League Players, white players were very well paid.	I thought it was not fair that white baseball players were paid more the Negro baseball players.
Vigilante groups, like the Ku Klux Klan, reacted violently against those who tried to change the way blacks were treated	I felt like the terrorist groups such as the Ku Klux Klan were acting inappropriate towards those who were against Racism. I also think it was not fair that the terrorist groups did not want the black people to be treated equally.
Then there was silence.	I felt like the crowd was amazed, surprised and in shock because Pee Wee Reese had put his arm around Jackie Robinson. I think the point was that Pee Wee was a rich and famous baseball player and he didn't have to be Jackie's friend but he wanted to.

Figure 8-6. LaShai's Double-Entry Journal

A highly strategic and reflective thinking procedure presented earlier was the "questioning the author" activity (Beck & McKeown, 2002; Beck, McKeown, Hamilton, & Kucan, 1997; Kucan & Beck, 1997). The type of thinking required by this activity is one of seven cited by the National Reading Panel (2000) for having a solid scientific base for improving reading comprehension. This is the thinking that generates questions as readers ask themselves about the meaning of a text. Thus, for instance, if the author of a social studies text was describing a particular historical figure, the students would be trained to make queries such as these: "What is the author trying to tell me about this person?" "Why did the author provide that information?" "What's the author's meaning here?" "How is the author writing this to make us think or feel a certain way?" "What does the text mean when it says . . .?" The use of such techniques as "questioning the author," double-entry responses, and study guides encourage students to think beyond the literal and develop interpretive and creative levels of comprehension.

Discussion and Interaction

Once the reading is complete, the teacher might begin the discussion stage by returning students to the purpose question. Since the purpose question is generally related to the whole meaning or main idea of the selection, the students may begin with the central concept and then connect related, subordinate ideas and information. For instance, the teacher could say, "What did you learn about animal responses that help animals survive or live better?" The teacher might display a concept map structure on the chalkboard to connect the students' answers to the reading. Then the purpose question might be parsed down to elicit other subtopic categories, such as "What do some animals do when the seasons of the year change?" or "How do animals prepare for their young?"

During the discussion and clarification of concepts, the teacher may skillfully integrate oral rereading for specific purposes. This does not mean that the entire selection is read again orally, it just means that the teacher asks for specific parts to be read aloud. The teacher's general strategy here is to ensure the under-standing of the selection for all by asking for particular parts to be read aloud. Students have to demonstrate that they know what to look for in order to answer the question. Thus, if the teacher says, "Find the sentences that tell us why animals migrate" and asks that they be read aloud, the teacher is ensuring that the students will learn the concept of migration from the oral reading and the discussion that follows. Through questioning, the teacher is encouraging students to engage in higher levels of comprehension and to make connections among sentences.

If one of the split-page procedures was used during the reading stage, the teacher should integrate the students' written comments into the discussion stage. Otherwise, the students won't feel that their work was of any particular importance and will not be motivated to write questions and look for answers again. Since techniques like the study guide and "questioning the author" are a sure way to promote the comprehension of complex material, the teacher should call on students to see what questions they posed as they read and what the general group thinks of the answers. Many times students take the quick way out and just jot down a word or phrase for an answer. They don't elaborate on the complexity of the issues or the connections among concepts. With whole-class interaction on the quality and robustness of an answer, there is a greater likelihood that a higher level of understanding will be attained for all.

Strategic Skills Development

Skills development can encourage strategic ways to think about the textual information. Teachers often think that it's necessary to move from literal to interpretive to applied and creative levels of comprehension, in that order, but that's not the case. Since so much comprehension work was accomplished in the discussion stage, the teacher might plan to focus, in this fourth step of the DRA, on one strategic skill that has transfer value.

The general purpose question provided a schema for an overarching view of the topic. Many readers, accordingly, read the text with concepts and generalizations in mind and plug in inferences and details as they read, making it very important for the teacher to understand that students' reading levels are quite varied (Vacca & Vacca, 2002). Finally, as so many literacy educators advise, teachers shouldn't get bogged down with subskills activities, usually done with work sheets and copied pages, because they will take away from higher level, problem-solving thinking, the creative engagement, and the plain enjoyment of reading to learn (May, 2001).

Skill and strategy work should be in tune with what the text offers. For example, if social studies readings are done on the exploration and colonization of the Americas, the rise of inventions during the industrial age, or even westward expansion, then sequential organization would appear to be a key way to join the events within each topic. Supporting the skill of sequential organization would be such activities as the use of time lines and flow charts, which have transfer value to other chronologically ordered topics.

For topics like rocks, volcanoes or earthquakes, causal thinking is very predominant in order to follow the chain of events and effects. Thus a cause-and-effect chart, with the use of connector words such as *because, since, therefore, thus,* and *accordingly,* would be a good strategic activity, because the students can transfer the skills they learn to other causal readings and writings.

Table 8-3 shows a cause-and-effect chart that could be constructed for a unit on ancient civilizations. This unit is often studied in the intermediate grades, and its content provides important cause-and-effect relationships that have influenced generations of cultures. This is a good time

Table 8-3. Cause-and-Effect Chart

Directions: Complete the following chart for the topic of ancient civilizations. You can look back in your text to find the answers. Where there is a cause, write an effect. Where there is an effect, write the cause. Use the connector words to make good sentences.

CAUSE	EFFECT
Development of tools	
	Growth of population
Hunting and gathering	
Discovery of fire	
	Surplus of food
	Development of civilizations
Domestication of animals	
Spread of agriculture all over the world	
	People having more time on their hands

to have a list or chart of important connector words available so that students can construct meaningful sentences that reveal the cause-and-effect relationships.

Enrichment, Extensions, and Follow-Ups

This stage of the DRA can support and extend any of the concepts, content, or strategies developed through the lesson. This extension can take many forms, engage some or many domains of the language arts, and involve individual or group effort. This might be the stage where real deep learning of a concept idea takes place, because students are actively involved in doing a project and/or additional work they themselves have selected. For example, when the topic of early Native American cultures was taught in one fourth-grade social studies class, the students generated many "want to know" questions that weren't covered in the text readings. There were so many questions generated that the teacher was able to assign each one to be researched by a student who was interested in investigating the answer.

The following list provides samples of follow-up and enrichment activities that the teacher can use as springboards for additional ideas:

- Complete the discussion or the "things to do" section that often concludes most content area text readings.

- Complete the L and the S column of the KWL(S) activity.

- Complete a concept or semantic map by filling in the related coordinate, subordinate, and detailed information.

- Complete an anticipation guide and confirm the answers.

- Complete time lines or charts by adding dates, events, and other data.

- Write a report, do a complete newspaper article, or plan a multimedia project based on the content or concepts of the reading.

- Write an editorial in the form of an opinion or persuasive paper, such as "After our reading, do you think that Puerto Rico should remain a commonwealth or become a state?"

- Complete a cloze selection in which words have to be appropriately placed back into a reading selection. Teachers often do this activity by writing a summary selection of a previously completed reading and omitting the key concept vocabulary. Students demonstrate their semantic understanding of the new vocabulary by using it correctly in the new context.

- Fill in a semantic feature analysis grid with plus and minus signs. The teacher should set this up by arranging subtopic coordinate ideas in a left-hand column. Thus, for the topic of animal behavior, down the left-hand column of chart paper the teacher might have written *snake, gray whale, woodchuck, opossum,* and *chameleon.* Across the top column would be attributes and characteristics of the various animals, such as *warm-blooded, cold-blooded, migrates, uses camouflage, pretends death, hibernates,* and *burrows.* When an animal is characterized by a trait, the student places a plus sign for that interaction. Students are further benefited by using the new concept vocabulary in sentences that join the two ideas.

- Create acrostic poems. Such poems use the letters of a topic word to create an imaginative poem about the ideas and vocabulary of the topic. A poem could be fashioned on the words *animals, rocks, and planets.* Here's an acrostic poem for the word *leaf:* lovely even after falling.
- Connect concepts and/or content with artwork in the form of the visual arts, music, or dance.
- Use dramatizations and turn rewritten text into plays.
- Conduct additional readings on the topic with feedback from the rest of the class.
- Have students do oral readings of content relating to the topic.
- Do crossword puzzles, with new vocabulary.
- Take field trips, with observational notes of students used to report their findings.
- Do written activities in the form of letters, diary entries, persuasive paragraphs, and news reports (the idea is to provide alternative writing forms in expressing content information).
- Use forms of poetry to express content ideas (see chapter 5).
- Use panel reporting as news summary or debate (with or without technology; see chapter 4).
- Do hands-on, manipulative projects such as making a "volcano" in the classroom.
- Use any other games, puzzles, or activities in which students use the ideas, content, concepts, and vocabulary of the topic.

The reader will also note that many of these activities were discussed in earlier chapters of this book for use in other contexts. Some fit quite nicely for meaningful work at Kidstations, and some provide excellent presentation vehicles for the oral communication schedule presented in Chapter 4.

Summary

This chapter has focused on expository, or informational, writing, which is the distinguishing writing style of the subjects studied in school, read in businesses and professions, and found on the Internet. The chapter has pointed out that the informational style can be problematic because of the way it is presented to be read and because of factors contributed by the students themselves. We noted that students' experiential backgrounds, their conceptual understanding, their range of vocabulary, and their motivation to engage are important factors in their understanding of informational topics.

Throughout the chapter remedies were presented to help students read and write about informational topics more effectively and efficiently. The suggestions and strategies we presented were authentically grounded in the texts of study. The use of transition words, concept mapping, writing activities, and read-alouds occurs as a topic or theme is being addressed in the classroom. If a study guide or a "questioning the author" activity occurs, it happens within the context of a particular social studies or scientific reading. The directed reading activity was offered in this chapter as a guided reading and writing instructional format that allows teachers to bring in a number of contextually related, relevant activities that will engage students in meaningful and reflective ways. Throughout the book are instructional formats, strategies, and activities that connect well to the DRA sequential procedure. We hope you will use some of these suggestions and strategies in assisting your students become more proficient and reflective readers, writers, and oral presenters.

Anticipation Guide Revisited

After reading this chapter, confirm your initial predictions about each statement. List the page number that supports each response.

Statement	Agree	Disagree	Verification
1. The expository or informational style of writing is quite similar to the writing style of fiction or stories.	_____	_____	_____
2. Such strategies as "questioning the author" and double-entry responses help students engage with informational text and reflect more deeply on the content.	_____	_____	_____
3. A teacher's instructional style has little influence on how students learn informational content.	_____	_____	_____
4. Background familiarity with particular content topics can influence how well they are understood during reading and how well students write about them.	_____	_____	_____
5. Students' knowledge of word meanings has little bearing on how well they comprehend text.	_____	_____	_____
6. Engaging students in authentic writing activities can assist the comprehension of content readings.	_____	_____	_____
7. Students' perception of themselves and their intentions about learning have little influence on teachers' effectiveness during content instruction.	_____	_____	_____
8. The directed reading activity (DRA) instructional format offers an efficient structure for engaging students reflectively in learning a content topic.	_____	_____	_____

Additional Resources

For Further Reflection

1. Try to use the classification concept map or tree structure design when a topic that includes "kinds of," "types of," "groups of," or "categories of" is studied. Have your students establish the top-level concept, the next most important ideas (which are coordinate to one another), and then subordinate and detailed ideas. The explicit factual information should be placed at the bottom of the map design. Have students do oral or written recitations connecting the top level to the detailed ideas in a coordinated way.

2. Focus your class on a topic, theme, concept, or principle relative to science, history, or mathematics. Place the students in groups and see how each group arrives at a plan to teach the lesson. Ask them to chart or map the lesson sequence and explain why it would make sense to accomplish the lesson in the particular way they chose. Have each group present its lesson configuration and plan to the entire class.

References

Allen, R. (2000, Summer). Before it's too late: Giving reading a last chance. *Curriculum Update*, pp. 1–3, 6–8.

Ancona, G. (1985). *Sheep Dog*. New York: Lothrop, Lee & Shepard.

Beck, I. L., & McKeown, M. G. (2002). Questioning the author: Making sense of social studies. *Educational Leadership, 60*, 44–47.

Beck, I. L., McKeown, M. G., Hamilton, R., & Kucan, L. (1997). *Questioning the author: An approach for enhancing student engagement with text*. Newark, DE: International Reading Association.

Beck, I. L., McKeown, M. G., & Kucan, L. (2002). *Bringing words to life*. New York: Guilford Press.

Bernstein, H. T. (1988). *America's textbook fiasco: A conspiracy of good intentions*. Washington, DC: Council for Basic Education.

Blackwell, P. (2003). Student learning: Education's field of dreams. *Phi Delta Kappan, 84*, 362–367.

Burns, P., Roe, B., & Ross, E. (1999). *Teaching reading in today's elementary* schools (7th ed.). Boston: Houghton Mifflin.

Cherryholmes, C. H. (1993). Readers research. *Journal of Curriculum Studies, 25*, 1–32.

Cronin, H., Sinatra, R., & Barkley, W. F. (1992). Combining writing with text organization in content instruction. *NASSP Bulletin, 76*, 34–45.

Del Fattore, J. (1992). *What Johnny shouldn't read: Textbook censorship in America*. New Haven, CT: Yale University Press.

Dickson, S. (1999). Integrating reading and writing to teach compare-contrast text structure: A research-based methodology. *Reading & Writing Quarterly, 14*, 49–79.

Donahue, P. L., Voelkl, K. E., Campbell, J. R., & Mazzeo, J. (1999). *NAEP 1998 reading report card for the nation and states*. Washington, DC: National Center for Educational Statistics, U.S. Department of Education.

Dreher, M. (2003). Motivating struggling readers by tapping the potential of information books. *Reading & Writing Quarterly, 19*, 25–38.

Enciso, P. (1994). Engagement in reading. In A. C. Purves (Ed.), *Encyclopedia of English studies and language arts* (pp. 426–427). New York: Scholastic.

Englert, C., Raphael, T., Anderson, L., Anthony, H., & Stevens, D. (1991). Making strategies and self-talk visible: Writing instruction in regular and special education classrooms. *American Educational Research Journal, 28*, 337–372.

Feathers, K. M. (1998). Fostering independent, critical content reading in the middle grades. In K. Beers & B. G. Samuels (Eds.), *Into focus: Understanding and creating middle school readers* (pp. 261–280). Norwood, MA: Christopher-Gordon.

Fielding, L. G., & Pearson, P. D. (1994). Reading comprehension: What works. *Educational Leadership, 51*, 62–67.

Fitzgerald, S. (1994). Textbooks, design and use. In A. C. Purves (Ed.), *Encyclopedia of English studies and language arts* (pp. 1204–1206). New York: Scholastic.

Fowler, D. (1998). Balanced reading instruction in practice. *Educational Leadership, 55*, 11–12.

Freeman, E., & Person, D. G. (1998). *Connecting informational children's books with content area learning*. Boston: Allyn & Bacon.

Galda, L., & Cullinan, B. (1991). Literature for literacy: What research says about the benefits of using trade books in the classroom. In J. Flood, J. M. Jensen, D. Lapp, & J. R. Squire (Eds.), *Handbook of research on teaching the English language arts* (pp. 529–535). New York: Macmillan.

Gillat, J., & Temple, C. (2000). *Understanding reading problems: Assessing and instructing* (5th ed.). New York: Longman.

Golenbock, P. (1990). *Teammates*. New York: Voyager Books.

Graves, M. (1994). Vocabulary knowledge. In A. C. Purves (Ed.), *Encyclopedia of English studies and language arts* (pp. 1246–1247). New York: Scholastic.

Guastello, E. F., Beasley, T. M., & Sinatra, R. (2000). Concept mapping effects on science content comprehension of low-achieving, inner-city seventh graders. *Remedial and Special Education, 26,* 356–365.

Guillaume, A. (1998). Learning with text in the primary grades. *The Reading Teacher, 51,* 476–486.

Gunning, T. (2002). *Assessing and correcting reading and writing difficulties* (2nd ed.). Boston: Allyn & Bacon.

Gunning, T. (2003). *Building literacy in the content areas.* Boston: Allyn & Bacon.

Guthrie, J., & Davis, M. (2003). Motivating struggling readers in middle school through an engagement model of classroom practice. *Reading & Writing Quarterly, 19,* 59–85.

Hammond, W. (1994). Directed reading activities. In A. C. Purves (Ed.), *Encyclopedia of English studies and language arts* (pp. 378–380). New York: Scholastic.

Hirsch, E. D. (2003). Reading comprehension requires knowledge of words and the world. *American Educator, 27,* 10–22, 28–29, 48.

Irwin, J. W. (1991). *Teaching reading comprehension processes* (2nd ed.). Upper Saddle River, NJ: Prentice Hall.

Kamberelis, G. (1999). Genre development and learning: Children writing stories, science reports, and poems. *Research in Teaching of English, 33,* 403–460.

Kucan, L., & Beck, I. (1997). Thinking aloud and reading comprehension research: Inquiry, instruction, and social interaction. *Review of Educational Research, 67,* 271–299.

Lenski, S. D., & Nierstheimer, S. L. (2004). *Becoming a teacher of reading: A developmental approach.* Upper Saddle River, NJ: Pearson/Merrill Prentice Hall.

Mandeville, T. (1994). KWLA: Linking the affective and cognitive domains. *The Reading Teacher, 47,* 679–680.

Margolis, H., & McCabe, P. (2003). Self-efficacy: A key to improving the motivation of struggling learners. *Preventing School Failure, 47,* 162–169.

May, F. B. (2001). *Reading as communication: To help children write and read* (6th ed.). Upper Saddle River, NJ: Prentice Hall.

McAllister, P. (1994). Using K-W-L for informal assessment. *The Reading Teacher, 47,* 510–511.

McCormick, S. (2003). *Instructing students who have literacy problems* (4th ed.). Upper Saddle River, NJ: Merrill Prentice Hall.

McKenna, M. C., & Robinson, R. D. (2002). *Teaching through text: Reading and writing in the content areas* (3rd ed.). Boston: Allyn & Bacon.

Metzer, M. (1994). *Nonfiction for the classroom.* New York: Teachers College Press.

Meyer, B. (1975). *The organization of prose and its effect on memory.* Amsterdam: North-Holland.

Meyer, B. (1984). Organizational aspects of text: Effects on reading comprehension and applications for the classroom. In J. Flood (Ed.), *Promoting reading comprehension* (pp. 113–138). Newark, DE: International Reading Association.

Meyer, B. (2003). Text coherence and readability. *Topics in Language Disorders, 23,* 204–224.

Moore, D. W., Moore, S. A., Cunningham, P. M., & Cunningham, J. W. (2003). *Developing readers and writers in the content areas, K–12.* Boston: Allyn & Bacon.

National Assessment of Educational Progress (NAEP). (1998). *Nation's report card in reading.* Washington, DC: Author.

National Reading Panel. (2000). *Teaching children to read: An evidence-based assessment of the scientific literature on reading and its implications for reading.* Bethesda, MD: National Institute of Child Health and Human Development.

Newman, S., & Celano, D. (2002). Access to print in low-income and middle-income communities: An ecological study of four neighborhoods. *Reading Research Quarterly, 36,* 8–26.

Norton, D. (1997). *The effective teaching of language arts* (5th ed). Upper Saddle River, NJ: Merrill.

Ogle, D. (1986). K-W-L: A teaching model that develops active reading of expository text. *The Reading Teacher, 39,* 564–570.

Ogle, D. (1989). The know, want to know, learn strategy. In K. D. Muth (Ed.), *Children's comprehension of text: Research into practice* (pp. 205–223). Newark, DE: International Reading Association.

Ornstein, A. (1992). The textbook curriculum. *Educational Horizons, 70,* 167–169.

Palmer, R. (1997). Nonfiction trade books in content-area instruction: Realities and potential. *Journal of Adolescent and Adult Literacy, 40,* 630–641.

Paris, S. G., Lipson, M. Y., & Wixson, K. K. (1994). Becoming a strategic reader. In R. B. Ruddell, M. R. Ruddell, & H. Singer (Eds.). *Theoretical models and processes of reading* (4th ed., pp. 788–810). Newark, DE: International Reading Association.

Pearson, P. D., & Camperell, K. (1994). Comprehension of text structures. In R. B. Ruddell, M. R. Ruddell, & H. Singer (Eds.) *Theoretical models and processes of reading* (4th ed., pp. 448–468). Newark, DE: International Reading Association.

Piaget, J. (1963). *The origin of intelligence in children.* New York: Norton.

Readence, J., & Moore, D. (1994). Content area reading. In A. C. Purves (Ed.), *Encyclopedia of English studies and language arts* (pp. 287–290). New York: Scholastic.

Reutzel, D. R., & Cooter, R. Jr. (1996). *Teaching children to read: From basals to books.* Upper Saddle River, NJ: Prentice Hall.

Reutzel, D. R., & Cooter, R. B., Jr. (1999). *Balanced reading strategies and practices: Assessing and assisting readers with special needs.* Upper Saddle River, NJ: Merrill.

Rice, D. (2002). Using trade books in teaching elementary science: Facts and fallacies. *The Reading Teacher, 55,* 552–565.

Richards, J. (2003). Facts and feelings response diaries: Connecting efferently and aesthetically with informational text. *Reading & Writing Quarterly, 19,* 107–111.

Richgels, D. (2002). Informational texts in kindergarten. *The Reading Teacher, 55,* 586–595.

Rosenblatt, L. (2004). The transactional theory of reading and writing. In R. B. Ruddell & N. J. Unrau (Eds.), *Theoretical models and processes of reading* (5th ed., pp. 1363–1398). Newark, DE: International Reading Association.

Rowan, K. (1994). Expository writing. In A. C. Purves (Ed.), *Encyclopedia of English studies and language arts* (pp. 474–477). New York: Scholastic.

Ruddell, M. (2005). *Teaching content reading and writing* (4th ed.). San Francisco: Wiley/Jossey-Bass.

Ruddell, R. B., & Ruddell, M. R. (1994). Language acquisition and literacy processes. In R. B. Ruddell, M. R. Ruddell, & H. Singer (Eds.), *Theoretical models and processes of reading* (4th ed., pp. 83–103). Newark, DE: International Reading Association.

Ryan, A., & Patrick, H. (2001). The classroom environment and changes in adolescents' motivation and engagement during middle school. *American Educational Research Journal, 38,* 437–460.

Ryan, R., & Deci, E. (2000). Intrinsic and extrinsic motivations: Classic definitions and new directions. *Contemporary Educational Psychology, 25,* 54–67.

Ryder, R. J., & Graves, M. F. (2003). *Reading and learning in content areas* (3rd ed.). San Francisco: Wiley/Jossey-Bass.

Sampson, M. B. (2002). Confirming a K-W-L: Considering the source. *The Reading Teacher, 55,* 528–532.

Schoenbach, R., Braunger, J., Greenleaf, C., & Litman, C. (2003). Apprenticing adolescents to reading in subject-area classrooms. *Phi Delta Kappan, 85,* 133–138.

Schoenbach, R., Greenleaf, C., Cziko, C., & Hurwitz, L. (1999). *Reading for understanding.* San Francisco: Jossey-Bass.

Scott, J. A., & Nagy, W. E. (1994). Vocabulary development. In A. C. Purves (Ed.), *Encyclopedia of English studies and language arts* (pp. 1242–1244). New York: Scholastic.

Spor, M. W., & Schneider, B. K. (1999). Content reading strategies: What teachers know, use, and want to learn. *Reading Research & Instruction, 38,* 221–231.

Strickland, D. (1998). What's basic in beginning reading? Finding common ground. *Educational Leadership, 55,* 6–10.

Tompkins, G. E. (1998). *Language arts: Content and teaching strategies* (4th ed.). Upper Saddle River, NJ: Merrill.

Vacca, R., & Vacca, J. (2002). *Content area reading: Literacy and learning across the curriculum* (7th ed.). Boston: Allyn & Bacon.

Venezky, R. (2000). The origins of the present-day chasms between adult literacy needs and school literacy instruction. *Scientific Studies of Reading, 4,* 19–39.

Villaume, S. K., & Brabham, E. G. (2002). Comprehension instruction: Beyond strategies. *The Reading Teacher, 55,* 672–675.

Wong, B.Y.L. (1997). Research on genre-specific strategies for enhancing writing in adolescents with learning disabilities. *Learning Disability Quarterly, 20,* 140–159.

Worthy, J. (2002). What makes intermediate-grade students want to read? *The Reading Teacher, 55,* 568–569.

Zemelman, S., Daniels, H., & Hyde, A. (1998). *Best practice: New standards for teaching and learning in America's schools* (2nd ed.). Portsmouth, NH: Heinemann.

Chapter 9

An Integrated Literacy Approach

Throughout this book the authors have presented a number of teaching suggestions, strategies, and workable activities to engage students through the primary and intermediate grades in authentic and reflective literacy practices. We have also shown that many of these literacy practices are connected to and enhance the intent of many of the English language arts standards. In this final chapter, we would like to showcase an integrated literacy approach that can be followed every time a new text selection is listened to or read. The approach also supports some of the best suggestions of the National Reading Panel (2000) and the National Commission on Writing (2003). At the core of this reusable format, which is called the 6Rs Approach, are the thinking processes of retelling or reconstructing accomplished through story or concept map usage. These maps provide the continuum glue that connects the reading and the writing.

The At-Risk Population

We have used this approach primarily with second- to intermediate-grade children often considered to be at risk for literacy success. The risk derives from their circumstances. Most are economically disadvantaged, and we've found that even though they are poor according to economic standards, they are not poor in mind and willingness to perform. Many are poor in their state's language arts rankings. A great many are English language learners, and a sizable group has been in or still is in special education settings. A rather new group is at risk because these students aren't adequately provided for under normal parenting conditions; they are known as sheltered or homeless children.

The 6Rs approach has been implemented with these categories of children during an out-of-school program called CampUs. The approach occurs in small-group settings after the regular school day, on Saturdays, and in the summer at a college campus. The children and youth served through affiliation with various government agencies and programs have been as follows:

1. *Housing development or "project" children.* The New York City Housing Authority (NYCHA) provides affordable and safe housing for more than 174,000 families with an average income of $15,685 living in its 346 housing development sites located throughout the city's five boroughs. In the last 9 years, roughly 1,000 children from different housing sites have been bused to the Queens campus of St. John's University. They attend a 10-day CampUs program, which features the 6Rs approach during half a school day in small-group settings and in a state-of-the-art computer lab. The second part of the day is spent at chess, swimming, and athletics.

2. *Homeless or sheltered children.* Hundreds of children from five or six facilities operated by the Department of Homeless Services (DHS) have attended the CampUs program at the City University of New York campuses located at Kingsborough Community College or City College of New York (CCNY). These children follow the same 10-day schedule as the public housing children.

3. *Low-achieving students in the English language arts (ELA).* One hundred children from two inner-city public schools participated in a full-day, 21-day CampUs program at St. John's University. One elementary school had 94% of its population eligible for free lunch and 80% of its fourth graders not meeting the state ELA standards, and a nearby intermediate school had 98% of its population eligible for free lunch and 86% of its eighth graders achieving below acceptable performance on the ELA standards.

4. *Economically disadvantaged children eligible served under the No Child Left Behind Act in a Supplemental Educational Services (SES) provider program.* The 6Rs approach has been implemented with children from grades 2 through 8 attending 20 different New York City schools for a 2-hour period on 23 Saturdays. Most SES children have been intermediate-grade children.

The Literacy Plan

Because the children are with us for short but highly controlled amounts of time, we have focused on the use of trade books as the initiating literacy spark of the 6Rs unfolding sequence. Trade books are those that are found in library and classroom collections all over the world, and their various category formats were discussed in Chapter 7. The use of children's literature selections, biographies, and information books provides us with a number of advantages. These books, purchased to make sets of 8–12 copies, are packaged in attractive ways, are easy to use in short periods, and seem to be user-friendly for children who must study in the summer and on Saturdays. Their use also allows us to support our state's English language arts standards, which require students through the grades to read at least 25 books a year.

Another major advantage is that we can locate enough books to support the three major themes of our summer programs. These themes ask children to become aware of the dangers of substance abuse by saying no to illegal drugs, alcohol, and cigarettes; to be a good person at home, at school, and on the playing fields; and to show respect for the environment and community by not littering and polluting. By focusing on these three socially relevant themes through reading, we want to help children overcome the negative influences of inner-city life and provide positive guidance in their lives. This is an issues approach to themes, as Saltman (1985) noted. Furthermore, such a thematic focus helps teachers and students to think about meaning while promoting positive attitudes toward the acts of reading and writing (Burns, Roe, & Ross, 1999). In future summer programs, we plan to add trade book sets that deal with the socially relevant themes of bullying and gangs.

While engaged in the themes, we increase children's reading and writing interactions with strategies that will help them in the formal arena of schooling in the fall. Our approach of Read, Reason, Retell and Reconstruct, Rubric, (w)Rite, and Revise (Figure 9-1) is based on a series of six interconnecting, cumulative steps aimed at promoting development in the four domains of the language arts and visual representation. It supports a number of our state's performance standards because children read a number of books, read about issues or topics in which they have to produce evidence of understanding, write responses to literary works, learn to use narrative procedures, and create a multimedia computer project in which they have to write, format, gather, and organize information (Board of Education of the City of New York, 1997, 2001).

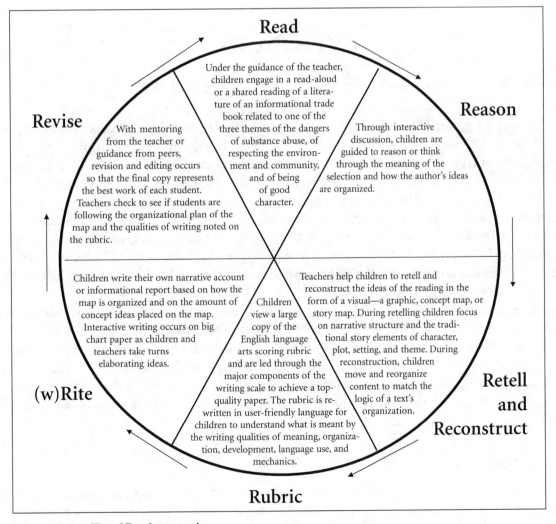

Figure 9-1. The 6Rs Approach

The 6Rs steps integrate many of the components of a balanced literacy framework (see chapter 3). Viewing, listening, speaking, reading, writing, and visual representation are featured as children and teachers engage in shared reading and writing and guided reading and writing and work through different text styles. Furthermore, vocabulary develops out of the textual readings, and students have many opportunities to practice and apply their new word knowledge through narrative and informational writing activities.

The summer literacy work is accomplished in two settings. One is a traditional school setting in which the small groups of children are taught through the 6Rs approach by preservice teachers under the supervision of licensed, veteran teachers during a 90-minute block each day. The second is held in one of three computer labs for an additional 45-minute period. Here children complete an individually generated computer project under the supervision of the computer teacher, lab assistants, and the preservice teachers who accompany their small groups to the larger lab. Children engage in the 6Rs steps as they work through their projects.

The Six Rs

Reading

Fiction and informational trade books are used on a daily basis as the motivating vehicle to engage the children with the messages of the three themes. Of the 35 books previewed and selected to be used as small-group text sets, 23 relate to the character development theme, 6 to the substance abuse theme, and 8 to the environmental theme. The books are further categorized by reading level and content for younger children (7–9 years old), older children (10–13 years old), and for students from other cultures who are learning English as a second language. The character development books are all children's literature and picture books in the narrative, story tradition, whereas the other two themes use both informational books and storybooks. Because many of the children are still beginning readers, such as those who have just completed first grade, are English language learners, or have been in special education settings, a read-aloud is generally done first, followed by a shared oral reading, and then the students are led through the reasoning and reconstruction processes.

Varied readings are a major way to increase the children's meaning and reading vocabularies. Because each book offers a rich source of words, new words are added each day to a growing list of theme words. The new words are most often printed on 5 x 8 cards and mounted on a word wall under the appropriate theme heading. Both the thematic book readings and the vocabulary reinforcements are aimed at organizing the children's knowledge of concepts and helping them to see the relevance and connectedness of the information. Gunning (2003) calls this organized focus "principled understandings."

Reasoning

During reasoning, teachers engage children in thinking about the text and its message. Questioning and verbal discussion that occur during and after the reading make this step very lively. Children interact freely with the text, the teacher, and one another as they talk about book ideas, new vocabulary, the relationship to the theme, and their personal reactions to meaning. Here we apply the three levels of thinking about a reading—experiencing, connecting, and extending—as noted by Finders and Hynds (2003). They experience the reading through the pictures, words, and mental images aroused by the text; they connect the reading to impressions in their lives regarding substance abuse, what makes a good person, and local environmental issues of littering and pollution. They begin to think about how they will extend the reading into a graphic map format, a writing project, an art project, or a computer project.

Retelling and Reconstructing

The thinking and reasoning processes involved in this aspect of the plan make use of the visual representation of ideas through graphic organizers and maps. Concept and story maps (discussed in Chapters 7 and 8) serve as a major strategy to help children formulate and organize their ideas after reading and before and during writing. Teachers move students smoothly into retelling and reconstructing stories and informational readings by verbally engaging the students in map construction. Information based on the reading is written within the graphic figures either by the teacher, who elicits this information during verbal discussion, or by the children themselves as they puzzle out the sequence of events of a story or the concepts and ideas of an informational reading.

Researchers have reported that students with and without learning problems have improved in reading comprehension and planning for writing when they have been shown how text ideas are organized in narrative and expository readings and when they have been provided with visual models of text organization (Davis, 1994; Swanson & DeLaPaz, 1998; Vallecorsa & deBettencourt, 1997; Wong, 1997). Many researchers have also reported the positive effects of concept map use for vocabulary and reading comprehension development when small groups of children and youth are taught in controlled settings (Boyle, 1996; Englert & Mariage, 1991).

Teachers use different map structures that represent how various readings and writings are organized. The maps used with literature or story readings reflect the common story grammar features of character, plot, setting, problems or conflict, outcomes or consequences, resolution, and theme. These maps generate a retelling of a story's events as children write down the sequencing and causal interactions. Some of these were shown in Chapter 7.

The maps used with expository, informational readings reflect cause-and-effect, sequential, compare-and-contrast, and topic-development text patterns and have been used successfully in other large-scale literacy projects to boost reading and writing achievement (Cronin, Meadows, and Sinatra, 1990; Cronin, Sinatra, & Barkley, 1992; Sinatra, 2000; Sinatra & Pizzo, 1992). These maps help children reconstruct information from a reading by allowing them to see the connections among ideas and concepts and by relating details and new vocabulary appropriately. Two of these maps, the Steps-in-a Process and the Many Causes of One Effect, are shown in Figure 9-2.

One example is provided by 10-year-old Landes, who developed a sequence of ideas written in her Steps-in-a Process Sequence Map. Because she learned that reading was fun from her teacher in the CampUs classroom setting, she took the modeling ideas home. In her second event, she revealed that what she learned "was special to me because I use [sic] to not like reading. . . . So when I came home I try [sic] to invent the same thing for my little brother." Her third event told about how she felt: "I feel happy . . . because I like reading more. Also my vocabulary is getting better." The final event concluded her

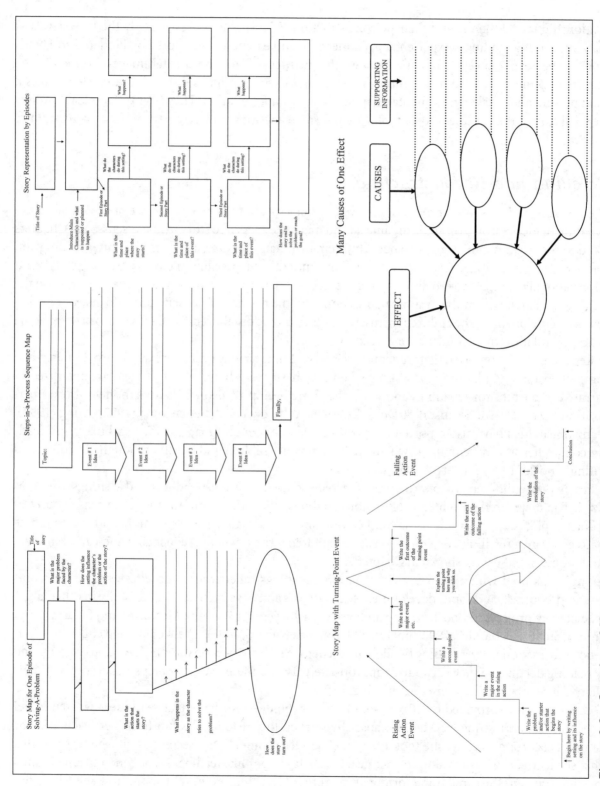

Figure 9-2. Samples of Maps Used in 6Rs Approach

thoughts about having "a great time being with new people" and having an excellent person and teacher to guide her. Many students used the Many Causes of One Effect map with the "say no" and protect the environment themes. They would place words like *littering, pollution, smoking, taking drugs* in the effect circle and then show and explain the multiple causes that arise from each of those effects.

Rubrics

The mapping step is followed by a discussion about writing and how reading can provide a number of ideas to develop in writing. Children are then presented with the five qualities of writing and the four-point scale used by our state in its rubric scoring system. The five qualities of writing, generally universal in nature, ask children to take note of meaning, development, organization, language use, and mechanics. The components of the rubric are written in a more user-friendly way, and large copies of the children's rubric are made and hung in each of the project's classrooms. Teachers and students discuss what features of writing will make a good paper as they view the rubric, and children return to look at the rubric as they engage in the ongoing writing or revision processes.

(w)Riting

Writing and planning for writing after reading and mapping is a central feature of the 6Rs approach. We believe that the benchmark standard of writing an acceptable paper and thinking deeply about a topic is a task of worth and value. The ability to write well has long-term significance in school and in one's professional life. Wolf and White (2000) described such a benchmark performance as the writing of a report as a "valued" performance, which does not attempt to meet each and every individual standard but represents a rich performance based on in-depth learning that occurs over time.

Children write their own individual papers while viewing either a group-constructed map or their own filled-in map as they are reminded of the qualities of writing noted in the displayed rubric. Project teachers interact freely with the children as they write, often answering questions posed by the children about their writing, such as "Does it sound good?" or "Is this correct?" After teacher interaction and revision suggestions, a rewriting is done. The first two pictures on the next page show how teachers integrate the qualities of writing with the revision process. The first picture shows the user-friendly rubric in the background to which the teacher and student can refer, and the second picture shows how the teacher, Laura Gavida, used pictures of boat construction to represent how papers would be scored on a 1–4 scale.

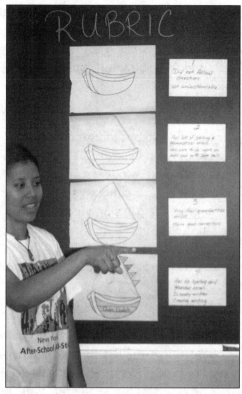

Revising

Rewriting is, more often than not, accomplished by a highly motivating, visual, and artistic activity that connects to the meaning of the book. For instance, with the book *Playing Right Field* (Welch, 2000) aligned to our character development theme, young children constructed a pop-up book. On the accordion panels of a folded strip of paper to which a paper ball was attached on one end and a paper baseball glove on the other, children wrote their episodes of the right fielder's story. For older children, the culminating writing activity with the novel *The Other Side* (Woodson, 2001) was to rewrite the story on panels on a cutout picket fence. The fence represented the divide between a black and white neighborhood and the setting where two young girls of different races overcome the barriers set by the segregationist climate of the times. For *The Great Kapok Tree* (Cherry, 2000), children wrote their version of what the animals told the young man about

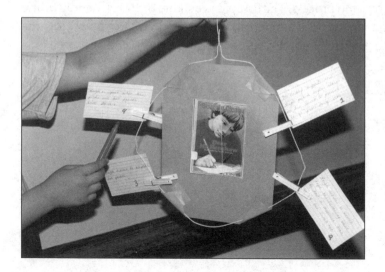

the dangers of deforesting on tree leaves and then hung their "leaves" on a drawing of a large tree constructed on chart paper. The picture to the left shows a student integrating the visual with the verbal in his sequential retelling of a Beverly Cleary book.

Once revision and editing are completed, children share their reading with a buddy or the whole group, with the paper finally becoming displayed on the classroom wall under the appropriate theme title. Children complete four to seven papers based on the readings of different trade books and the use of the different organizational maps. Young children and level 1 writers generally produce a paragraph-length paper, but the teachers work on elaborating content details, expanding sentences and transforming phrases and clauses to achieve sentence variety, and constructing good topic sentences to introduce paragraphs. The reading, mapping, and writing process of the 6Rs steps support and build on one another. The literacy engagement is cumulative and recursive; written products are the visible outcomes of each trade book reading, and the cycle begins again with the new offering of a trade book related to another theme. In this approach, children's expectations are that reading, reconstructing, writing, and revision are one unifying event. As noted by Piazza (2003), a routine is established that writers become accustomed to in their expectations and requirements.

Expectations and routine continue in the computer lab, where children work on a multimedia project connected to one of the three CampUs themes. Popular children's software programs allow the children to write, use visuals and illustrations, link to Internet informational resources, and make appealing page layouts. A 4-point scoring rubric was generated and used by computer teachers to evaluate each child's computer project. This rubric is scored in relation to the following five qualities: project completeness in exemplifying a CampUs theme; organization and structure; originality; graphical presentation; and written presentation.

To help children accomplish a more thoughtful and rich project in the short amount of time, computer teachers find it wise to initiate the project with a two-page planning work sheet that supports the 6Rs steps. The work sheet helps students integrate their prior knowledge, plan where they are going, and compose their writing project. After a teacher-led discussion of the meaning of each of the themes and how they might be addressed, children follow these planning steps: (a) they select an aspect of a theme to investigate; (b) they generate an idea web or concept map of the components of the theme that are known at the time (in recent years we have used the Kidspiration program for this step); (c) they construct an outline of how screens might be planned based on the number of concepts shown on the map; (d) they link the outline to Internet sites related to the three themes provided by the teacher and begin to gain information and take notes; and (e) they write their initial scripts for each screen or card, incorporating their notes and possible ideas of visuals that will complement the text.

Measuring Effectiveness

In the 6Rs program configurations, we have attempted various evaluations to determine if changes in student achievement or behavior occurred. The staple assessment measure throughout all the programs was to compare a prewriting essay with a postwriting essay. Students wrote both papers on the same topic. They were required to tell about a favorite experience, and their papers were evaluated by outside raters who followed the state scoring procedure based on the rubric of 1–4 points. By judging each of the qualities of writing—meaning, development, organization, language use, and mechanics—on the 4-point system, we were able to arrive at a focused holistic score for each paper.

When a large number of student papers written in the various program configurations were analyzed, the exiting papers were found to be stronger at significant levels. Not all students improved in writing, and many duplicated their pre- and post-rubric scores. The mean range of improvement for large groups in 10-day, 21-day, and 50-day programs was from .26 to .69 points based on the 4-point scale. We also generally found that the better the attendance, the higher the gain in writing ability. For instance, in the

NCLB SES program, in which children read, map, and write 2 hours each Saturday morning, the children who attended 41–50 hours improved by .65 points, whereas the children who attended 21–30 hours improved by .22 points.

The results for Spanish bilinguals and children identified as needing special-education services were most heartening; significant increases in writing occurred. From 2000 to 2003, 478 Hispanic children increased in a range from .33 to .40 points, and the 287 children receiving special-education services increased by .23 to .40 rubric points in the same 3-year period. These comparison results were not based on a control group, but rather on expected levels of achievement found in historical patterns or standards of reasonableness.

One might also think that a half day of intensive reading, writing, and project-oriented computer work would be a turnoff for many children during the traditional summer vacation time. This was not necessarily so! In the last 3 years we have found that the DHS-sheltered children made very strong gains in writing progress, ranging from .32 to .69 points each summer; the poor-performing ELA students increased by .61 points, with the greatest gain made by the intermediate-grade students, from 2.28 to 2.92.

There are other indicators that children's perceptions and behavior change for the better. In the summer of 2004, we experimented with the use of the Reader Self-Perception Scale (RSPS) developed by Henk and Melnick (1995). These authors developed a 33-item scale, the norms of which they based on 1,479 fourth, fifth and sixth graders. The scale's 33 items were categorized into five areas: general perception, progress, observational comparison, social feedback, and physiological states. A table was provided to indicate descriptive statistics for each category area and grade level.

For our purposes, we selected the category areas of general perception (with 1 item), progress (with 9 items), and social feedback (with 9 items). In all, students read 19 items at the very beginning and end of each program, and they responded with how much they agreed or disagreed with each statement. If they strongly agreed with the item statement, they were given 5 points; if they agreed, 4 points; if undecided, 3 points; if they disagreed, 2 points; and if they strongly disagreed, 1 point. The highest score achievable for each category area was as follows: general perception, 5 points; progress, 45 points; and social feedback, 45 points.

The general perception of oneself as a reader was prompted by the item "I think I am a good reader." Progress in reading, containing 9 items, was measured by such statements as "When I read, I don't have to try as hard as I used to," "I am getting better at reading," "I understand what I read better than I could before," and "When I read, I recognize more words than I used to." Progress related to how students felt about themselves as they improved or became stronger in their reading and overall literacy abilities. Social Feedback, measured by 9 items, contained such statements as "My teacher thinks I am a good reader," "People in my family think I am a good reader," "Other kids think I am a good reader." This category was concerned with how the student perceived what others thought about the improvement of his or her ability.

With both the low-functioning ELA students and the DHS-sheltered children, we found that the children's perceptions of themselves as competent readers improved significantly. Because the guided reading and writing approach was the only formal approach offered to these children during the summer, they responded to the 19 items on the scale based on what they believed happened to themselves as readers. The structured reading of the trade books, the reading during the mapping and writing components, the rereadings during the revision stage, and the reading of other children's papers accounted for a high degree of daily engagement, which the children thought was a positive influence on their reading growth.

An analysis of the children's written responses to a questionnaire at the end of each cycle indicated that they internalized many of the major objectives of the program and were able to express these in writing. For instance, when asked to tell about some of the things they learned, 700 children wrote that they learned about the dangers of drugs, alcohol, and smoking; 330 learned how to use computers; 295 learned how to protect the environment; 405 learned how to write better; 304 learned how to read better; 190 learned how to use maps; and 275 learned about respect and teamwork. When asked to tell about how their writing got better, 765 children indicated that they wrote and practiced writing a lot; 235 learned to use maps and to organize; 175 learned new vocabulary; 495 learned grammar, spelling, and penmanship; and 88 learned to add details. When asked if mapping helped them plan to write a better paper, 435 wrote that mapping helped them organize their ideas and writing; 281 said that mapping gave them ideas to think about before writing; and 104 said that they could understand what they were writing about.

The Benefits of a Coordinated Approach

The use of story and concept mapping is a key strategy for the organization of textual ideas and is supported by the verbal and map-building interaction in the small-grouping patterns. Teachers guide students to translate narrative structure and information from readings into visual graphic arrays, thereby creating blueprint plans of the reading to be followed by a written retelling, reconstruction, or summary. Use of such maps, in which readers construct mental representations of print ideas, supports three of the seven National Reading Panel's (2000) recommendations to improve reading comprehension: (a) mapping graphic representations of the material being read; (b) learning the structure of stories as a means of remembering story content; and (c) summarizing to integrate and generalize ideas gained from text.

We also found the mapping and note-taking steps to be extremely important in the overall success of each child's multimedia project, because a mindset was provided for each individual student of where he or she is going with the project. For instance, sixth-grade Jose, who selected the good character theme, included these major topics on his concept map to be developed in forthcoming screens: respecting others, helping people, listening to show respect, controlling anger, no bullying, and finding peaceful solutions to problems. Children also reported in their writing that they learned from the short but intensive program. They indicated that they read, mapped, wrote, used computers, and learned about the dangers of drugs, alcohol, and smoking. They indicated that their writing became stronger because they practiced it a lot and that they used maps to organize the ideas they gained from reading before they wrote.

We strongly believe, as others do, that when students write, they learn the "big ideas" and "enduring understandings" that connect broad bands of knowledge and processes, both of which can live on in the mind to be applied in the future (Kameenui & Carnine, 1998; Wiggins & McTighe, 1998). Writing is a meaning-making process in which students have to construct meaningful messages in accordance with their stored knowledge of language conventions, vocabulary, and text styles. The mind focuses on the messages to be written, calls up words and sentence patterns to express meaning, revises meaning, edits conventions, and looks ahead to make connections to forthcoming written ideas presented in a particular way. When young writers act like readers and young readers act like writers, both the reading and writing processes strengthen.

Writing itself influences thinking and learning as students explore, clarify, and process the meanings, concepts, and ideas in textual sources. When reading and writing occur in unison, they create a powerful bond that influences learning in ways that are not possible when students read without writing and write without reading. The prominent view of The National Commission on Writing (2003) is that writing enhances learning. The commission noted that in order for students to make knowledge their own, "they must struggle with the details, wrestle with the facts, and rework raw information and dimly understood concepts into language they can communicate to someone else. In short, if students are to learn, they must write" (p. 9).

The 6Rs instructional format is a reusable strategy that can be implemented throughout the traditional school disciplines during the regular school day. Teachers select standards or curriculum-based topics from their content disciplines of language arts, science, social studies, and mathematics. Topics selected by teachers should be based on a text source, such as an anthology reader, a trade book, a textbook, or an Internet source, as well as a text-structure pattern that can be logically represented by a graphic organizer or concept map. For instance, "Types of Biomes" or "Types of Aquatic Habitats" can be represented by a classification (tree) map, the "Plant and Animal Cells" by a comparison-and-contrast map, and "The Lewis and Clark Expedition" by a time line, flow chart, or sequence concept map.

Teachers can also scaffold the use of graphic organizers from modeling to independent practice in a whole-part-whole instructional setting or one that uses kidstations (see chapter 3). Initially the teacher introduces a particular graphic organizer that helps students reconstruct the information of a topic reading. The teacher builds the map or organizer in a whole-class setting. The organizer is used as a vehicle with which to elicit information from the reading as the organizer is constructed (with explicit or implicit words or phrases from the text included) on the chalkboard, chart pages, or overhead projector. The students then produce an essay based on the organization plan and information displayed on the map. Since this is a whole-class, cooperative activity, the written papers are generally quite similar in macrostructure pattern but dissimilar in sentence structure and connectness. The teacher presents the state scoring rubric and discusses the qualities of the writing. Revisions follow under teacher guidance or through peer or small-group interactions in which students assist each other.

In the second stage, guided practice, students work in groups to analyze a reading and build a concept map or graphic organizer cooperatively. Students most often use a graphic organizer previously introduced by the teacher during the initial modeling stage. Students then work on a joint written essay in which each writer writes one or several paragraphs to explain the topic. As the students work, they assist one another in the revision and editing processes.

After the guided reading stage, the students are asked to work independently with a text source. They follow the 6Rs procedure on their own. They may select a previously introduced graphic organizer or a visual plan to reconstruct the reading, or they may modify or create a different map plan to represent the meaning of the text. Then they write a paper to express the meaning represented by their visual organizer. At this stage, the teacher may have the students present their maps and written works to the class, with discussion and interaction to follow.

Particularly for low achievers and at-risk students, the 6Rs instructional format has been found to be very beneficial. This may be especially so with respect to potential lack of prior knowledge, the vocabulary understanding brought to the topics, and the need to strengthen memory processing. Concept maps can assist the learning of content for underachievers in three ways: (a) they portray model plans of text organization so that students have a mental plan of comprehending and composing as they read and write; (b) they help teachers and students to connect preexisting knowledge in a visual or graphic way, thereby helping students form new knowledge constructs; and (c) they help learners to connect knowledge in a network of propositions that have a unified meaning.

References

Blake, B. E., & Sinatra, R. (2005). The 6Rs approach: Developing "critical" writers among poor, urban students in a summer literacy program. *The Language & Literacy Spectrum, 15,* 62–79.

Board of Education of the City of New York. (1997). *Performance standards, New York* (1st ed.). New York: Author.

Board of Education of the City of New York. (2001). *Performance standards, first edition: Applied learning.* New York: Author.

Boyle, J. (1996). The effects of a cognitive mapping strategy on the literal and inferential comprehension of students with mild disabilities. *Learning Disability Quarterly, 19,* 86-98.

Burns, P. C., Roe, B. D., & Ross, L. P. (1999). *Teaching reading in today's elementary schools* (7th ed.). New York: Houghton Mifflin.

Cherry, L. (2000). *The great kapok tree.* New York: Vanguard Books.

Cronin, H., Meadows, D., & Sinatra, R. (1990). Integrating computers, reading and writing across the curriculum. *Educational Leadership, 48,* 57–62.

Cronin, H., Sinatra, R., & Barkley, W. F. (1992). Combining writing with text organization in content instruction. *NASSP Bulletin, 76,* 34–45.

Davis, Z. T. (1994). Effects of pre-reading story mapping on elementary readers' comprehension. *Journal of Educational Research, 87,* 353–360.

Englert, C. S., & Mariage, T. V. (1991). Making student partners in the comprehension process: Organizing the reading "POSSE." *Learning Disability Quarterly, 14,* 123–138.

Finders, M. J., & Hynds, S. (2003). *Literacy lessons: Teaching and learning with middle school students.* Upper Saddle River, NJ: Merrill Prentice Hall.

Gunning, T. (2003). *Building literacy in the content areas.* Boston: Allyn & Bacon.

Henk, W., & Melnick, S. (1995). The reader self-perception scale (RSPS): A new tool for measuring how children feel about themselves as readers. *The Reading Teacher, 48,* 470–479.

Kameenui, E., & Carnine, D. (1998). *Effective teaching strategies that accommodate diverse learners.* Upper Saddle River, NJ: Merrill.

National Commission on Writing. (2003). *The neglected "R": The need for a writing revolution.* Princeton, NJ: College Board.

National Reading Panel. (2000). *Teaching children to read: An evidence-based assessment of the scientific literature on reading and its implications for reading.* Bethesda, MD: National Institute of Child Health and Human Development.

Piazza, C. L. (2003). *Journeys: The teaching of writing in elementary classrooms.* Upper Saddle River, NJ: Pearson.

Saltman, J. (1985). *The Riverside anthology of children's literature* (6th ed.). Boston: Houghton Mifflin.

Sinatra, R. (2000). Teaching learners to think, read, and write more effectively in content subjects. *The Clearing House, 73*, 266–273.

Sinatra, R., & Pizzo, J. (1992). Mapping the road to reading comprehension. *Teaching Pre-K–8, 23*, 102–105.

Swanson, P. N., & DeLaPaz, S. (1998). Teaching effective comprehension strategies to students with learning and reading disabilities. *Intervention in School and Clinic, 33*, 209–218.

Vallecorsa, A. L., & deBettencourt, L. U. (1997). Using a mapping procedure to teach reading and writing skills to middle grade students with learning disabilities. *Education and Treatment of Children, 20*, 173–188.

Welch, W. (2000). *Playing right field.* New York: Scholastic.

Wiggins, G., & McTighe, J. (1998). *Understanding by design.* Alexandria, VA: Association for Supervision and Curriculum Development.

Wolf, D. P., & White, A. M. (2000). Charting the course of student growth. *Educational Leadership, 46*, 6–11.

Wong, B.Y.L. (1997). Research on genre-specific strategies for enhancing writing in adolescents with learning disabilities. *Learning Disability Quarterly, 20*, 140–159.

Woodson, J. (2001). *The other side.* New York: Putnam.

About the Authors

Richard C. Sinatra

Authors, from left to right: Brett Elizabeth Blake, Joanne Marie Robertson, E. Francine Guastello, and Richard C. Sinatra.

Richard Sinatra is Professor, Director of the reading and writing education center, and Chairman of the Department of Human Services and Counseling at St. John's University in Queens. He has been an educator for over 45 years, serving as an English teacher in the junior-high grades, a third and fourth grade teacher, a reading specialist, a district reading coordinator, and university literacy professor. He has authored and co-authored books, book chapters, and journal articles. He has been a literacy consultant to many school districts. For the past 10 years he has been the project director of the after-school all-stars "Camp-Us" Project which provides literacy, computer, cultural, and athletic programs to thousands of housing development children from New York City. In 1987, he received the College Reading Educator Award given annually by NYS Reading Association, and in the spring of 2000, he received the prestigious St. Vincent DePaul Teacher-Scholar award from St. John's University. In 1972, he received his Ph.D. in reading education from Hofstra University.

Brett Elizabeth Blake

Brett Elizabeth Blake is the Coordinator of the Graduate Adolescent Education Programs and a Senior Research Fellow in the Vincention Center for Social Justice and Poverty at St. John's University in New York. She holds an M.A. in linguistics from Northwestern University and a Ph.D. from the University at Illinois, Chicago. Dr. Blake has worked and written extensively about the challenges urban English language learners face in their literacy learning, including four other books. Her most recent book, "A culture of refusal: The lives and literacies of out-of-school adolescents" (2004) highlights the struggles these learners face in jail and migrant camp classrooms in both urban and rural settings.

E. Francine Guastello

Dr. Francine Guastello is an Associate Professor of Literacy, Coordinator of the Graduate Literacy Program at St. John's University in New York, and Chair of the School of Education's Curriculum Committee. Dr. Guastello is a two time recipient of a federal grant under Title IIA "No Child Left Behind." She is the Supervisor of the Graduate Practicum Program of diagnostic and prescriptive remediation of children with learning disabilities and diverse learners. She initiated the first Orton-Gillingham training Course at SJU in the summer of '04 and is presently working with the 3rd Cohort. Prior to becoming a university professor, Dr. Guastello was an elementary school teacher for 12 years, an elementary school principal for 16 years, and taught as an adjunct professor of literacy at Fordham and St. John's for 6 years. Her research interests and professional publications include topics that focus on effective instructional practices in literacy development for low-achieving students and diverse learners and the promotion of family literacy.

Joanne Marie Robertson

Dr. Robertson is an Assistant Professor at St. John's University, School of Education. Her current research explores students' perceptions of self-efficacy and motivation to read and write in the primary grades, as well as the integration of inquiry based instruction and action research projects to support students' critical thinking in the elementary grades. Her research is conducted in culturally and linguistically diverse classrooms serving as authentic contexts for literacy. Dr. Robertson explores ways to enhance understandings about theorized practice, optimal learning environments, and the benefits of mentoring and shared inquiry to retain and support excellent teachers in the profession.